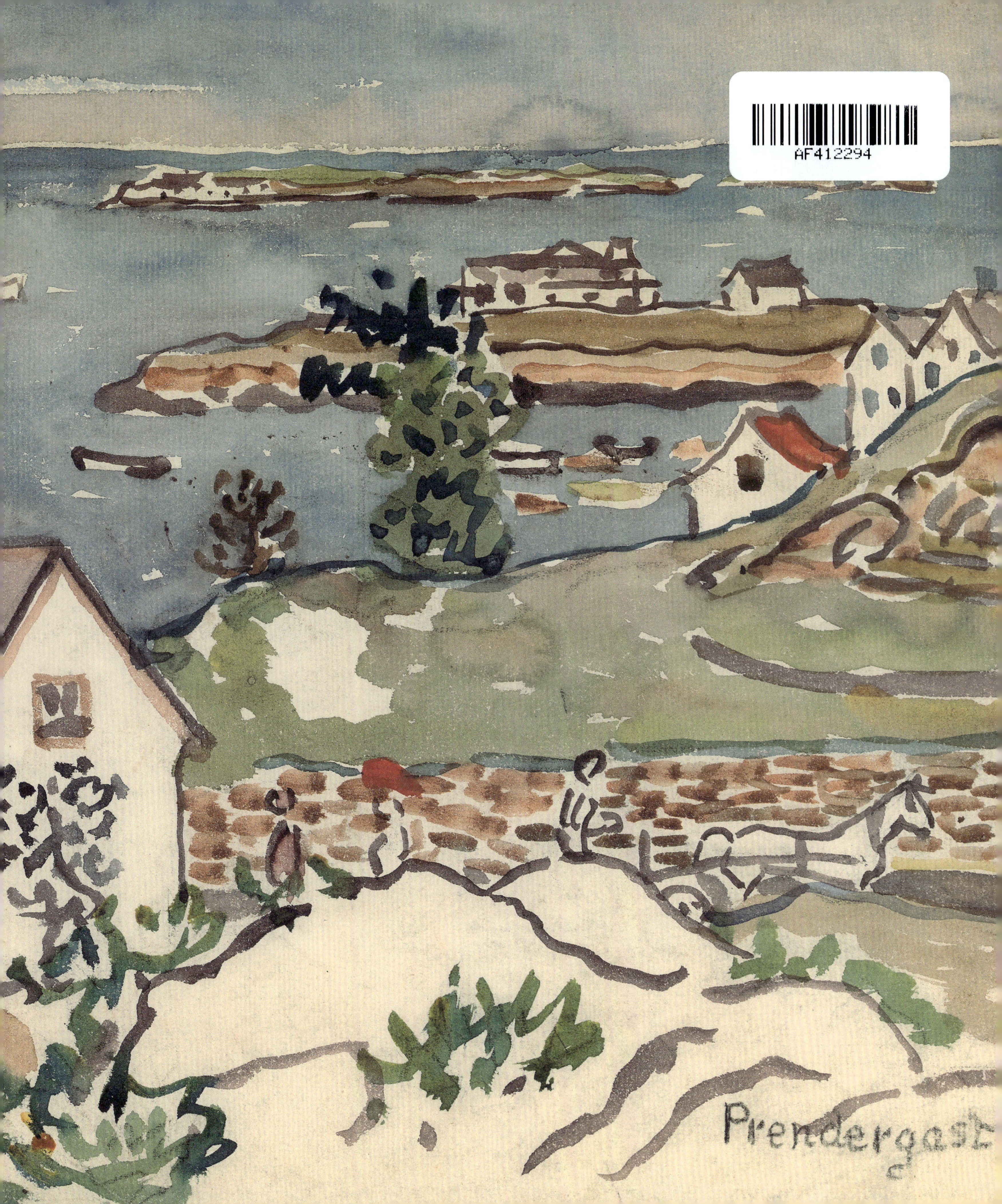
Prendergast

Maurice Prendergast
By the Sea

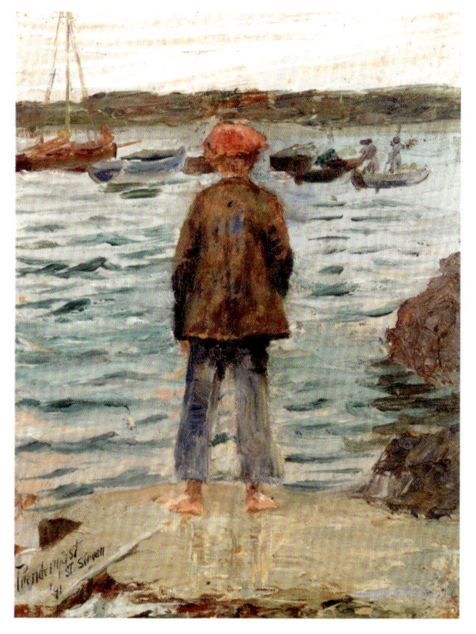

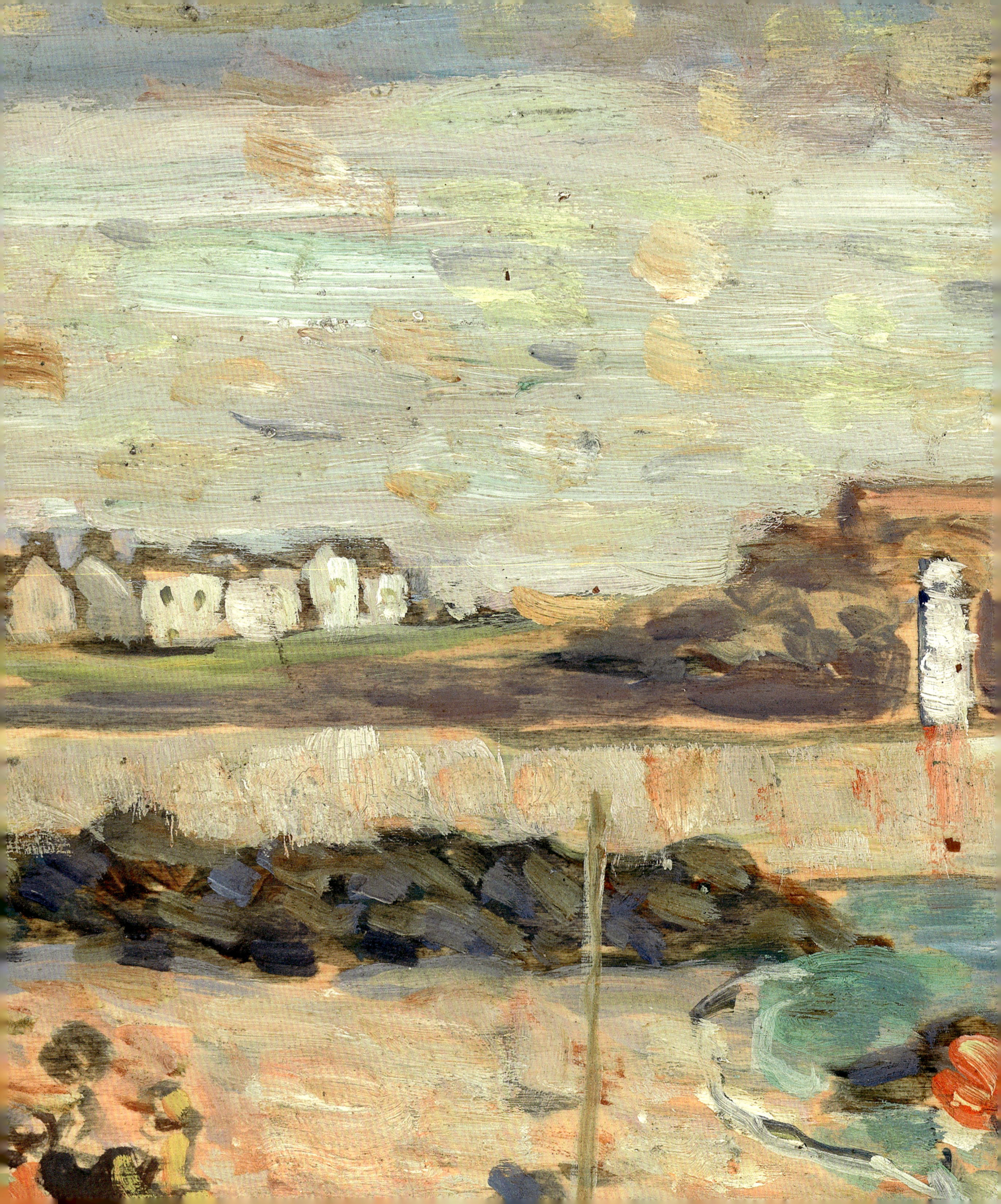

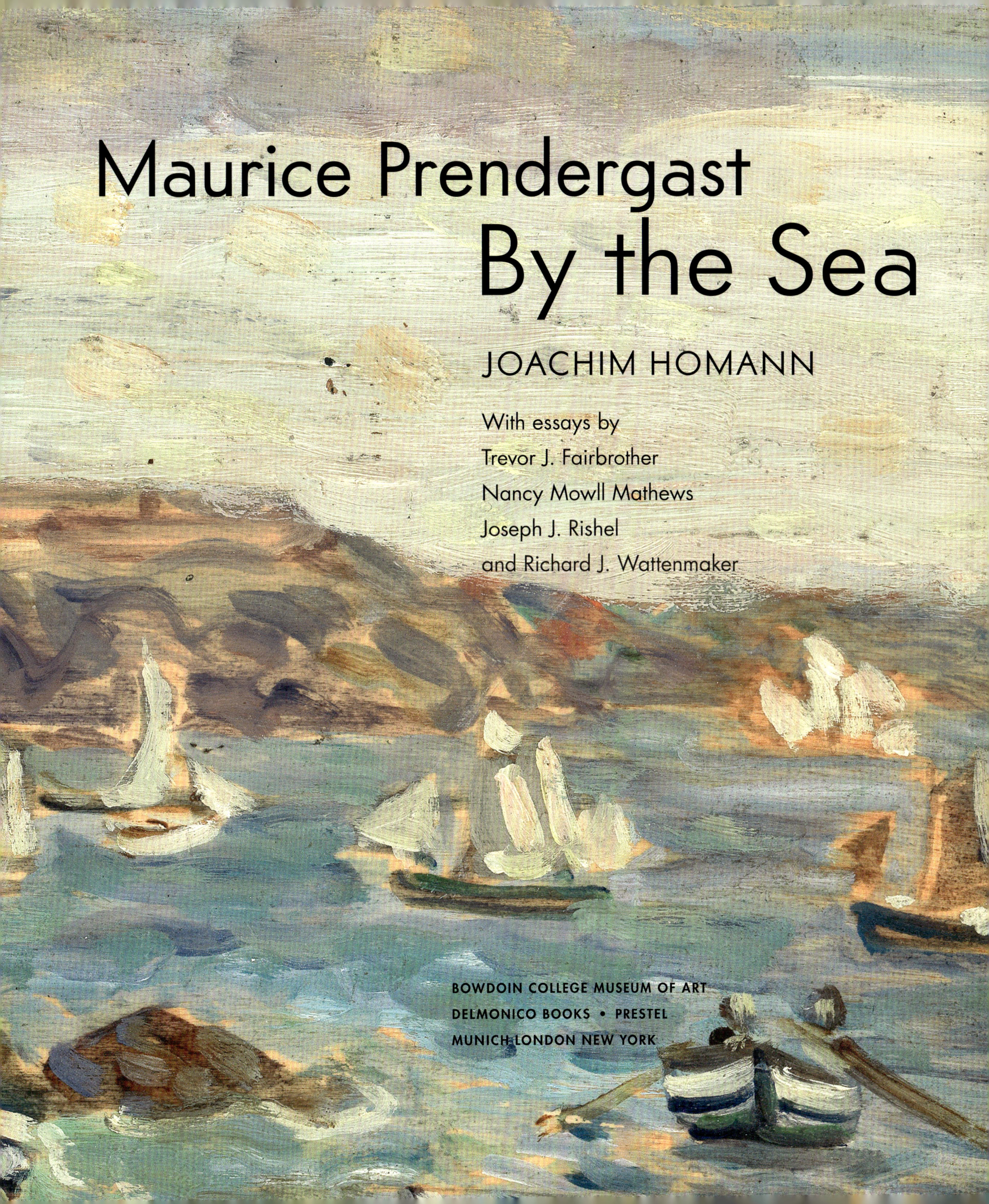

Maurice Prendergast
By the Sea

JOACHIM HOMANN

With essays by
Trevor J. Fairbrother
Nancy Mowll Mathews
Joseph J. Rishel
and Richard J. Wattenmaker

BOWDOIN COLLEGE MUSEUM OF ART
DELMONICO BOOKS • PRESTEL
MUNICH·LONDON NEW YORK

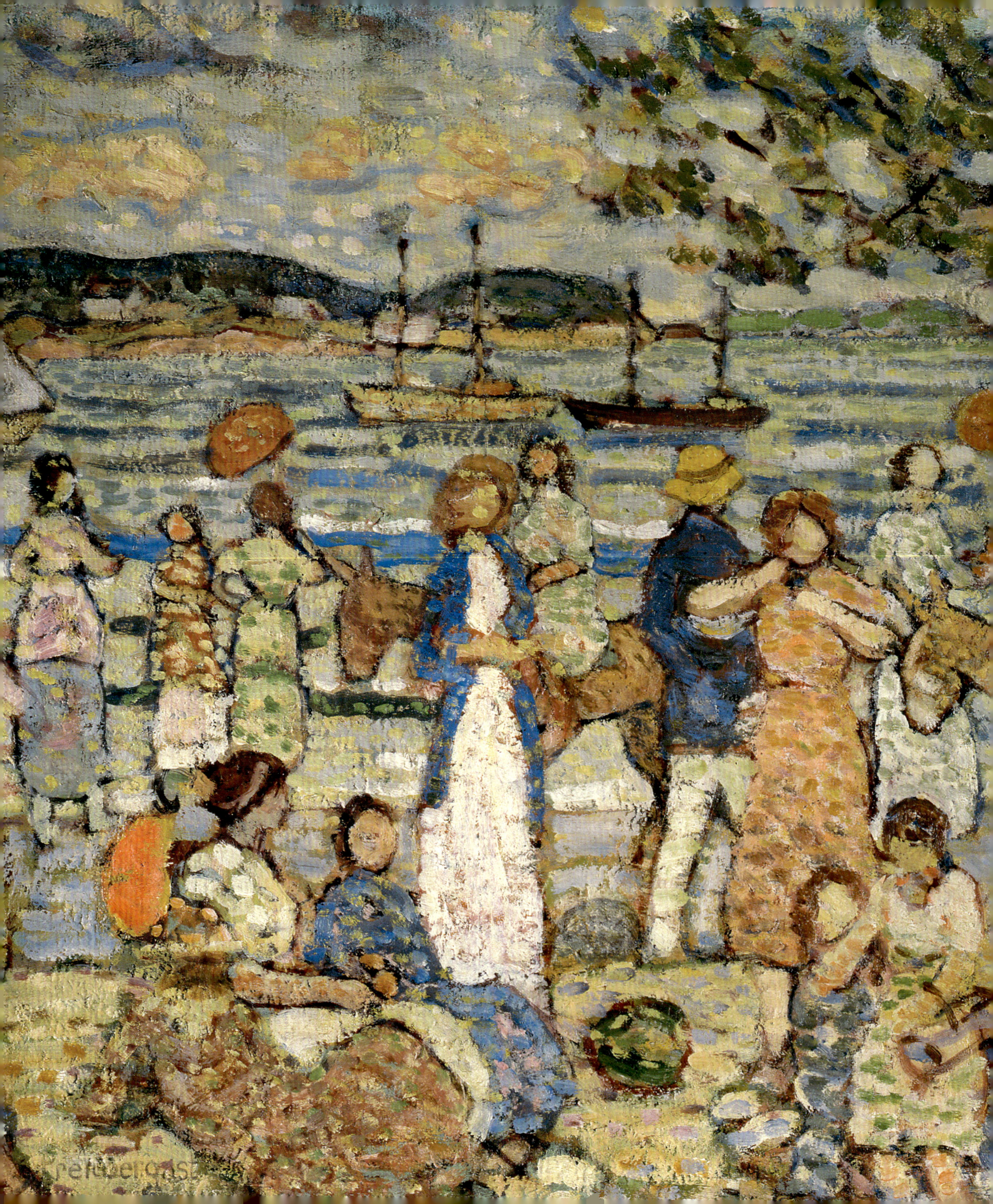

CONTENTS

FOREWORD

Maurice Brazil Prendergast (1858–1924) was one of the millions of seasonal visitors who frequented the beaches and resort towns of New England between the 1890s and the 1920s. Throughout his life, the seaside inspired his art. Prendergast captured the atmosphere of summer holidays along the coast in brilliant watercolors, animated monotypes and oil sketches, and sumptuous paintings whose originality and experimental character earned the artist early recognition as a leading American modernist. Prendergast evoked in his work the exhilarating effects of intense sun, salty breezes, and the open ocean, in constant motion in the changing tides; he rendered the exuberant colors of the summer crowds traversing promenades, piers, and rocky shores. Viewers of his art experience the unbridled happiness of splendid summer days on the coast with a visceral intensity.

In the thirty years of his engagement with the seaside, Prendergast's interpretations of it evolved significantly, from his much loved early watercolors and monotypes recording the leisure culture of the 1890s to the late visionary paintings, viewed by contemporaries as his major achievement. This volume illustrates for the first time the full arc of Prendergast's development of his seaside imagery, including not only his perceptions of the environs of Boston and the shores of Massachusetts, New Hampshire, and Maine but also works inspired by the Normandy coast and by two iconic Italian destinations, the Lido in Venice and the island of Capri. But localities did not always matter to Prendergast. Although in some of his works he provided recognizable geographical details, in many others the particular site cannot be identified. It appears that the ocean itself—not a specific place but an opening to the world—allowed Prendergast to strive for the universal.

Keenly aware of art historical precedents as well as current artistic trends, Prendergast engaged productively with art from the early Italian Renaissance to the French avant-garde. He was a cosmopolitan who had received training in art schools in Paris and took every opportunity to travel to France, England, and Italy. His ability to respond to international impulses with a steady stream of innovation earned Prendergast admirers among critics and much younger peers and enabled him to participate in major exhibitions that were perceived as cutting-edge. Yet for all its sophistication, Prendergast's art remained deeply invested in the populace as both a subject and an audience, a preoccupation illustrated throughout this book in his many images of crowded beaches and promenades along the shore. Whether densely packed or harmoniously choreographed, dressed in their Sunday best or bathing suits, Prendergast's multitudes are always peaceful, admiring the shore, enjoying each other's company, and engaging in play. To Prendergast's crowds the ocean provides the ideal backdrop, an uninterrupted horizon that establishes compositional coherence and instills in viewers a sense of unity among the people.

The following essays open up multiple perspectives on Prendergast and his seaside visions. Nancy Mowll Mathews provides a panorama of artistic developments and societal changes that informed Prendergast's continuously changing work. Trevor Fairbrother focuses on the artist's position in the cultural climate of Boston, his home for most of his life. In a close-up of pivotal moments in Prendergast's career, Richard Wattenmaker makes apparent the artist's striking visual intelligence. Joseph Rishel, in a final note, puts a question mark behind any attempt to explain conclusively Prendergast's unique sensibility for and commitment to the seaside: a lifelong fascination for the artist and a riddle to posterity.

Prendergast's gentle and enchanting art touches anyone who encounters it, not the least those of us who realized this catalogue and the companion exhibition. I am deeply thankful to the exceptionally generous public and private lenders and to my fellow authors, whose affection for Prendergast in some cases goes back decades but still feels fresh. Numerous generous funders have made possible this first retrospective of Prendergast's work in twenty years. Major sponsors include the Devonwood Foundation, The Mr. and Mrs. Raymond J. Horowitz Foundation for the Arts, Eric '85 and Svetlana Silverman, and the Elizabeth B. G. Hamlin Fund at Bowdoin College. Additional support has been provided by The Robert Lehman Foundation, Carolyn Logan P'12, the Morton-Kelly Charitable Trust, Thomas A. McKinley '06, and an anonymous donor; we are also grateful to Furthermore: a program of the J. M. Kaplan Fund for support of our exhibition catalogue. Nancy Mowll Mathews, co-curator, has been a crucial contributor to the realization of every phase of this project, and I am profoundly grateful to her. We are delighted to present this book to a new generation of readers as an introduction to Prendergast's experimental and innovative art.

Joachim Homann
Curator, Bowdoin College Museum of Art

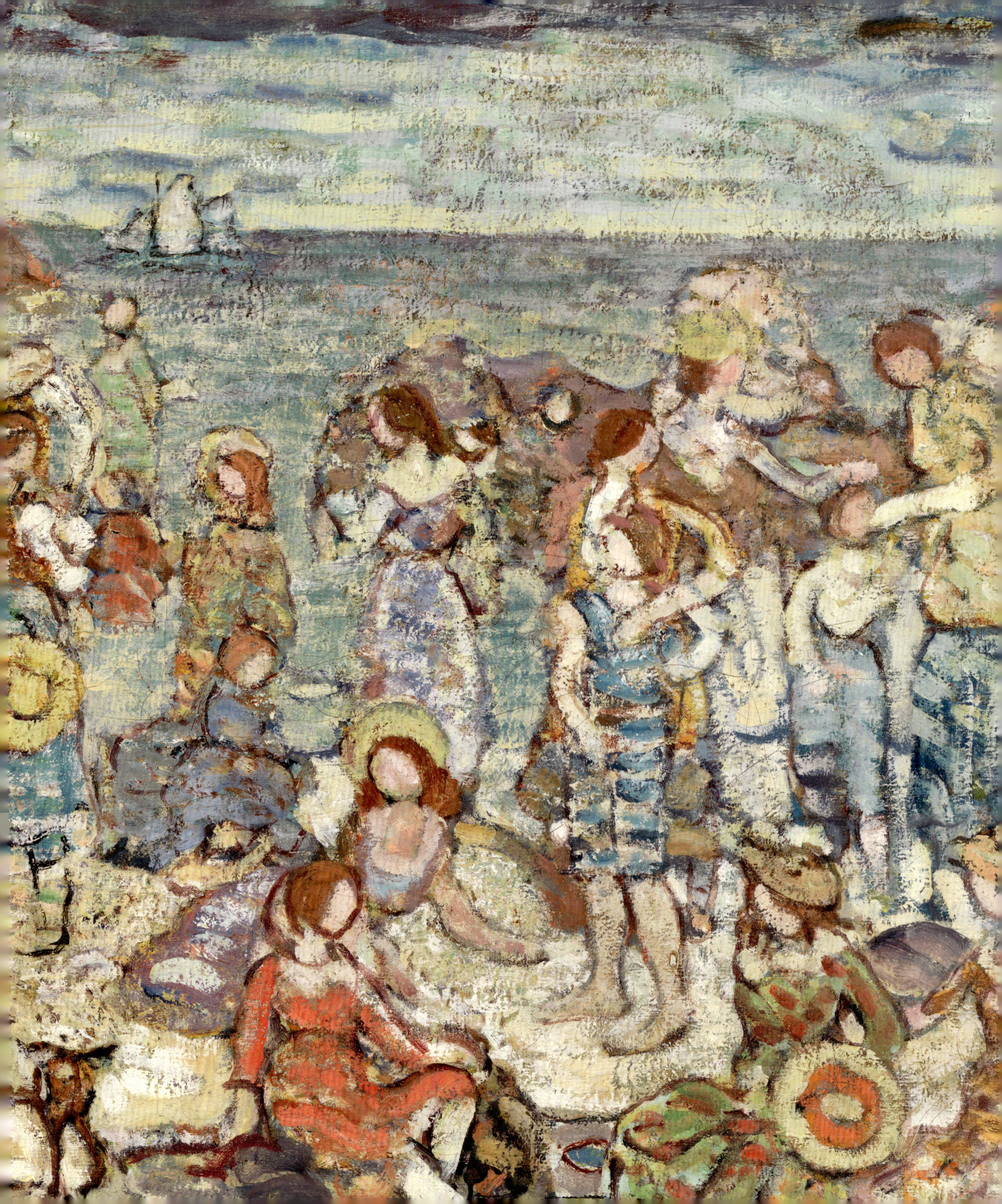

Crowds by the Sea

JOACHIM HOMANN

> Circumambulate the city of a dreamy Sabbath afternoon. . . . What
> do you see?—Posted like silent sentinels all around the town, stand
> thousands upon thousands of mortal men fixed in ocean reveries. . . .
> They must get just as nigh the water as they possibly can without
> falling in. . . . Inlanders all, they come from lanes and alleys, streets
> and avenues—north, east, south, and west. Yet here they all unite.
>
> —Herman Melville, *Moby Dick; or, The Whale*

Maurice Prendergast's lifelong pursuit was the rendering of crowds by the sea. Once he had acquired the artistic skills necessary to capture multitudes of people near the water, primarily through academic training in Paris and constant practice during the summers he spent along the Normandy coast, he never allowed himself to be distracted from the topic for long. Beginning in 1894, his first year as a professional artist in Boston, Prendergast could be seen on the piers and beaches and in the harbors and seaside parks of the region, filling his sketchbooks with studies of women, children, and men enjoying the water's edge. While no viewer of Prendergast's work has failed to identify crowded coasts as the artist's primary subject, interpretations of this thematic choice are scarce. The critics who helped cement Prendergast's reputation as a modernist focused on his formal repertoire rather than his motifs. Others valued the artist as a chronicler of the culture of leisure that emerged in the Progressive era (1890s–1920s) but did not distinguish in their interpretations between the seashore and the other sites of public recreation depicted in his works. Neither perspective accounts completely for Prendergast's almost single-minded exploration of multiple, usually faceless figures by the sea over the most productive thirty years of his adult life.[1]

Most people today picture themselves enjoying pristine ocean beaches either by themselves or in intimate company. Our perception of the ocean is shaped in part by a tradition of seascape painting that invited the lonely contemplation of timeless nature

Detail, *The Cove*, 1916 (plate 71)

and preferred the sublime above the beautiful.[2] For Prendergast, however, the colorful summer visitors—engaged in play and exploration (plates 11, 26) and attracted
by such seaside amenities as piers (plate 22), promenades (plate 6), and hot air
balloons (plate 23)—added to the allure of the coast. Throughout his prolific career,
Prendergast's interpretations deepened; the artist stripped away what he deemed ines-
sential. In the early years of the twentieth century he painted children riding wooden
horses on a popular merry-go-round in the resort town of Nahant (plate 21). In his late
work, riders on horseback appear in backgrounds of paintings that are as imaginative
as child's play (plate 53). And where the younger Prendergast delighted in sketching
ruffled dresses (plate 9), the aging artist presented some female figures in the nude
(plate 51). His landscapes, detailed with local specifics in an earlier phase, general
and simplified later, underwent a parallel transformation. As Prendergast's renderings
became more dreamlike, they rarely failed to integrate multiple figures within the land-
and seascape.

Among his peers, Prendergast stands out for his commitment to capturing the
crowds on the shore. In 1905, Hermann Dudley Murphy, a close friend, painted an
untouched beach as three bands of sky, ocean, and sand (fig. 1).[3] Supremely decorative and deliberately economical in its means, the painting could be read as a com-
ment on Maurice's peopled pictures. Equally telling is a comparison with John Sloan's
most ambitious beach scene, dated to 1908 (fig. 2). In stark contrast to the oil sketches
of Saint-Malo beaches (plate 36) that Prendergast had exhibited that same year in the

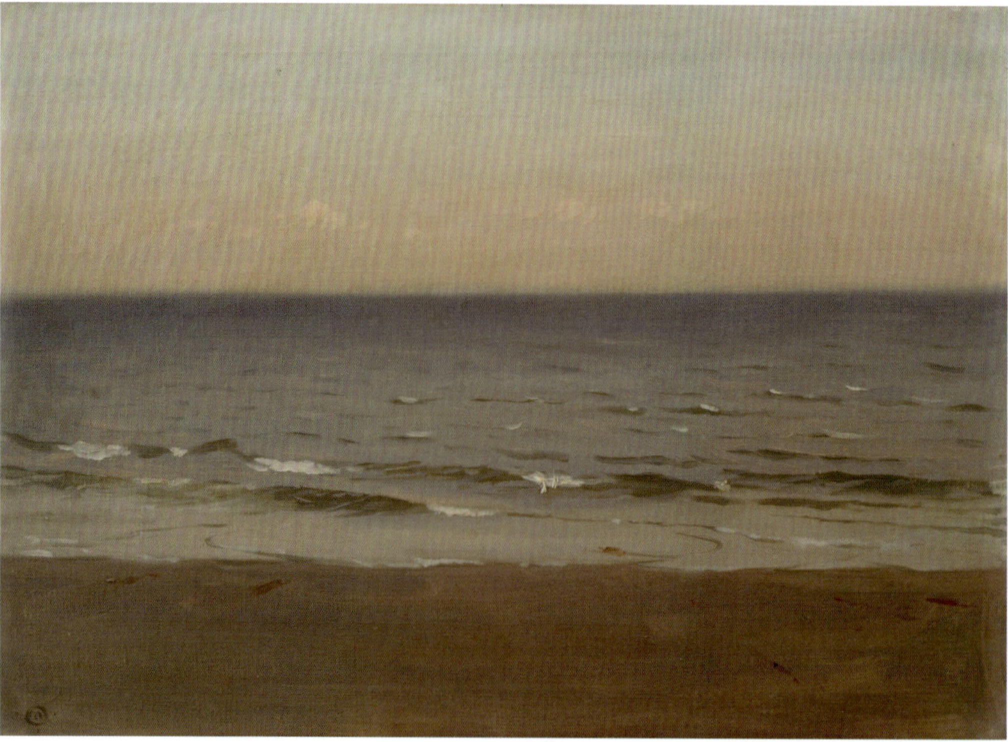

Fig. 1. Hermann Dudley Murphy,
The Beach, 1905. Oil on canvas,
20 × 27⅛ in. (50.8 × 68.9 cm). Bowdoin
College Museum of Art, Brunswick, Maine;
Bequest of Mrs. Ella Pratt (1969.43)

JOACHIM HOMANN

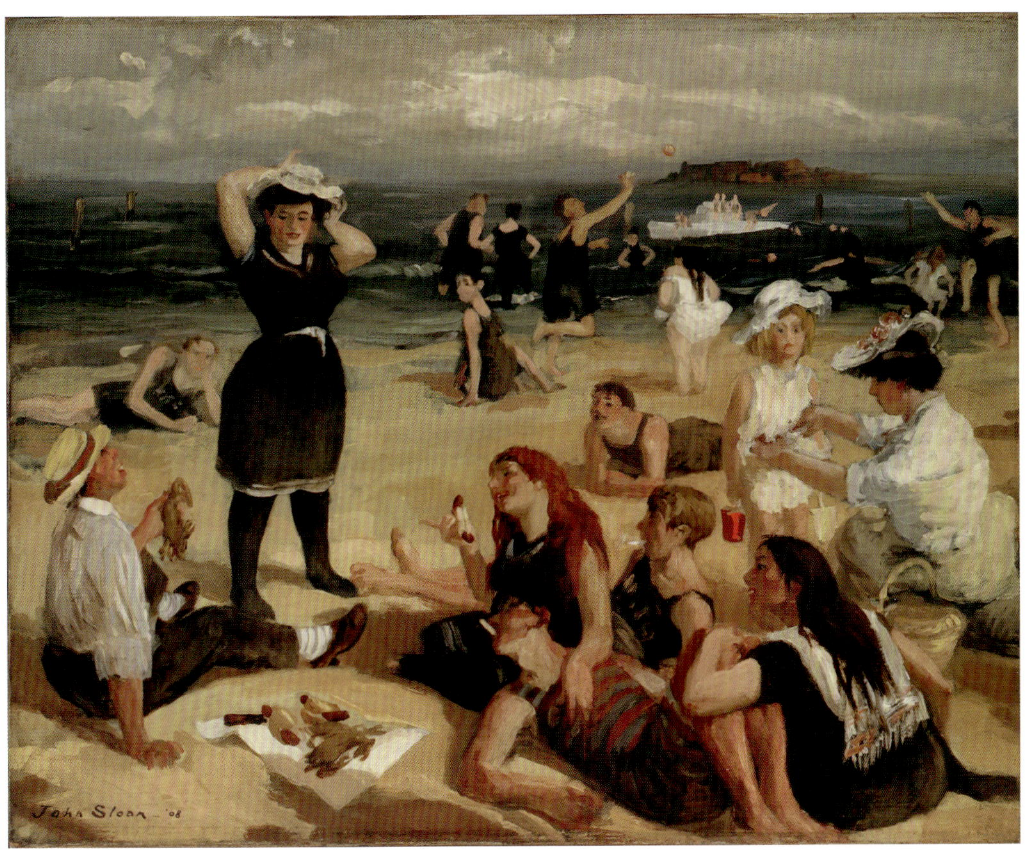

Fig. 2. John Sloan, *South Beach Bathers*, 1907–8. Oil on canvas, 31¹³⁄₁₆ × 36 in. (80.8 × 91.4 cm). Walker Art Center, Minneapolis; Gift of the T. B. Walker Foundation, Gilbert M. Walker Fund, 1948 (1948.27)

landmark exhibition "The Eight," to which Sloan also contributed, Sloan's large paint-ing revels in anecdotal details. Casual poses, fashionable costumes, and humorous props make this an entertaining document of the customs of its time, and more reveal-ing than any of Prendergast's coastal works. Sloan purposefully showed not a crowd but a cast of types representative of their class. As Sloan later reminisced, "This Staten Island resort had few visitors compared to Coney Island, and gave better opportunity for observation of individual behavior. It is amusing to recall how very chic the bathing costume of the girl standing seemed at that time."[4] Or consider the seaside works of William J. Glackens from the same period. Partly inspired by Prendergast's Saint-Malo production, this close friend had delighted in painting bathers since 1908, especially after he started summering in Bellport, New York, on Long Island, in 1911. *Captain's Pier* is characteristic of Glackens' ability to bring together figures and seaside architec-ture in paintings that give a vivid impression of what a day at the beach at the turn of the century might have been like (fig. 3).[5] While all three colleagues were closely asso-ciated with Prendergast in pivotal moments of his career, none shared Prendergast's fascination with crowds along the water.

It would be unfair, however, to conclude that Prendergast was an outsider. Like many of his American colleagues, Prendergast rejected academic art that evoked

and idealized the classical heritage (fig. 4).[6] He looked instead at French Impressionism and Post-Impressionism to develop new perspectives on the landscape, especially
the city and the coast. Prendergast transformed the French impulse into a genuinely
American response that, ultimately, contributed to his generation's effort to establish
a new cultural identity for a country confronted with mass immigration and urbaniza-
tion.[7] Prendergast must have situated his ambitions within the "big picture" of national
aspirations. For many contemporary critics, the holiday spirit in Prendergast's work was
its defining character, and the association with national celebrations never far-fetched:
"Mr. Prendergast was born to paint fêtes, and he carries a whole Fourth of July in his
color-box."[8] The artist's works need to be understood in correlation to a cultural climate
that valued patriotism and high educational ideals and made many artists receptive to
"euphemism, optimism, nationalism, and nostalgia."[9]

In his community-affirming art, Prendergast drew on a literary rather than a
pictorial tradition that associated crowds metaphorically with the sea, one that had
been firmly established long before he picked up his brush. Charles Baudelaire, in
The Painter of Modern Life (1863), had encouraged artists to capture the essence of
modernity by studying the urban masses. He echoed Jean-Jacques Rousseau, who
in his critique of the theater had postulated that the most compelling spectacle for
a large crowd was the crowd itself. Rousseau described a popular festival: "Plant a

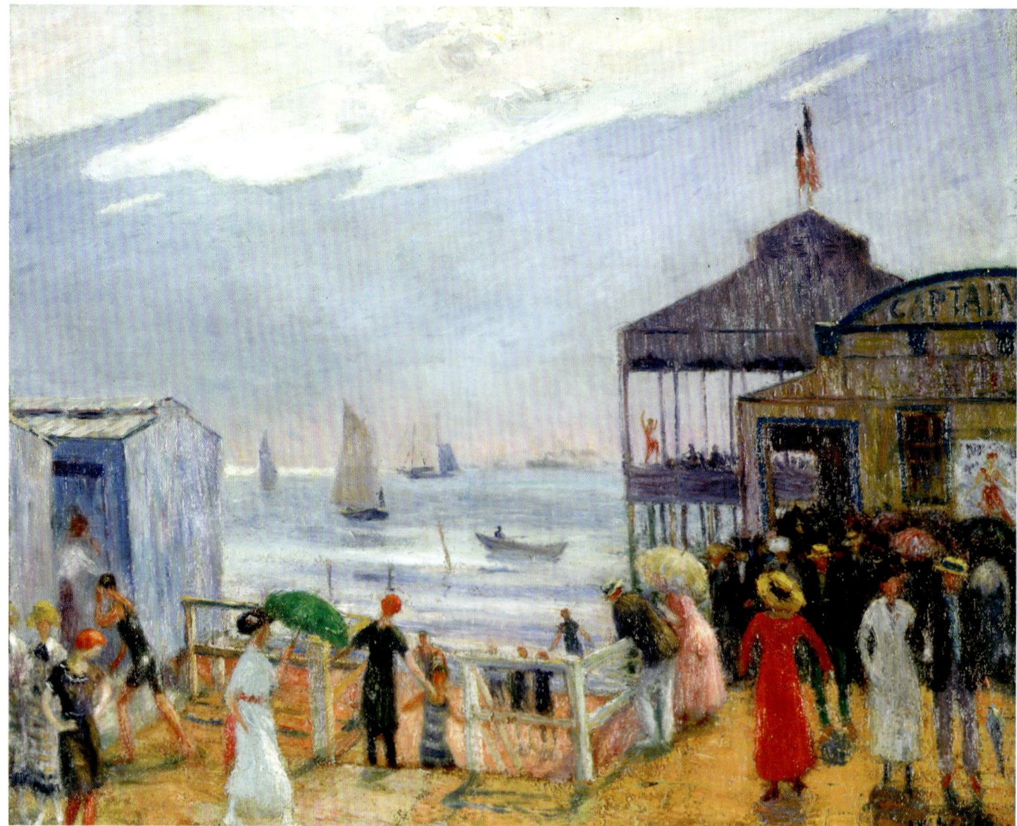

Fig. 3. William J. Glackens, *Captain's Pier*, 1912–14. Oil on canvas, 25⅛ × 30⅛ in. (63.8 × 76.5 cm). Bowdoin College Museum of Art, Brunswick, Maine; Gift of Stephen M. Etnier, Honorary Degree, 1969 (1957.127)

JOACHIM HOMANN

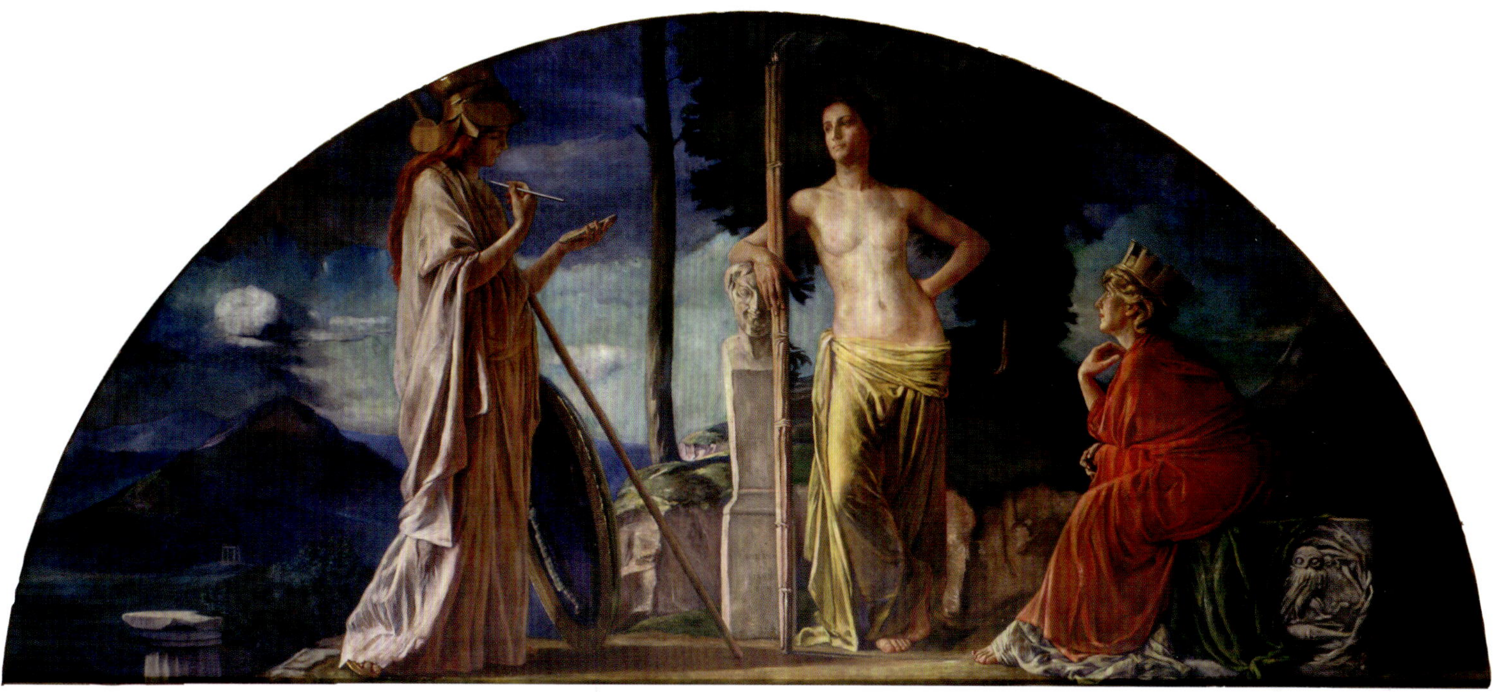

post crowned with flowers in the center of a site, assemble the people there and you will have a festival. Do even better: display the spectators as spectacle; make them actors themselves, make each of them see himself and love himself in the others, in order that all will be better united."[10] Baudelaire, in turn, described the urban crowd as a spectacle for the artist. "For the perfect *flâneur*, for the passionate spectator, it is an immense joy to set up house in the heart of the multitude, amid the ebb and flow [*l'ondoyant*] of movement, in the midst of the fugitive and the infinite."[11] To describe the masses, he resorted to an image that connected the modern and urban phenomenon of crowds to the timeless natural forces and immensity of the ocean. The metaphor had appeared even earlier in Walt Whitman's poem "Crossing Brooklyn Ferry," first published in 1856.[12] Whitman's daring vision conflates the intensely sensual perception of the crowd with the ebb and flow of the tides:

> Flow on, river! flow with the flood-tide, and ebb with the ebb-tide!
> Frolic on, crested and scallop-edged waves!
> Gorgeous clouds of the sunset! Drench with your splendor me, or the
>   men and women generations after me;
> Cross from shore to shore, countless crowds of passengers!

Open for debate, however, is whether crowds were a precondition to the rise of modern societies or, to the contrary, posed a threat to liberal democracies. Whitman was not isolated in his optimistic understanding of crowds, as Christian Borch has

Fig. 4. John LaFarge, *Athens*, 1898. Oil on canvas, 108 × 240 in. (274.3 × 609.6 cm). Bowdoin College Museum of Art, Brunswick, Maine; Gift of the Misses Harriet Sarah and Mary Sophia Walker (1893.35)

recently shown. Rather, the poet contributed to a school of thought that found positive energy in crowds "because they gave vent to bodily impulses and sexual desires; because they initiated affective, physical contact in public space. This was the reason why crowds may improve the future architecture of society."[13] Other commentators assessed the dangers inherent in crowds, which they believed tended to behave irrationally. Edward A. Ross, the most widely read social scientist of the time, defined the "mob" as "a crowd of people showing an unanimity due to mental contagion." Would art count among the "prophylactics against mob mind" that Ross sought to identify?[14] And would Prendergast's peopled beaches contribute to fostering community ties, providing an impulse to the crowd to lay the foundation of a future society?[15]

In an article about Prendergast that he published shortly after the artist's death, in 1924, collector Duncan Phillips described his perception of the work *Autumn* (plate 65): "I possess a canvas of the American fantasist—an improvisation, truly pagan of course, on the russets, purples and orange tones of autumn orchestrated with inexpressibly gorgeous peacock blues and greens—which has somehow the grave dignity in design and spacing of the abstract figures which makes me think of august church decorations of the best periods."[16] Comparing the painting to "frescoes presenting the most solemn Christian stories," Phillips not only praised its spiritual energy but also identified the "ecstasy" the canvas evoked in him as "more medieval than modern." In his new museum he planned to share this transformative experience with the public through a gallery and library space decorated with his large collection of Prendergast paintings, implicitly re-creating the communal experience of a medieval church in a secularized, modern setting.[17]

Crowds were not only a subject in Prendergast's art, they were also its intended audience. Prendergast witnessed the unprecedented growth in public enthusiasm for art that took place between the founding of the Museum of Fine Arts, Boston, in 1870, just two years after he arrived in the city, and 1924, the last active year of director Benjamin Ives Gilman, when attendance swelled above 400,000 annual visitors, including 9,000 participants in docent tours.[18] The artist contributed to this audience expansion by submitting his works to countless shows nationwide, eager to reach the broadest possible demographic.[19] In 1909 Gilman declared, "The problem of the present is the democratization of the museum: how they may help to give all men a share in the life of the imagination."[20] For Prendergast, this institutional "problem" was also an artist's charge. With increasing support from collectors driven by educational goals, such as Albert C. Barnes and Duncan Phillips, Prendergast wanted his work—which ironically was never collected by the Museum of Fine Arts in his lifetime—to be accessible to the urban populace.[21] He surely hoped to inspire his viewers to imagine themselves in his works as part of the crowd, in a moment of self-recognition that sparked their sense of community.

Prendergast's most successful works seem to bristle with energy and create the sensation of perpetual movement; they convey the exhilarating forces that shape the summery crowds in motion on promenades and along busy beaches. A modernist in terms of his formal innovations, Prendergast was also modern for embracing the condition of living his life as a "man of the crowd."[22] His images give shape to the faceless city dwellers, acknowledging them as an almost natural force and probing their ability to find a new unity and fulfilling beauty. In his imagination, the ocean is a mirror to the people, and that mirror provides the artist's modus operandi:

> And still deeper the meaning of that story of Narcissus, who because he could not grasp the tormenting, mild image he saw in the fountain, plunged into it and was drowned. But that same image, we ourselves see in all rivers and oceans. It is the image of the ungraspable phantom of life; and this is the key to it all.[23]

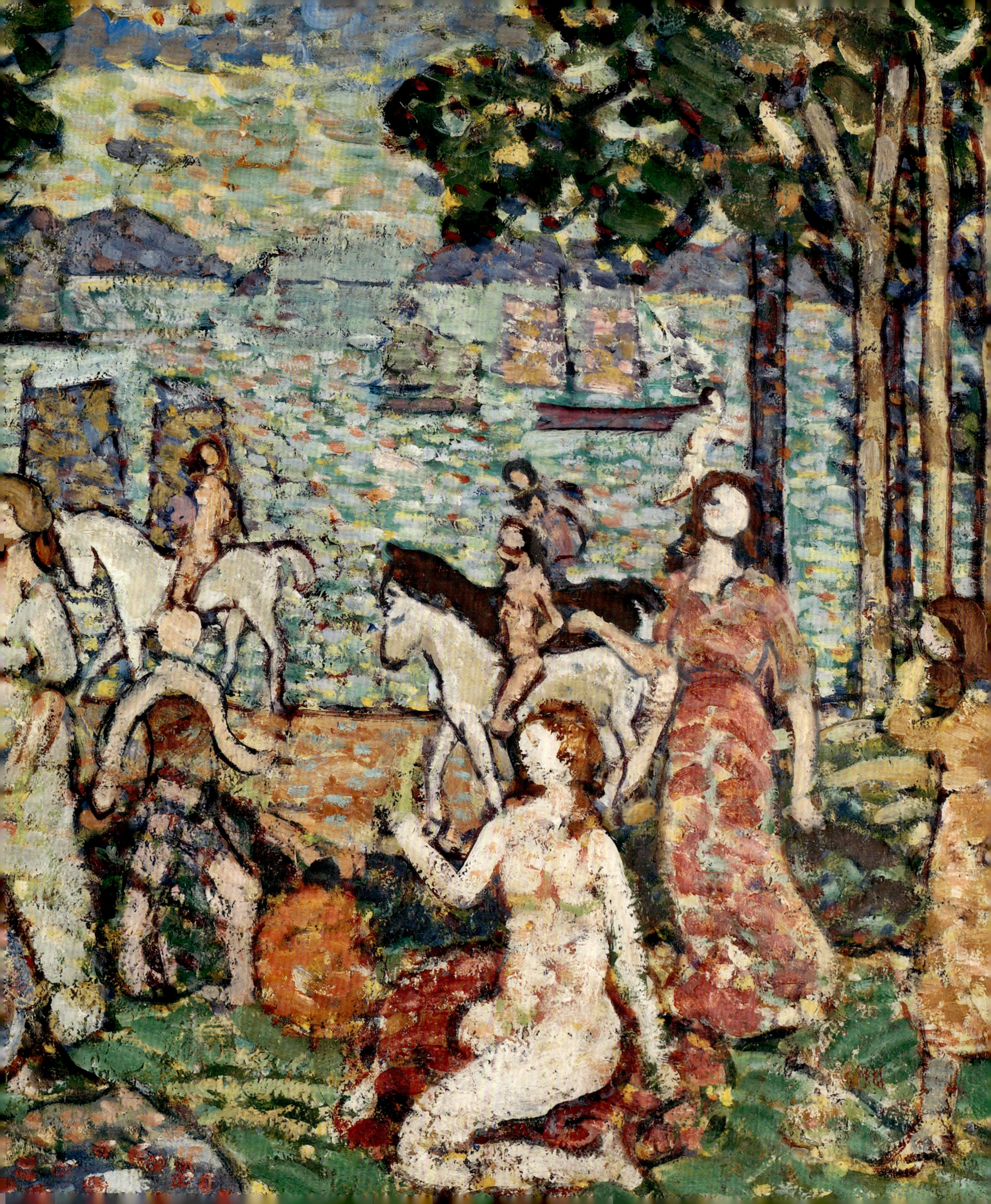

Prendergast:
Change and Sea-Change

NANCY MOWLL MATHEWS

Maurice Prendergast's paintings by the sea span one of the most dramatic periods in world history, and thanks to the artist's keen interest in new movements of all kinds, they testify not only to the emergence of modern art but to modern technology and society as well. Yet, for all Prendergast's interest in change, these paintings are remarkably similar to one another, as if he took the seacoast as a touchstone against which all new ideas would be tested. The result is a body of work best understood as changing in a special way, we might even say as a "sea change."

According to the dictionary, a "sea change" (used with or without hyphen) is a major transformation, visible to all, brought about by a seemingly inexorable natural force such as the sea. The term was brought into general use by Shakespeare in the hauntingly beautiful song delivered by the wind sprite Ariel in *The Tempest* (1610):

> Full fathom five thy father lies;
> Of his bones are coral made;
> Those are pearls that were his eyes:
> Nothing of him that doth fade,
> But doth suffer a sea-change
> Into something rich and strange.
> Sea-nymphs hourly ring his knell:
> Ding-dong.
> Hark! now I hear them—Ding-dong, bell.

The process that Ariel describes is radical—but metamorphic. Ferdinand's father does not disappear lying on the sea floor; rather, his body is changed from ordinary human substance into precious materials of luminous color (coral and pearl). The rhythmic ringing of the knell by sea nymphs echoes the rhythmic ebb and flow of the waves that caused this change to occur slowly and over time.

Detail, *The Promenade*, 1913 (plate 53)

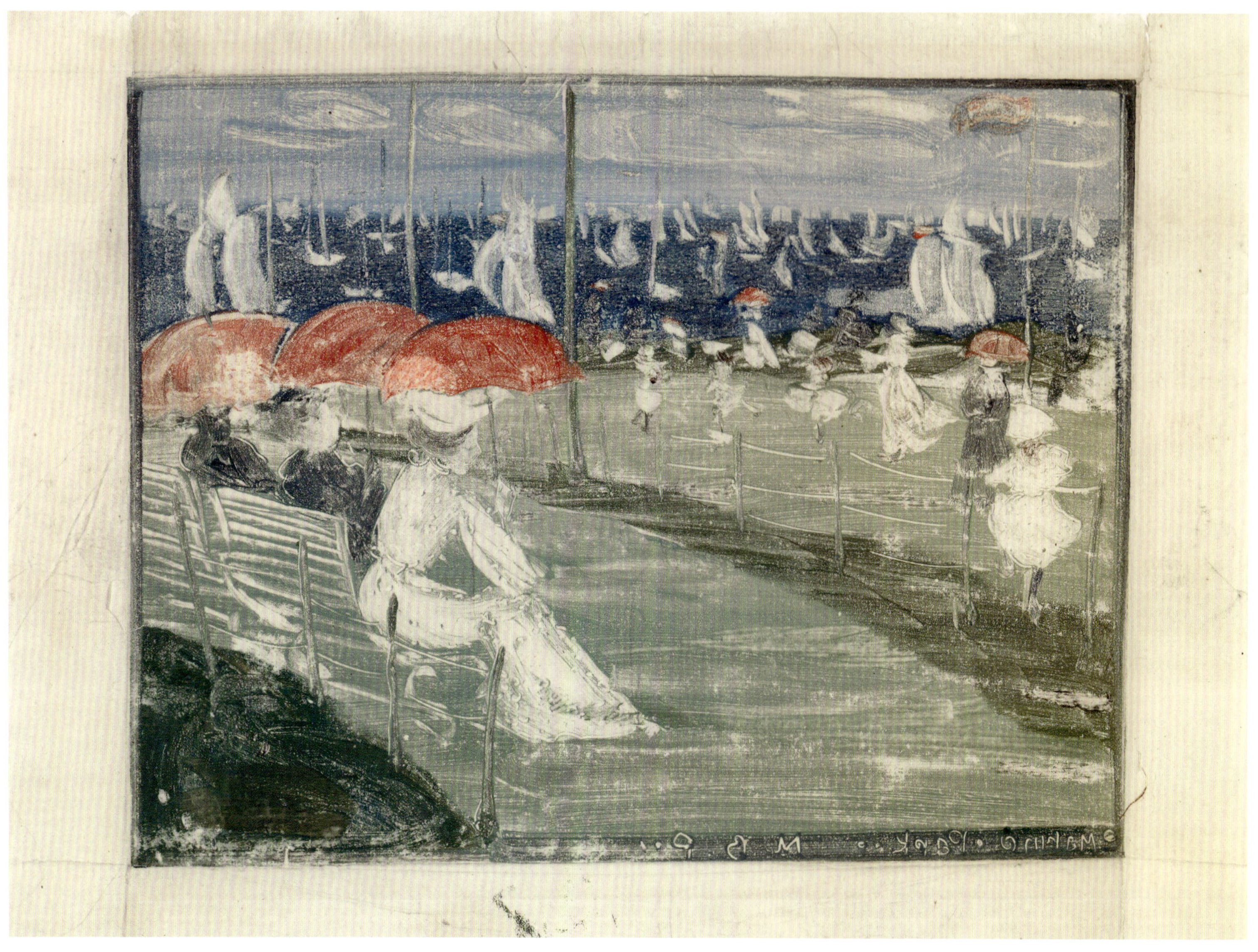

Fig. 5. Maurice Prendergast, *Marine Park, South Boston*, 1895–97. Monotype on paper with pencil additions, 9⅞ × 12⅝ in. (25.1 × 32.1 cm). Williams College Museum of Art, Williamstown, Massachusetts; Gift of George and Wilhelmina Batchelder (98.2)

This is the kind of change that we see in Prendergast's art. His signature motifs of seaside beaches and parks were established early in the 1890s, and, like Shakespeare's magical body, they remained until the end of Prendergast's life (plate 53). He returned to these themes with wave-like rhythm, each time transforming them into a new style as he responded to changes in modern art and historical circumstances. In the last phase of this metamorphic process, in the 1910s, the layers of paint are so visible that we actually see the paintings change in front of our eyes. With their complex brushstrokes, dabs of color, and wavy figures, it is fair to say that we see them "suffer a sea-change/Into something rich and strange."

Although his theme is the seaside, Prendergast cannot be called a landscape painter. He presents the coast as a place of intersections: between water and land, people and nature, and work and leisure. Transitions, zones, borders, and the

NANCY MOWLL MATHEWS

morphing of one substance into another become the essence of his art as they are the essence of his subject. In more than a thousand oils, watercolors, and monotypes devoted to the relationship of land and water, Prendergast penetrated, dissected, and clarified this transitional world. Different compositions emphasize different zones of the coastline: from immersion in the water (swimming), to floating on the water (boating), to the beach (rocky or sandy), to the promenade (boardwalk or other walkway by the beach), to the seaside park or harbor (overlooking the water), and finally to the seaside village (completely on land). Often the zones are graphically presented as bands from foreground to background, as in *The Promenade*, or, twenty years earlier, *Marine Park, South Boston* (fig. 5), whose concentric zones he portrayed as ripples of green spreading out until they meet the blue of the sea.

"Prendergast is essentially a part of the NEW MOVEMENT . . ."
Wrote Frederick James Gregg in a short essay for the catalogue of Prendergast's first major retrospective exhibition, in 1915, in which *The Promenade* was exhibited.[1] The two men had been working and socializing together since the Armory Show of 1913, and much of the text thus reflects statements made by Prendergast in his own letters. As a result, Gregg's essay—quotations from which serve as the subheads to the present essay—is invaluable in understanding how the artist and his associates saw his goals and leadership in the modern art world.

Gregg begins with a few striking essentials he wants the reader to know about Prendergast: (1) that he is the president of the Association of American Painters and Sculptors, the organization that had just pulled off one of the milestones of American art history, the "International Exhibition of Modern Art," or Armory Show, of 1913; (2) that in his hometown of Boston he is the *only* artist "affected by distinctly European influences;" and (3) that he has just moved to New York. In those few sentences, Prendergast is crowned king of modern art with its most important attributes: European influences and a New York base.[2]

As a leader for change, Gregg asserts, Prendergast is revered "particularly by the younger men" and is "regarded with deep respect abroad." Although his art may not be easily understood, he is equal to such giants of the Paris school as Cézanne and Matisse in innovation and may be called "a great master, one of the very few Americans to whom that term may be applied in sincerity and truth." The next generation can look at Prendergast's groundbreaking style and see "art in America in the near future."[3]

In this regard, it comes as a surprise to read that the subject of Prendergast's art is primarily the New England coast, specifically Massachusetts, not a subject that today we would consider groundbreaking. But Gregg's point is that Prendergast's paintings do not depend on representation but on "intrinsic art value" and the ability to create his own world through "intense personal expression."[4] Whether he is painting

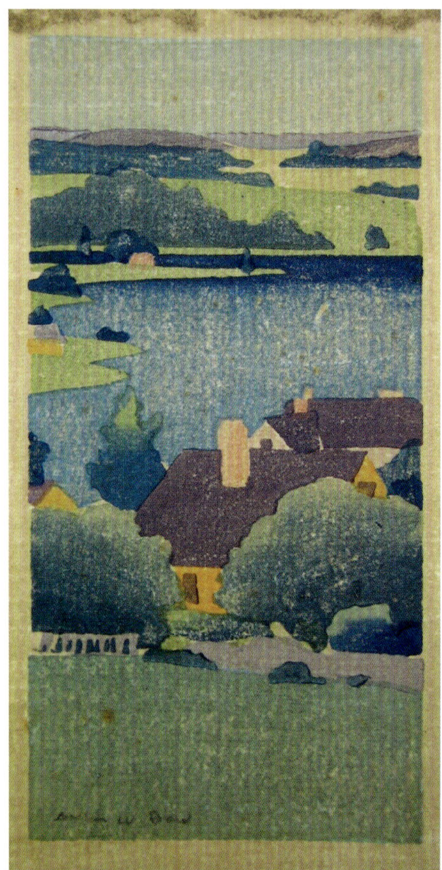

Fig. 6. Arthur Wesley Dow, *A Bend in the River*, c. 1895. Woodblock print, 2⅞ × 5⅝ in. (7.3 × 14.3 cm). Ipswich Museum, Massachusetts

in "Venice, Paris, or Marblehead, Massachusetts," says Gregg, Prendergast makes the subject his own. By 1915, the idea that the modern artist was charged with achieving personal expression (not representation) was very much in vogue. The artists featured in the Armory Show, such as Cézanne, Gauguin, Matisse, and Duchamp, had made that point vividly. Nevertheless, even if the subject of a painting should be transformed by personal expression, a subject must still be chosen. And in Prendergast's case, he chose land and water imagery two out of three times throughout the course of his almost forty-year career. And he chose the New England coast at least half the time. This was not just a matter of convenience. As Gregg points out, by 1915 Prendergast no longer lived in Boston, and he had to go out of his way to study the motif that he would transform again and again.[5] The coast in Prendergast's *The Promenade* was like a siren, luring him with her song and challenging him to possess this rocky margin between land and sea.

"Beginning with his earliest works"

Although in his essay Gregg refers to the art and ideas of 1915, he makes clear that the same principles can be seen throughout Prendergast's career, as he is an artist of unusually stable and deeply personal artistic goals. Of these, Gregg writes, the most important is Prendergast's interest in the abstract shapes of the composition, upon which artists of the emerging modernist styles believed the success of any painting depended. From Maurice Denis's often-quoted admonition of 1890, "Remember that a painting—before being a battle horse, a nude woman, or an anecdote of some sort—is essentially a flat surface covered with colors, put together in a certain order,"[6] to Arthur Wesley Dow's 1899 design textbook *Composition*, Prendergast's art was rooted in a climate of what Gregg calls "design, and again design, and yet again design."

Dow (fig. 6), who painted and taught in his own design summer school on the New England coast in Ipswich, Massachusetts (as well as at Columbia University), stressed the problems of "opposition, transition, subordination, repetition, and symmetry in art."[7] The "NEW MOVEMENT" of the 1890s in American art Gregg refers to included Dow's abstract theorizing as well as Impressionism, which had taken root among Boston artists who, like Prendergast, painted along the New England coast. Following in the footsteps of such midcentury specialists as Fitz Henry Lane, Childe Hassam and Frank Benson, both members of the "Ten American Painters," sought out seaside imagery. Hassam, who had been Prendergast's role model in the 1880s, returned from Paris in 1889 to live in New York. But from 1890 on, he spent many summers on the island of Appledore, Maine, just north of Cape Ann, where he painted the seaside gardens and rocky cliffs of this very private retreat of the wealthy and cultured (fig. 7). Benson found a summer getaway nearby in Newcastle, New Hampshire, in Portsmouth Harbor (fig. 8), where he ran a summer school with Edmund Tarbell.

NANCY MOWLL MATHEWS

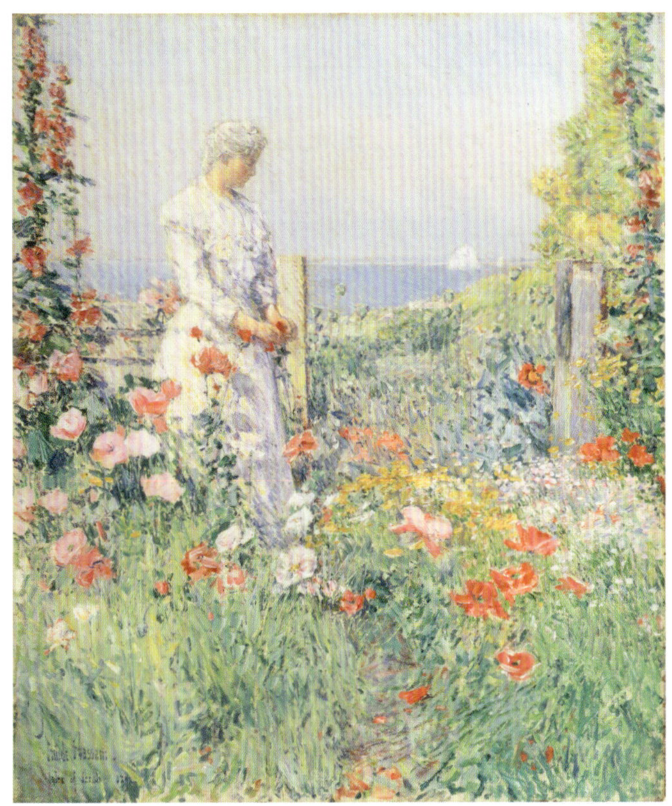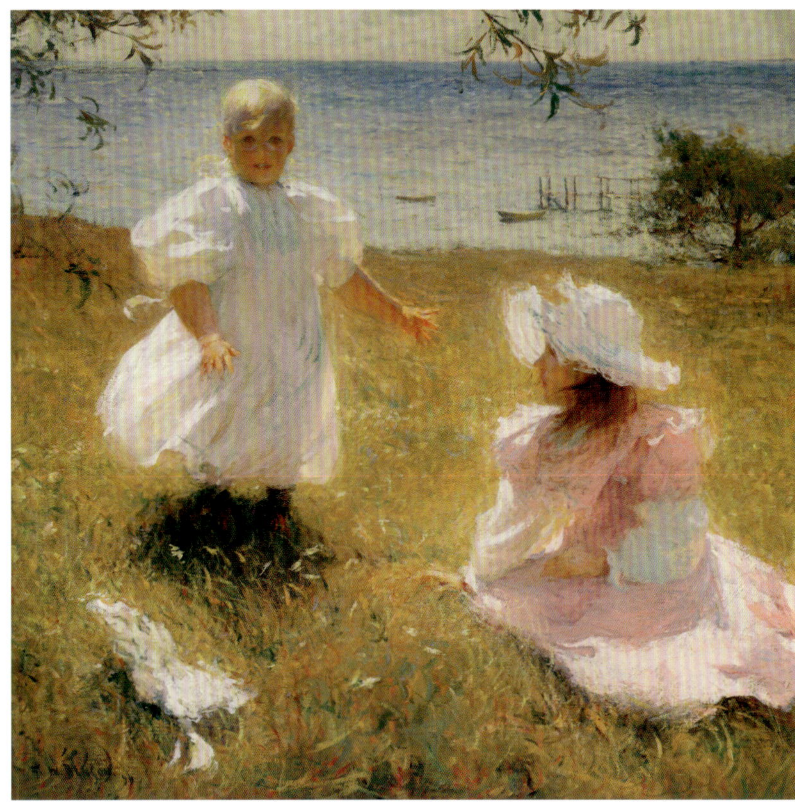

In 1900, he would move his summer location farther north, to North Haven Island in Maine.

But as wedded as the American Impressionists were to scenes by the sea, none was as obsessed by it as Prendergast, who saw more than just a beautiful setting for charming scenes of friends and family. In this regard, Prendergast's closest parallel in the 1890s was Winslow Homer. Although not an Impressionist, Homer's "modernity" was strong enough that he was invited to join Hassam, Benson, and others in forming the Impressionist-leaning Ten American Painters (Homer declined). Comparing Prendergast's *Handkerchief Point* (plate 12) to Homer's *Saco Bay* (fig. 9), it seems impossible that these two worlds could coexist. Yet, in fact, Homer would have needed to venture only a short distance from his house to see the very sights that Prendergast painted, for by that time large resort hotels and excursionists had invaded Prouts Neck, as they had everywhere else along the coast.[8] These two works could have been painted simultaneously, each artist turning his back on the other. Both men had what Gregg would call "the determination never to be moved from his own chosen path," and in this determination they both chose the New England coast as their grand theme, mining for a lifetime the endless subtleties of its ebb and flow.

Prendergast's seaside scenes began to show up regularly in Boston exhibitions beginning in 1895. Although he was almost forty, he was considered a newcomer. He

Fig. 7. Childe Hassam, *In the Garden (Celia Thaxter in Her Garden)*, 1892. Oil on canvas, 22¼ × 18 in. (56.5 × 45.7 cm). Smithsonian American Art Museum, Washington, D.C.; Gift of John Gellatly (1929.6.52)

Fig. 8. Frank Benson, *The Sisters*, 1899. Oil on canvas, 40 × 40 in. (101.6 × 101.6 cm). Terra Foundation for American Art, Chicago; Daniel J. Terra Collection (1999.11)

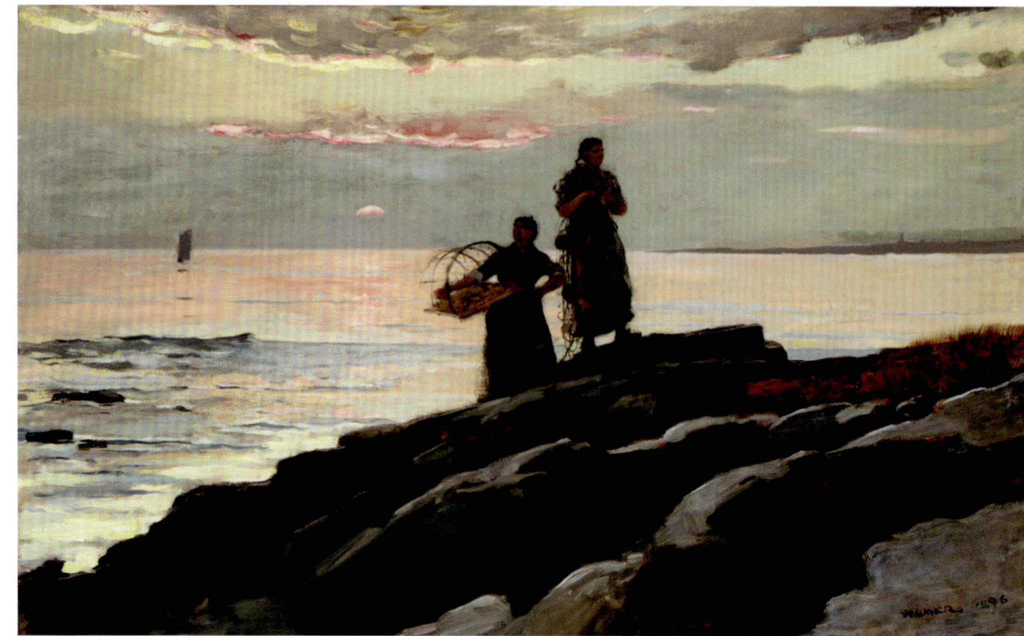

Fig. 9. Winslow Homer, *Saco Bay*, 1896. Oil on canvas, 23⅞ × 37 in. (60.5 × 96.4 cm). Sterling and Francine Clark Art Institute, Williamstown, Massachusetts (1955.5)

had spent the first two decades of his working life as a commercial artist, lettering and designing for an advertising company in Boston. By 1891, having accumulated enough cash reserves to make the switch to fine art, he spent almost four years studying and experimenting with new styles in Paris. When he returned to Boston, Prendergast was a master of his own watercolor style, one based heavily on what he had observed of new French art. By that time the seacoast itself had a newly modern appearance, thanks to the efforts up and down the shore to replace the outdated wharves and commercial equipment that had once been the hallmark of New England maritime industries. Whaling and the processing of whale oil, for instance, long a mainstay of the Massachusetts maritime economy, had been on the decline since crude oil was discovered in Pennsylvania in 1857. Railroads had taken away much of the shipping business that had transported goods from coast to coast and up the Mississippi in the United States. Supporting industries that had flourished along the thousands of coastal inlets in a maritime economy, such as ice and salt, simply disappeared. Prendergast's first coastal scenes were painted in Westport, Maine, along Brook's Cove (fig. 10).[9] Today nothing remains of the transport schooners, logging docks, and other local industries he depicted. Instead, the peninsula is entirely rural and the shore lined with vacation homes.

The transition had begun during Prendergast's lifetime. He observed the massive retooling of the seashore for the new leisure industries that grew simultaneously with the postmaritime New England economy. Railroads spread out from the cities to the coast to serve the holiday migrations that began to occur. Municipalities, in turn, offered visitors public beaches, seaside benches and restaurants, and amusement

NANCY MOWLL MATHEWS

parks. Steamboat lines out of the larger
ports ran regular excursion boats to harder
to reach locations. In the United States—by
1900 the largest economy in the world—
prosperity offered not only unheard-of leisure
but the money to support it, and soon leisure
became a political cause, with labor unions
agitating for forty-hour work weeks and guar-
anteed vacations.[10]

Prendergast chose to study the leisure
seekers, but he was not one of them. While
the tourists were enjoying extended holidays
roaming the beaches and taking pleasure
cruises, he was the workman, diligently plying
the sketchbooks and paint boxes that were
the tools of his trade. In his earliest paintings

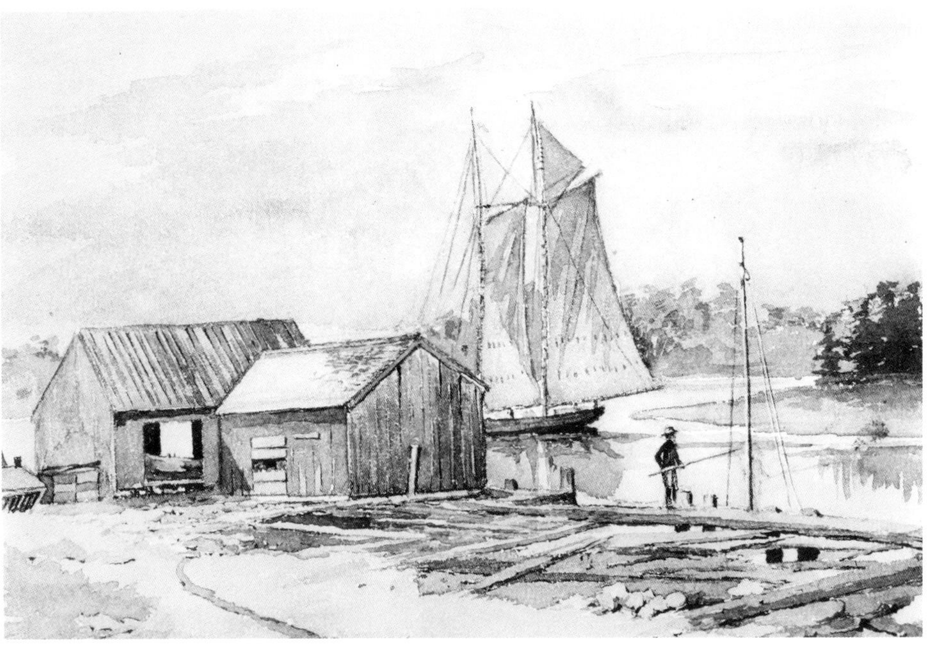

Fig. 10. Maurice Prendergast, *Brook's
Cove, Westport, Maine*, c. 1889.
Watercolor on paper, 7 × 10½ in.
(17.8 × 26.7 cm). Whereabouts unknown;
photograph courtesy Prendergast
Archive and Study Center, Williams
College Museum of Art, Williamstown,
Massachusetts

of people overlooking the sea, such as *St. Servan Fisherman* (plate 1), the lone fisherman standing on the shore, surveying the boats and weighing the success of his next
fishing trip, could be Prendergast himself, assessing the scene and wondering if he will
make a success of his next painting. Like the fishing community Homer painted so often
on those perilous rocks, Prendergast, too, was working tirelessly at a risky profession
based on that same Atlantic Ocean.

Leisure was not the frivolous theme that artists such as Homer avoided in their
pursuit of great art; it had become a serious subject for a newly mature society. With
his well-dressed idlers using their leisure time to drink in the exhilaration of that special
zone of wind and water, green and blue, Prendergast in the 1890s captured this spirit
of health and progressive thinking. A decade later, George Bellows would say of
Prendergast's paintings that "this fellow's works give a wonderful sense of quiet repose
which would add dignity to any place where repose was in order . . . one would love
to have a place decorated by his paintings where he could go and rest."[11]

"He never condescended to make his art easier for the public"

The repose Bellows talked about in Prendergast's paintings comes from the combination of carefully zoned compositions and evocative subject matter. But Prendergast's
desire to be part of the "new movement" pushed his art to a point where only others
interested in modernist experimentation could follow. Bellows's letter begins by say-
ing, "Prendergast, whose pictures are often laughed at, are to me the most refined of
decorations."[12] After 1900, when Prendergast moved away from the Impressionist seaside subjects, he enlarged his sphere to New York and kept a vigilant eye on Paris for

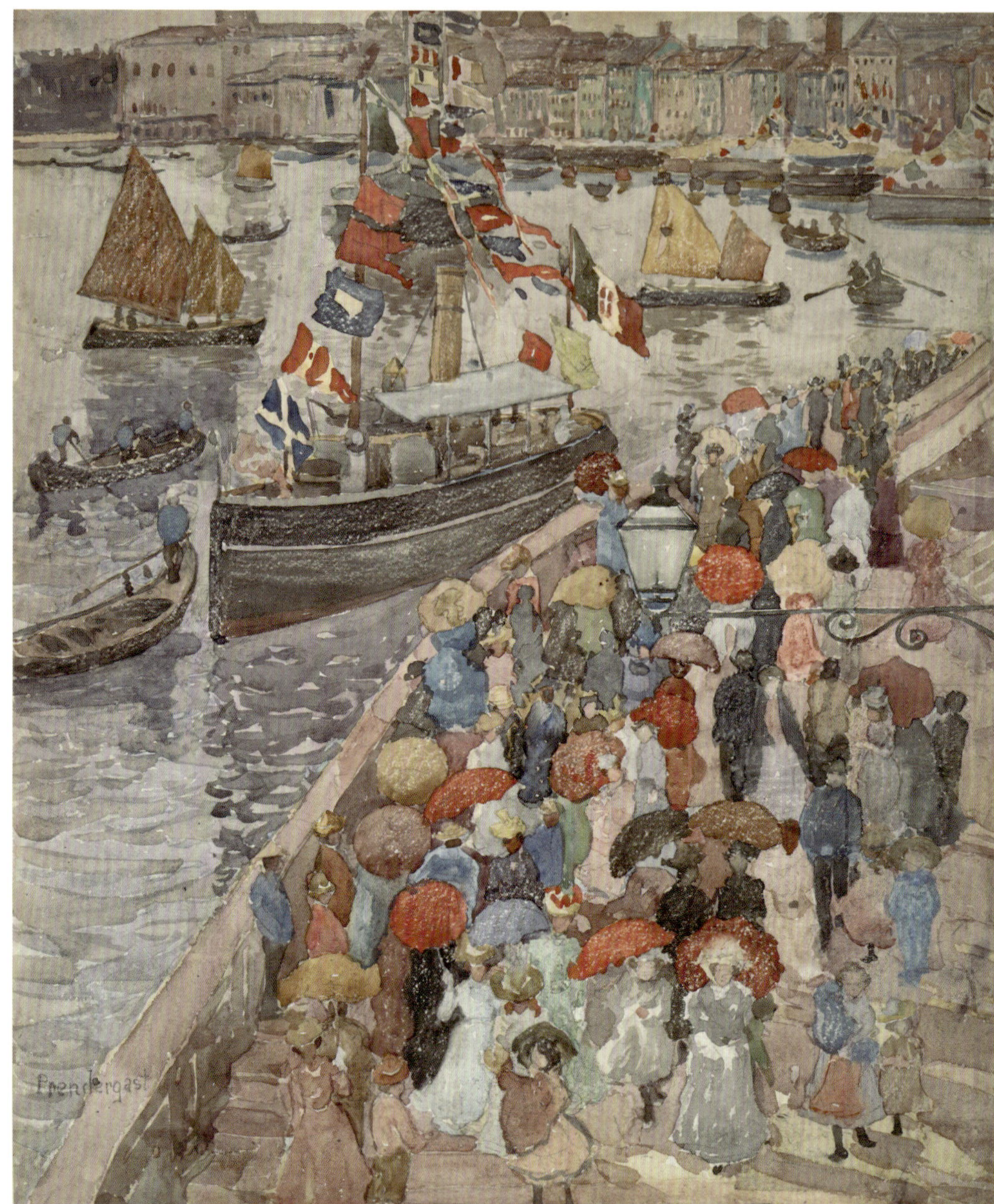

Fig. 11. Maurice Prendergast, *The Quai, Venice* (recto), c. 1899. Watercolor with graphite on paper, 15⅝ × 12¾ in. (39.7 × 32.4 cm). Yale University Art Gallery, New Haven; Gift of Arthur G. Altschul, B.A. 1943, and Diana Altschul (1991.87.1a–b)

new impulses. In doing so, he forged lifelong friendships with Robert Henri, Arthur B. Davies, and William Glackens—and discovered Cézanne. At this time, Prendergast's critical reception, which had been almost universally positive for the first ten years of his fine-art career, began to divide into those who appreciated Parisian modernism and those who did not. Furthermore, the early patrons, including Sarah Choate Sears, who funded his first trip to Italy in 1898–99, fell by the wayside, and he did not replace them with major collectors until after 1910.

In 1900, Prendergast had his first solo exhibition in New York, at the Macbeth Gallery.[13] The exhibition consisted almost entirely of his new watercolors, such as

   NANCY MOWLL MATHEWS

The Quai, Venice (fig. 11), which shows the canal city with its abstract lines and tourist crowds. Although the reviews were enthusiastic, Prendergast was nervous about his reinterpretation of such a well-known artistic subject. "Mr. Macbeth likes them," he wrote to Mr. and Mrs. Sears, "said he never had anything like them on his walls before." He added, however, that "somebody proposed having chairs in the gallery so they could sit down to recover from their shock."[14] Prendergast had exhibited in New York before and apparently already knew some of the progressive artists and critics, and this strong presence propelled him to the forefront of that aggressively modern art crowd.

By 1901, Prendergast had produced a series of New York scenes, such as *The East River* (plate 20), that shared Henri's interest in the rawness of the city. Although Prendergast went no further with Ashcan subject matter, he continued to sympathize with progressive social causes and participated in several art exhibitions in support of socialist organizations.[15] He was invited by Henri to join him, along with John Sloan, George Luks, William Glackens, and Arthur B. Davies, for an exhibition at the National Arts Club in 1904, which turned out to be a rehearsal for the exhibition of "The Eight" four years later.[16] This time he showed only oil panels of promenades along the beach, mostly studies of the coast near Salem, Massachusetts. Much more stylized than his earlier beach and park scenes, these works heralded a complete break with the art of his earlier years. The new prominence given the sky, now painted in thick, heavy brushstrokes, is a sign that the entire canvas is unified. There are no more distinctions between earth, sky, and water; they are all, as Maurice Denis put it, "a flat surface, covered with colors."

When the forthcoming exhibition of "The Eight" was announced in the spring of 1907, Prendergast had French modernist theory on his mind. He promptly sailed for France for a long summer of studying the exhibitions of modern art in Paris and painting on the Normandy coast. It was during this trip to Paris that Prendergast was finally able to see works by the French artists who until that time he had only read about in books and art magazines.[17] He was well aware that faithful representation of nature was increasingly under attack, but when he saw Cézanne's regularized broken brushstrokes and repeated subjects, as in the Mont Sainte-Victoire series, Prendergast realized that, although he was on the right track, he had not gone far enough. From Matisse and the Fauves he learned that color could be liberated from visual reality to have an emotional or symbolic meaning all its own. He immediately began experimenting while in Paris, and when he went out to the coast the full impact of the new ideas exploded into the extraordinary oils and watercolors of the Saint-Malo shoreline. Using his innate color sense and his new appreciation of the energy of broken planes arranged in

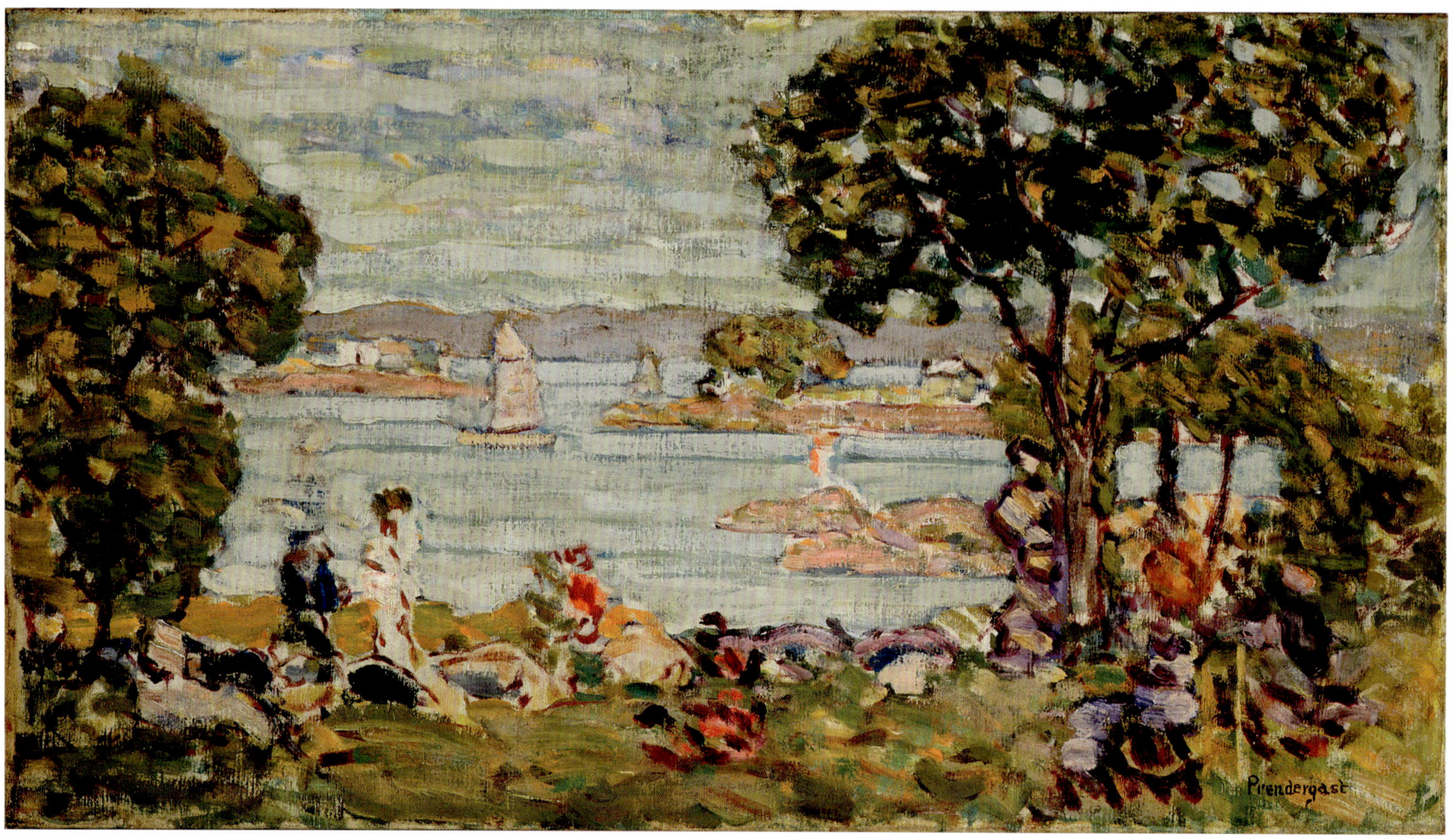

Fig. 12. Maurice Prendergast, *Cove, Maine*, c. 1907–10. Oil on canvas, 17⅜ × 30⅛ in. (44.1 × 76.5 cm). Los Angeles County Museum of Art; Gift of Mrs. Charles Prendergast (M.91.16.1)

horizontal bands from the top to the bottom of the canvas, Prendergast was able to create a new reality out of his old familiar theme.

A few months later Prendergast was able to show off his discoveries in "The Eight" show, which opened in New York at the Macbeth Gallery in February and traveled to several other cities (plate 36). His work, shown in this context, was polarizing. It stood out among the Ashcan paintings of Sloan (see fig. 2), Luks, Glackens (see fig. 3), and Henri, who had taken seriously the goal of the exhibition: to celebrate American art. Critics noticed the French subjects and influences, mentioning Cézanne specifically. Soon after the exhibition Stieglitz mounted a show of Matisse's drawings, which elicited comparisons to Prendergast's works: "[Matisse's] color work, like that of Maurice Prendergast's in the recent display of 'The Eight,' would seem to be simply spots of paint daubed on here and there, perhaps with some idea of form or composition, not at first recognizable."[18] Although Prendergast's co-exhibitors were delighted with the new work and supported his interest in French trends, the larger art community began to be split on whether it was an affront to homegrown artists and styles.

The summer after "The Eight" show, Prendergast submitted two paintings to the annual exhibition of contemporary art held at the Poland Spring Art Gallery in South Poland, Maine.[19] Several of his friends from Boston also exhibited their work at this venue, and it was probably through them that the connection was made. Prendergast likely traveled north that summer to spend a few days in Poland and out along the coast, since the following year he exhibited a work simply called *Maine* at the Macbeth Gallery.[20] There are several works with such titles, including *Cove, Maine* (fig. 12), that are dated by stylistic similarities to the Saint-Malo oils.

After Prendergast's return to painting along the New England coast, the Normandy coast was still on his mind. Although he had the American motif in front of him, he strove to work, like Cézanne, "in deeply meditative sessions, heightening the color sensations and elevating form into a decorative concept and color to its most harmonious register. Thus, the more the artist works, the further his work distances itself from the objective."[21]

"Puritanical, unemotional, and unimaginative environment of New England"

The seaside scenes of the New England coast that followed Prendergast's trip to France in 1907 began to incorporate an element that up to this point had been absent from his work: the nude bather (fig. 13). Although it is impossible to pinpoint when these small Cézannesque bathers first appeared along the rocky coasts of Prendergast's paintings, they made their public debut in New York in April 1910.[22] In the next few years, Prendergast would develop this motif into grander and more abstract compositions, ultimately exhibiting such work at the Armory Show of 1913 (fig. 14).[23] The mixture of nude and clothed figures in a bathing context in French modernist art can be traced to Manet's *Déjeuner sur l'herbe* (1862–63, Musée d'Orsay, Paris) and was quickly associated by critics with the European art that hung in the main galleries of the Armory Show. The deliberate awkwardness of the figures, meanwhile, was related to Cézanne, whose own were said to "evoke a shuddering sense of the bestial."[24]

The reinterpretation of classical themes in an abstract manner was a hallmark of most of the artists who had recently been dubbed Post-Impressionist, including Gauguin and Matisse (see the essays by Joseph J. Rishel and Richard J. Wattenmaker in this volume). For Prendergast, it had even more personal significance, since the liberation of his art was followed by a liberation in the form of his private erotic drawings of nudes, which can be found throughout his sketchbooks. Theorists on travel and tourism in recent

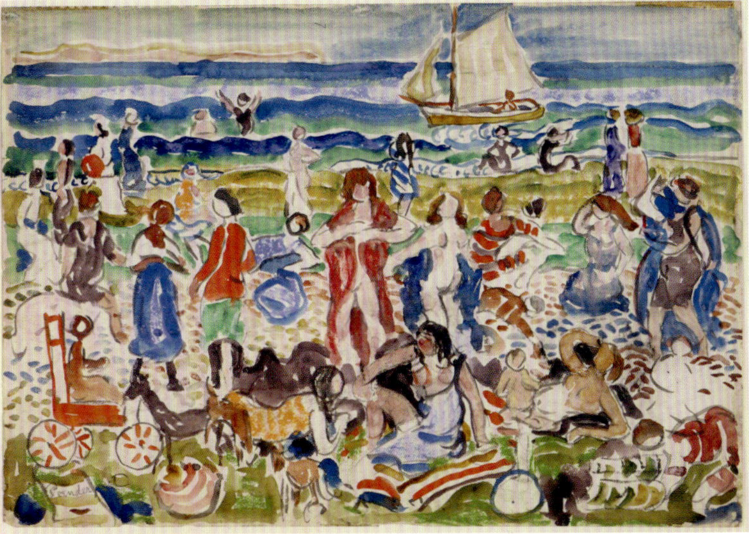

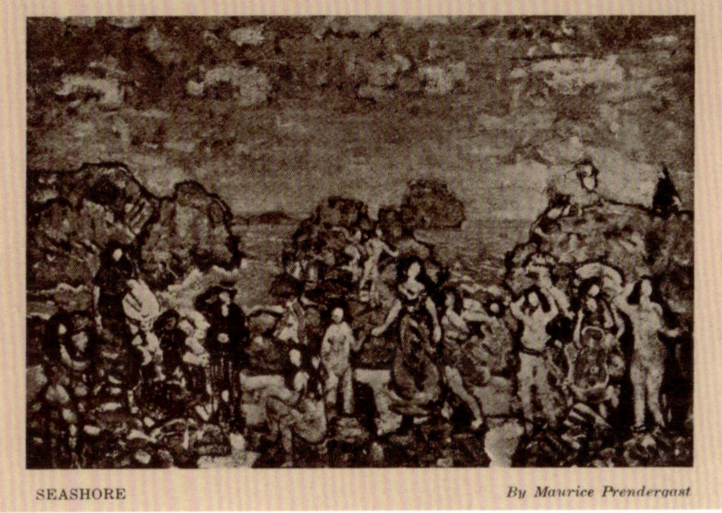

Fig. 13. Maurice Prendergast, *Bathers*, c. 1916–19. Watercolor, pencil, pastel, and black chalk on paper, 14 × 19⅞ in. (35.4 × 50.5 cm). Saint Louis Art Museum; Gift of Mr. and Mrs. G. Gordon Hertslet (55:1967)

Fig. 14. Maurice Prendergast, *Seashore*, c. 1913 (whereabouts unknown). Postcard produced in conjunction with the Armory Show, 1913. Walt Kuhn Papers, Archives of American Art, Smithsonian Institution, Washington, D.C.

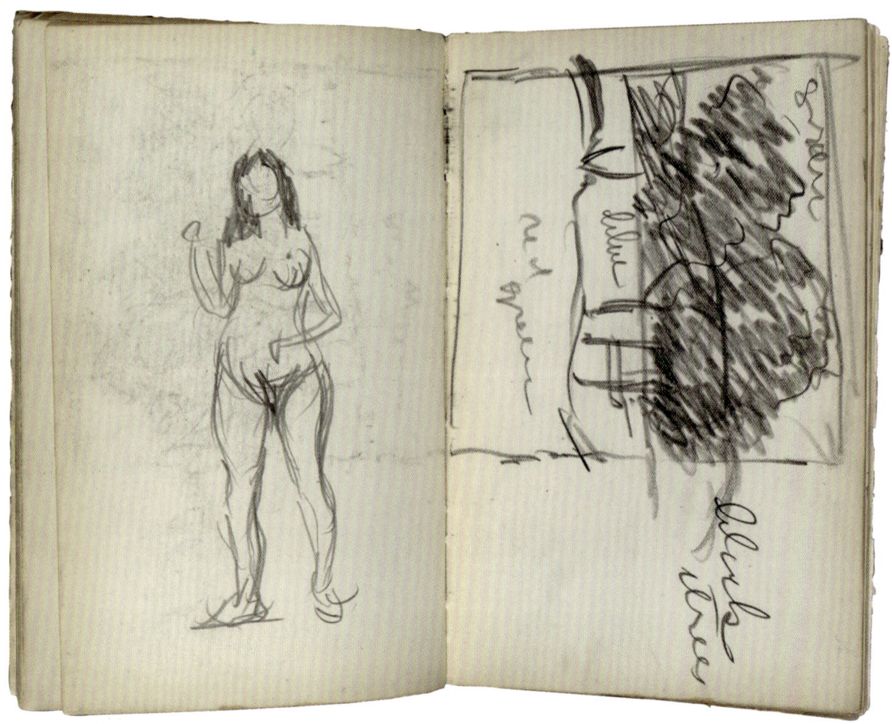

Fig. 15. Maurice Prendergast, *Sketchbook 34*, c. 1913. Graphite pencil on blank paper in notebook, 7 11/16 × 5 1/8 in. (19.6 × 13 cm). Museum of Fine Arts, Boston; Gift of Mrs. Charles Prendergast in honor of Perry T. Rathbone (1972.1124)

years have emphasized the sensation of being "elsewhere," of "crossing boundaries" when we leave our workaday worlds for the sensory pleasures of such holiday destinations.[25] Prendergast had always infused beach and seaside parks with female beauty, but by 1910 he had crossed the boundary into overt eroticism (plate 56). While his sketchbooks, like the one he used when he traveled back to Maine to visit Carl Cutler in Brooksville during the summer after the Armory Show (fig. 15), have landscape motifs on separate pages from suggestive drawings of women, in his paintings Prendergast merged the two into mythological but highly charged reinterpretations of the New England coast.

The association of erotic nudes with the chaste rocky peninsulas so recently painted in heroic splendor by Winslow Homer was difficult for some Bostonian critics. As Prendergast's friend Charles Hovey Pepper wrote to William Macbeth, "He is shocking good old Boston with a picture of ladies bathing in the garb of nature by a very dangerous craggy shore."[26] Pepper thought it was a good thing for Boston, but that narrow-mindedness marked a turning point for Prendergast. He soon began looking for a studio in New York, and by 1915 his friend Gregg could proclaim his outrage about how Prendergast was treated in the "Puritanical, unemotional, and unimaginative environment of New England."

"He has superb courage, consistency and determination"

Prendergast's final years, which he spent safely ensconced in the more sympathetic environment of the New York art world, were prosperous ones. He was invited to exhibit in several major shows that blended French and American modernists, and his works were eagerly collected by John Quinn, Albert Barnes, Lilly Bliss, Ferdinand Howald, and Edward Root, among others. As Gregg noted, the attitude of New England critics did not keep Prendergast away from his favorite sites, and every summer, until his failing health prevented it, he took sketching trips north to the coast. Almost ninety sketchbooks have survived, most of which are dated after 1910, and almost sixty were done after Prendergast moved to New York. Only a few of the sketches relate directly to finished works, but the exuberant drawing of beaches, parks, picnickers, and bathers translates into the liveliness of the final watercolors and oils.

NANCY MOWLL MATHEWS

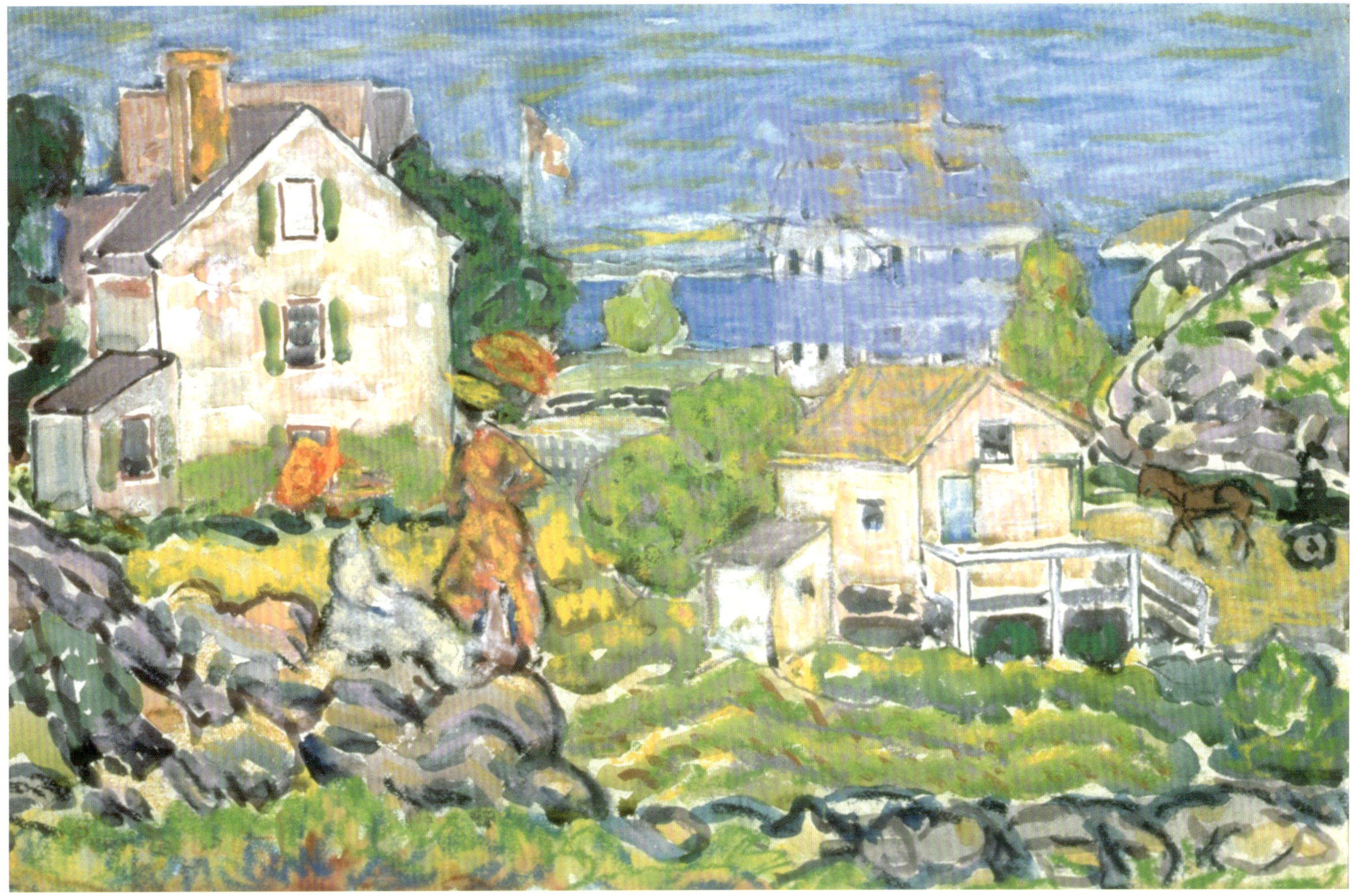

The titles of Prendergast's works suggest that the artist cast a wide net in his summer site selections. *Beach Scene, Maine* (plate 52), *New Hampshire* (plate 67), and *Marblehead Harbor* (fig. 16) seemingly represent visits to three states. And while he did paint in all three, the titles of Prendergast's works are not to be trusted.[27] The watercolors *New Hampshire* and *Marblehead Harbor*, for example, are obviously of the same site, probably Marblehead. In this remarkable pair, we can fully appreciate how metamorphic a painter Prendergast was. *New Hampshire* is in itself a fully conceived and well-drawn depiction of one of the final additions to Prendergast's coastal subject matter: the seaside village. But Prendergast could not help but rethink it, starting with roughly the same composition (although from a greater distance and somewhat changed architecture) and then making radical changes in almost every part. He redrew the figures, the rocks, the texture of the lawns and houses, and, most astoundingly, transformed the entire background into a body of water that matches the sky.

In the years since the new resorts sprang up in the 1890s, much had changed in coastal tourism. The huge hotels built directly on the beach had a short lifespan,

Fig. 16. Maurice Prendergast, *Marblehead Harbor*, 1916 (n.d.). Watercolor and pastel on paper, 13¹³⁄₁₆ × 19⅞ in. (35.1 × 50.5 cm). The University of Michigan Museum of Art, Ann Arbor; Gift of Mrs. Charles Prendergast (1963/2.60)

victims of flooding, fire, and societal change. The waves of immigrants into the United States in the first decades of the twentieth century had put a halt to the leisure advocacy on the part of the labor unions. Eager to work, they would not support the movement toward longer vacations for rest and relaxation, and thus the typical American vacation stalled at two weeks. It remains today the shortest vacation time for workers in any first-world country. Another change in American travel habits occurred with the spread of the automobile, which enabled leisure seekers to travel independently rather than en masse by public transportation and to find their own, less-crowded vacation spots.[28]

Change had always been a positive attribute of Prendergast's art, but in late canvases such as *Sunset and Sea Fog* (plate 72) one senses an elegiac note, as if he were praising a way of life that was now in the past. Symbolist imagery had become part of his aesthetic, and now Prendergast added the New England coast to his list of ancient cultures. The thick paint, built up over time and, perhaps, over another, earlier composition, keeps the artist's hand moving in our imagination.[29] Charles Hovey Pepper remembered Prendergast painting on his loosely stretched canvases and the rhythmic "flop, flop" of the brush.[30] The result, he said, was "such color. Now the opal . . . now a topaz, now a lapis. Trays of jewels."[31] The sea change had reached its final stage.

Over the course of his long career, Prendergast celebrated change in many ways. Drawing on the fluid characteristics of the sea, whose transformative rhythms and zones as it meets the land are so evident in his compositions and brushwork, he was able to imbue his painting with a force that was impossible for other artists to adopt. As Gregg put it, "An imitation Prendergast is almost unthinkable." Consequently, in terms of long-term change in the history of American modern art, Prendergast's stylistic influence was limited. But because of his prominence at a crucial moment in the New York art world, and because of the hypnotic charm of his seaside paintings, Prendergast was able to advocate for modernist theory, particularly the emphasis on personal expression, and to play a part in the sweeping transformation of modern culture that was taking place in front of his eyes.

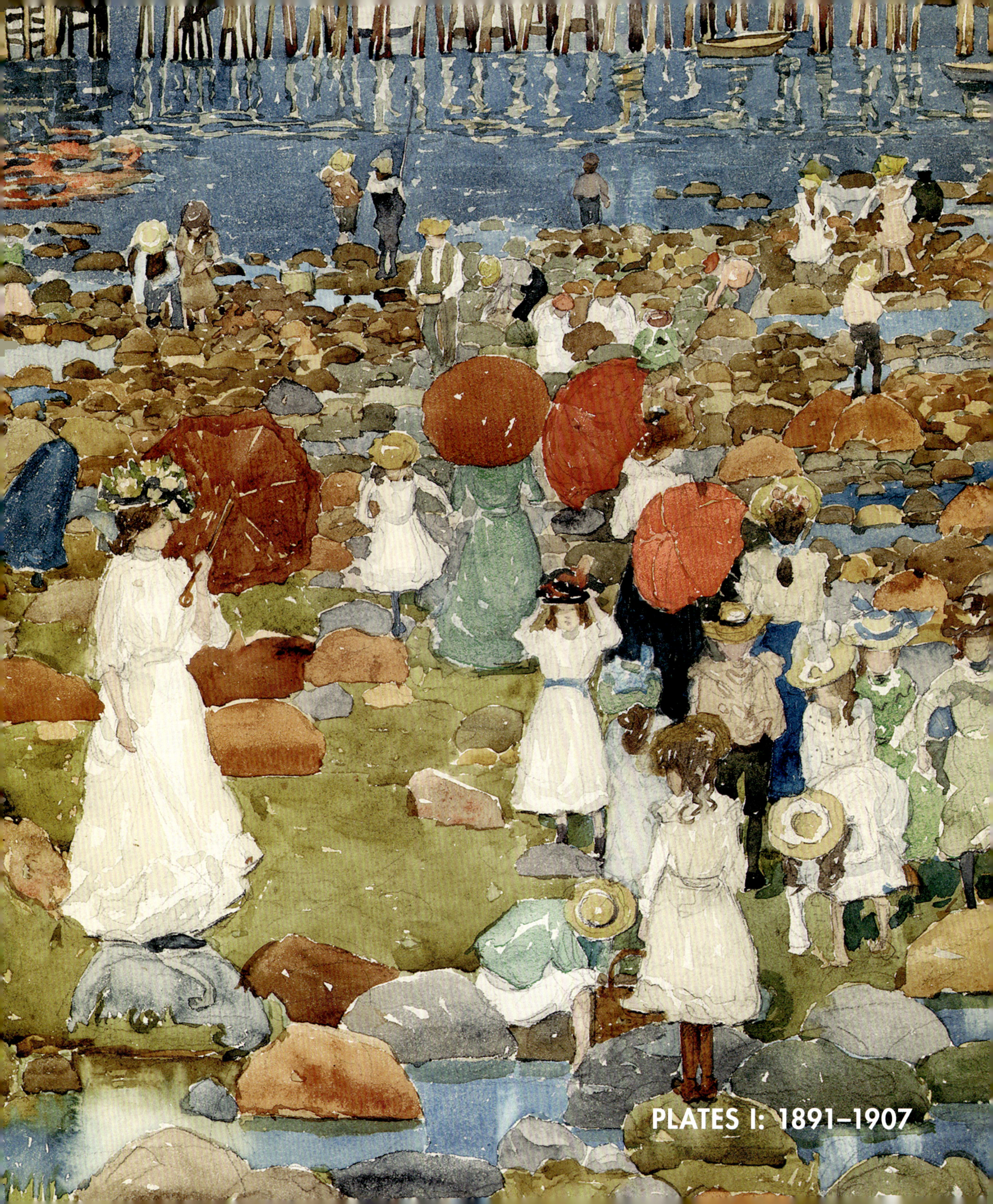

PLATES I: 1891–1907

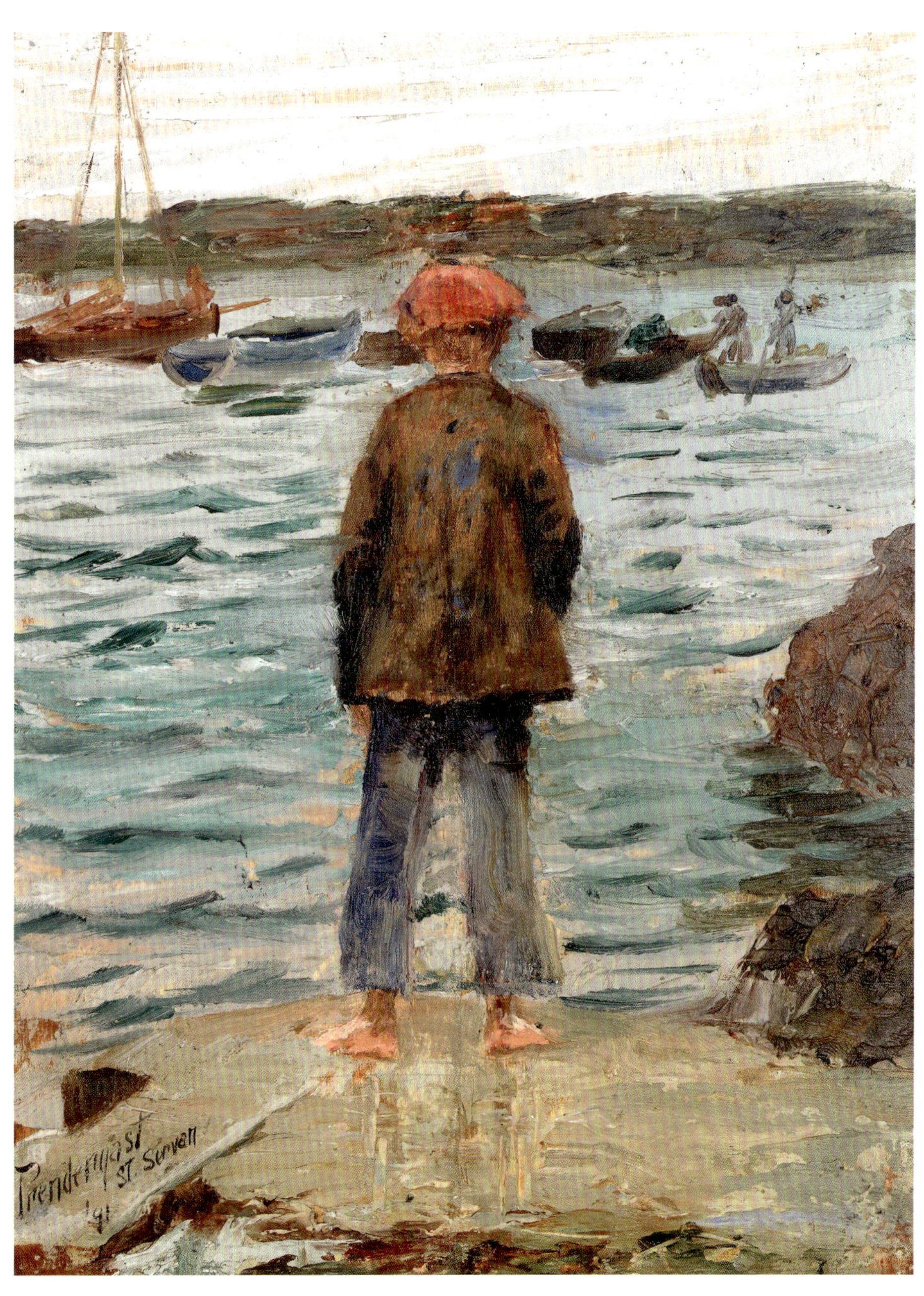

1. *St. Servan Fisherman*, 1891

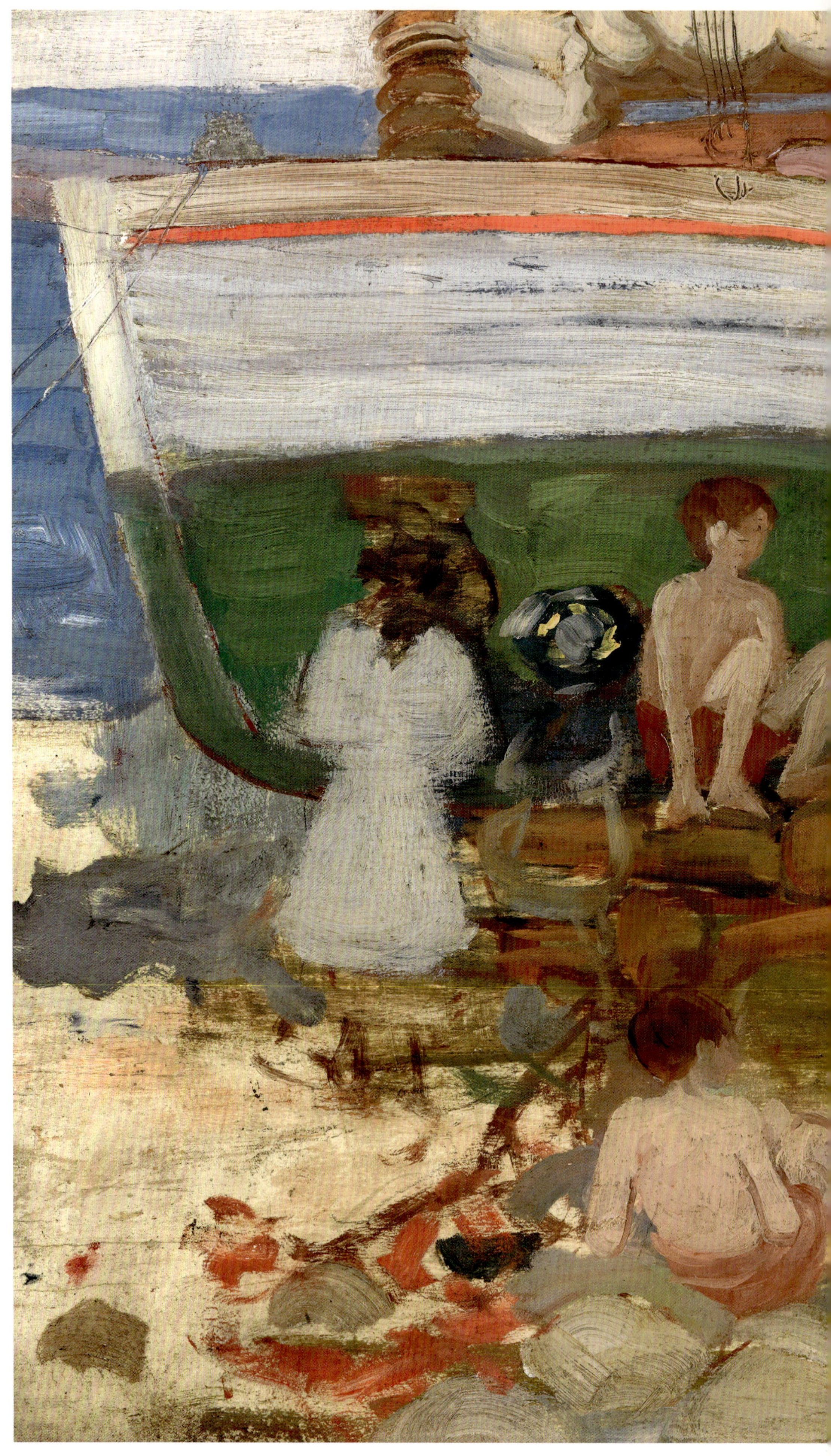

   2. *Low Tide*, c. 1897

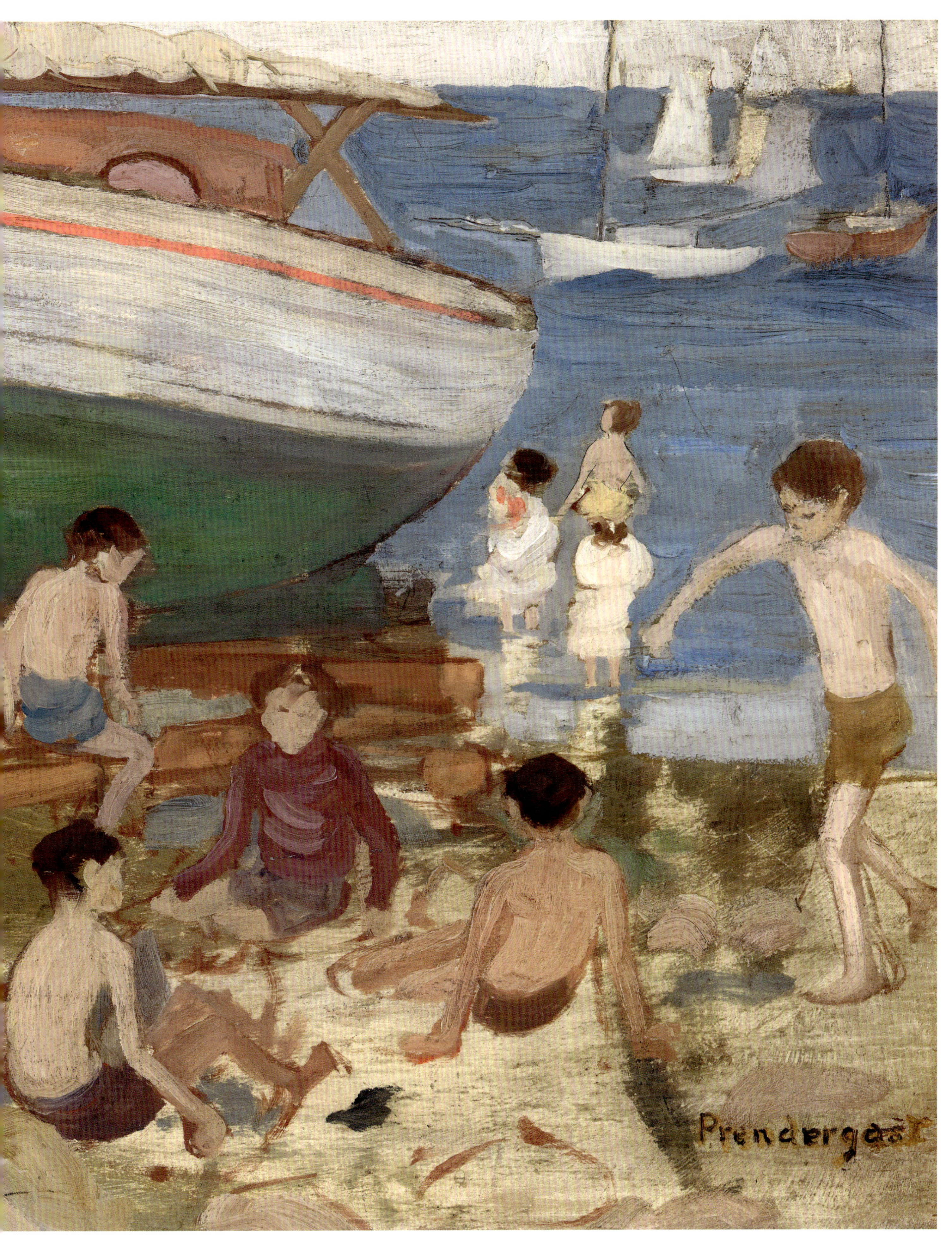
Prendergast

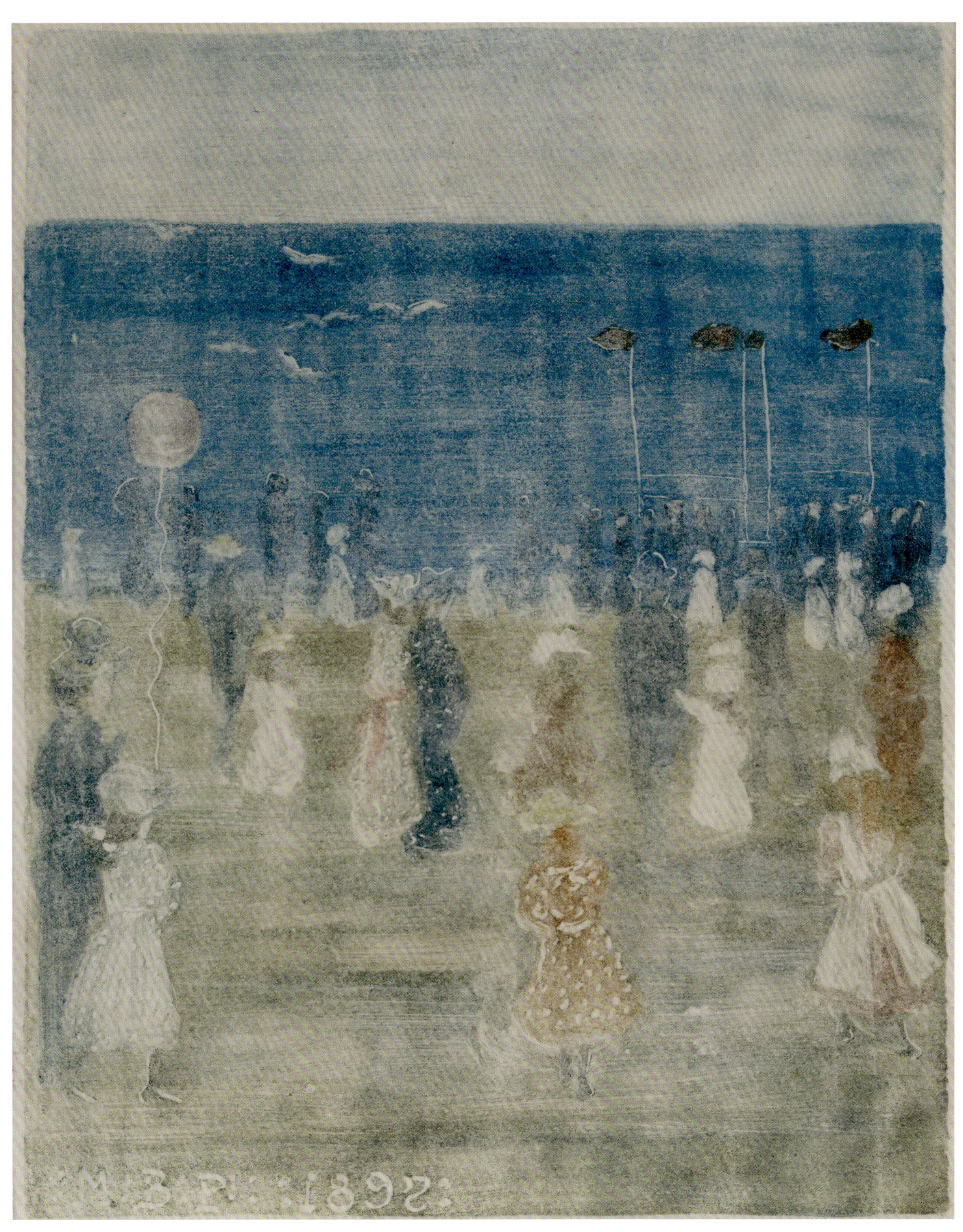

3. *At the Seashore,* 1895

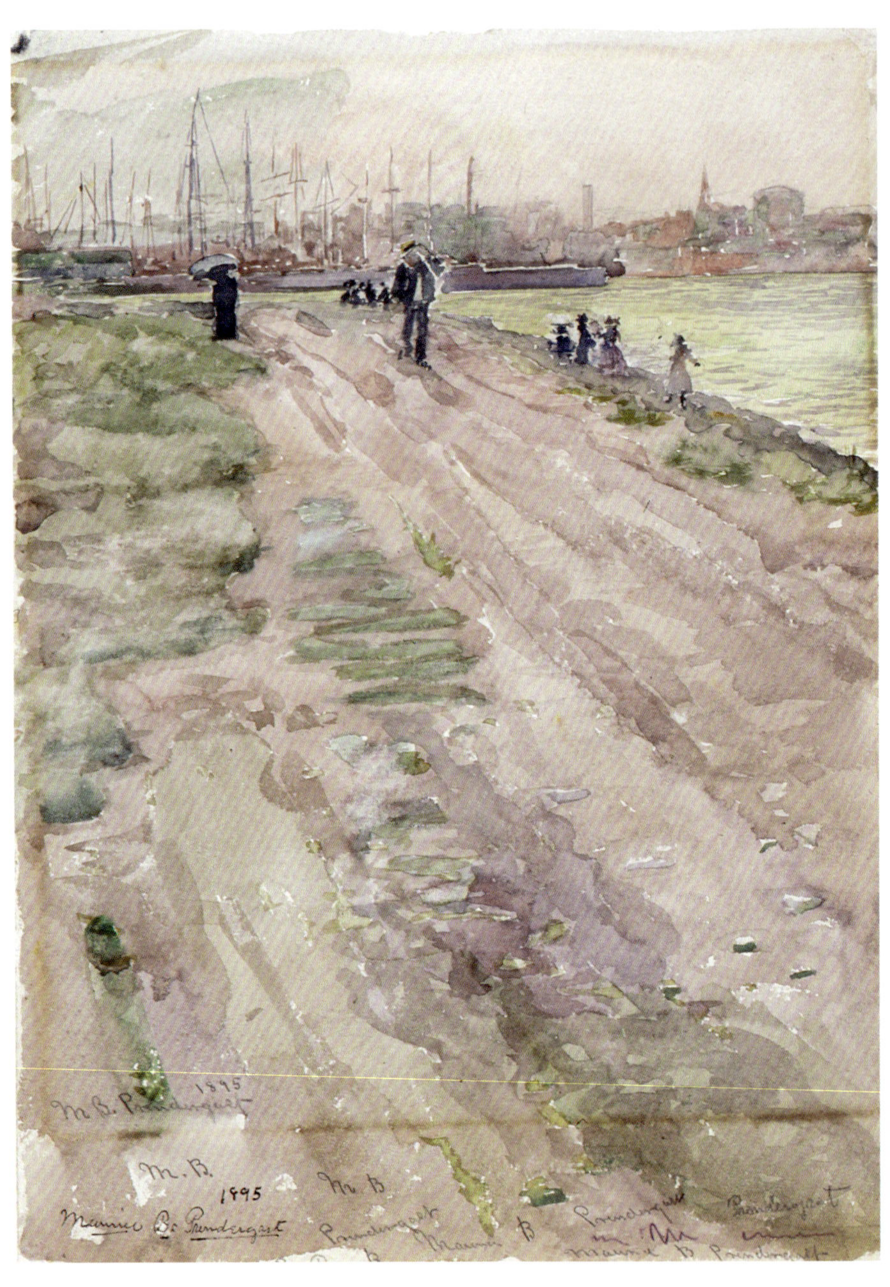

4. *The Harbor from City Point (New England Shore and Harbor Scene)*, 1895

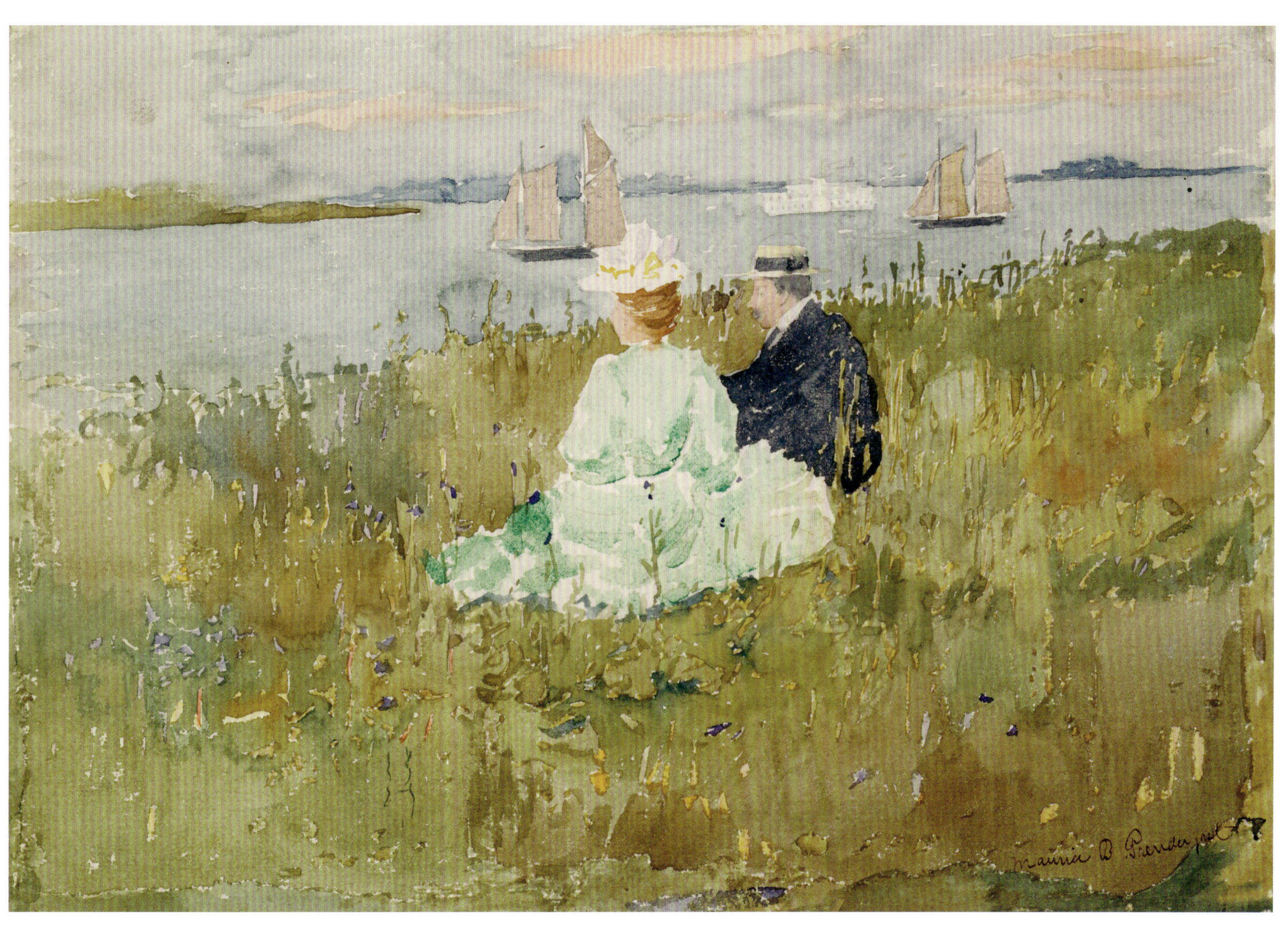

5. Viewing the Ships, c. 1895–97

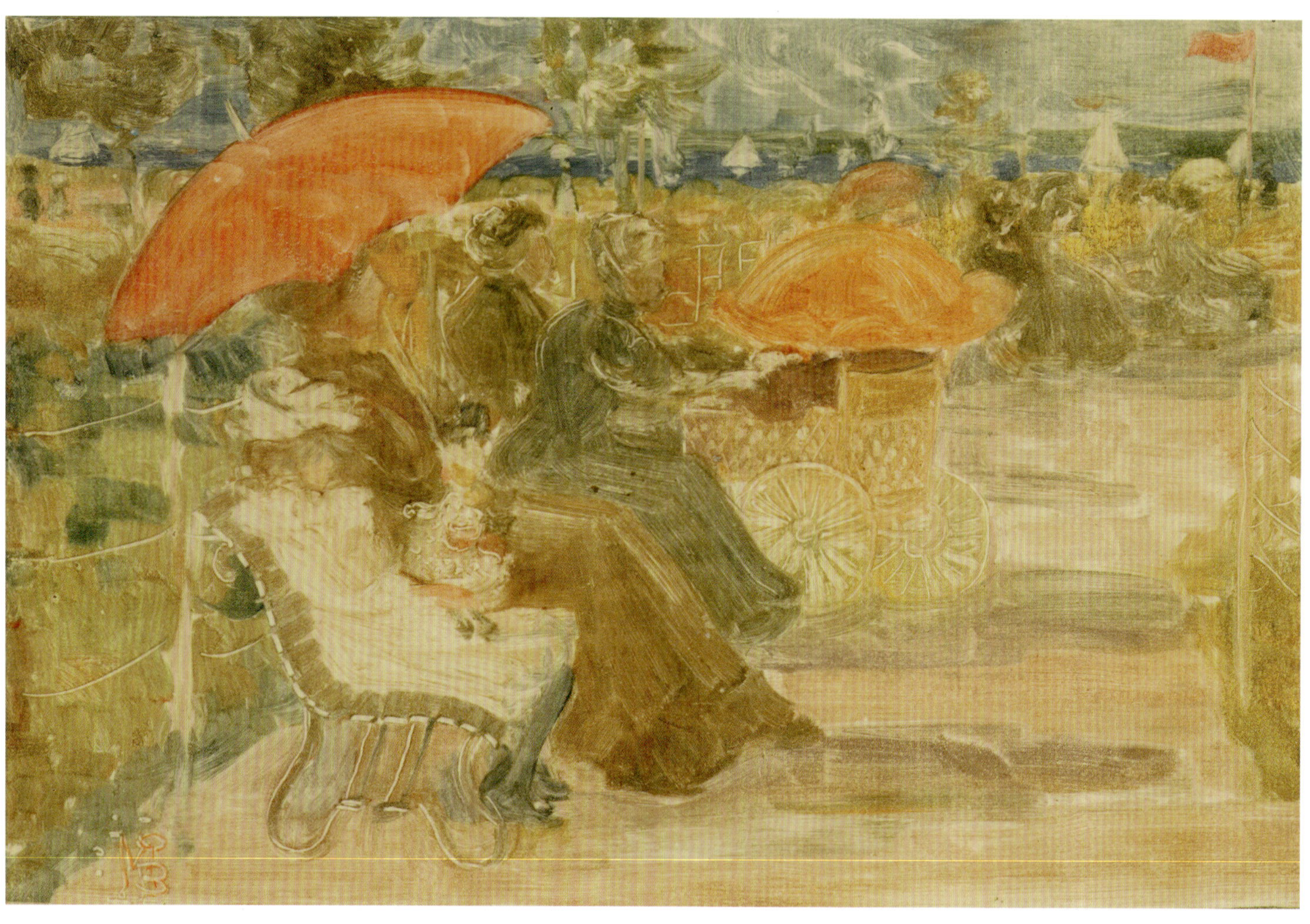

6. *Marine Park*, c. 1895–97

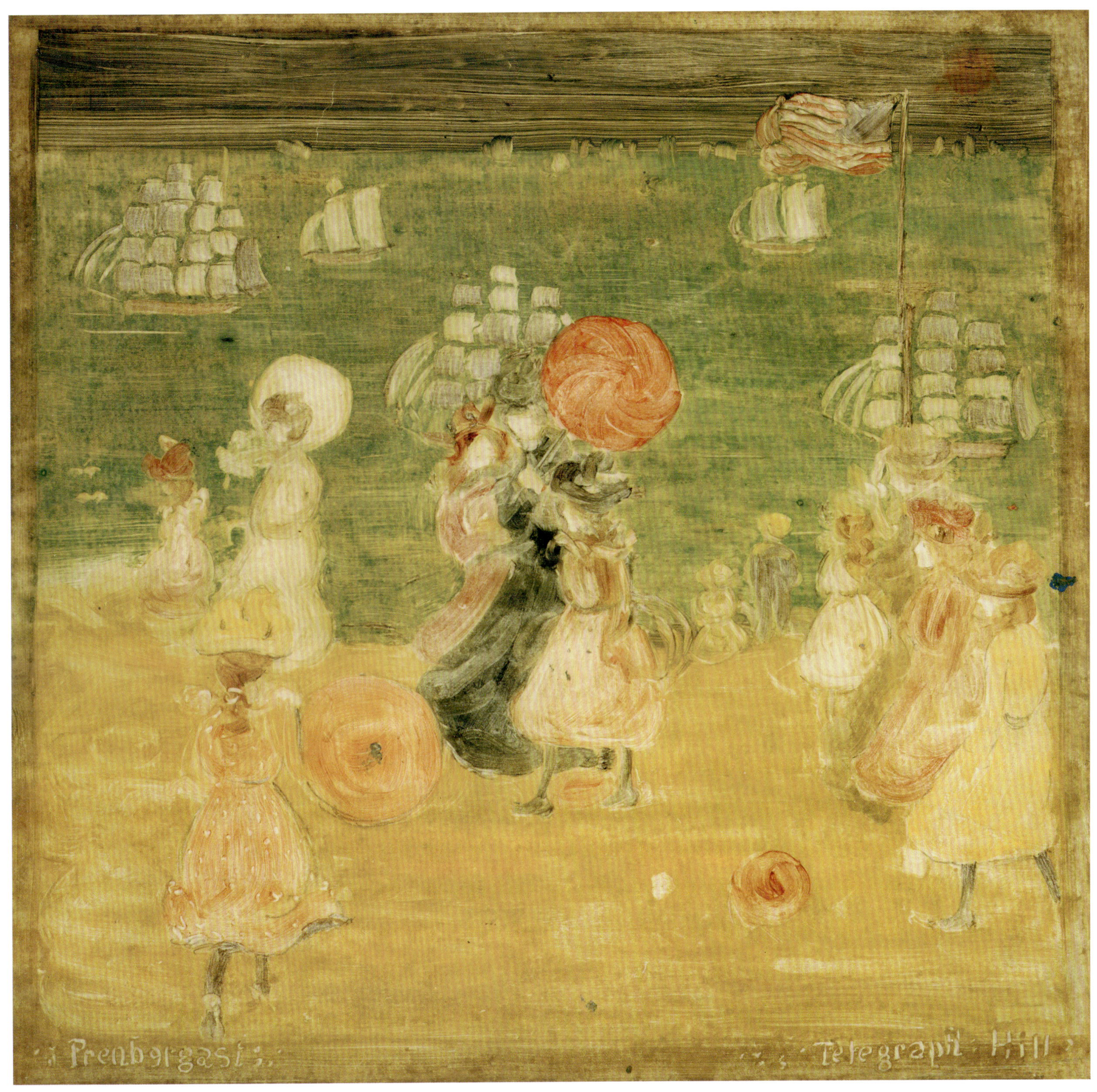

7. Telegraph Hill I, c. 1895–97

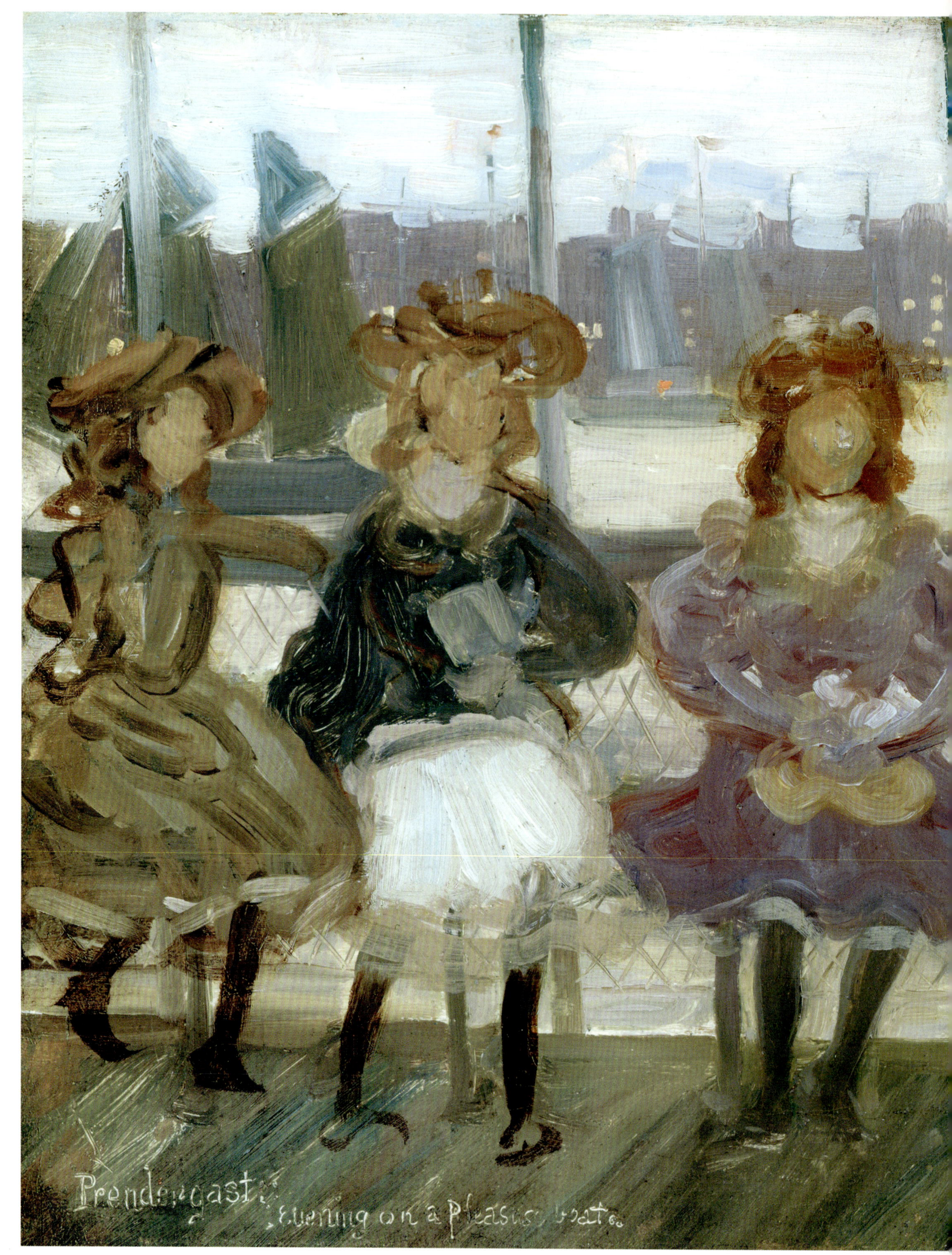

8. *Evening on a Pleasure Boat,* c. 1895–97

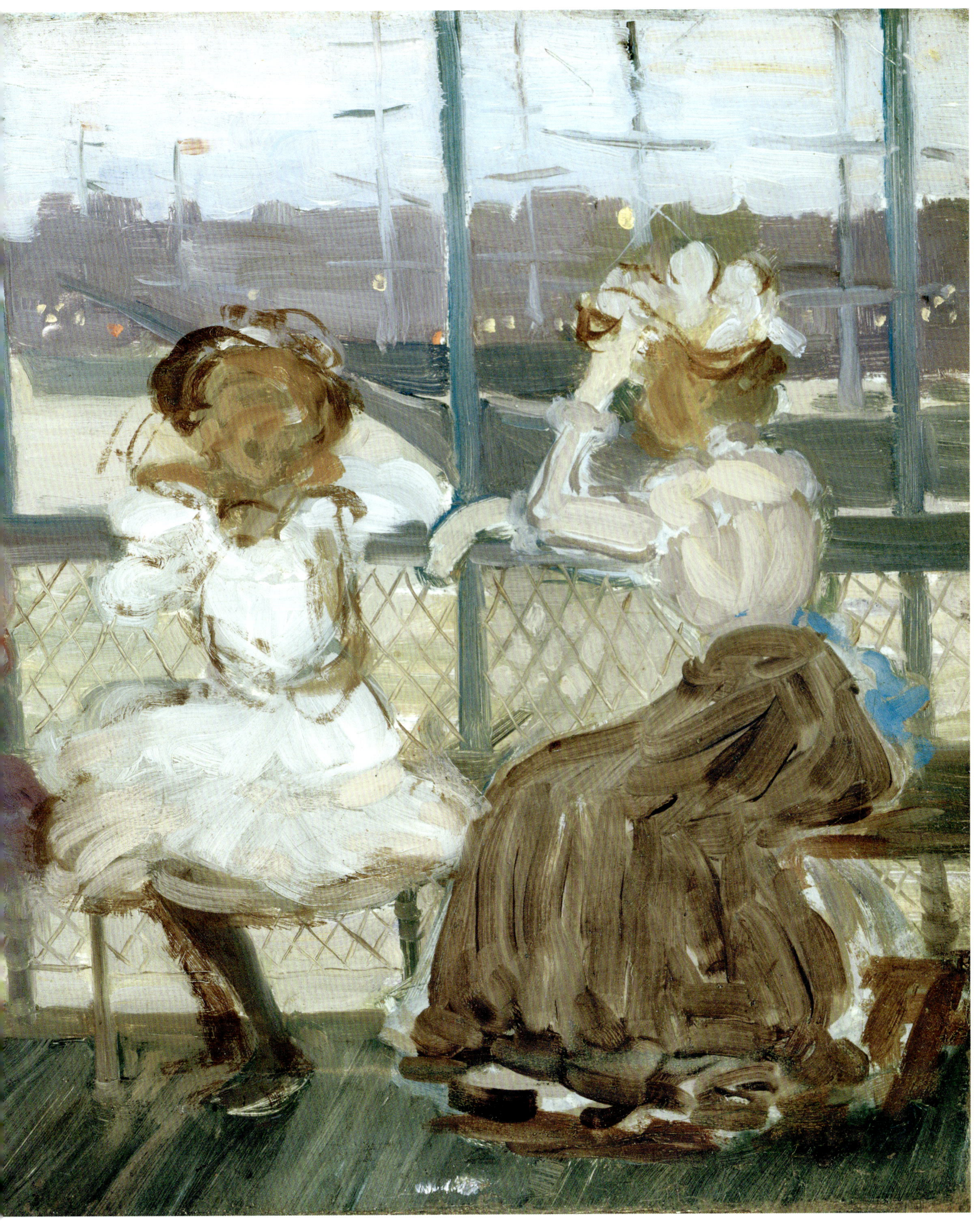

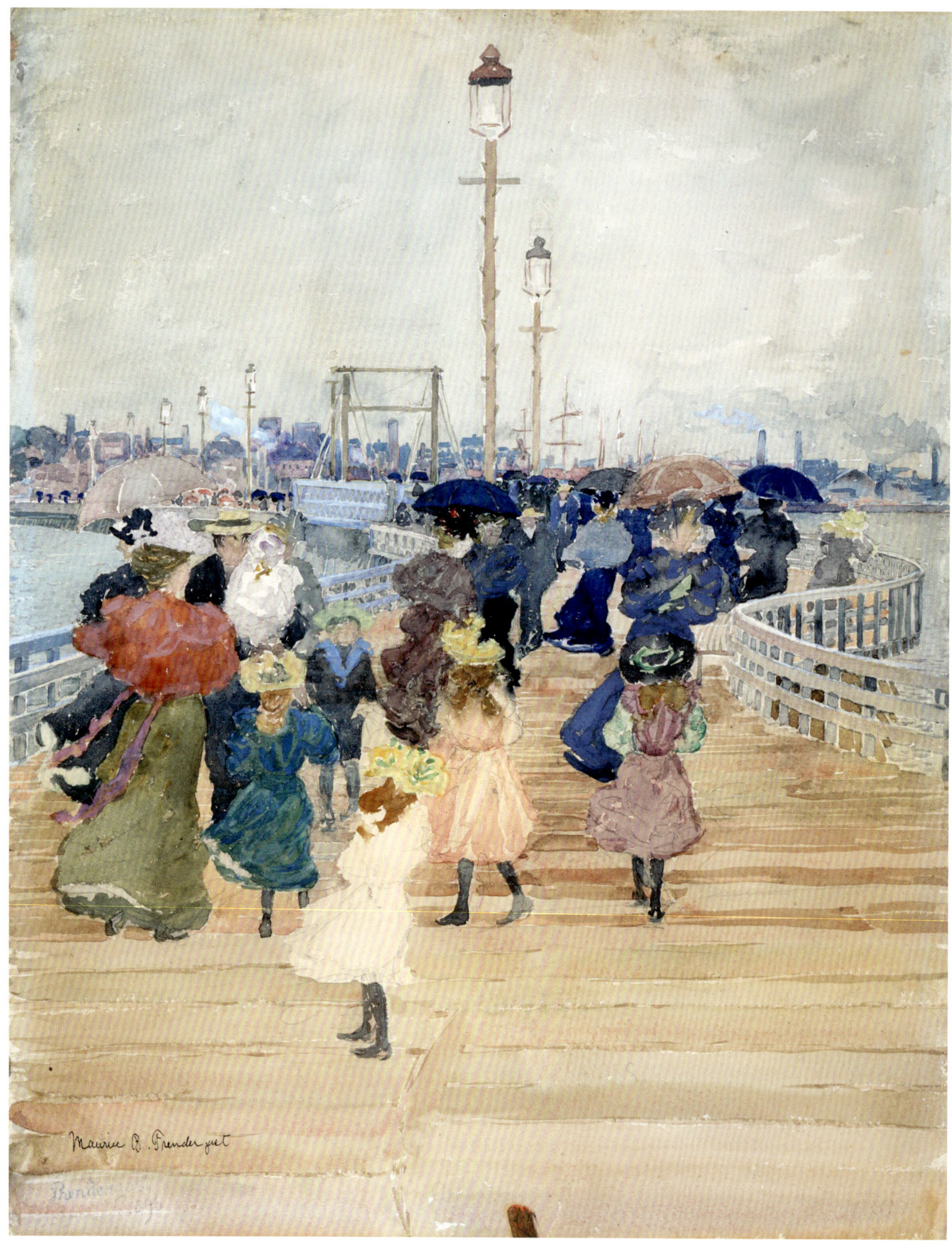

9. *South Boston Pier*, 1896

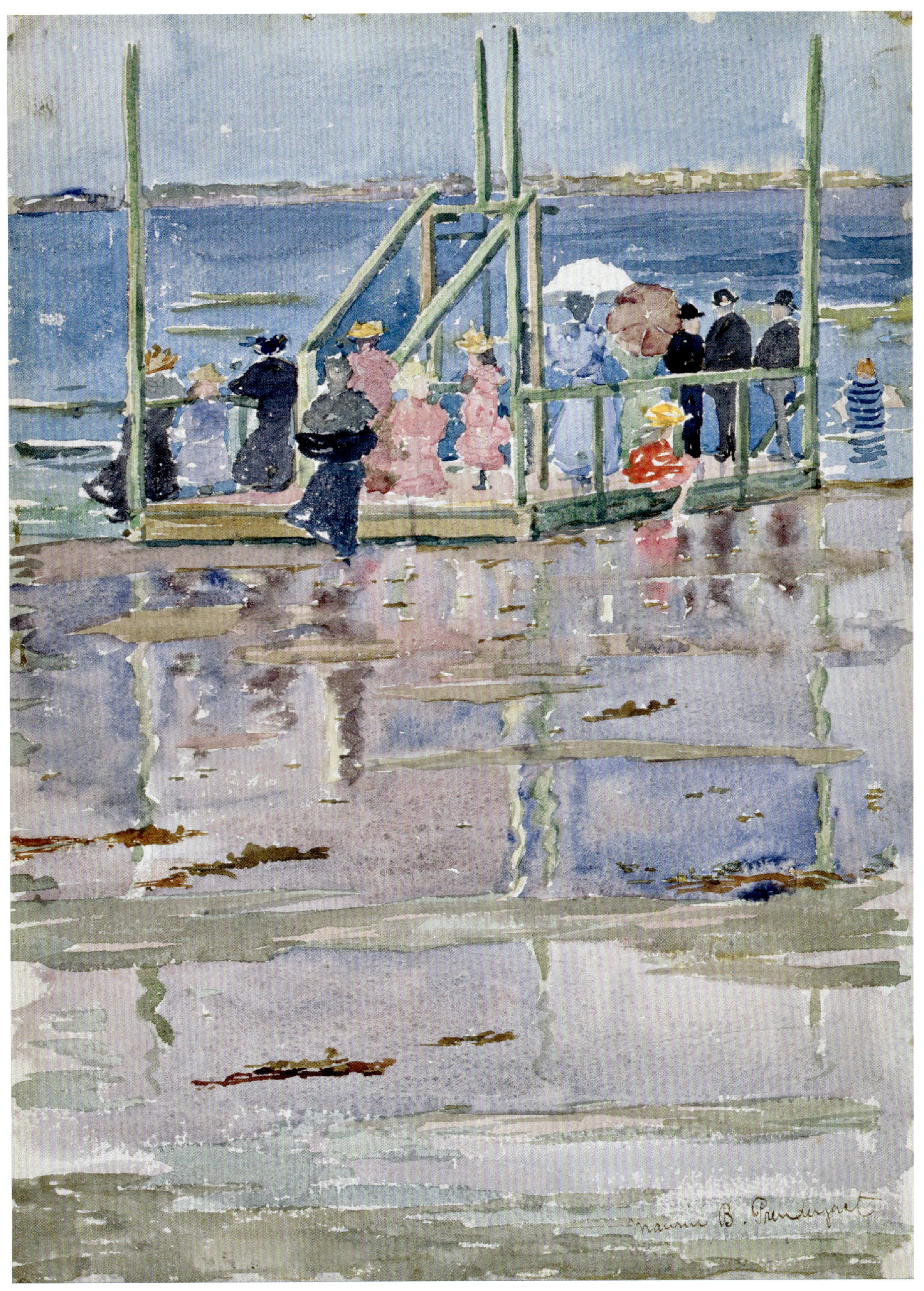

10. *Float at Low Tide, Revere Beach, c. 1896–97*

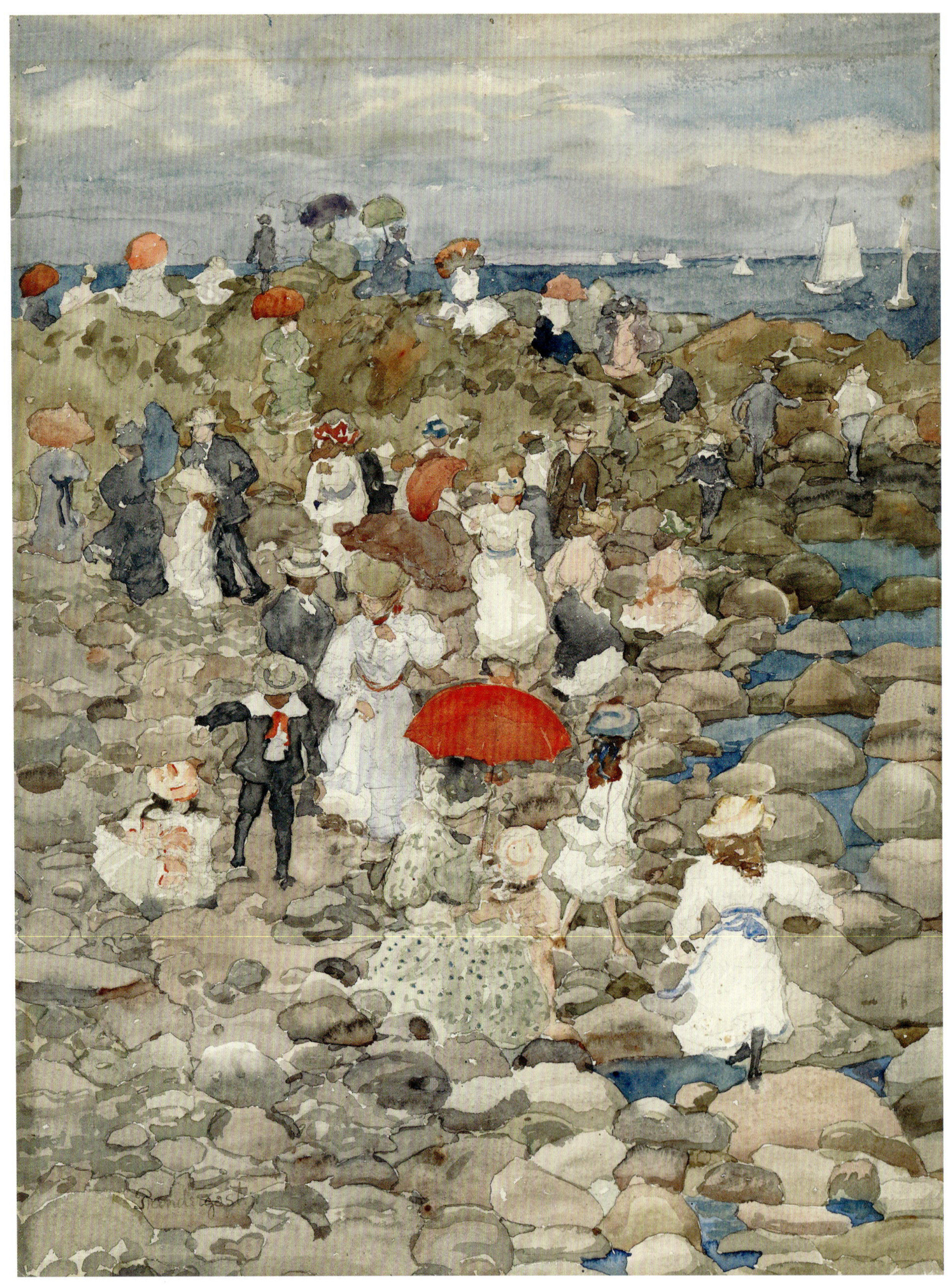

 11. *Rocky Shore, Nantasket, c. 1896–97*

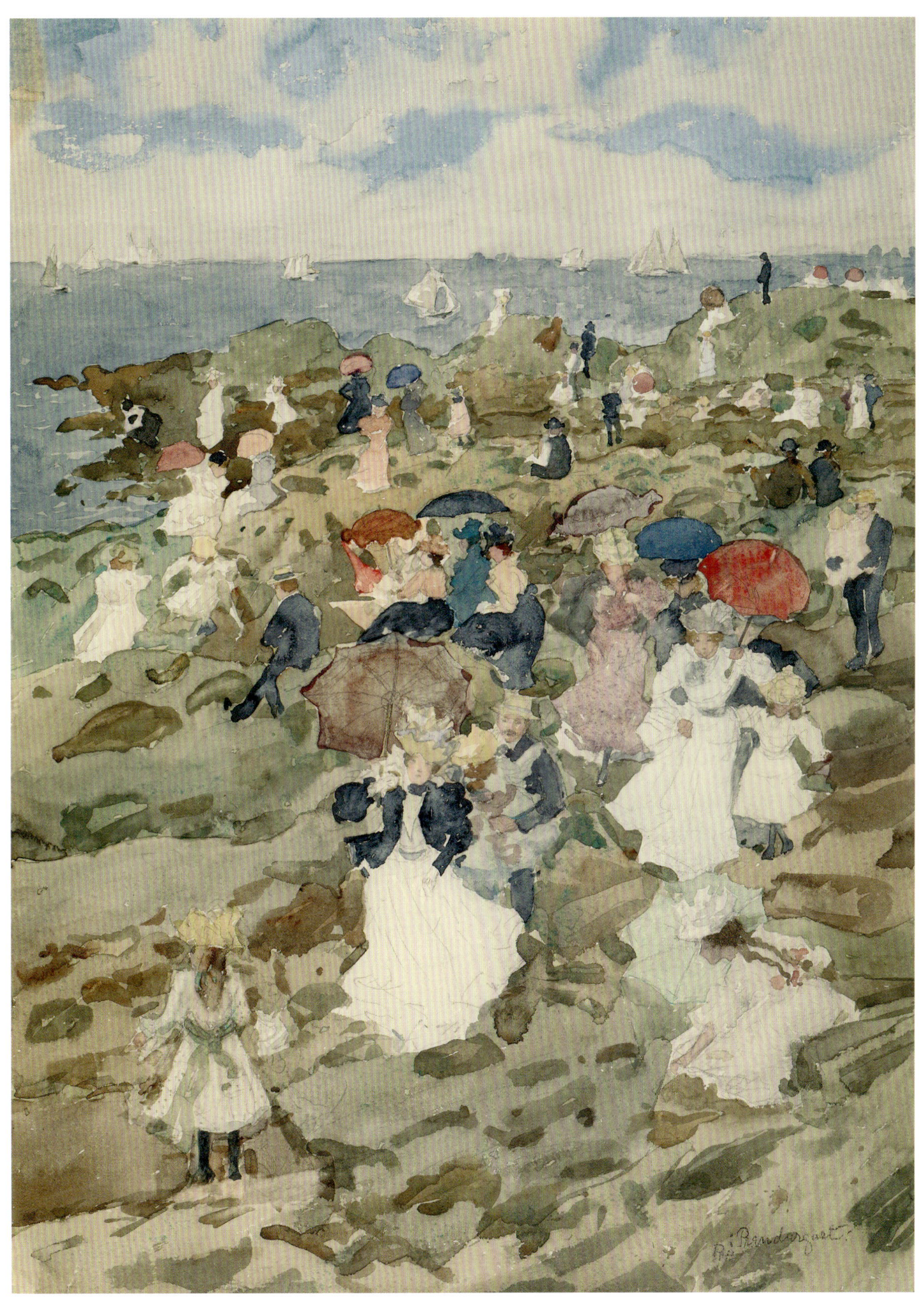

12. *Handkerchief Point*, 1896–97

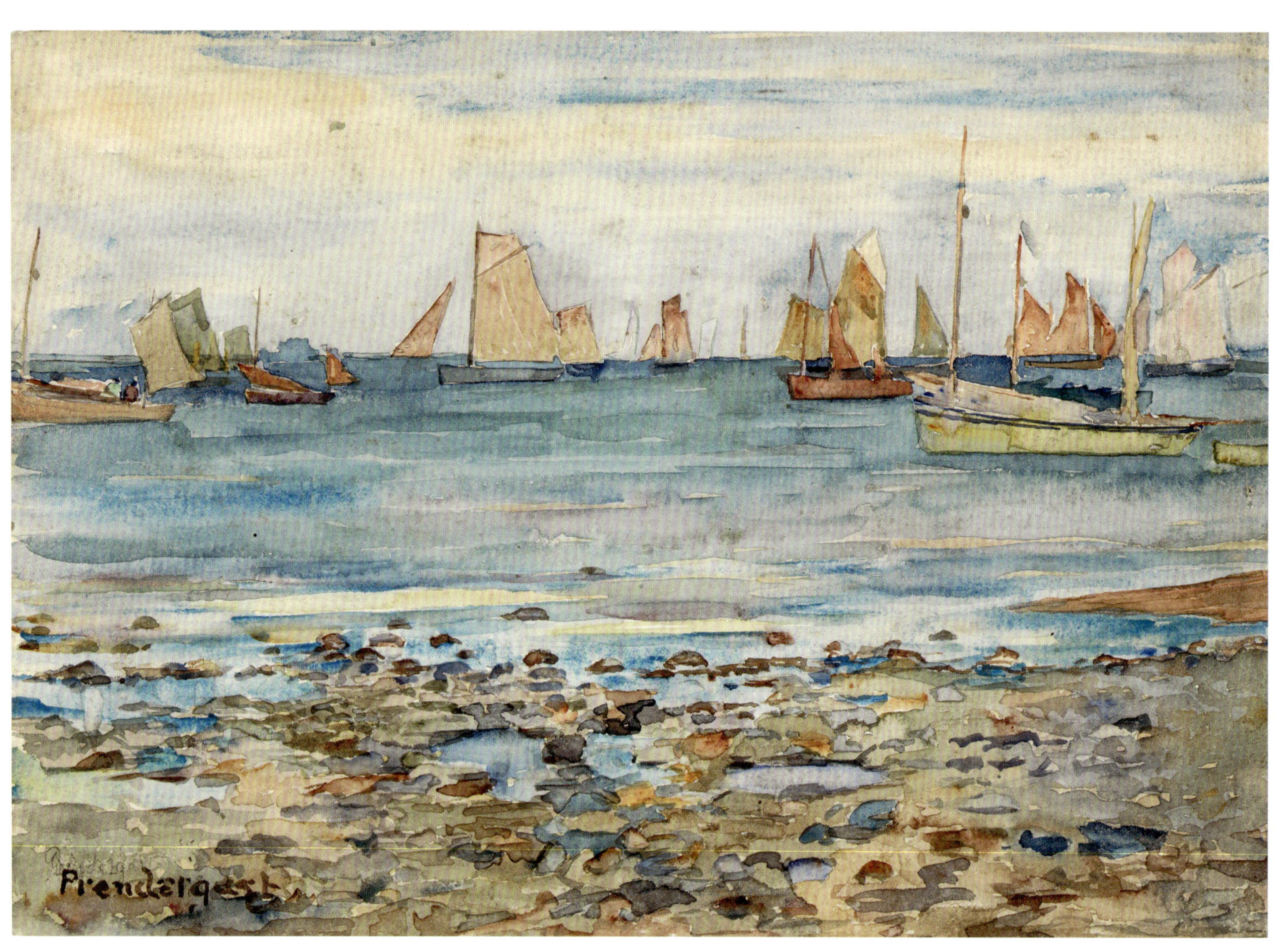

     13. *Sunny Morning, Low Tide at the Beach,* c. 1896–97

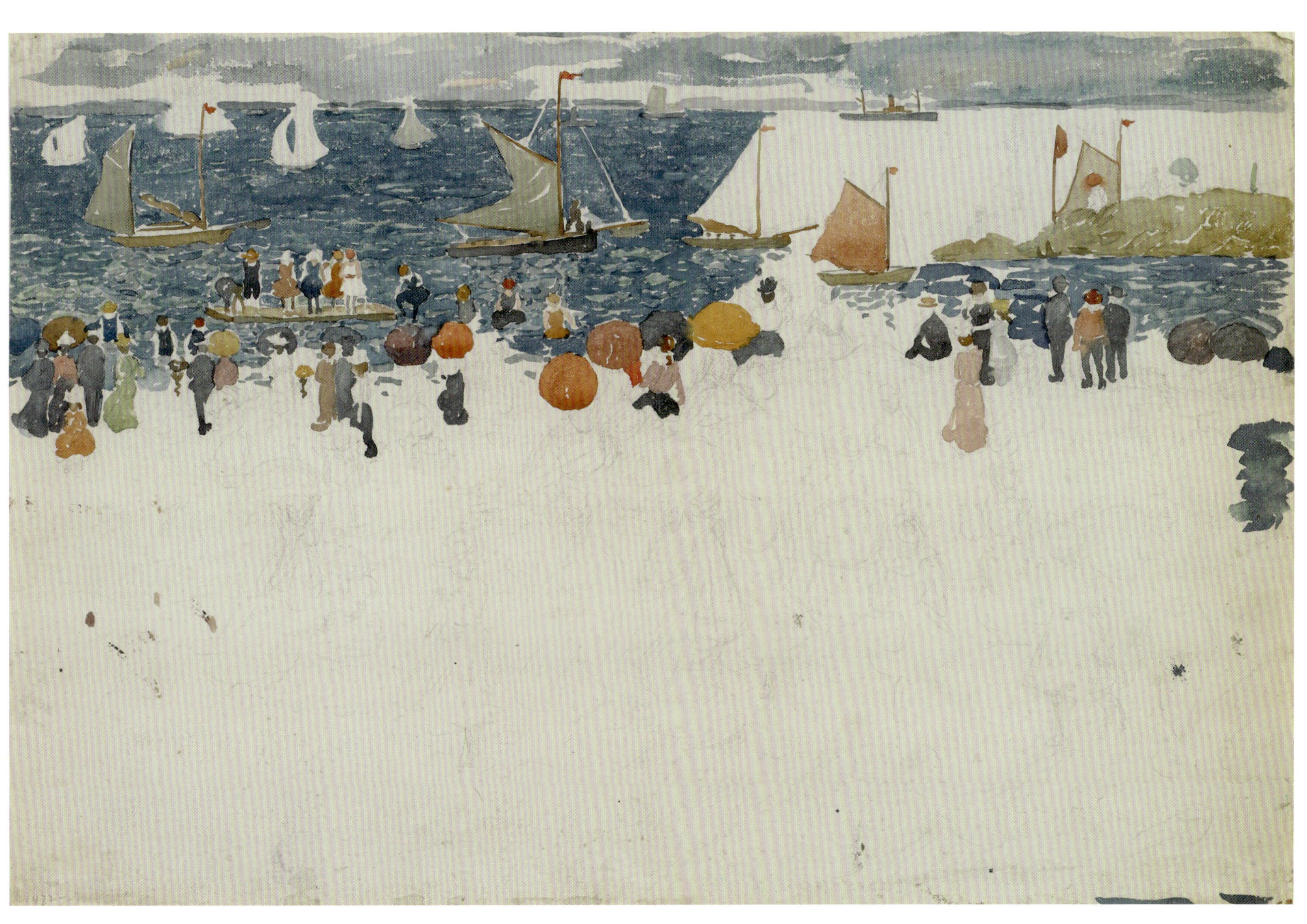

14. *Beach Scene with Boats*, c. 1896–97 (recto: *Five Figures*, c. 1910–13, plate 54)

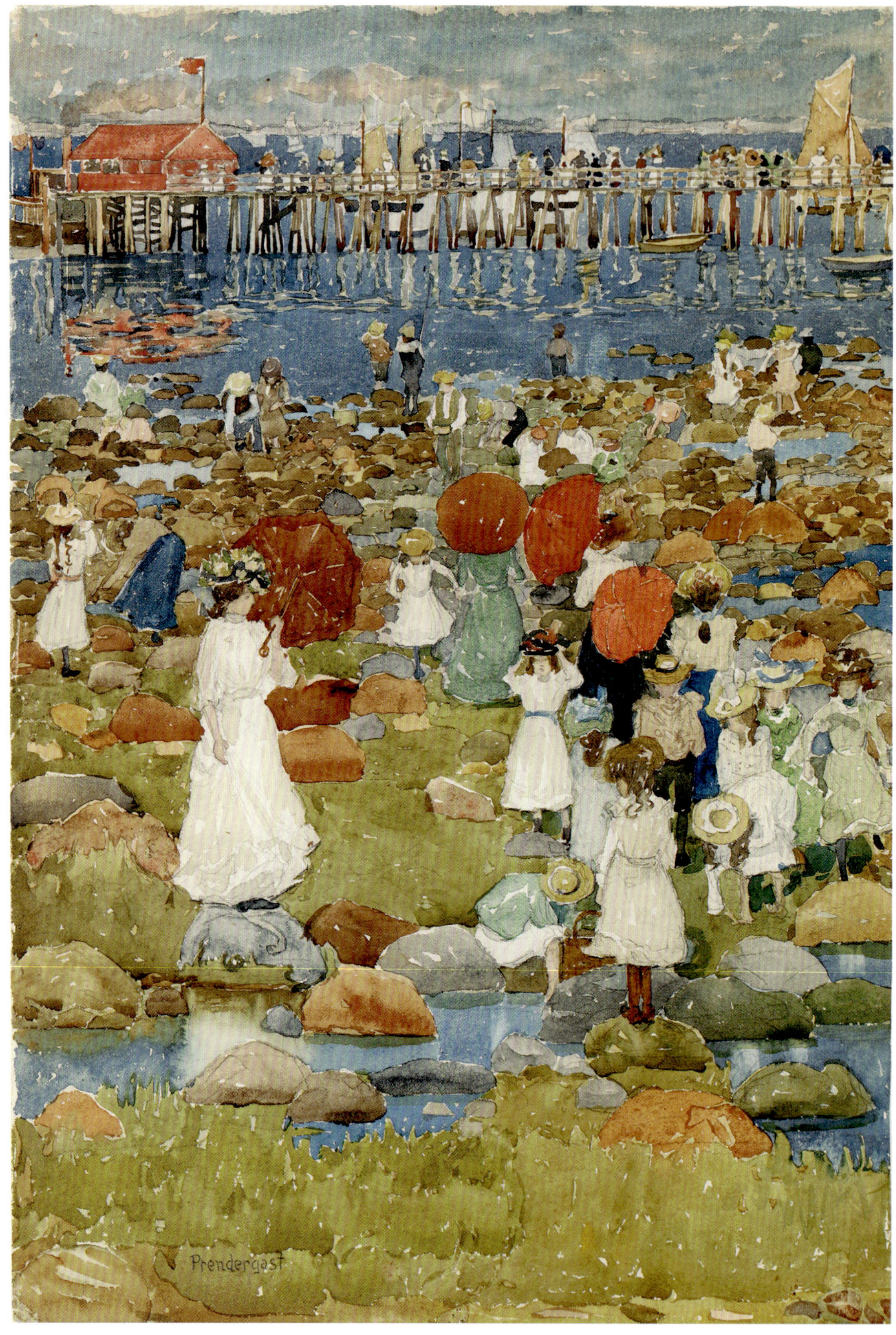

15. *The Stony Beach, Ogunquit,* c. 1896–97

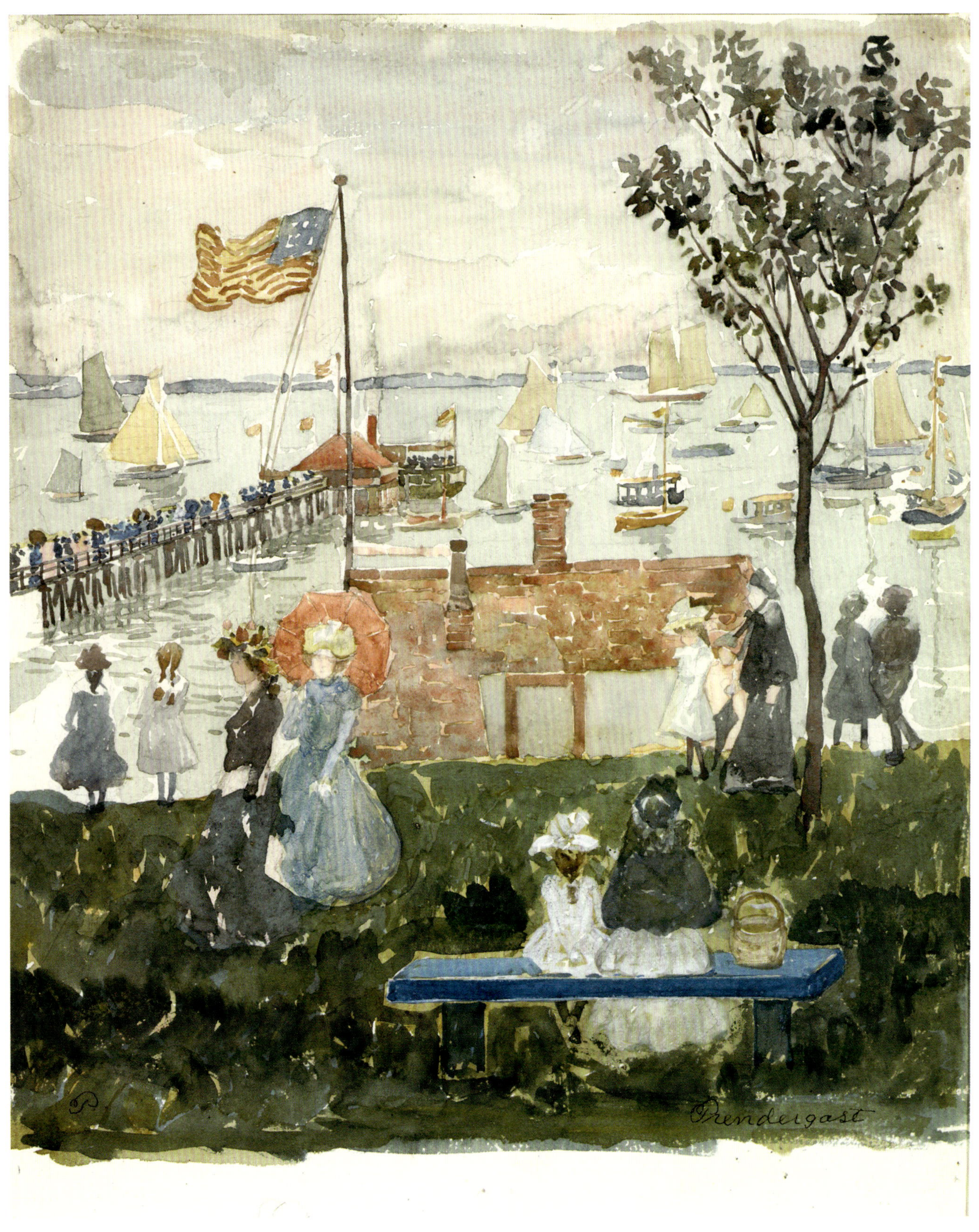

16. *Excursionists, Nahant,* c. 1896–97

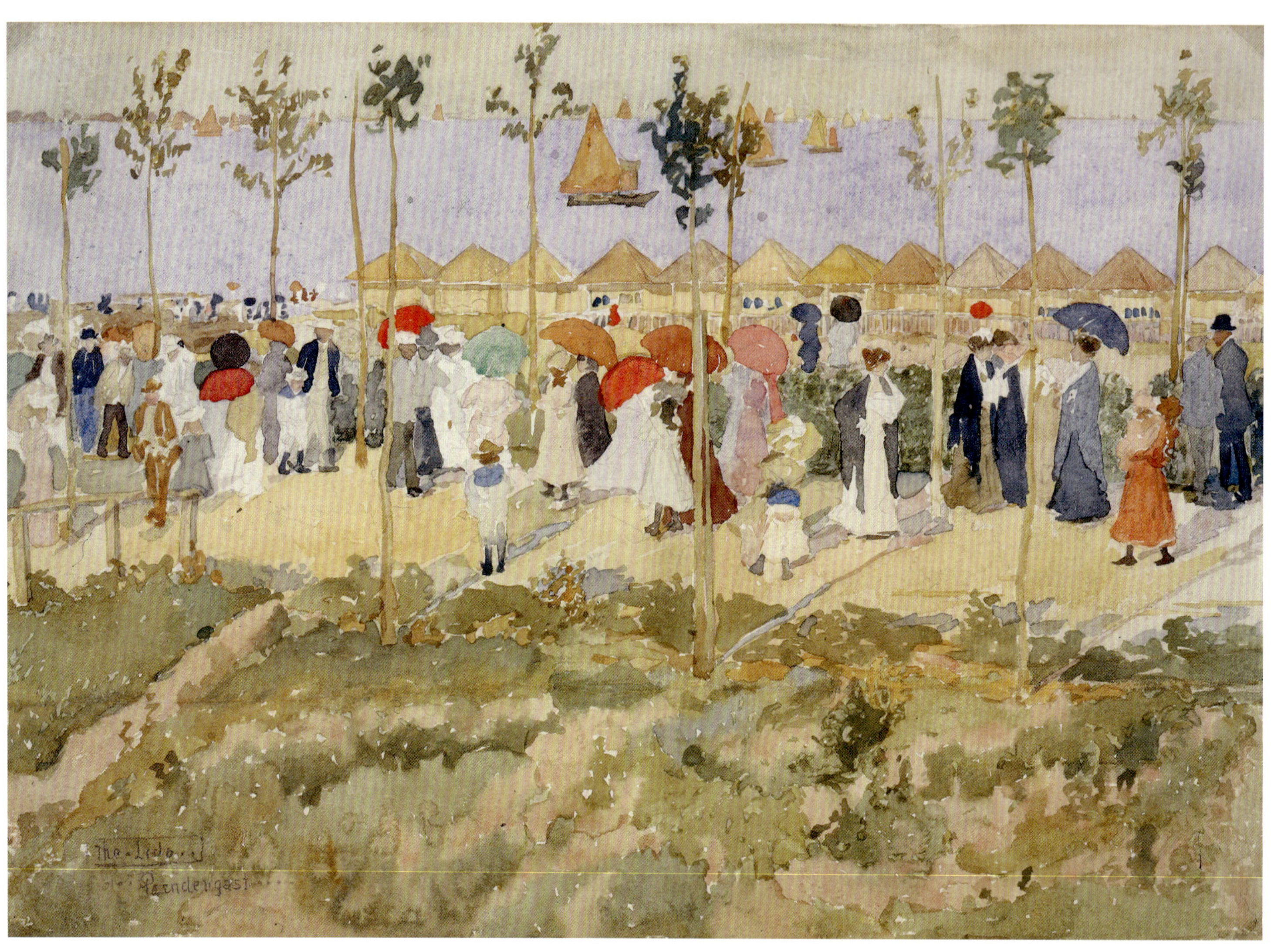

17. *The Lido, Venice, c. 1898–99*

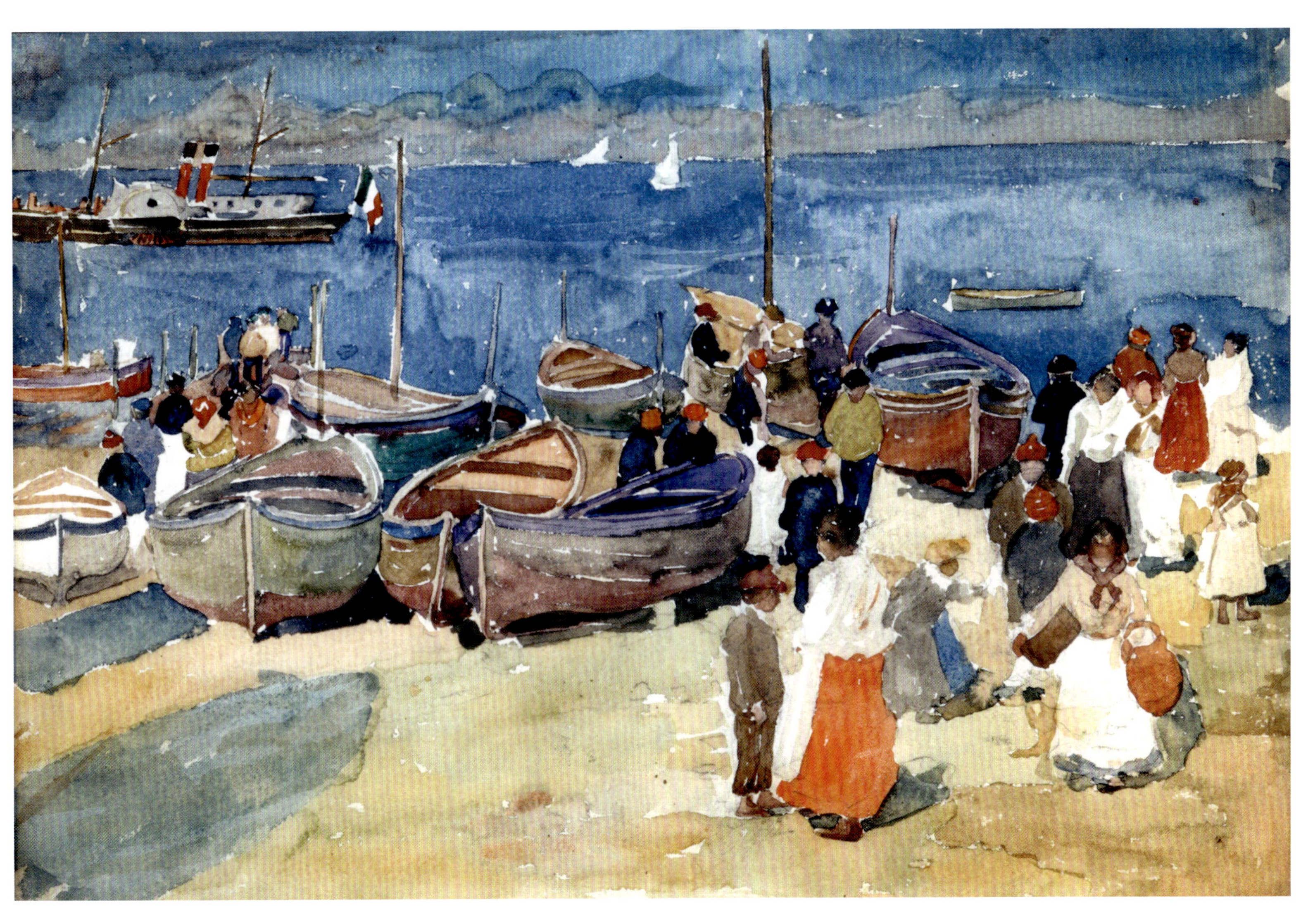

18. *At the Shore (Capri)*, c. 1898–99

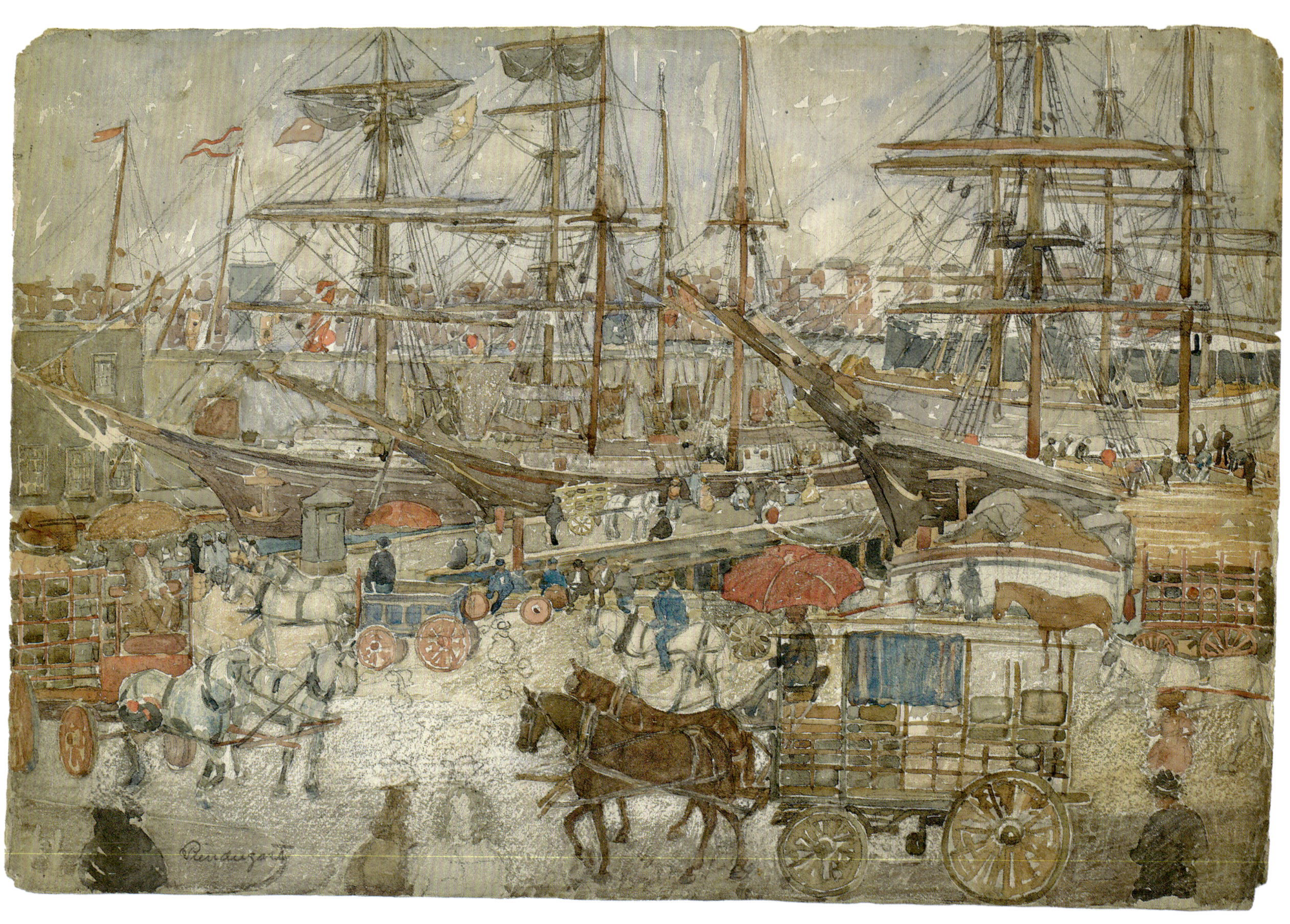

19. *Docks, East Boston*, c. 1900–1904

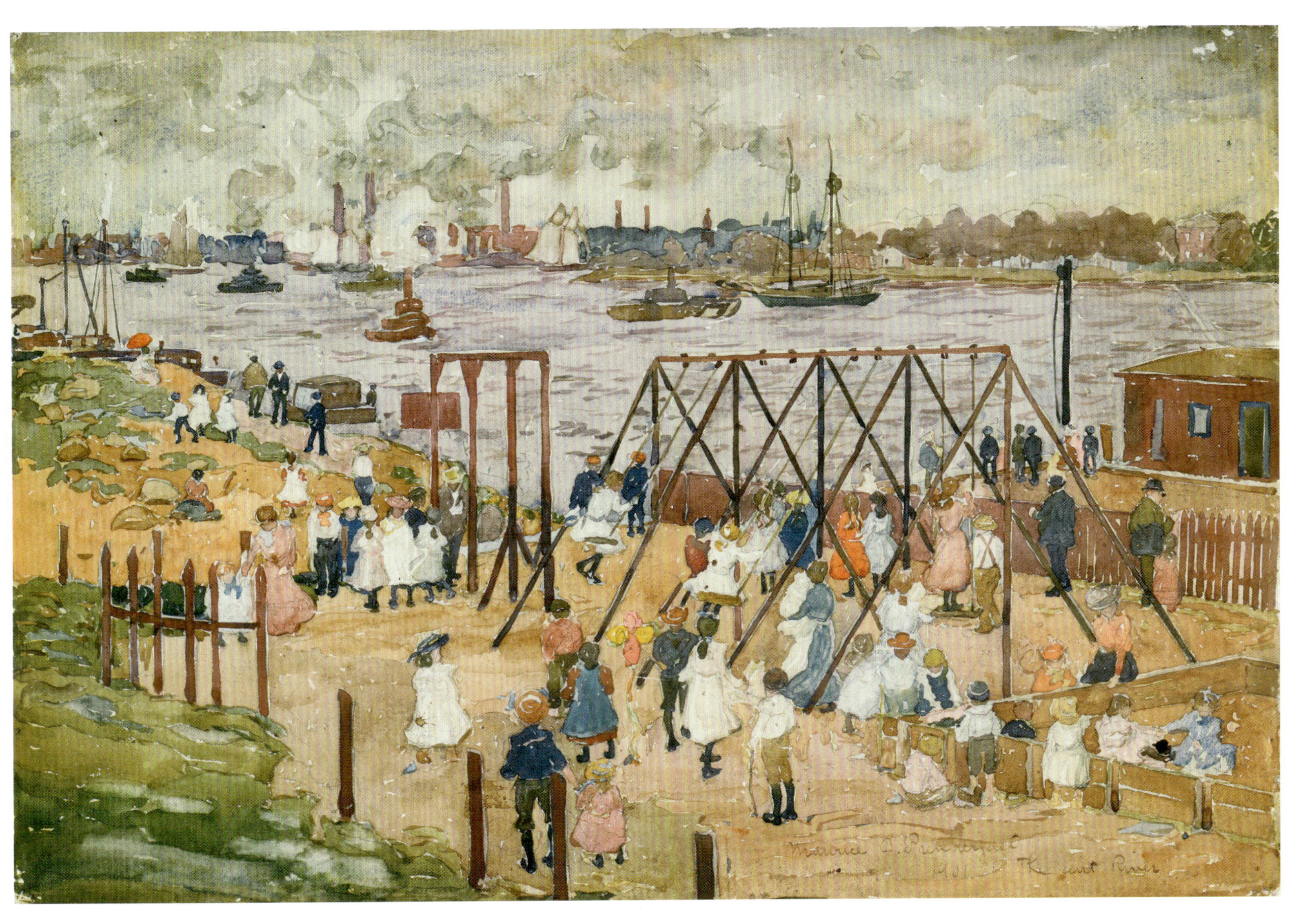

20. *The East River,* 1901

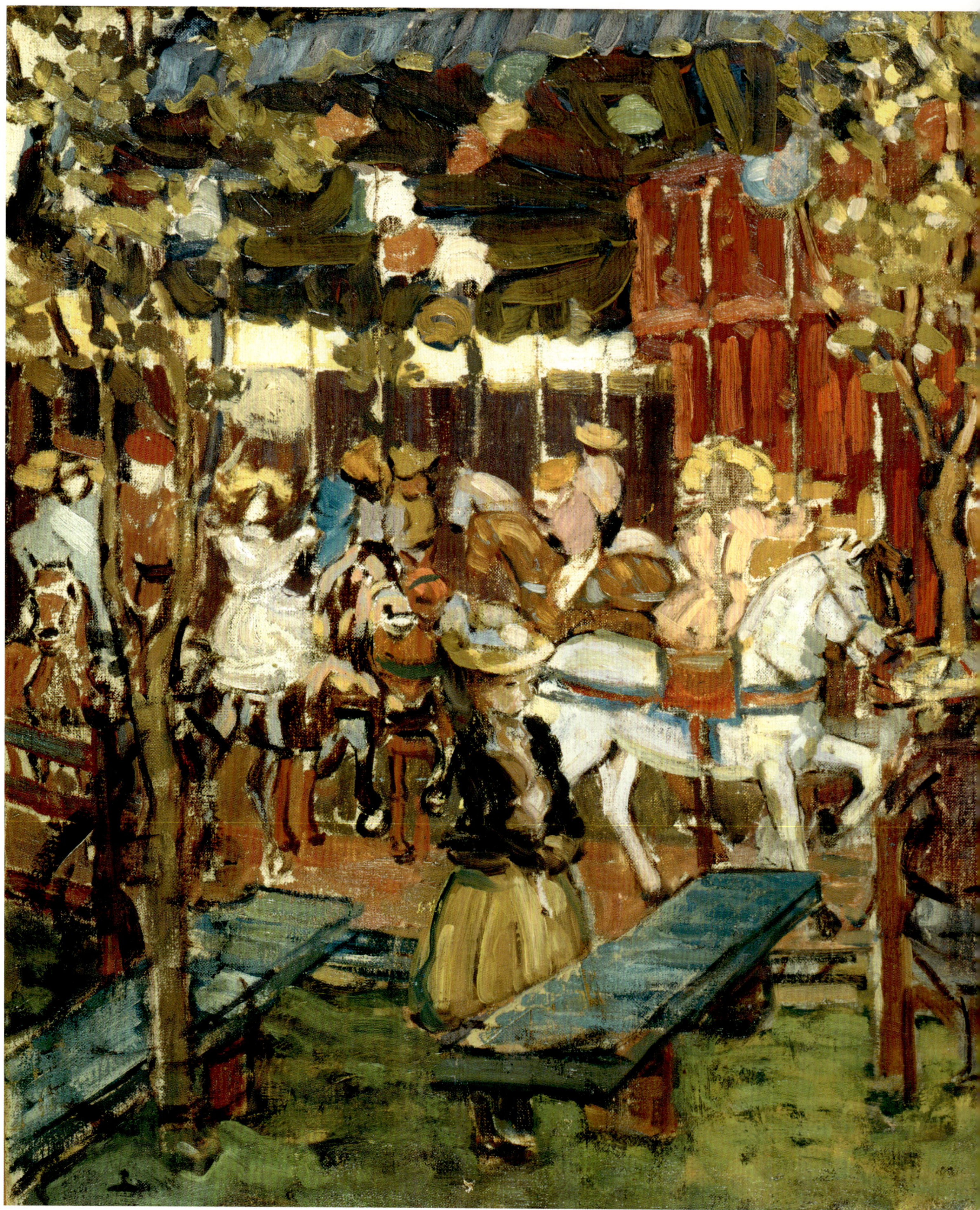

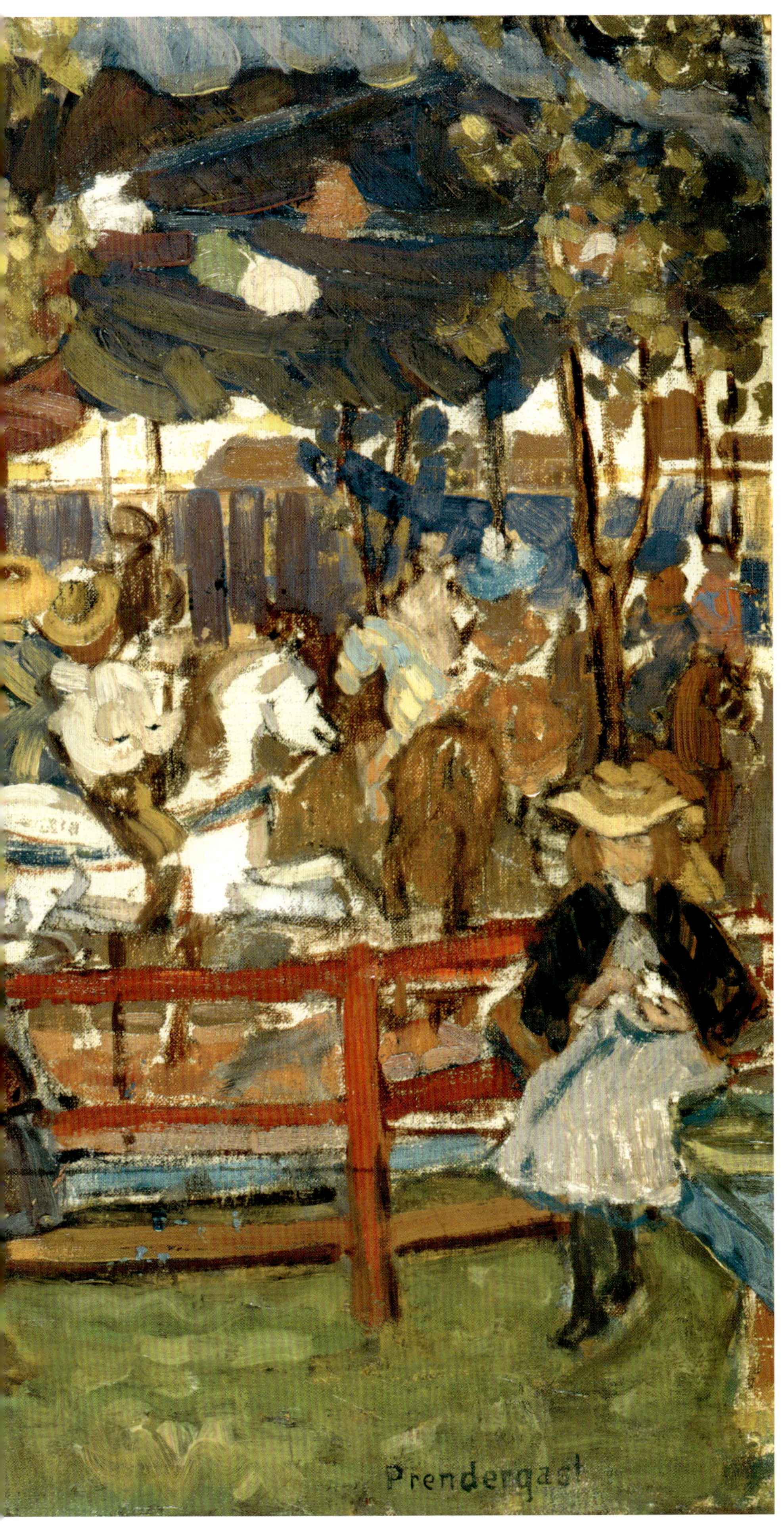

21. *The Flying Horses*, c. 1902–6

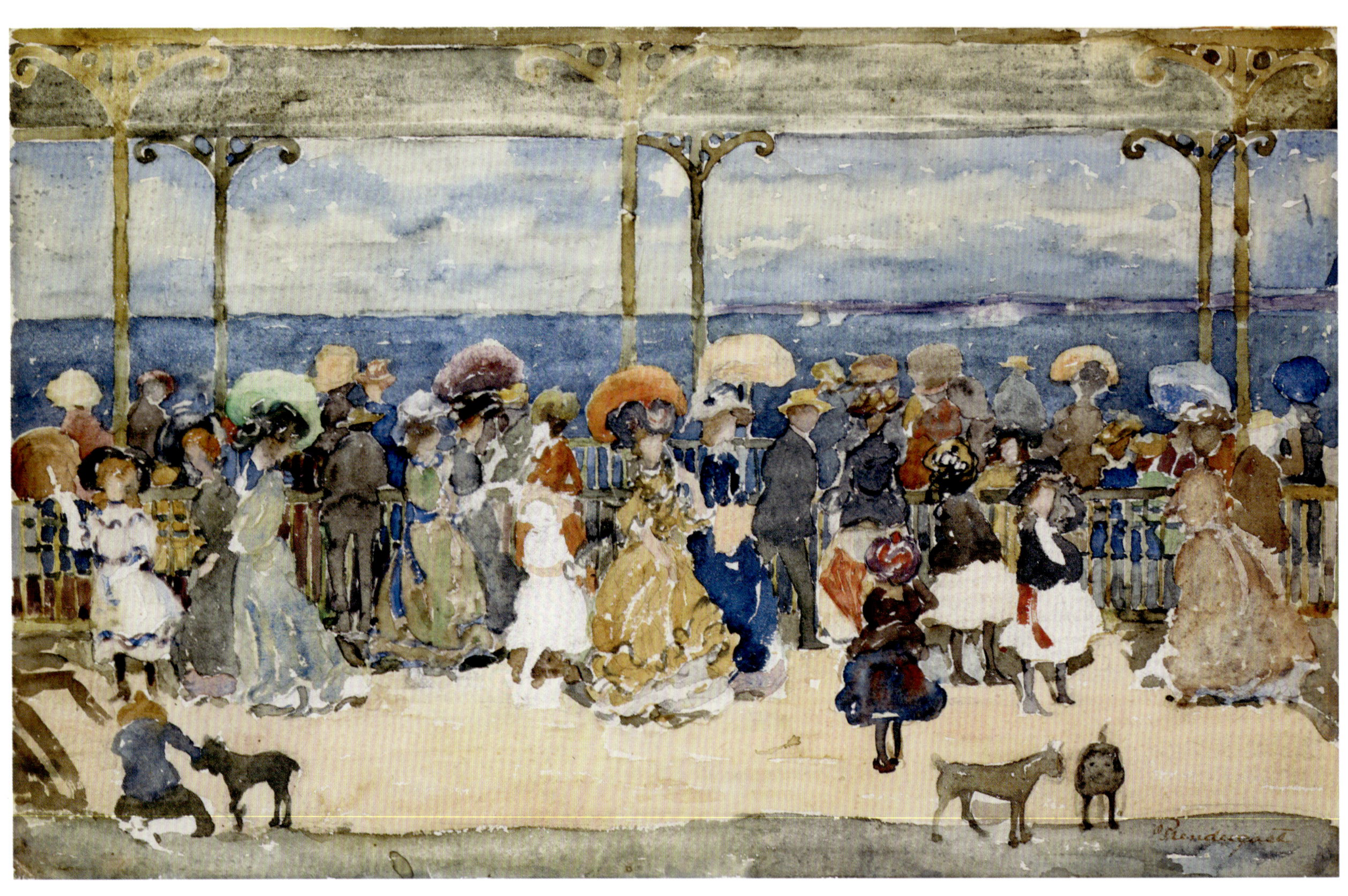

22. *On the Pier, Nantasket,* c. 1900–1905

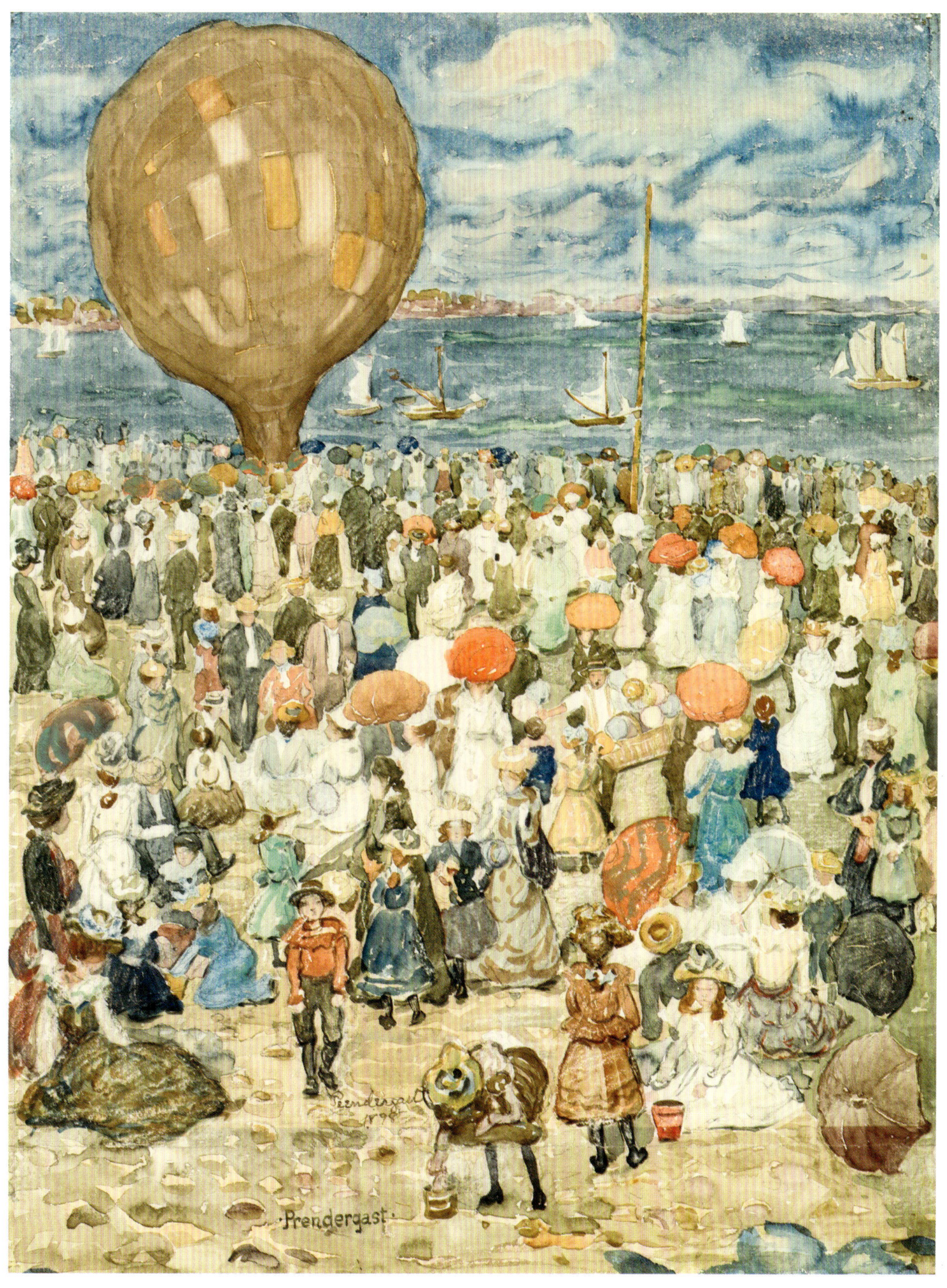

23. *The Balloon*, c. 1901

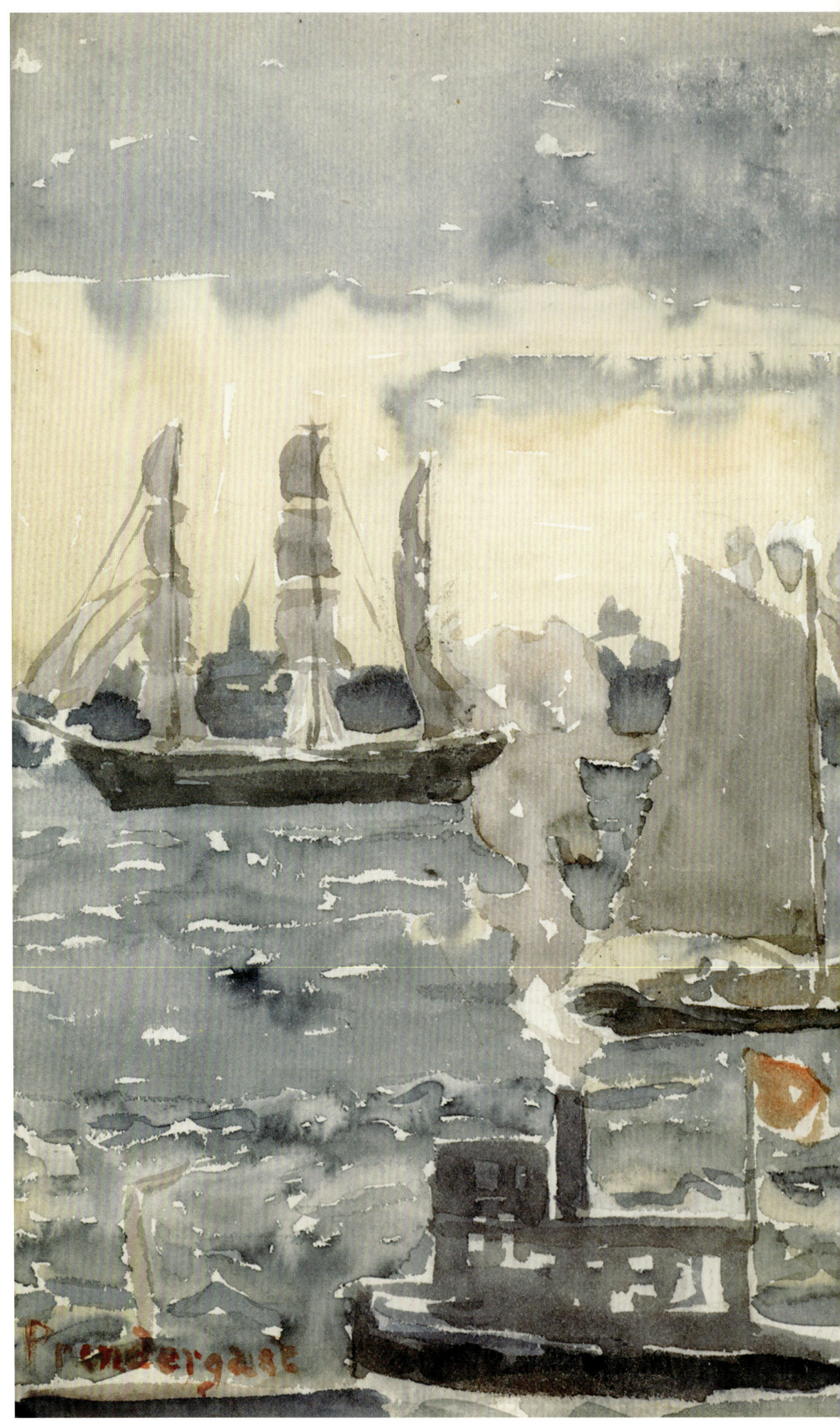

     24. *Boston Harbor*, c. 1900–1905

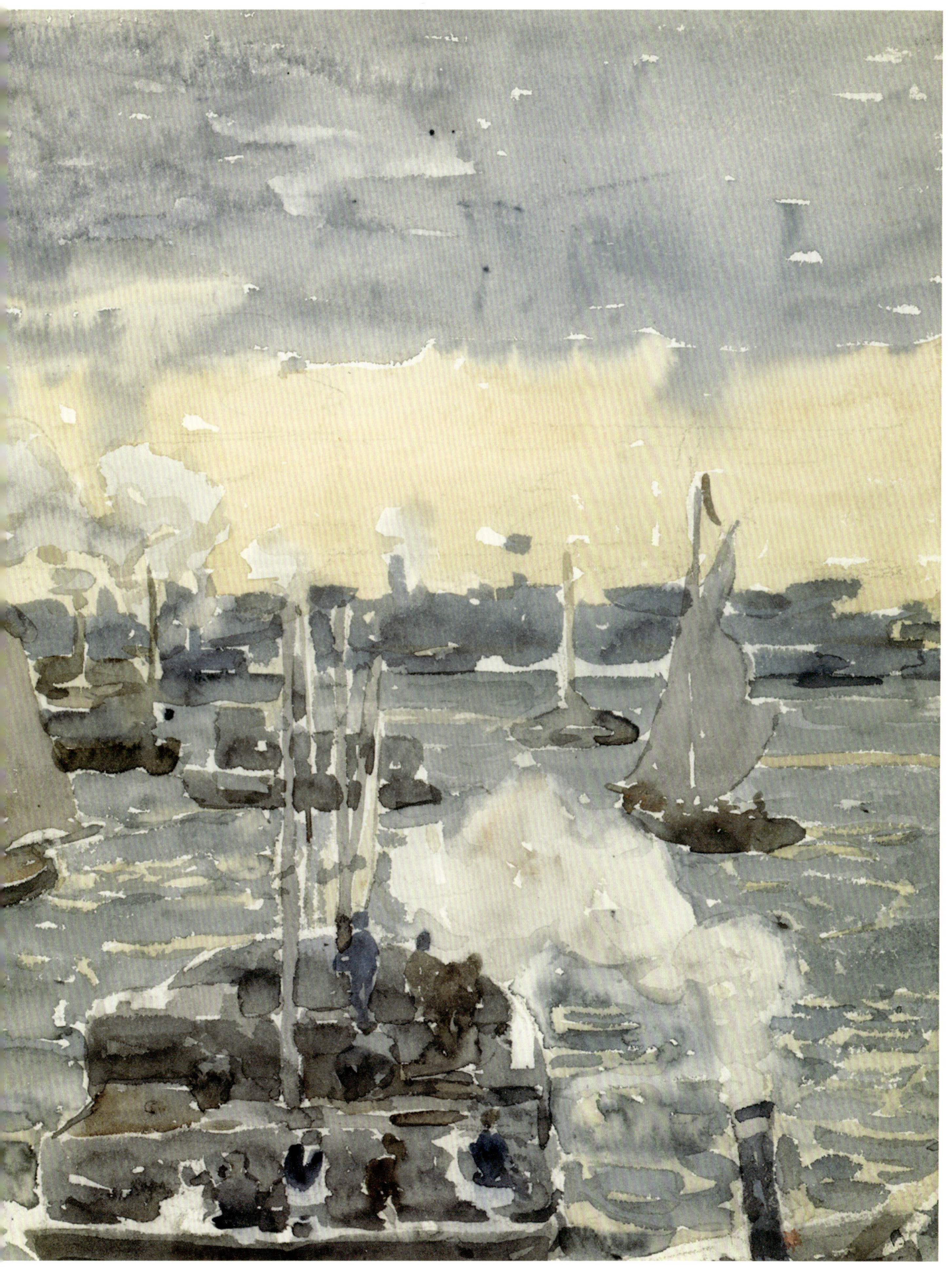

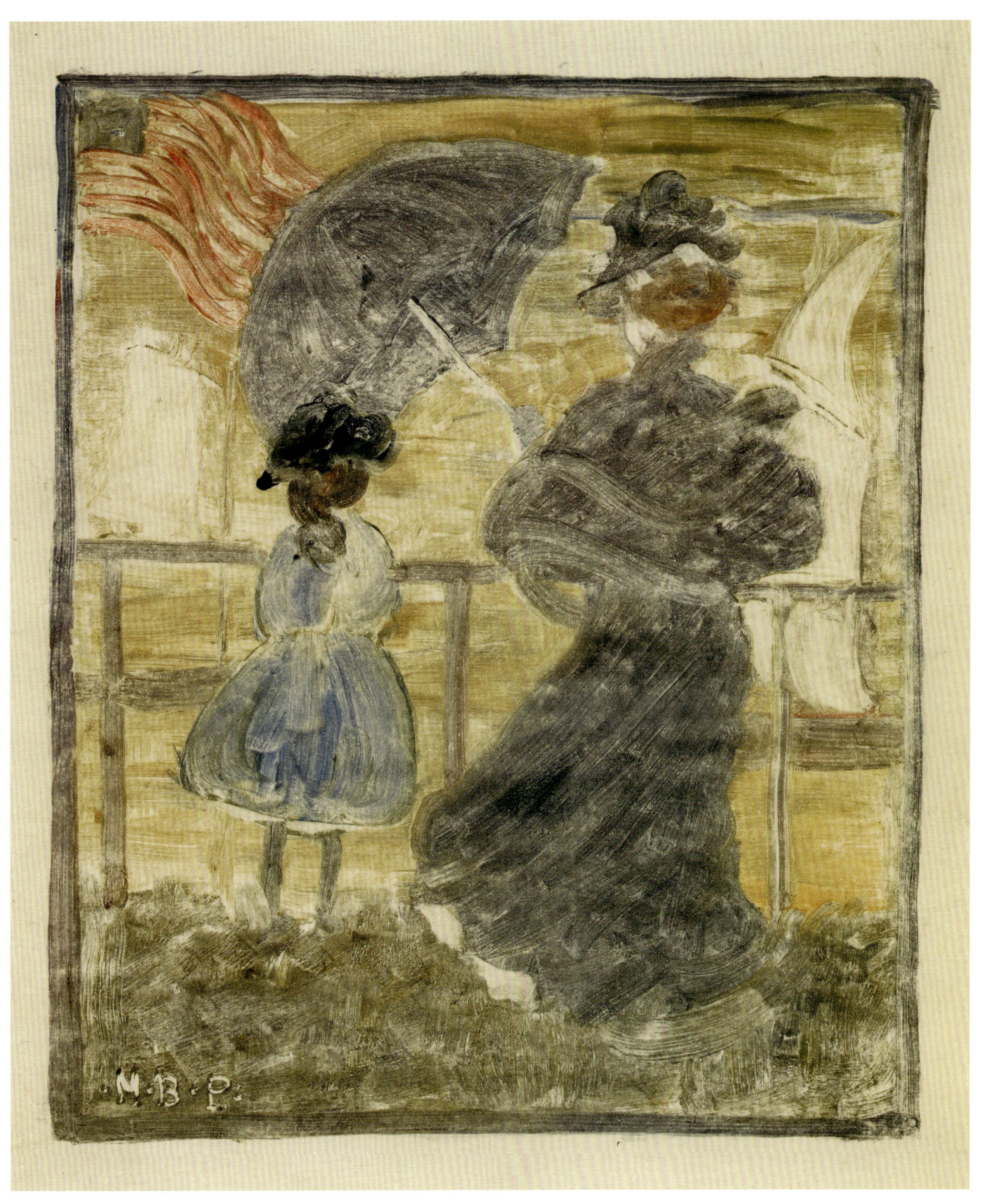

25. *On Deck, Boston (Nantasket Ferry?)*, 1902

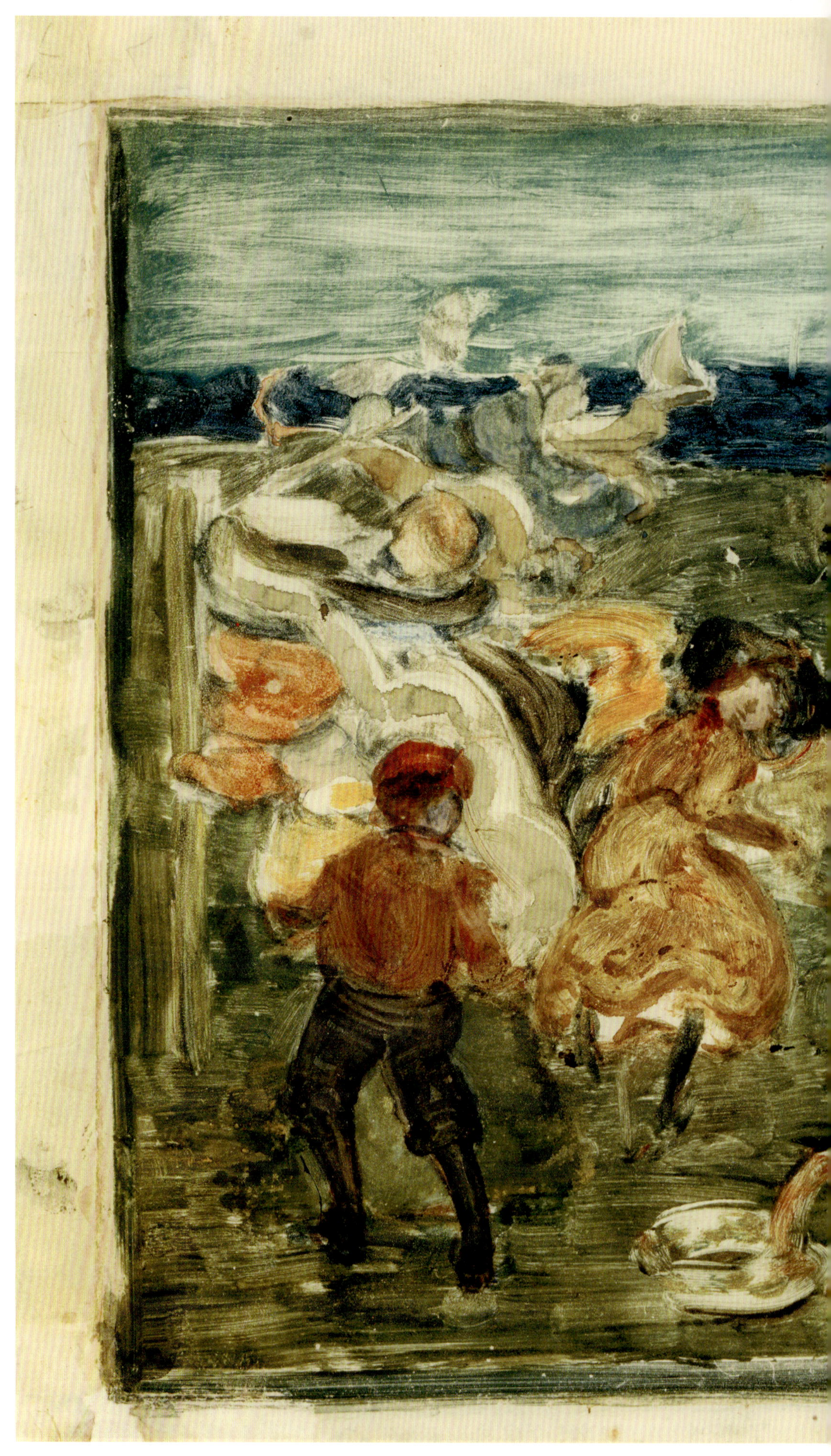

26. *Lighthouse,* c. 1900–1902

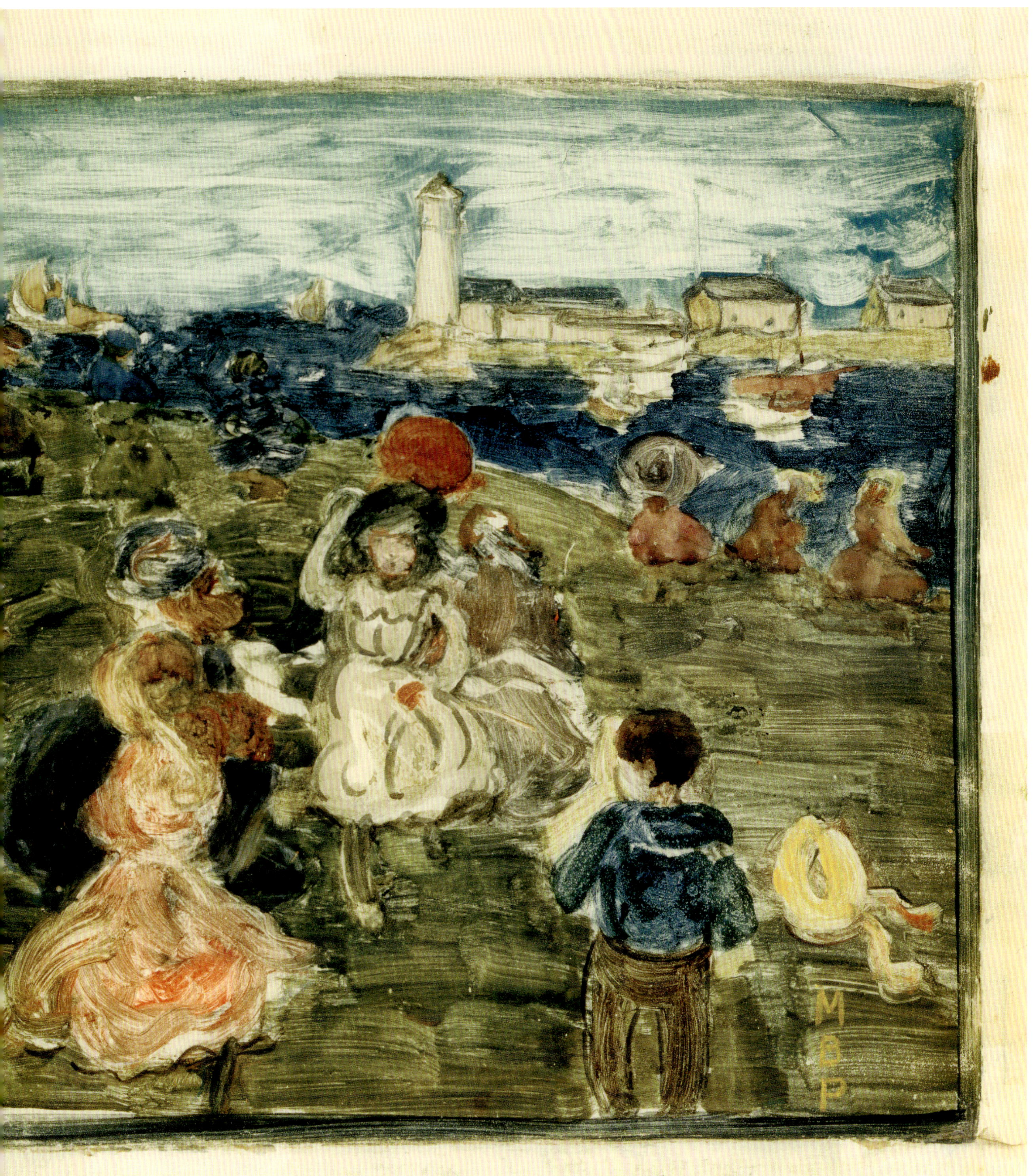

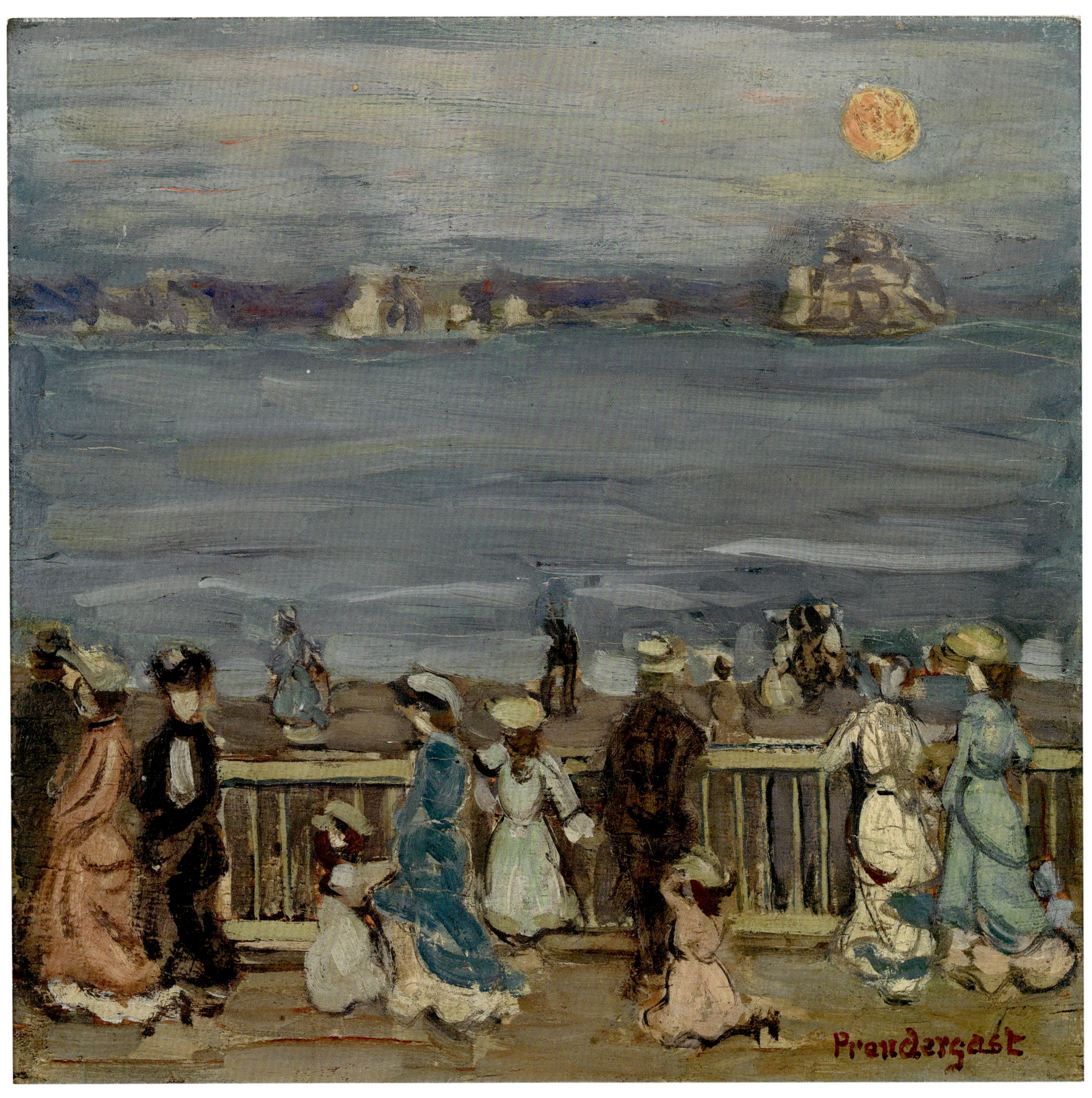

27. *Salem*, c. 1902–4

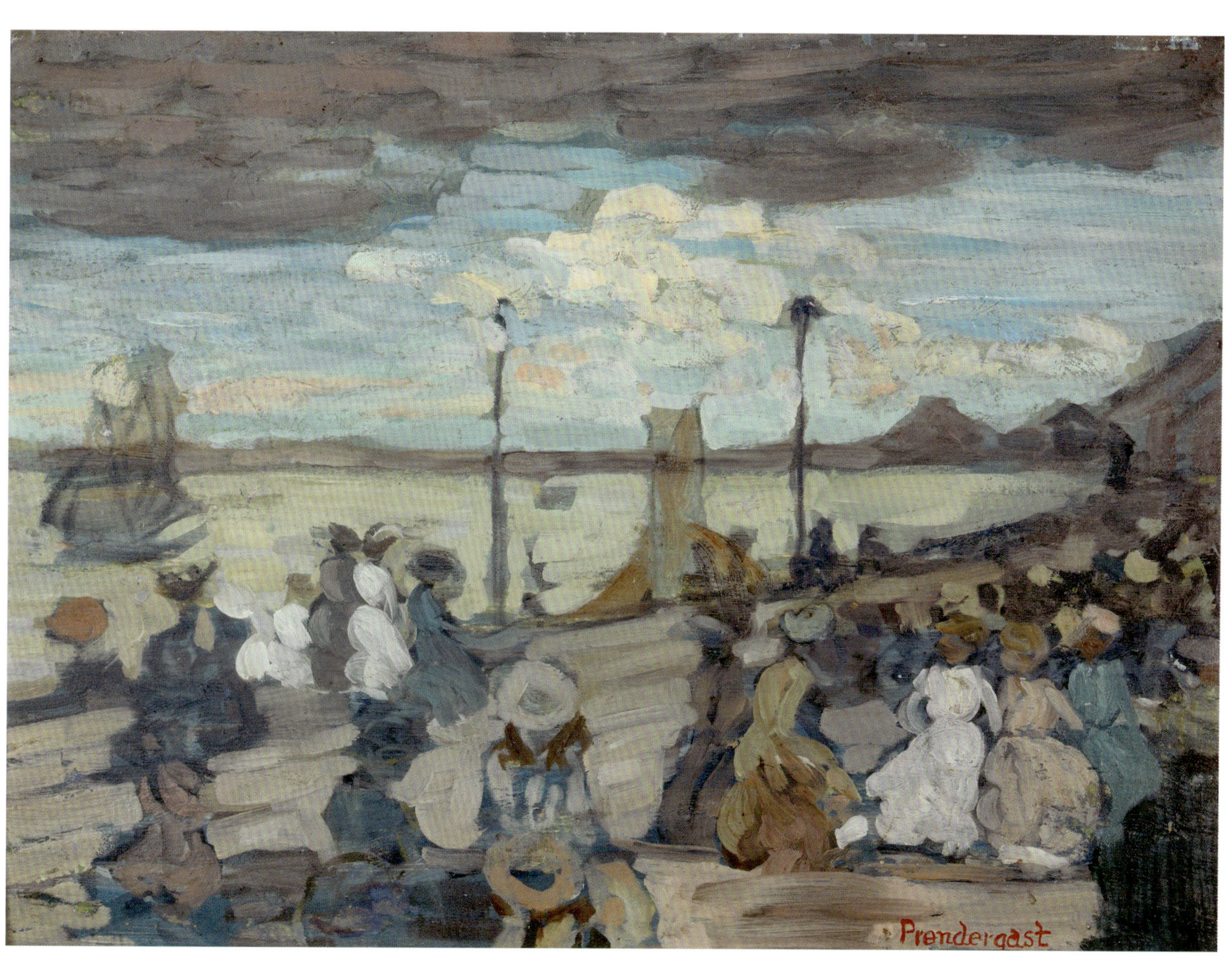

28. *Approaching Storm*, c. 1902–4

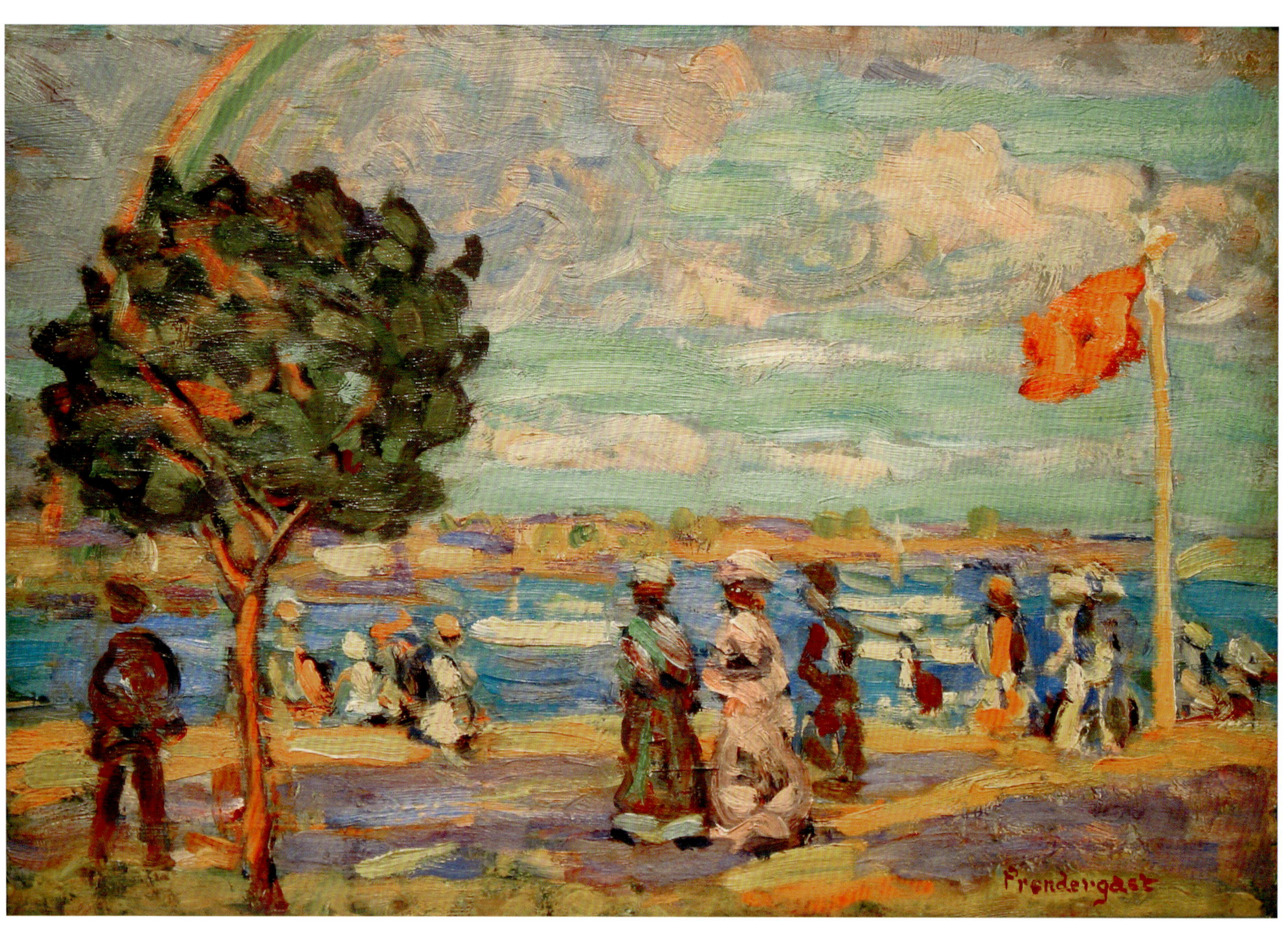

29. *Yacht Race, c. 1902–4*

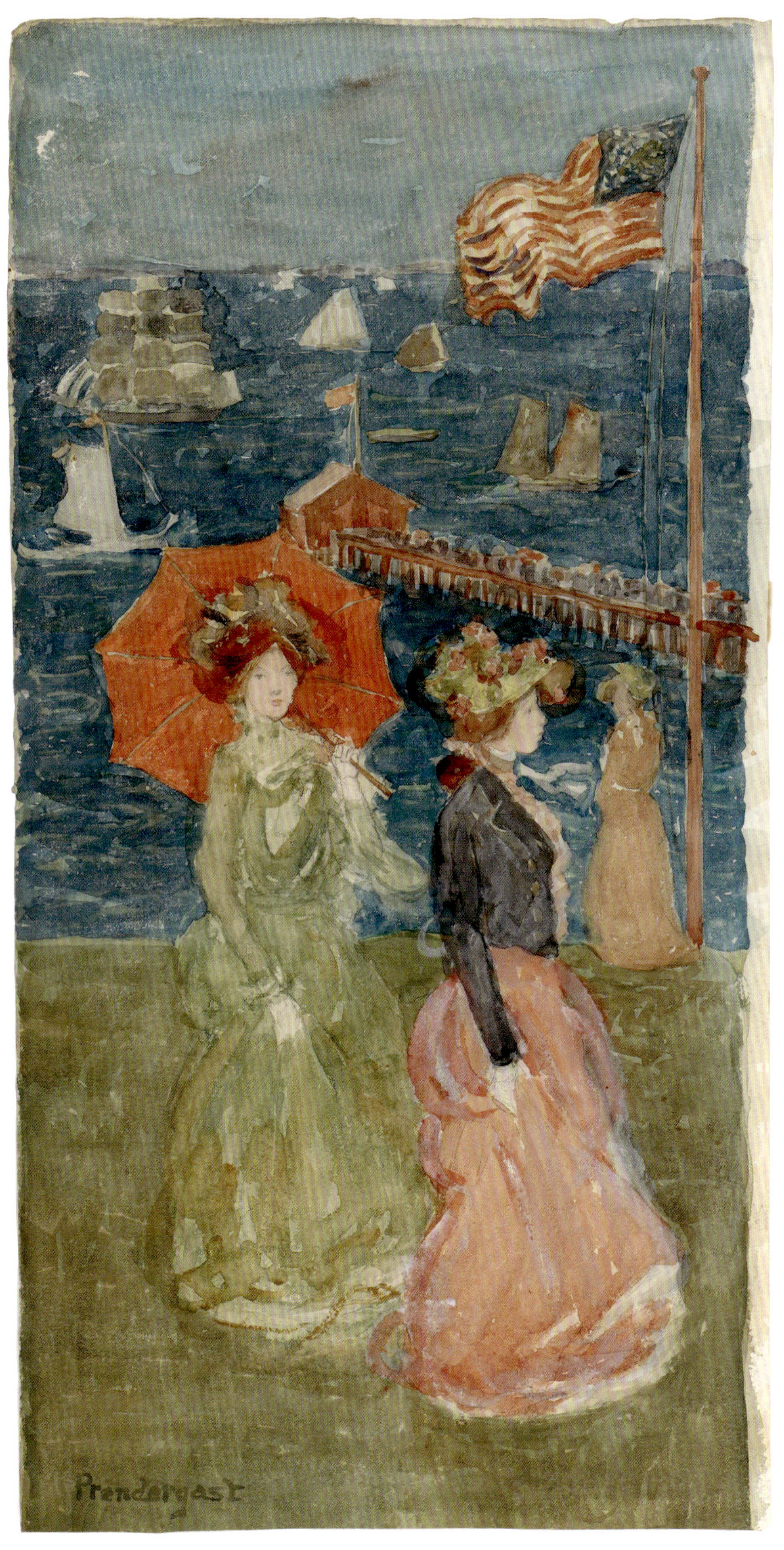

30. *Figures Under the Flag*, c. 1900–1905

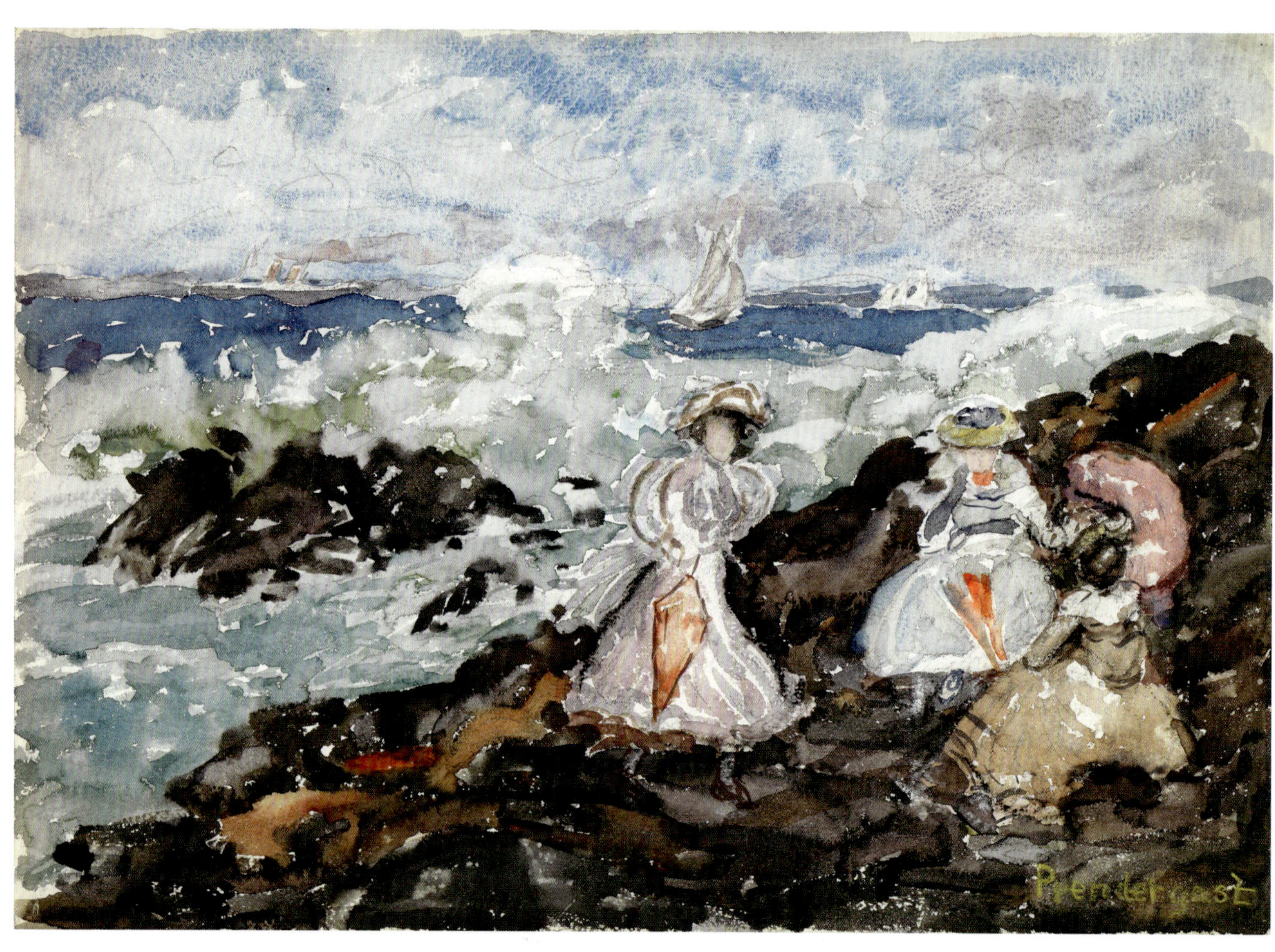

31. *Surf, Cohasset*, c. 1900–1905

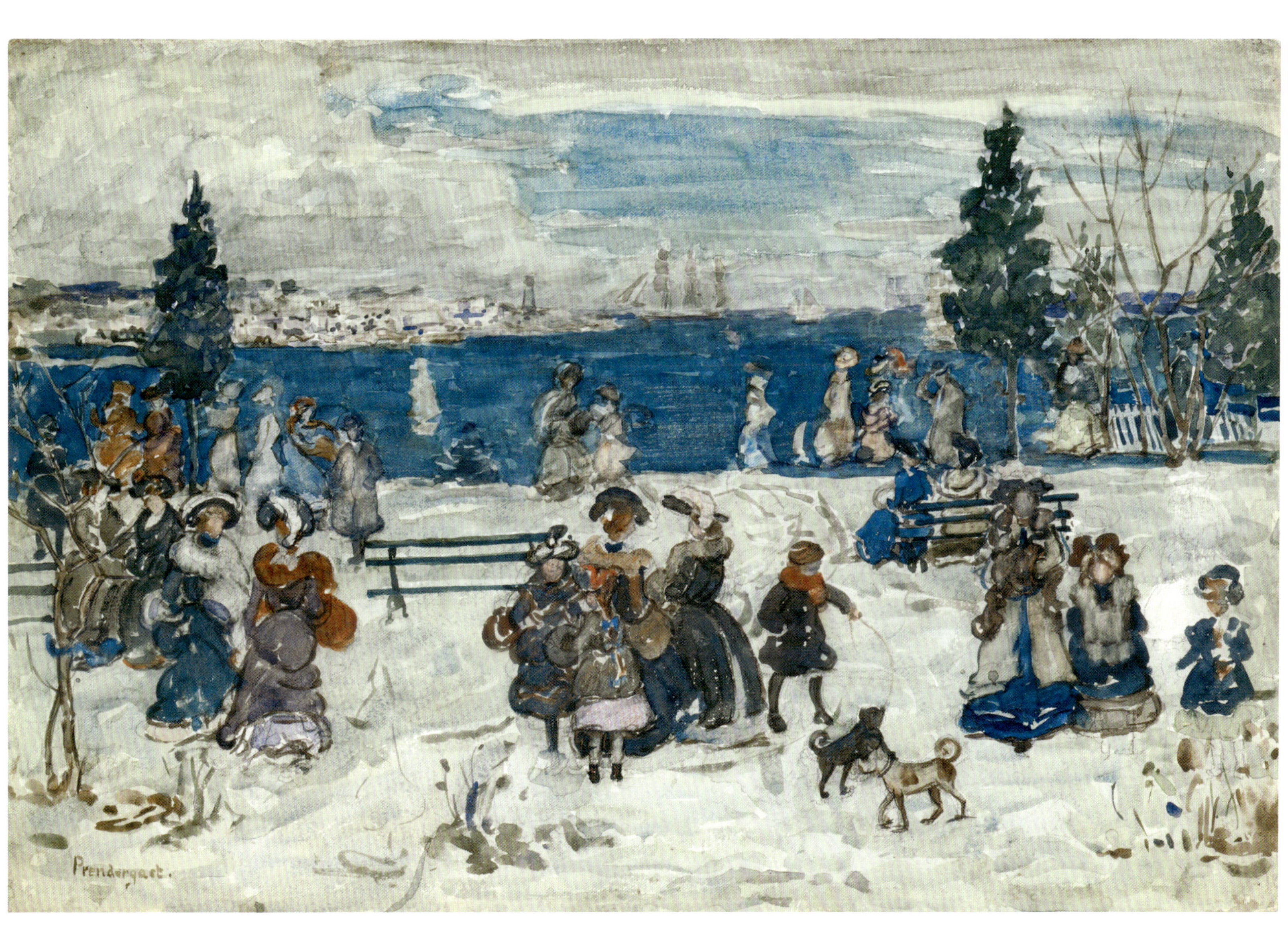

32. *April Snow, Salem*, c. 1906–7

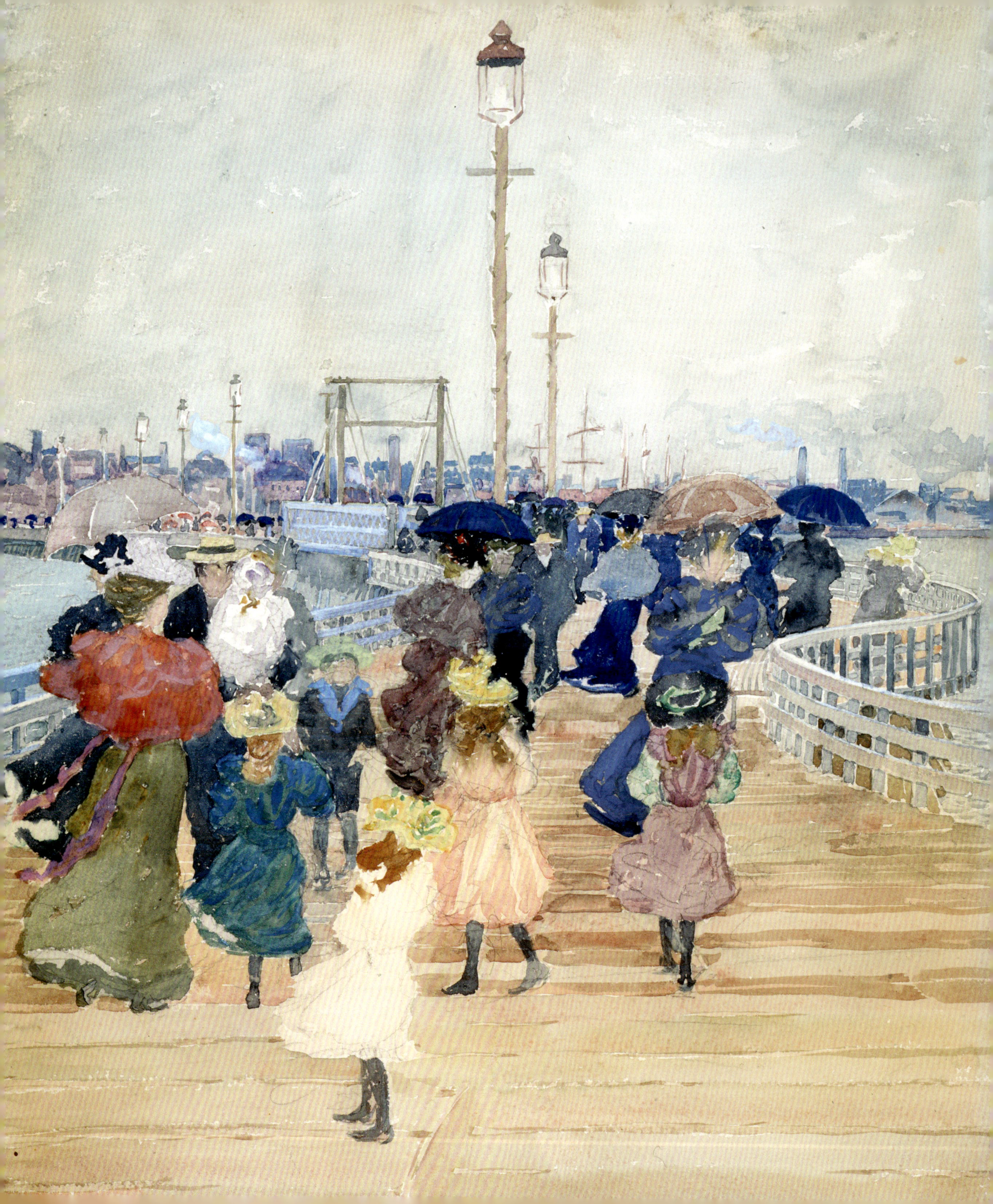

"Audacities": Maurice Prendergast and the Culture of Fin-de-Siècle Boston

TREVOR J. FAIRBROTHER

The son of an Irish father and an American mother, Maurice Prendergast was born in 1858 on the island of Newfoundland, then a far-flung British outpost. When he was ten, his father's grocery shop failed, causing the family to relocate to his mother's hometown, Boston. About four years later, Maurice left school and found employment in a dry goods store. Gravitating to the realm of advertising, he spent several years lettering the show cards used in ephemeral commercial displays. Both Maurice and his younger brother, Charles, aspired to be artists, however, and even though Boston offered various options for training, the Prendergast brothers retained their amateur status until they had saved enough money for an extended stay in France.

Beginning in 1891, Maurice and Charles took classes in Paris at two art schools that catered to the international clamor for professional credentials: the Académie Julian and the Académie Colarossi. The following year Charles returned to Boston, where he eventually established a workshop that produced hand-carved frames inspired by historic sources. Maurice remained in France until 1894, studying, painting, and exploring a broad spectrum of art, from the historic collection at the Louvre to the gamut of contemporary work. He probably saw paintings by the Neo-Impressionists, for example, who combined structural clarity with a disciplined, Pointillist technique, and by the Nabis (including Maurice Denis and Pierre Bonnard), who venerated Vincent van Gogh.

Prendergast returned to Boston resolved to specialize in pictures of streets, parks, and seaside vistas in which fleeting humankind (from one individual to a crowd) is at leisure. He embarked on a career that would be centered on images of anonymous residents enjoying their municipal bounty, and he did so in a town whose leaders were

Detail, *South Boston Pier*, 1896 (plate 9)

justly proud of their legacy of national distinction in education, medicine, transportation, public parks, and cultural endeavors. A man of humble background, Prendergast flourished in a community where starchy Brahmins set the cultural tone. But Boston, to her credit, proved cosmopolitan enough to keep this freethinking artist in residence until 1914, when he moved to New York. In 1938, fourteen years after Prendergast's death, New York artist and writer Walter Pach characterized the evolution of his friend's art as a steady shift from "vaporous tone and poetry" to a pictorial sturdiness in which "the pigments kept all their fire." Pach noted the "silver" aspect in Prendergast's earlier Boston works ("the daintiness of some fairy figure by the sea") and attributed the robust stability of the later phases to things Maurice learned from the works of Cézanne, "the Persians," and Giotto.[1]

To perceive the artistic diversity Boston fostered during Prendergast's formative years one need only consider the styles of the grandest edifices in Copley Square: Gothic Revival (Old South Church, 1873, and the Museum of Fine Arts, 1876); Romanesque Revival (Trinity Church, 1877), and Beaux-Arts classicism (Boston Public Library, 1895). The mural decorations commissioned for the Public Library included a serene and refined classical ensemble by Pierre Puvis de Chavannes, the French painter whose work had inspired the emerging Symbolist movement.[2] It is safe to assume that Prendergast, in keeping with his wide-ranging artistic interests, was familiar with many of the currents in modern art because they were aired so thoroughly in Boston, from the French Impressionist style of painting, exemplified by Claude Monet, to the "art for art's sake" philosophy championed by James McNeill Whistler, to the aesthetic "otherness" of Japanese fine and decorative arts, which, as it happens, also shaped Monet and Whistler.

On returning from Paris in 1894, Prendergast's most demanding project was to create almost a hundred images for an illustrated edition of *My Lady Nicotine*, J. M. Barrie's tales of young men who worship tobacco. This Boston publication drew praise in *The Studio*, a London-based magazine, whose reviewer saluted the "clever young artist" for work of such "rare delicacy." After applauding the book's "admirably simple and very well lettered" title page, the writer insisted that to experience Prendergast at his finest one should see "the amazing excellence" of his watercolors.[3]

In the early watercolor *The Harbor from City Point* (plate 4), dated 1895, Prendergast showed a slightly scruffy section of the waterfront in South Boston. Passersby occupy but a small part of the composition; the artist paid more attention to evoking a rapid diagonal recession into space, from an empty foreground to a distant urban-industrial horizon with numerous ships and buildings. The overcast weather may have spurred Prendergast to focus on the drama of the isolated setting, and the muted light certainly inspired a quirky assortment of transparent greens, purples, and blues. There is a general kinship with Monet's spatially innovative landscapes, such as

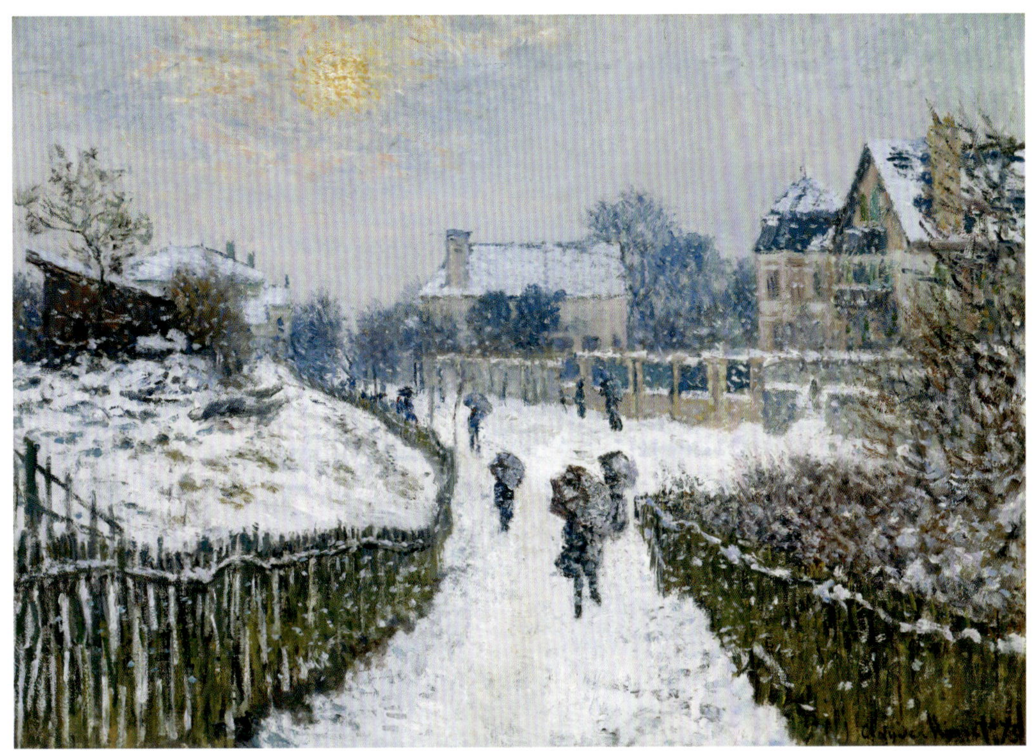

Fig. 17. Claude Monet, *Boulevard Saint-Denis, Argenteuil, in Winter*, 1875. Oil on canvas, 24 × 32⅛ in. (60.9 × 81.6 cm). Museum of Fine Arts, Boston; Gift of Richard Saltonstall (1978.633)

Boulevard Saint-Denis, Argenteuil, in Winter (fig. 17). Monet painted this exhilarating Impressionist canvas of falling snow in 1875, after he had begun to collect Japanese woodcuts, and it entered a private Boston collection in 1890 thanks to the scouting efforts of local painter Frederick Porter Vinton. Boston, in fact, offered numerous opportunities to experience modern French art; early in 1898, for example, the dealer Durand-Ruel lent pictures by Manet, Degas, Monet, Pissarro, Renoir, and Puvis de Chavannes to an exhibition hosted by the Boston Art Students' Association.[4]

South Boston Pier (plate 9), from just one year later, attests to Prendergast's rapid evolution with its more nuanced articulation of space. Note, for example, how the curved fences animate the middle ground, and the lampposts and ship masts pierce the skyline to establish two diagonal axes. The work depicts a newly constructed footbridge on wooden pilings that allowed city folk to promenade from the mainland to Castle Island. The larger setting is Marine Park, an extensive municipal "pleasure ground" developed to provide opportunities for healthy recreation.

The artistic delights of *South Boston Pier* define Prendergast's signature style: an appreciation of the milling crowd; a seemingly casual approach to composition; a playful manner with the brush; and a capricious flair for notes of bright color. His initial desire to depict a cross-section of city dwellers was likely roused in the previous decade by the work of Childe Hassam, a successful Boston artist, just a year younger than Maurice, who had established a local reputation before he sought professional training abroad. After studying at the Académie Julian during a stint in Paris, Hassam

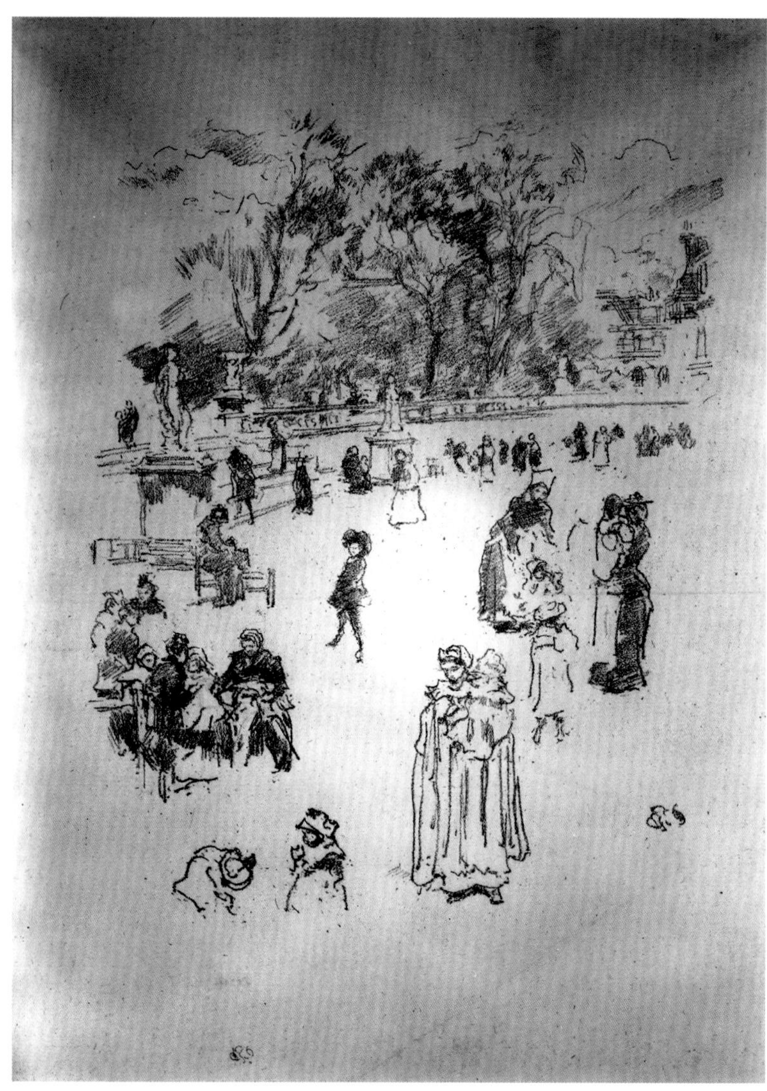

Fig. 18. James Abbott McNeill Whistler, *Nursemaids of Luxembourg*, 1894. Lithograph on paper, 11¾ × 8½ in. (29.8 × 21.6 cm). Brooklyn Museum; Gift of the Rembrandt Club (15.393)

moved to New York in 1889. A plush book titled *Living New England Artists* (1888), which illustrated his city views and praised his ability to translate Boston's "prosaic thoroughfares" into "pictorially poetic" images expressive of "modern life," attests to Hassam's prominence at the time.[5]

Prendergast's style was a little less slavish to "proper" draftsmanship than Hassam's, and by the mid-1890s he was more attuned to the endlessly innovative Whistler, whose compositional "eccentricities"—evident in his 1894 lithograph of women and children in a Parisian park, *Nursemaids of Luxembourg* (fig. 18)—appealed to Prendergast at this juncture in his development. When painting *Rocky Shore, Nantasket* (plate 11), for example, Maurice populated his landscape with freestanding and overlapping figures in a manner that recalls Whistler's *Nursemaids*. Following a judicious and presumably additive method, each artist constructed a composition that feels casual, momentary, and pleasantly incomplete. Through careful editing, their pictures convey the sensation of an unhurried glimpse. Although both artists took a Japoniste, quasi-abstract approach to rendering groups of people, today Whistler's effort comes across as the more daring because it is monochrome and because he used an empty expanse of white paper as the ground on which he "floated" many of his figures. Another shared trait was an aversion to giving overly descriptive detail to a given figure. While they might well stress a particular outline of a dress or the gesture of a foot, both artists were apt to pay scant attention to a person's face. A similar freewheeling strategy guided their use of color. In *Rocky Shore*, Prendergast arranged certain vibrant hues—the different notes of red on parasols, hats, and neckerchief, the whites of dresses and sails, and the blue and turquoise pools of sea water—to keep the viewer's eye on the move.

The development of artistic posters in the early 1890s had a crucial impact on Prendergast. Although traditionalist critics pooh-poohed "poster mania" when it took off, the phenomenon nonetheless unleashed tremendous creativity. In the United States, the purveyors of "little magazines," the publishers of books with ornate bindings and decorated pages, and such mass-market companies as Harper's, Scribner's, and Lippincott's all embraced the trend. Boston's first exhibition of pictorial posters, presented in 1895, encompassed works by an international group: Walter Crane, Aubrey Beardsley, and J. & W. Beggarstaff from England; Eugène Grasset and Jules

    TREVOR J. FAIRBROTHER

Chéret from France; and a young American contingent that included Edward Penfield, Louis Rhead, Will Bradley, and Thomas B. Meteyard. Prendergast was probably not an exhibitor, and he may not have even visited the show, but one of his posters appeared on a list in a booklet by the organizer.

Arthur Wesley Dow's poster *Modern Art* (fig. 19), which appeared in several early anthologies, remains a landmark in Boston's poster movement. The artist was a local figure who made a pilgrimage to Paris and the Académie Julian in the 1880s. His inquisitive and astute mind gave his art its independent path and steadfastly guided his career teaching and writing about nontraditional and cross-cultural approaches to becoming an artist. Dow produced *Modern Art* for a progressive magazine that had recently moved from Chicago to Boston. He made the inspired decision to surround his main design—a pastoral twilight—with a moody green border asymmetrically decorated with poppies. His juxtaposition of two components ("picture" and "ground") has an Asian quality, and the simple, almost schematic landscape simultaneously recalls Dow's dual devotion to Japanese woodblock prints and poetic Barbizon landscapes. To further enrich and complicate the work, Dow devised a vaguely Art Nouveau yet provocatively homemade lettering for the title.

Round Table Library (fig. 20), the poster Prendergast designed for a Boston publisher in 1895, demonstrates that he did not shy from experimental, unusual, or accidental effects. The objective, for both artist and client, was an enticing image of a pretty and fashionable woman who happens to be reading. Prendergast gave the model an imposing presence in the compositional frame but maintained the intimate sense of being lost in a book. A stand of daisies shields the bank where his model sat; he added an empty expanse of rippling water to echo her quietude and devised an energetic sky to compete with her sinuous coiffure. The bold use of yellow may have been inspired by Aubrey Beardsley, whose covers for the magazine *The Yellow Book* had made him notorious, but Prendergast's amiable manner of drawing was the antithesis of the young Englishman's firm, hyper-elegant, and sometimes risqué stylizations.[6]

Prendergast had a twin sister who died at the age of about nineteen. The lovely young woman in *Round Table Library* tempts one to wonder if this lost sibling inspired, either privately or subliminally, the artist's abiding fascination with the blithe female muse. Indeed, in his multifigure pictures from this period, it is easy to imagine that Prendergast is devoting slightly more attention to one or another young woman, as if she *might* become a face in the crowd.

During his ascent through the art establishment, Prendergast typically kept the mood of his pictures cheery and carefree, and in that respect there was a link between him and his established Boston peers Frank Benson and Edmund Tarbell, exponents of a pictorially affable and often innocuous line of Impressionist painting. But Prendergast's art was too wedded to quirky and individualist notes—whether

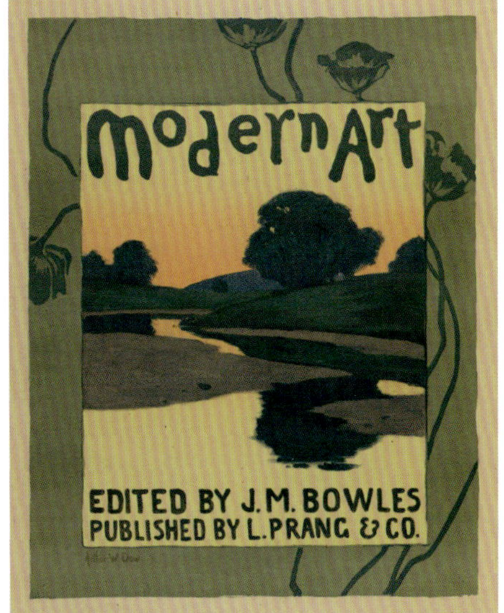

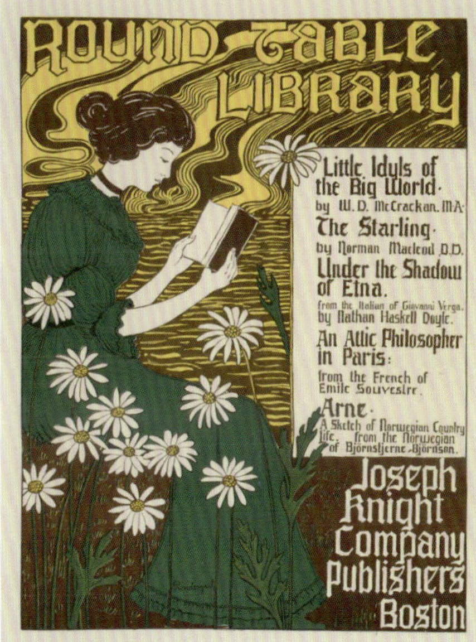

Fig. 19. Arthur Wesley Dow, *Modern Art*, 1895. Poster, color lithograph, 17⅝ × 13⅝ in. (44.7 × 34.6 cm). Museum of Fine Arts, Boston; Gift of L. Prang & Co., Boston, 1895 (M10688)

Fig. 20. Maurice Prendergast, *Round Table Library*, 1893–1924. Poster. The New York Public Library, Astor, Lenox, and Tilden Foundations (1259284)

the unfussy application of paint, the casual drawing, or the penchant for eccentric visual rhymes—to bring him into the fold of the "Boston School."[7] These aspects of Prendergast's art can be found in the watercolor *Figures Under the Flag* (plate 30), which, superficially at least, has several key ingredients of the Impressionism favored in Boston; most notably, it presents women wearing summer outfits on a lovely day as an opportunity to translate effects of sunlight into painterly touches. But Prendergast's two main figures may well be strangers, for there is no obvious anecdotal link between them. The fact that they are closely juxtaposed is surely the product of the artist's fancy as he worked up a picture that satisfied him as an arrangement of shapes, marks, and colors. Likewise, the artist cared more about relationships among the three horizontal divisions of the background—sky, sea, and grass—than whether his pier sat at a "believable" remove beyond his flagpole. It is important to remember that although Prendergast was an avid outdoor sketcher, he produced his more elaborate works in the studio. *Figures Under the Flag* is thus probably a typical example of a composition made with the aid of the arsenal of poses, silhouettes, gestures, and vignettes found in his sketchbooks.

Prendergast got his start with his charming works on paper, as these excerpts from reviews testify:

> 1897: "His subjects [are] full of dainty and buoyant action, and are painted with a most felicitous and suggestive touch. He is a brilliant and distinguished colorist."

> 1899: "He paints distinctly in his own style. Gaily dressed little people, and lots of them, and much bunting *bunt und feierlich* [colorful and festive] are his motives, and he develops them charmingly."

> 1901: "He is a delightful artist of the butterfly type, a sort of modern Watteau. The fun that he has in painting these scenes must be huge."[8]

Another gauge of Prendergast's growing reputation in Boston is the fact that his work was warmly spoofed in a group exhibition of caricatures presented at the Copley Society in 1902. In the catalogue, a picture by one "Norris Venezuela Pennygrass" titled *The Breezy Pond, Franklin Park* is accompanied by a blurb that observes: "[He] went to Paris and entered the ateliers of Bourgerboo. . . . His strong individuality is admirably shown by the lack of all traces of his master's influence in his painting, except the extremely mathematical character of his composition and drawing."[9]

As a means to reveal the stylistic elements that Prendergast did and did not embrace as a result of his first sojourn in Paris, consider a painting on paper by

TREVOR J. FAIRBROTHER

Henri de Toulouse-Lautrec, *Jane Avril Leaving the Moulin Rouge* (fig. 21). The subject of a woman walking at her leisure was dear to Prendergast, as was the heightening of the atmosphere (especially the colors) associated with public locales. But this work is pitched in a psychologically intense register; the seemingly slapdash rendering of the background is breathtaking, and the deft characterization of the figure qualifies the picture as an outstanding informal portrait. Jane Avril was a celebrated cancan dancer, and Toulouse-Lautrec was paying homage to the grace and poignancy of her offstage personality. His response to the introspective solitude behind the makeup and chic outfit is profound. Prendergast's *Figures Under the Flag*, on the other hand, shows no desire to "nail" or "capture" the two main figures: while charming in their different ways, they are relatively anonymous.

In *Jane Avril*, Toulouse-Lautrec rendered the floor and walls in contrasting patterns of irregular dots and lines. If Prendergast had gone that far at the start of his career, he would have flopped in Boston. As it turned out, the more moderate style he practiced won him critical acclaim and even attracted a few collectors, most notably the rich painter and photographer Sarah Choate Sears, owner of Maurice's *South Boston Pier.*[10] The Boston collector Isabella Stewart Gardner did not acquire a

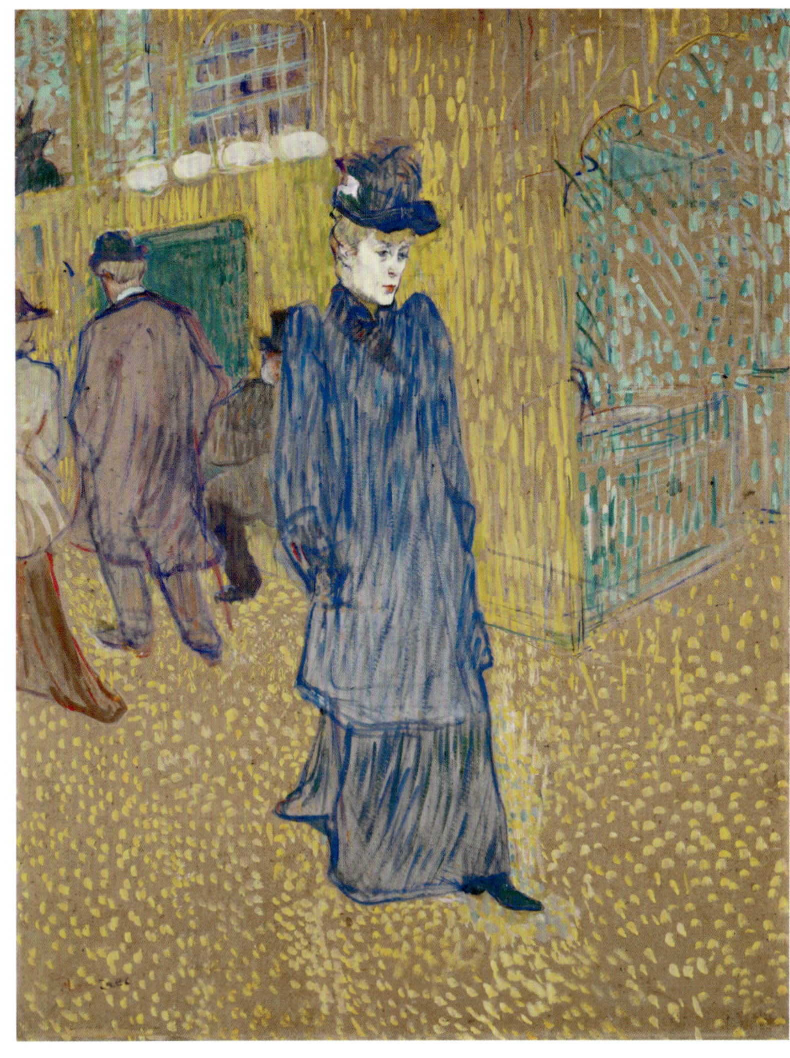

picture by Maurice, but one of her many paintings by John Singer Sargent (*Charles Martin Loeffler*, 1903) entered her collection in one of Charles Prendergast's carved and gilded frames. (Maurice and his frame-making brother were "different" enough, both as artists and lower-middle-class bohemian types, to guarantee that they retained their independence; in fact, they probably savored their ability to make a living on the fringes of polite society.) And while Maurice did not live to see his work displayed in or acquired by the Museum of Fine Arts, from a philosophical standpoint there were richer rewards. As Charles remarked in later years, "Nobody had as much fun as Monny and me."[11]

Over time, as he produced more oil paintings, Maurice developed and honed his working methods. He knew that there was more to modern art than he could find in either Boston or New York, and he made no bones of the fact that a trip to Europe was the best way to find artistic rejuvenation. By 1908 he had come to realize that the changes happening in his art were becoming unwelcome in Boston. In a review of a much ballyhooed New York exhibition of paintings by "independent" American artists, a Massachusetts critic referred to Prendergast as follows: "We are all familiar [with] Mr. Prendergast's audacities here in Boston, and we do not dislike them. In fact, with all their faults we love them still."[12] This verbiage seems to be as pointed as it is clever. Indeed, the writer sounds weary of cautioning Prendergast about his stubborn artistic autonomy. The remark probably betrays the smug conservative mindset prevalent in elite Bostonian culture. Happily, Prendergast had an enduring detachment from the wangling of critics, dealers, and collectors: no bourgeois he. In a letter of 1915, soon after his move to New York, he told a new patron that people engaged in business maneuvers left him bored and confused: "I only want to be let alone and to do the work."[13]

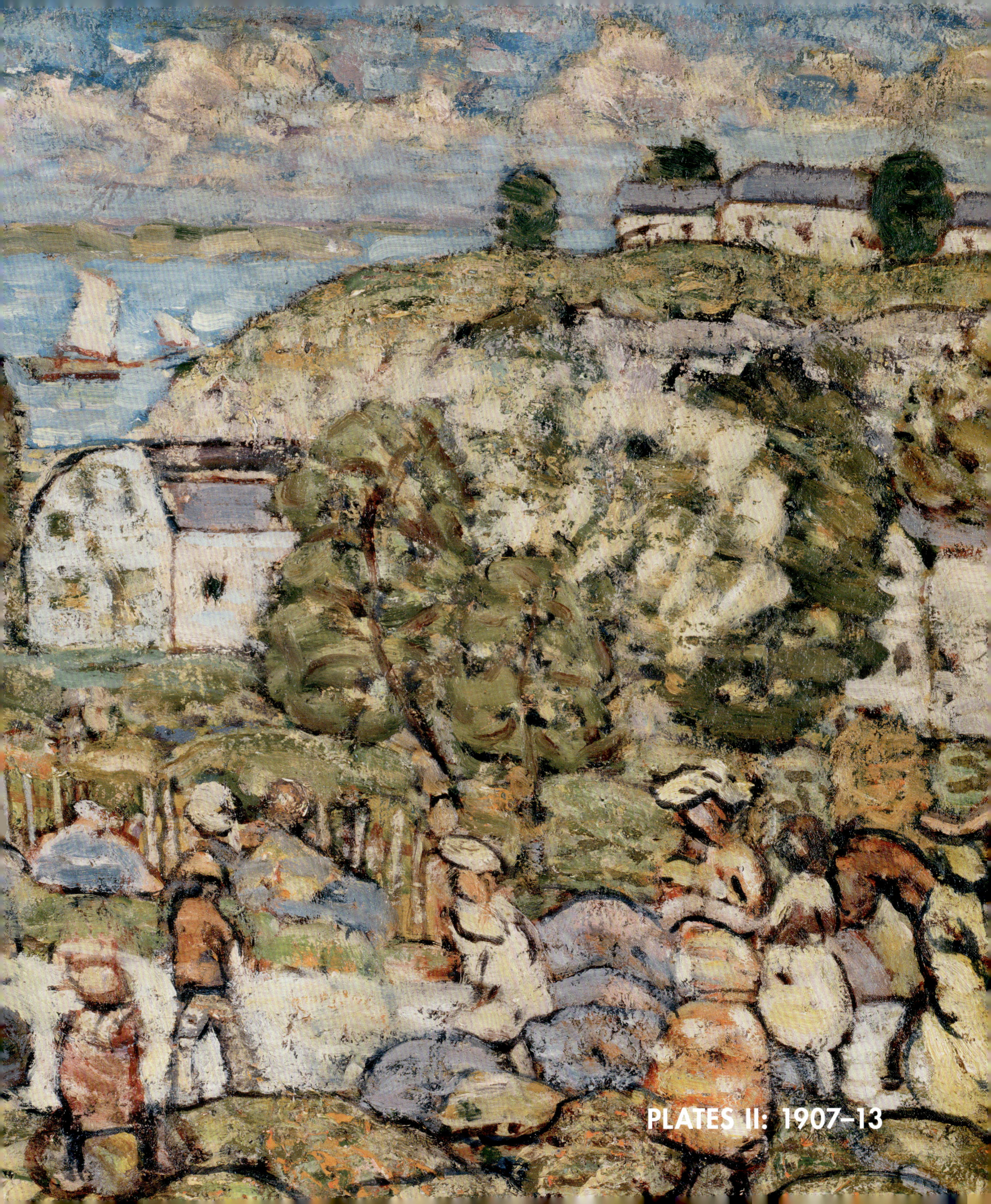

PLATES II: 1907–13

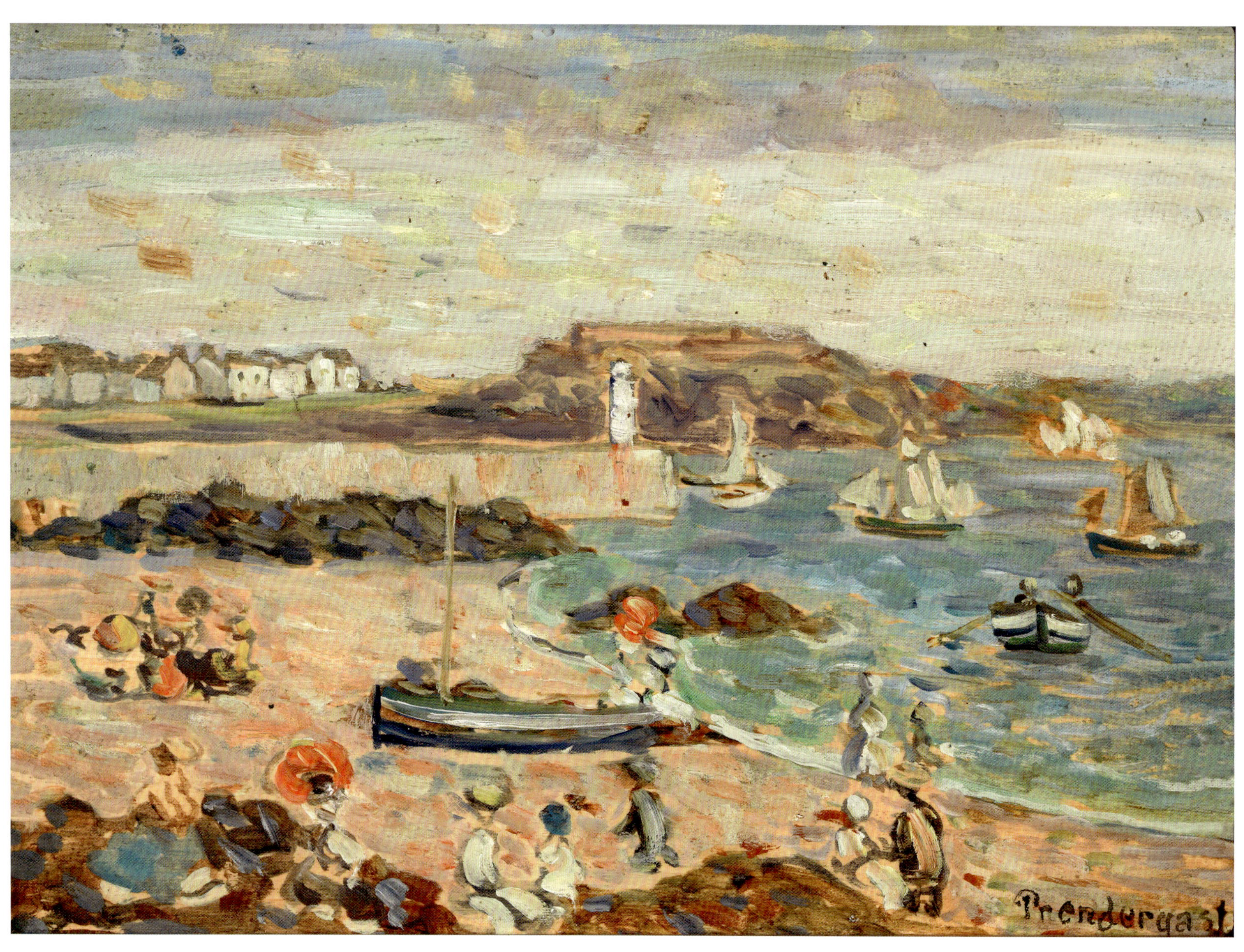

33. *Study St. Malo, No. 32*, c. 1907

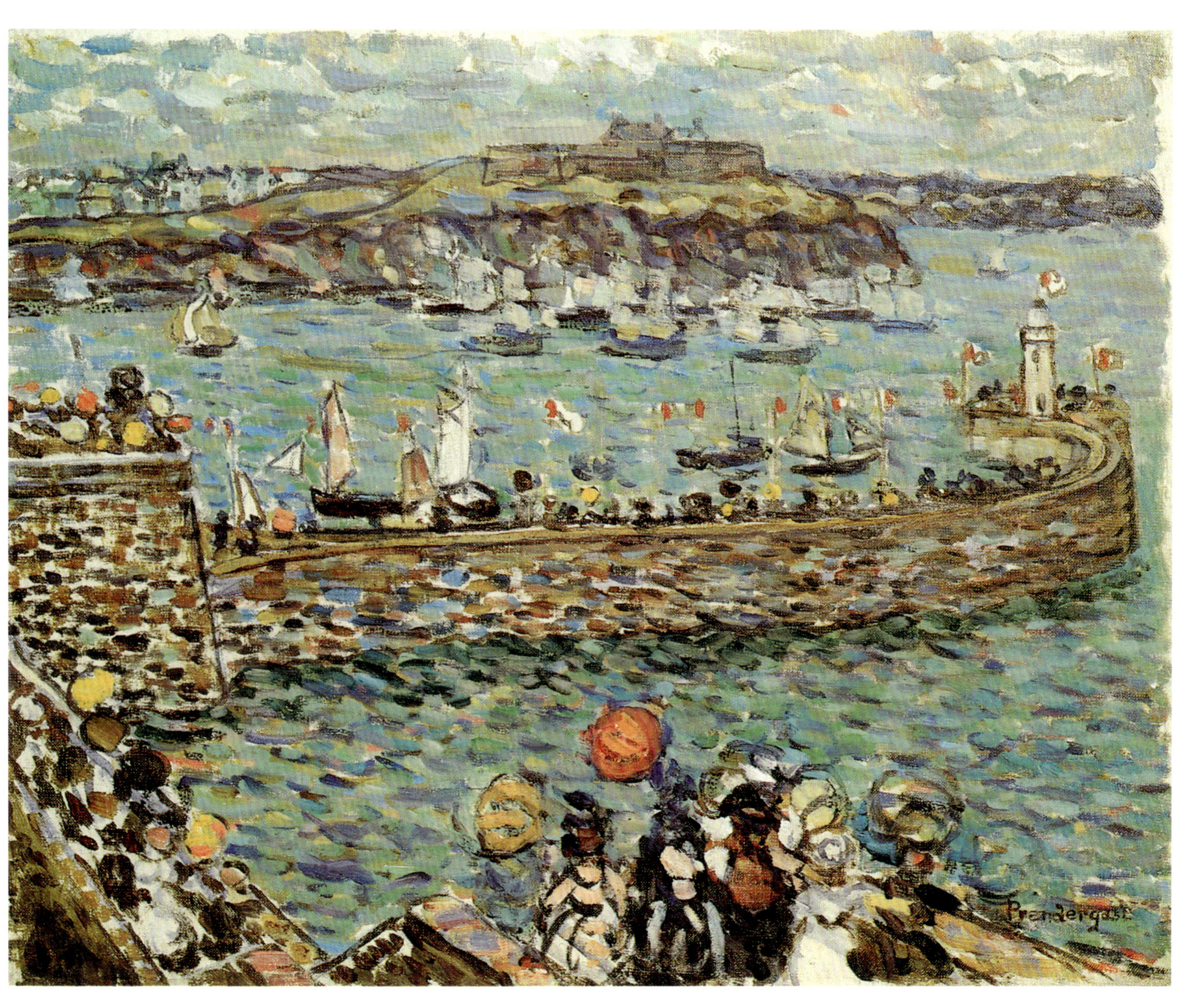

34. *Lighthouse at St. Malo*, c. 1907

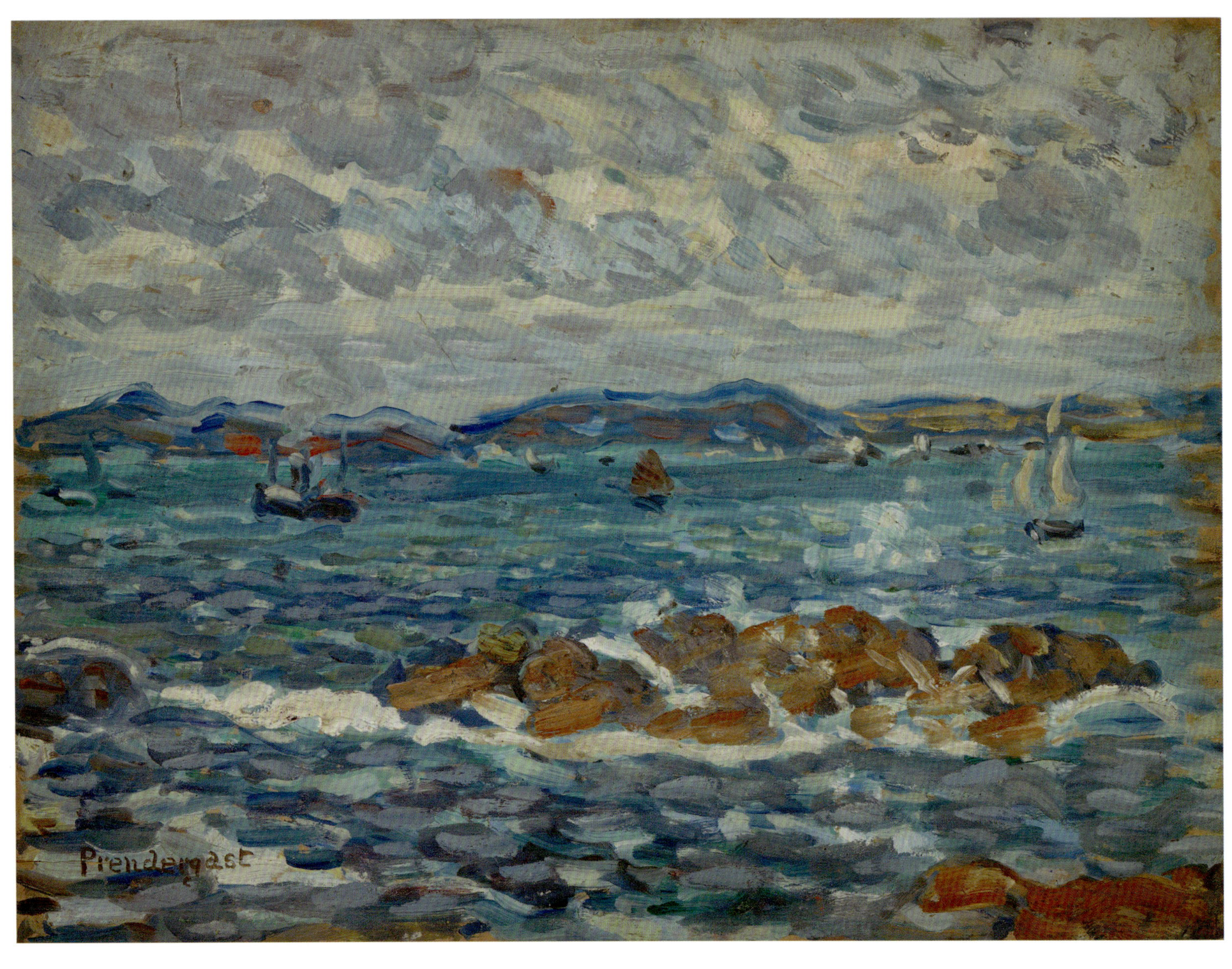

35. *St. Malo,* c. 1907

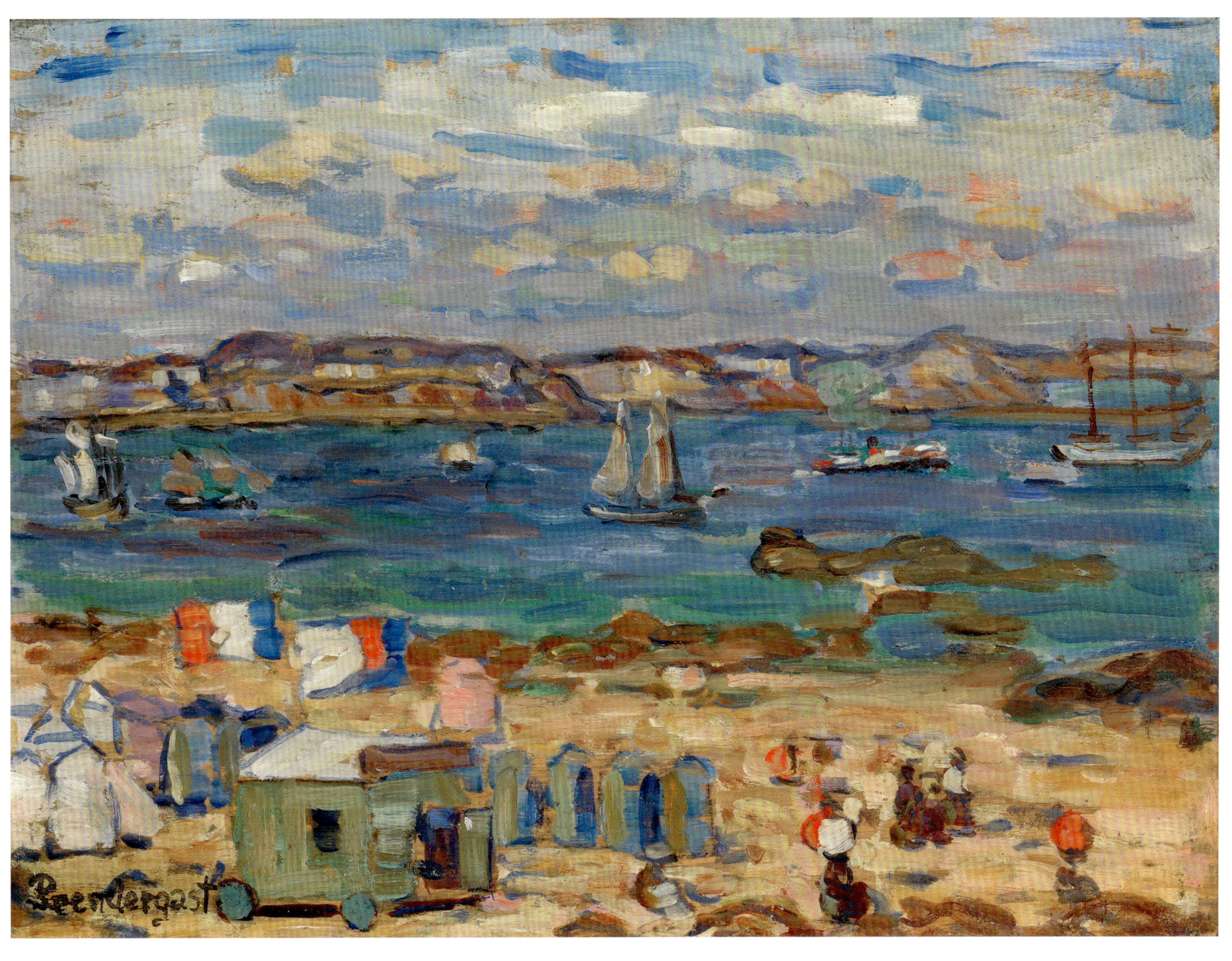

36. *Study St. Malo, No. 12,* c. 1907

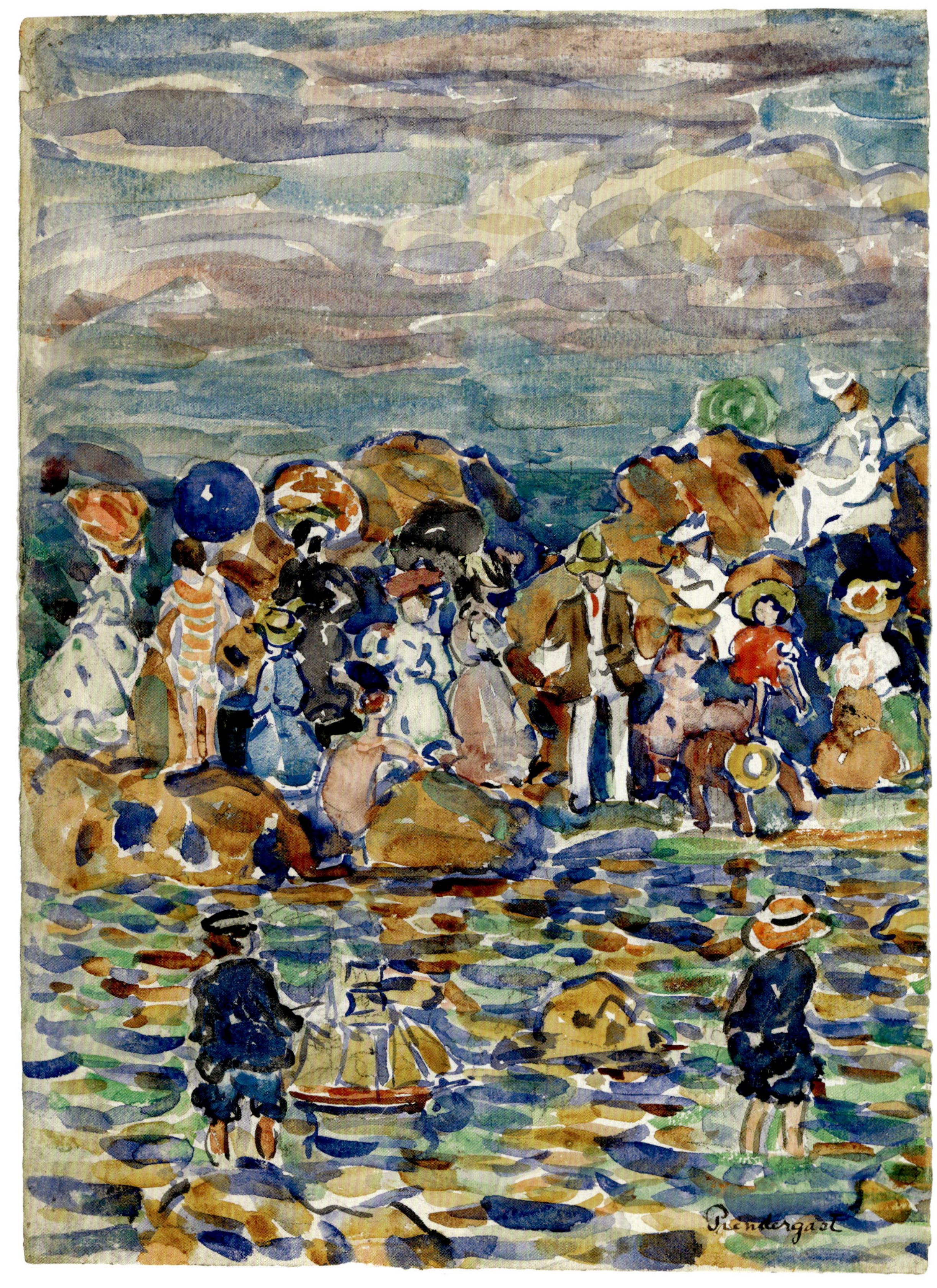

  37. *St. Malo*, c. 1907

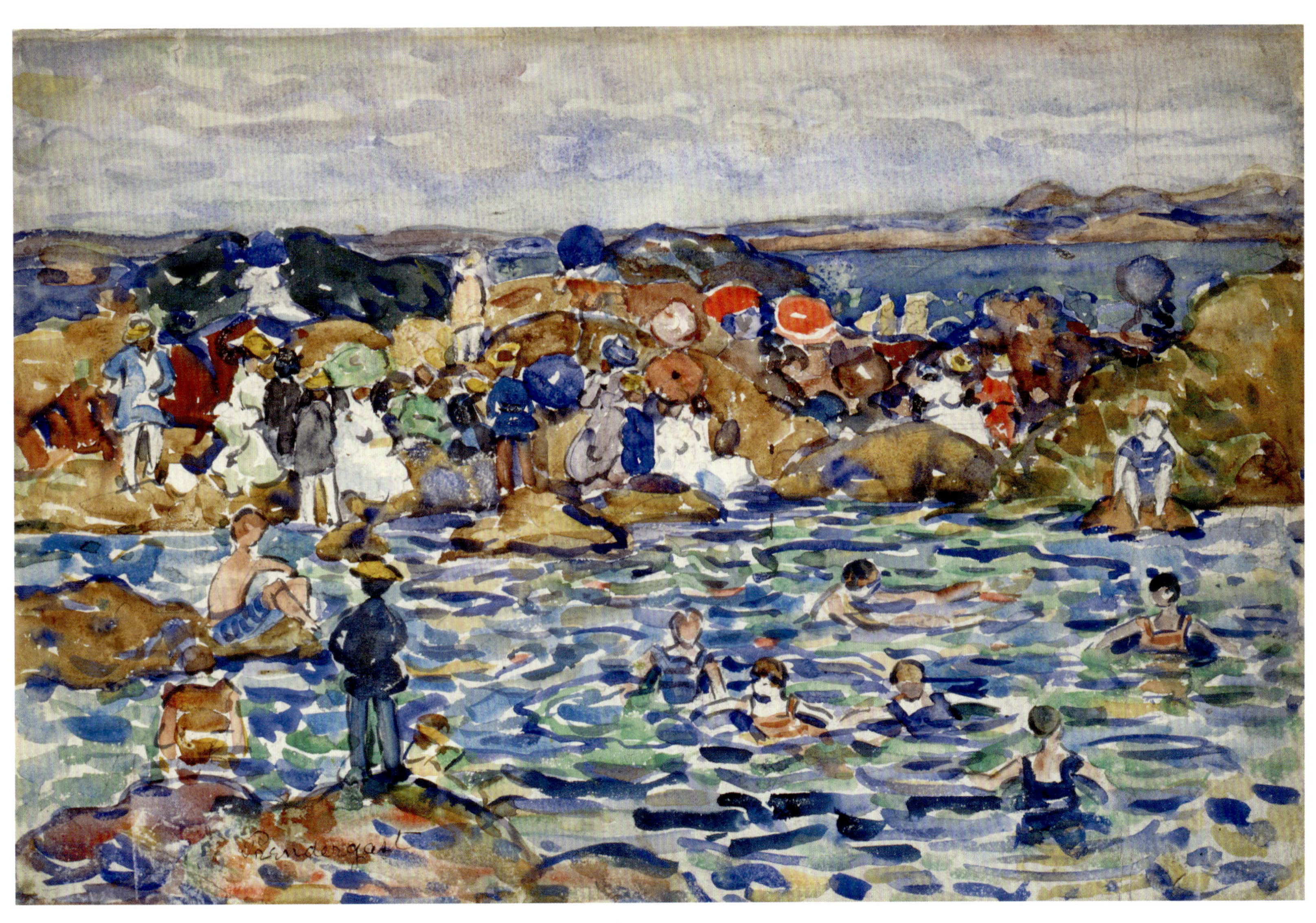

38. *At the Shore, St. Malo No. 1*, c. 1907

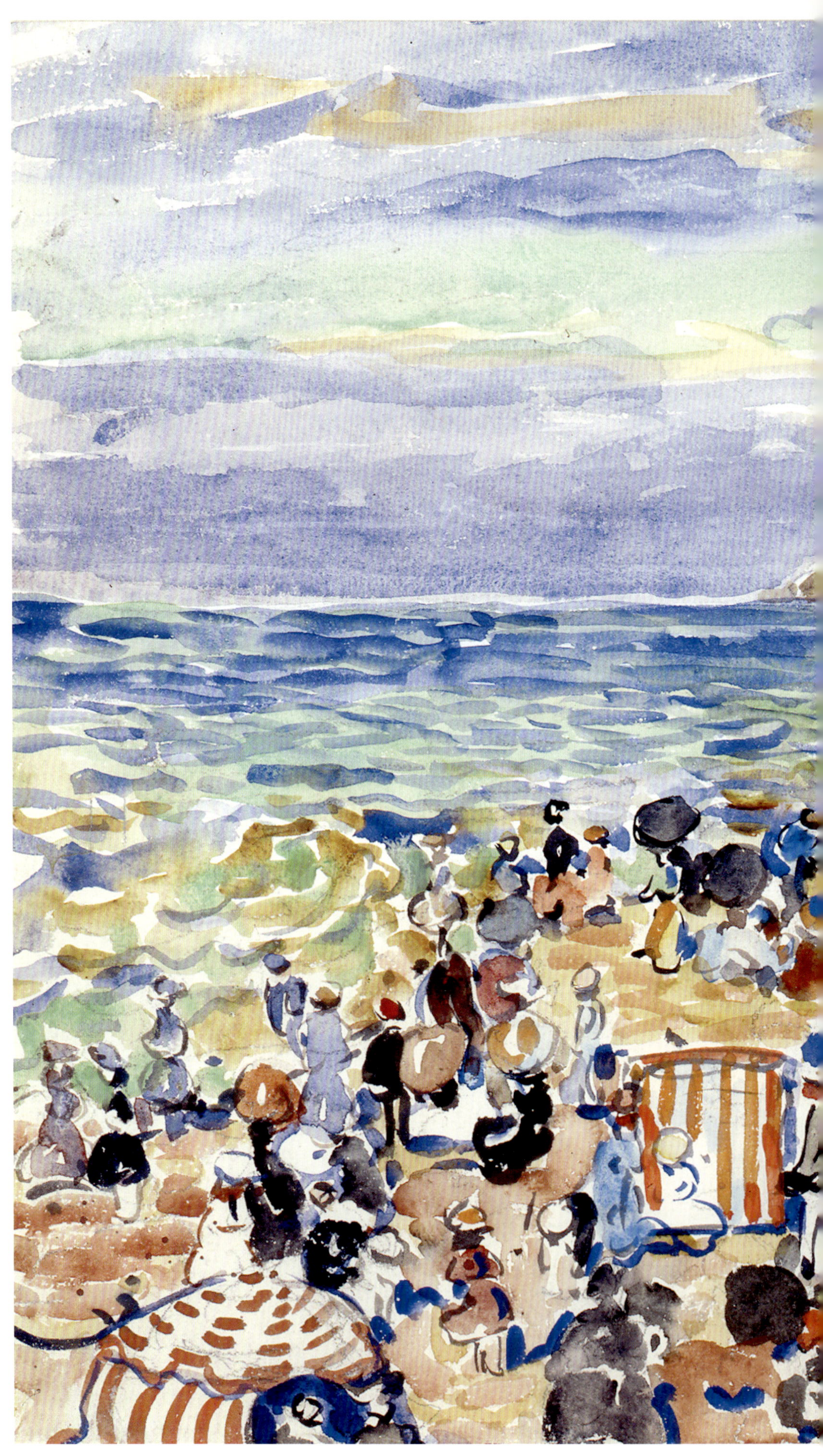

39. *St. Malo, No. 2,* c. 1907–10

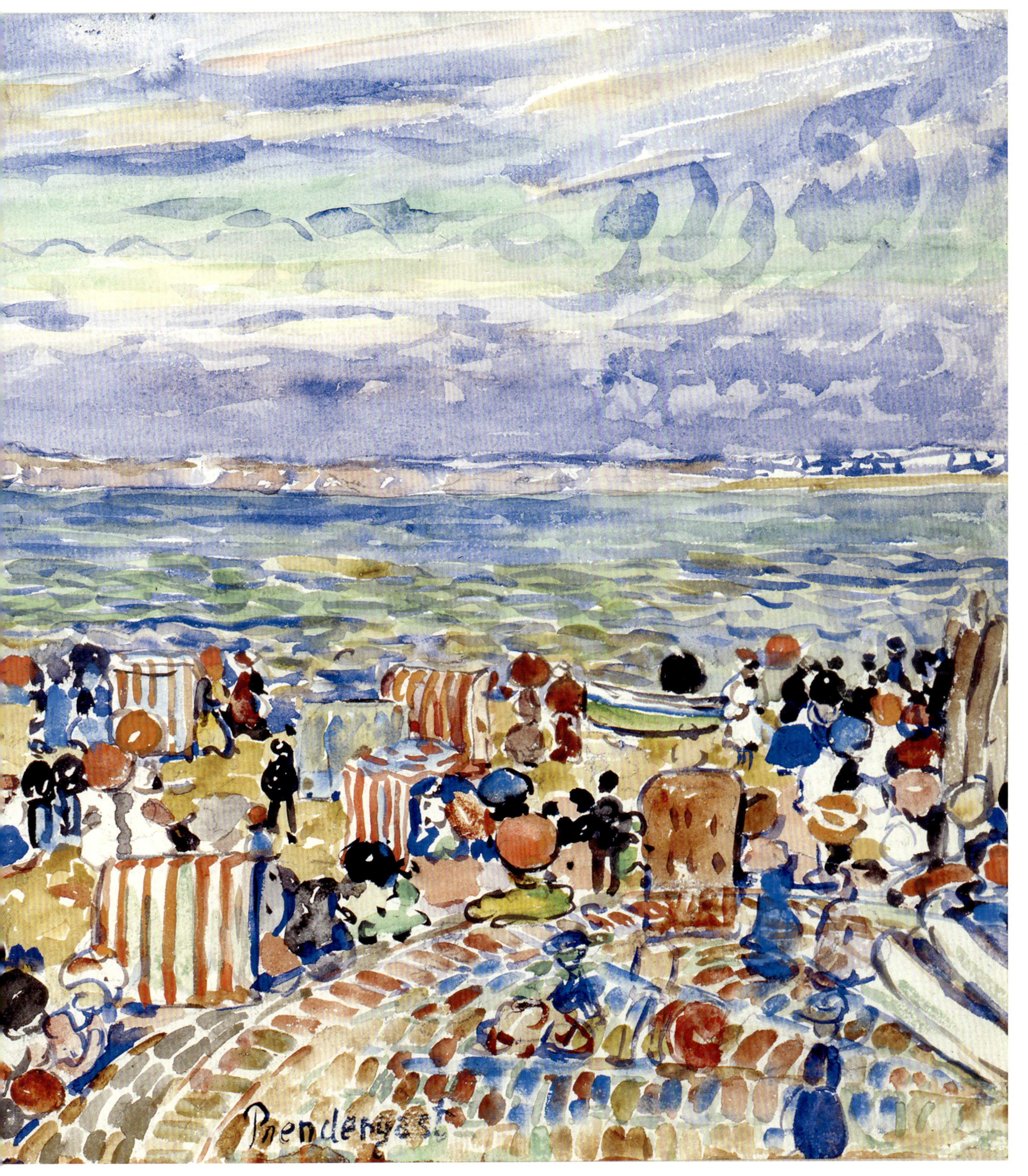

Prendergast

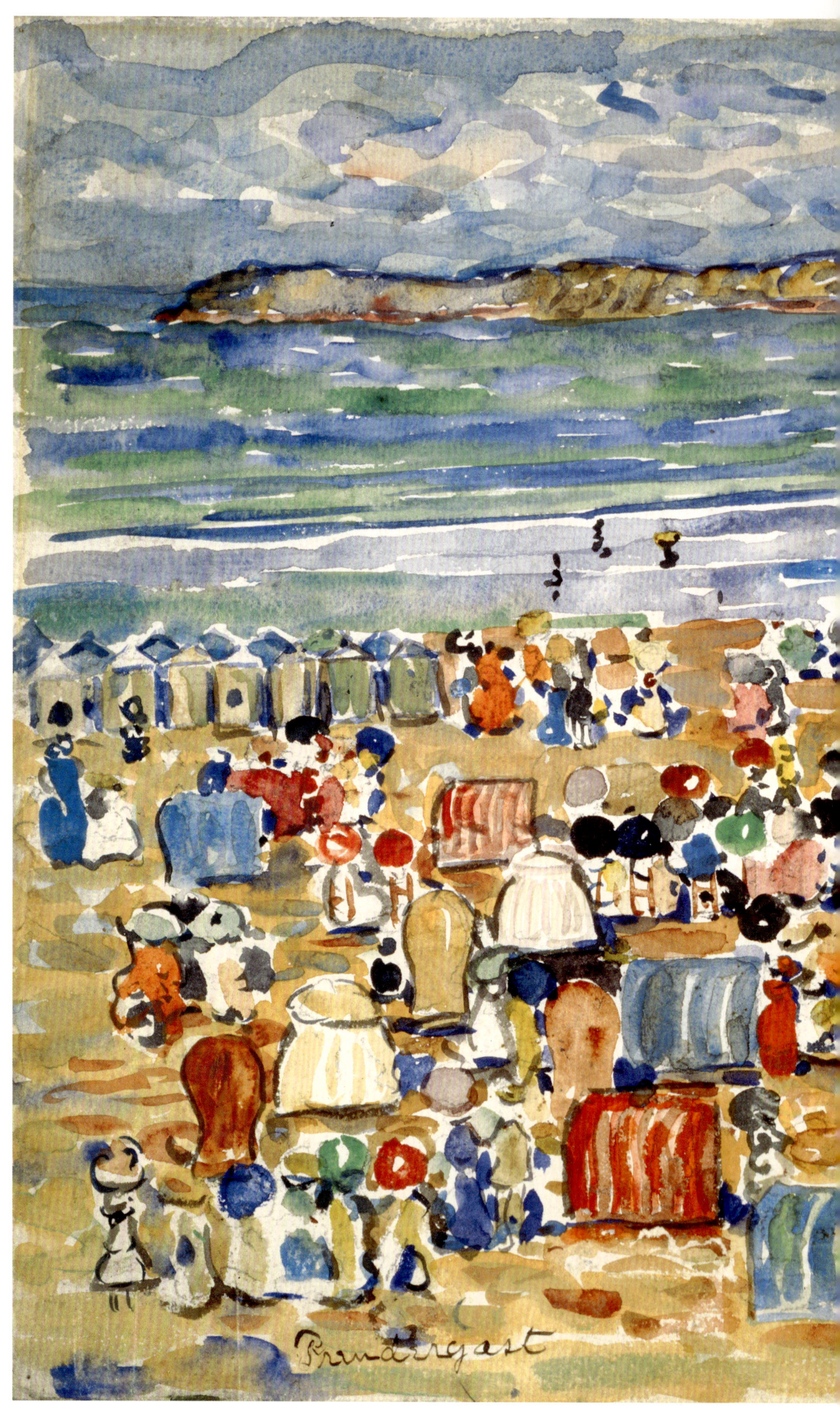

40. *On the Beach, St. Malo*, c. 1907

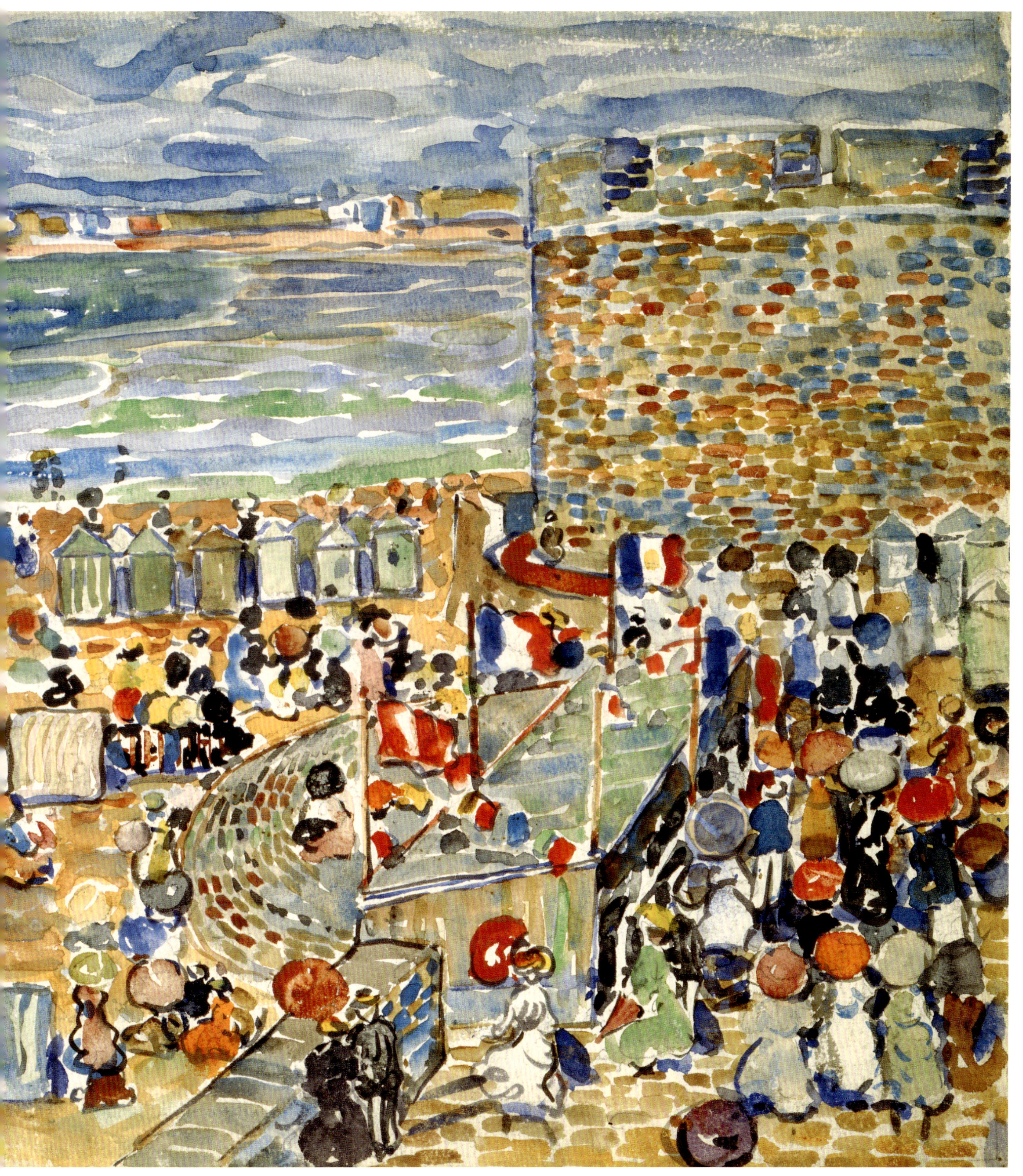

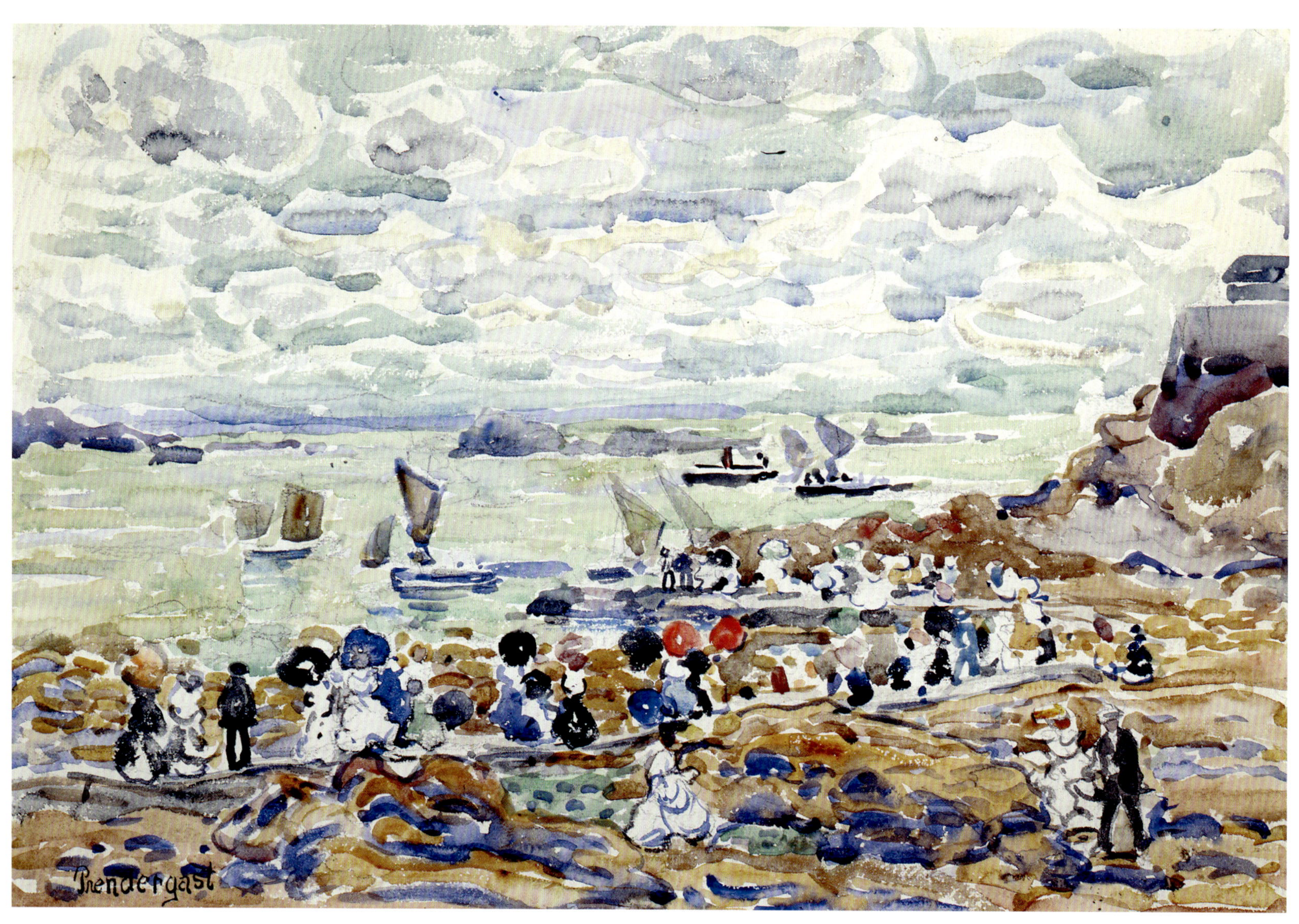

41. *St. Malo, No. 1*, c. 1907–10

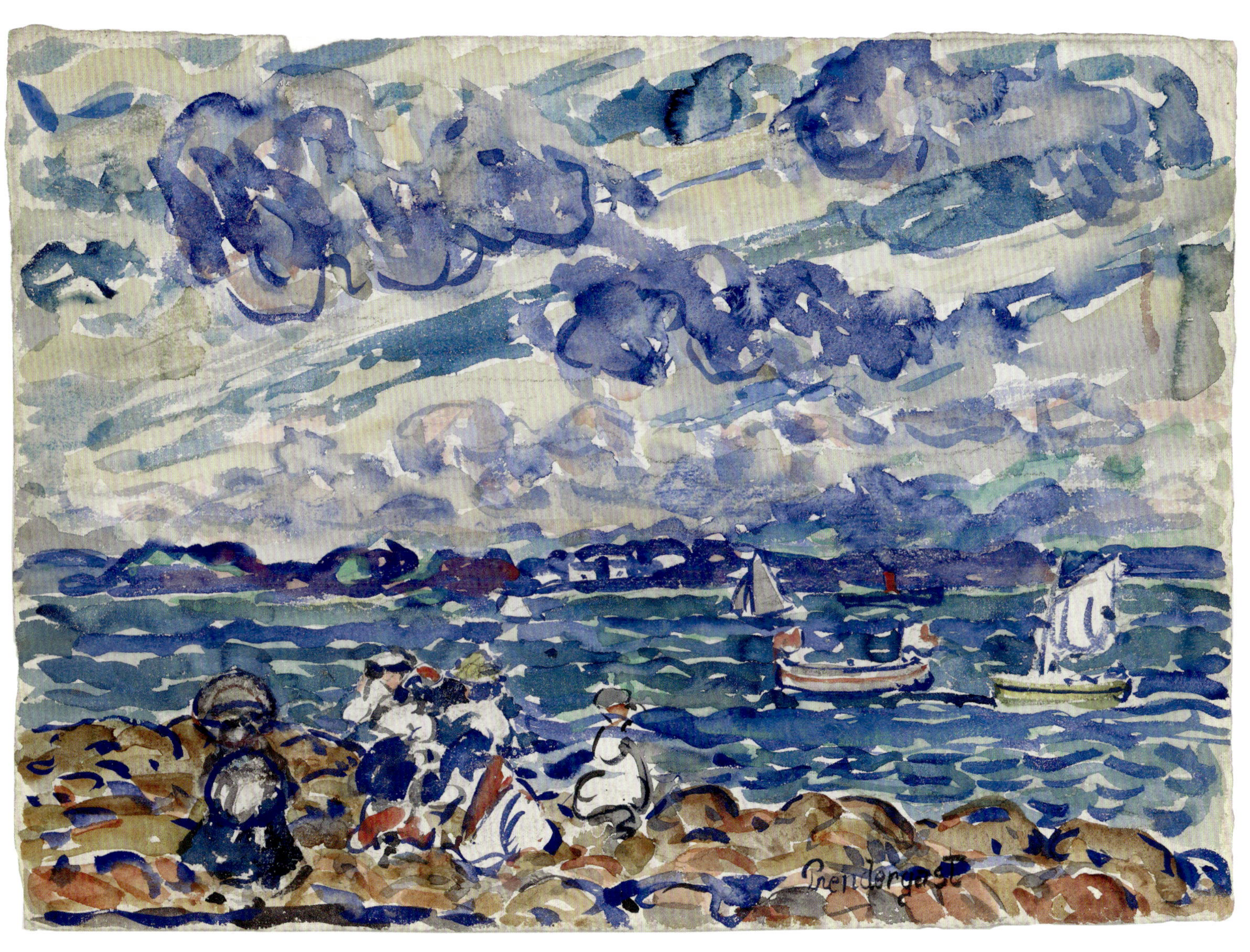

42. *St. Malo*, c. 1907

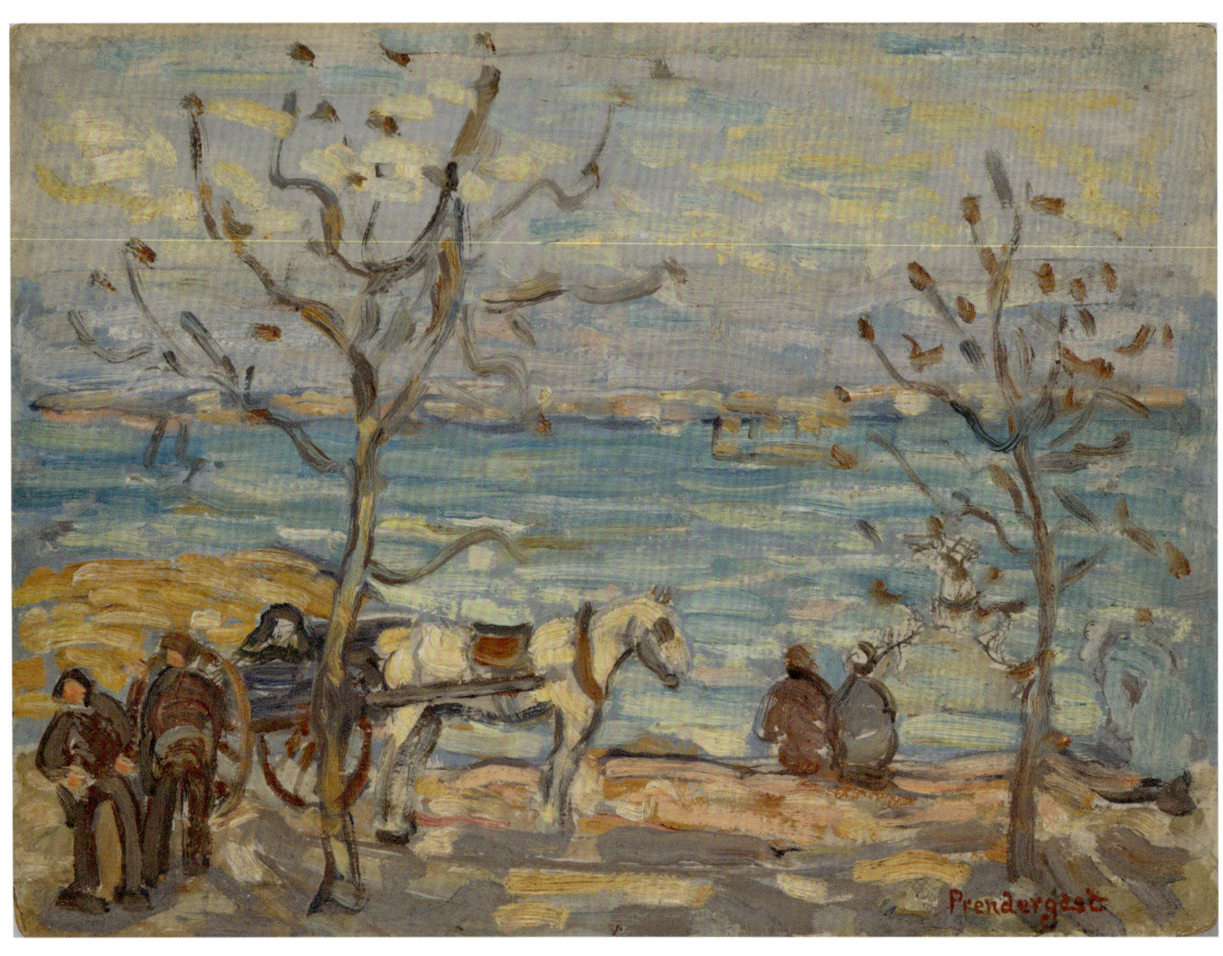

   43. *Winter Day*, c. 1908

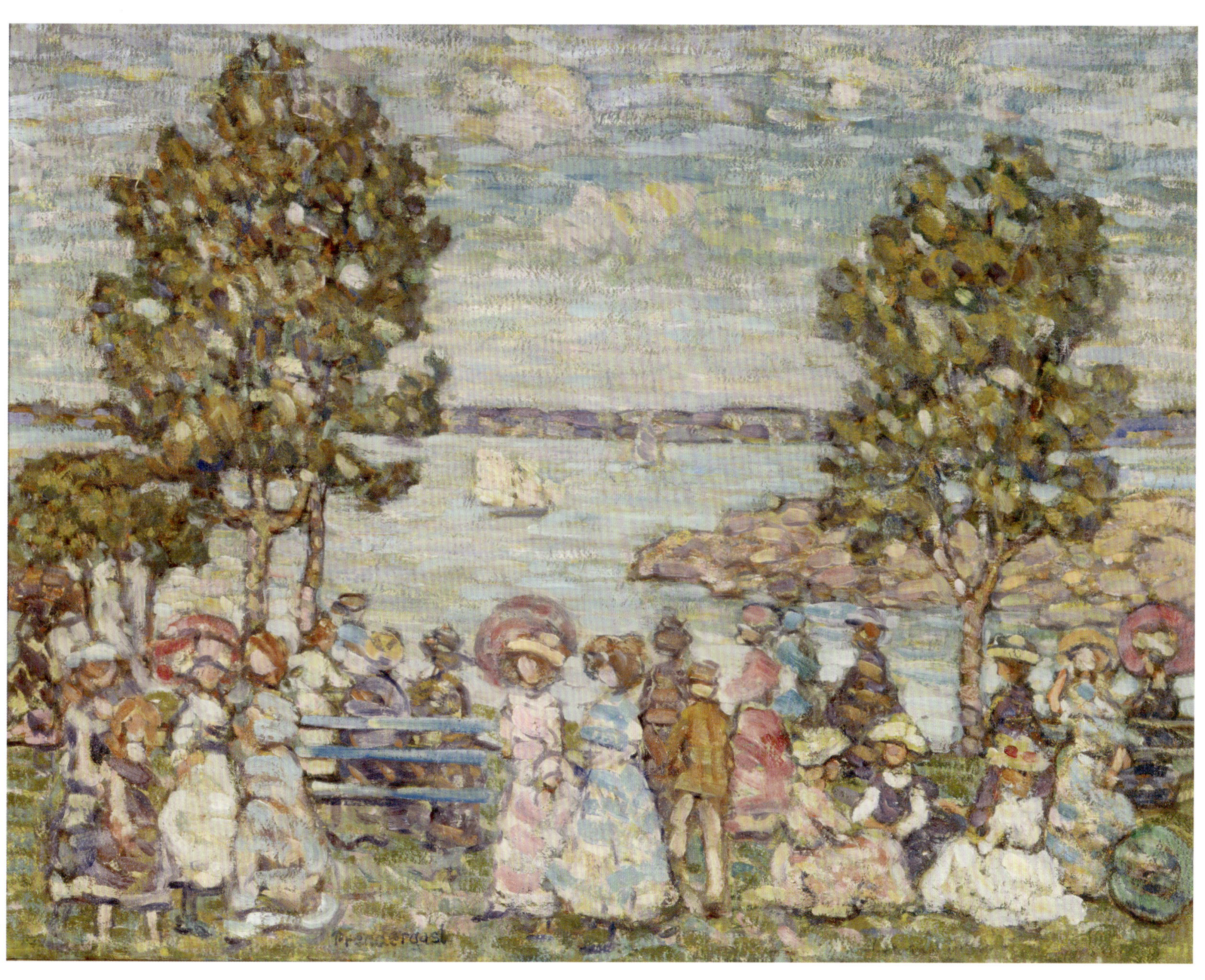

44. *The Holiday*, c. 1908–9

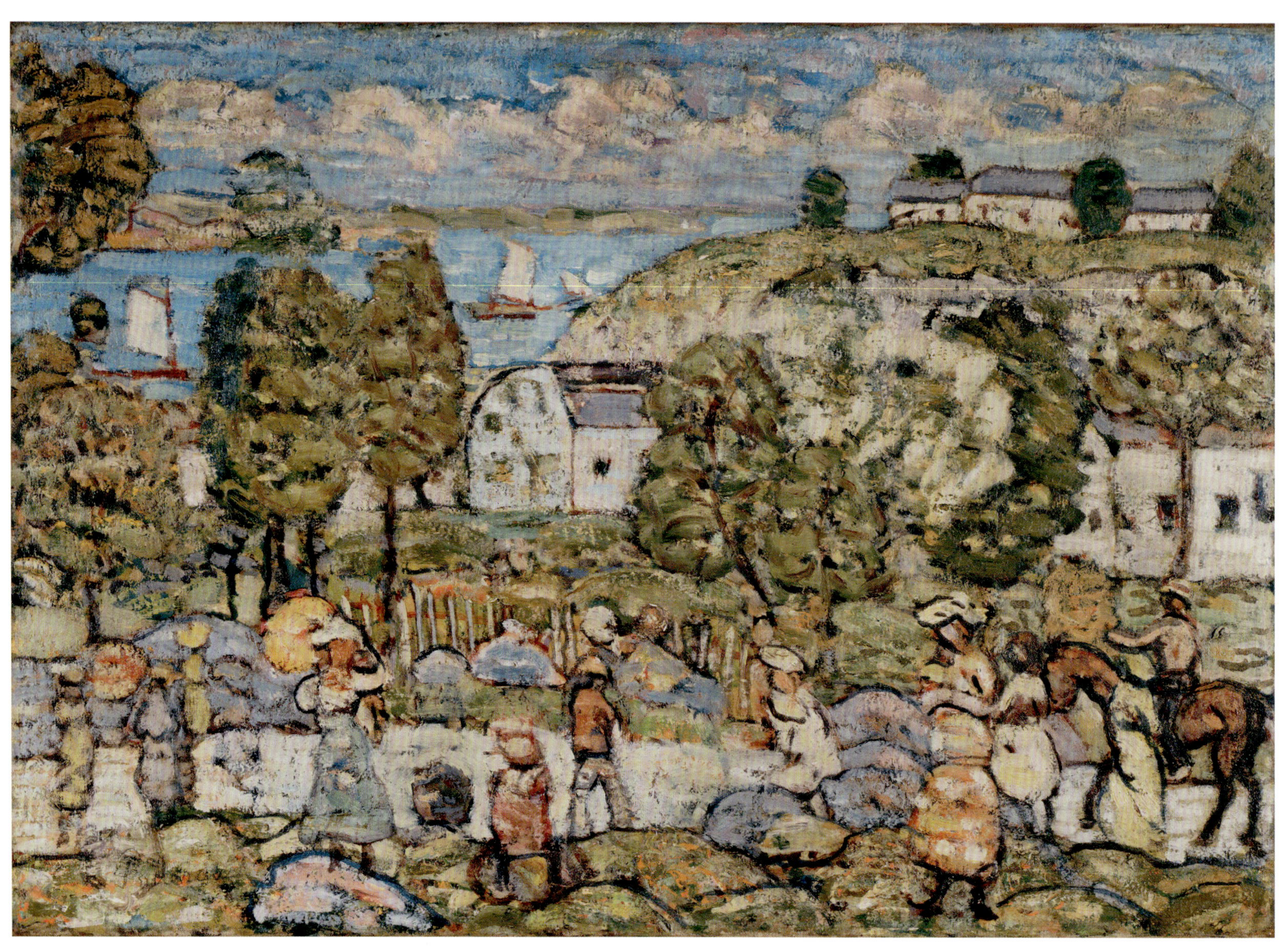

  45. *Landscape Near Nahant*, c. 1908–12

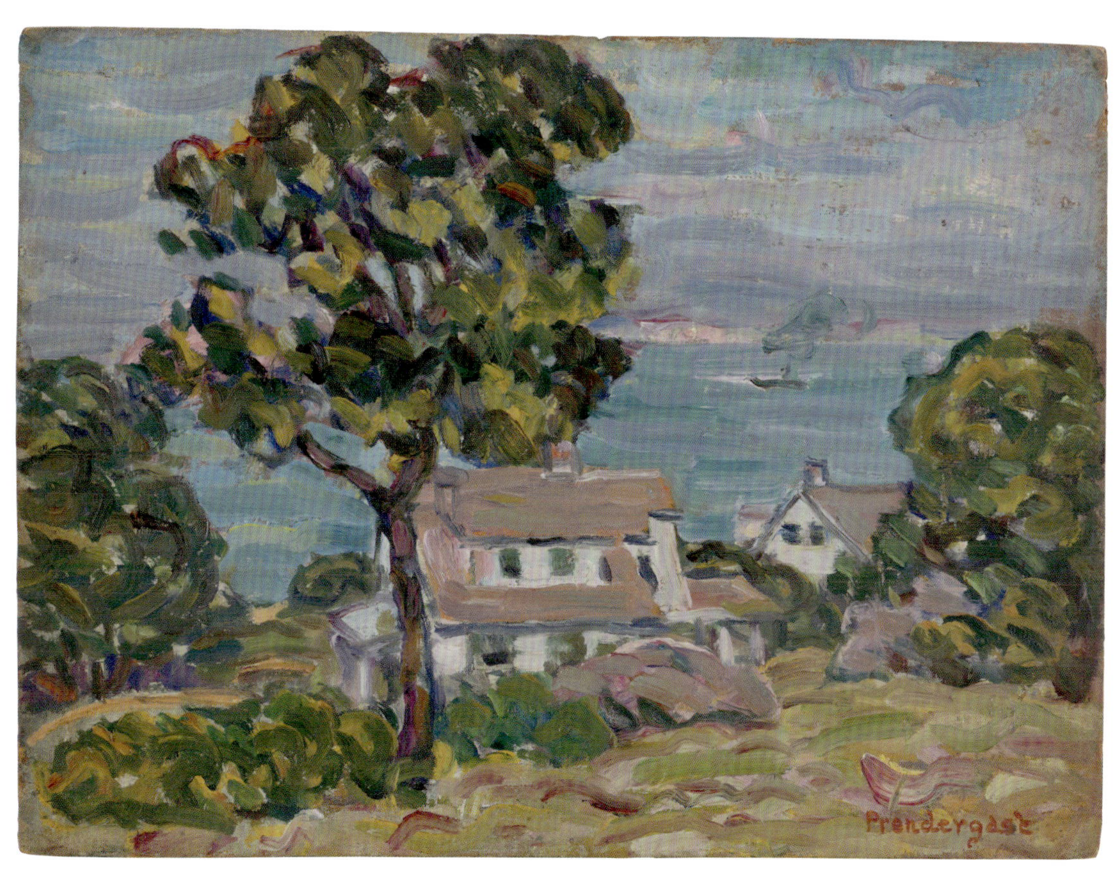

46. *Seaside, Maine*, c. 1911

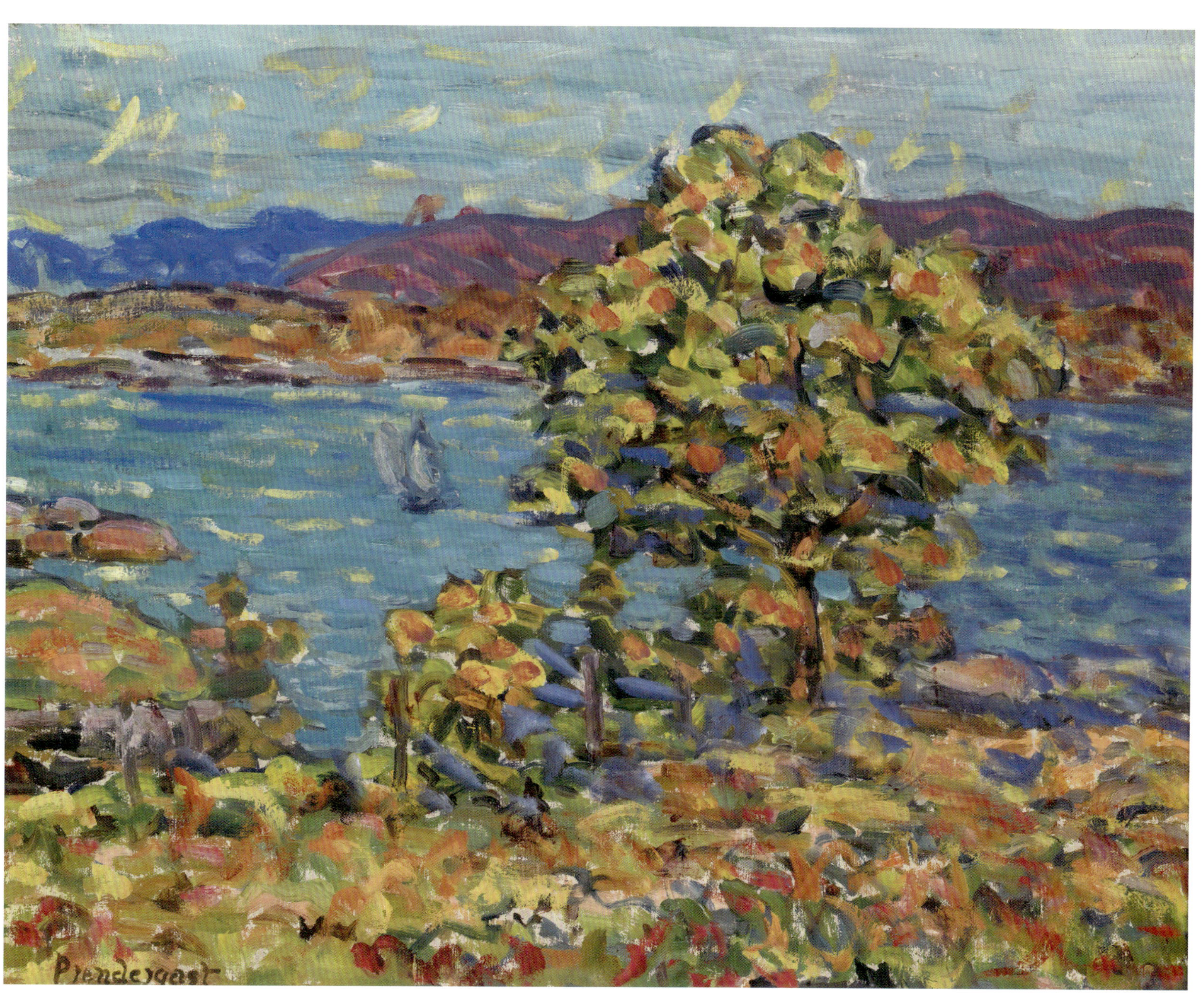

47. Lake in Maine, c. 1910–13

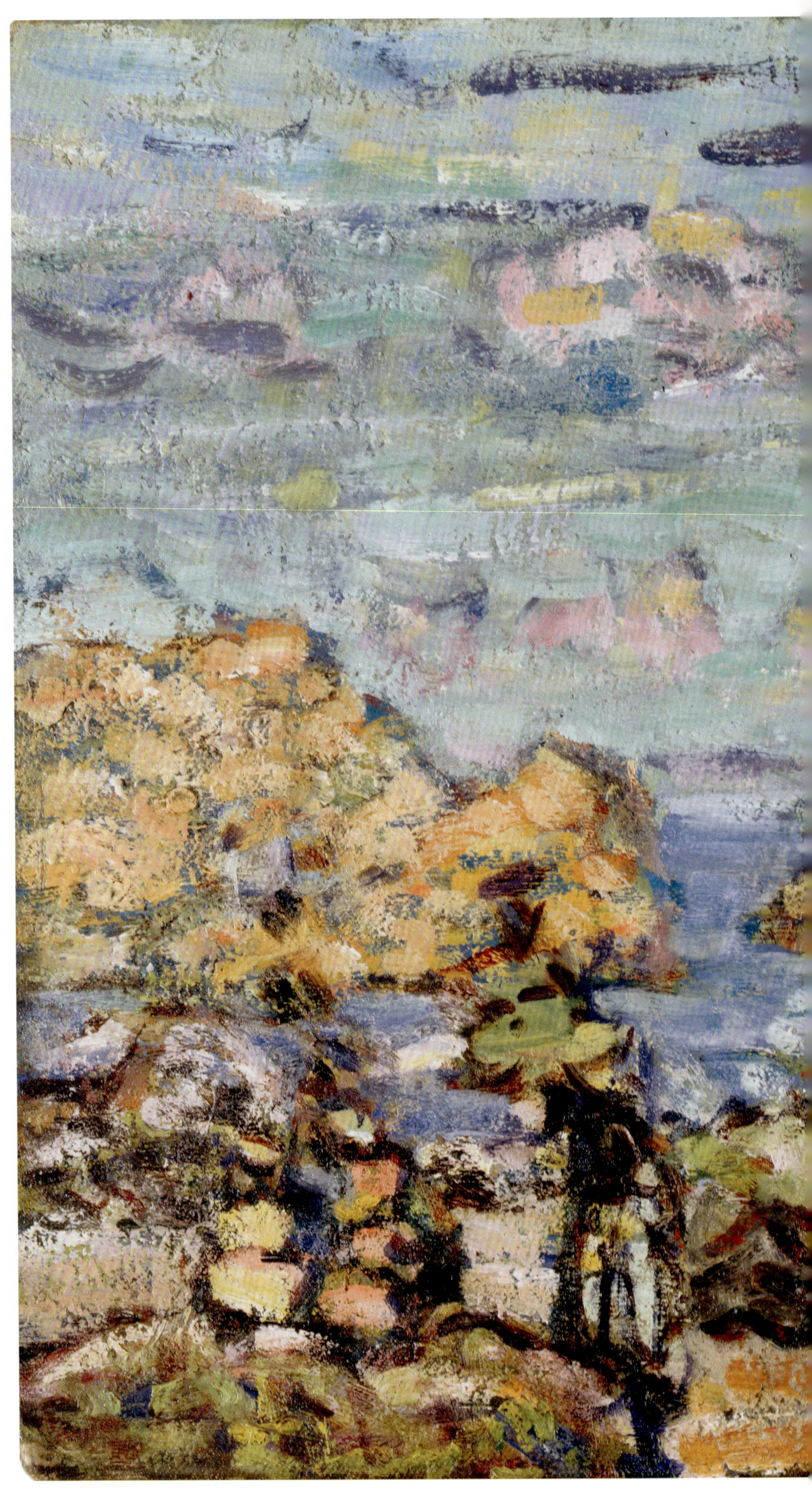

48. *Rocky Coast Scene*, 1912–13

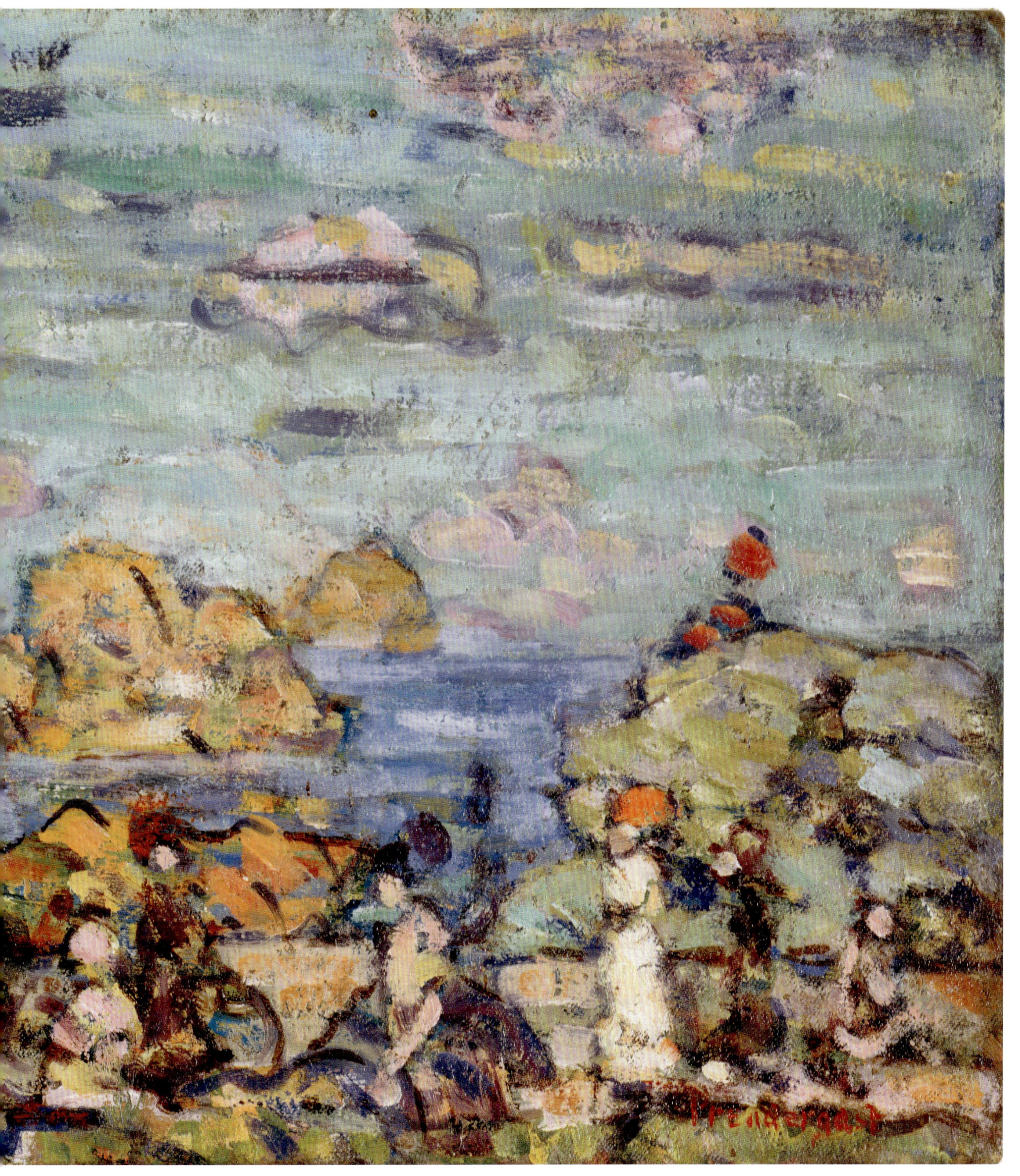

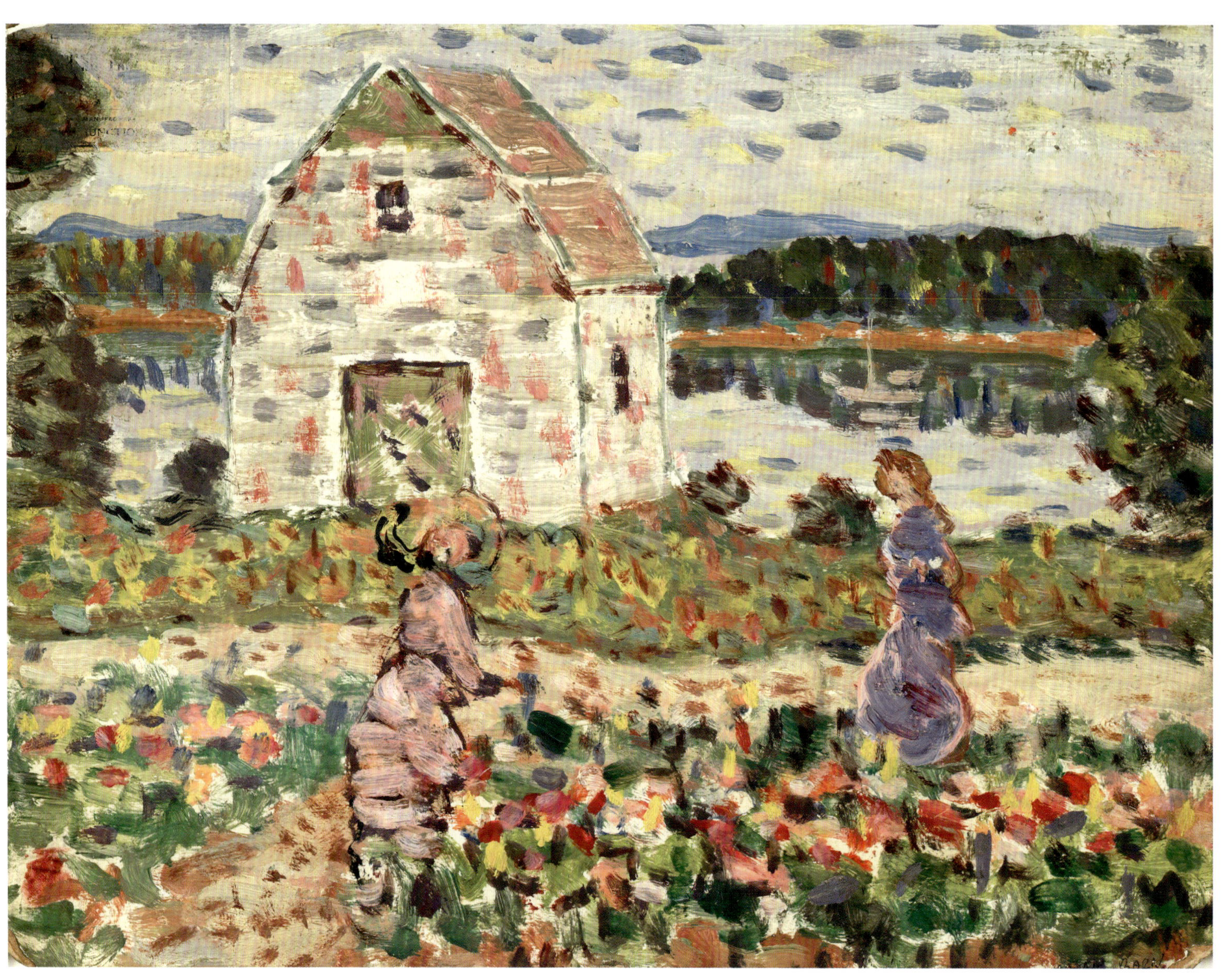

49. *Maine Barn*, c. 1910–13

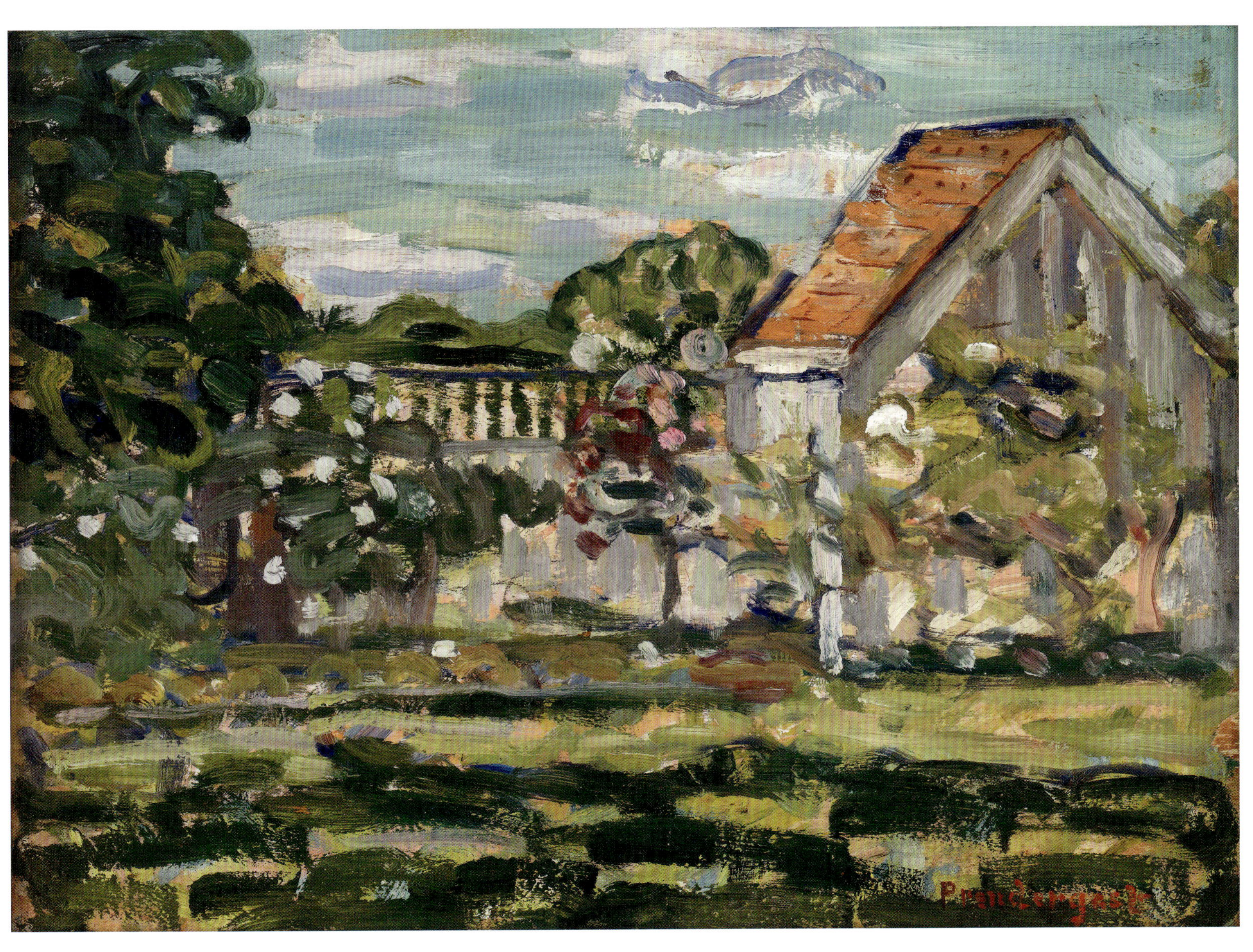

50. *Maine*, c. 1910–13

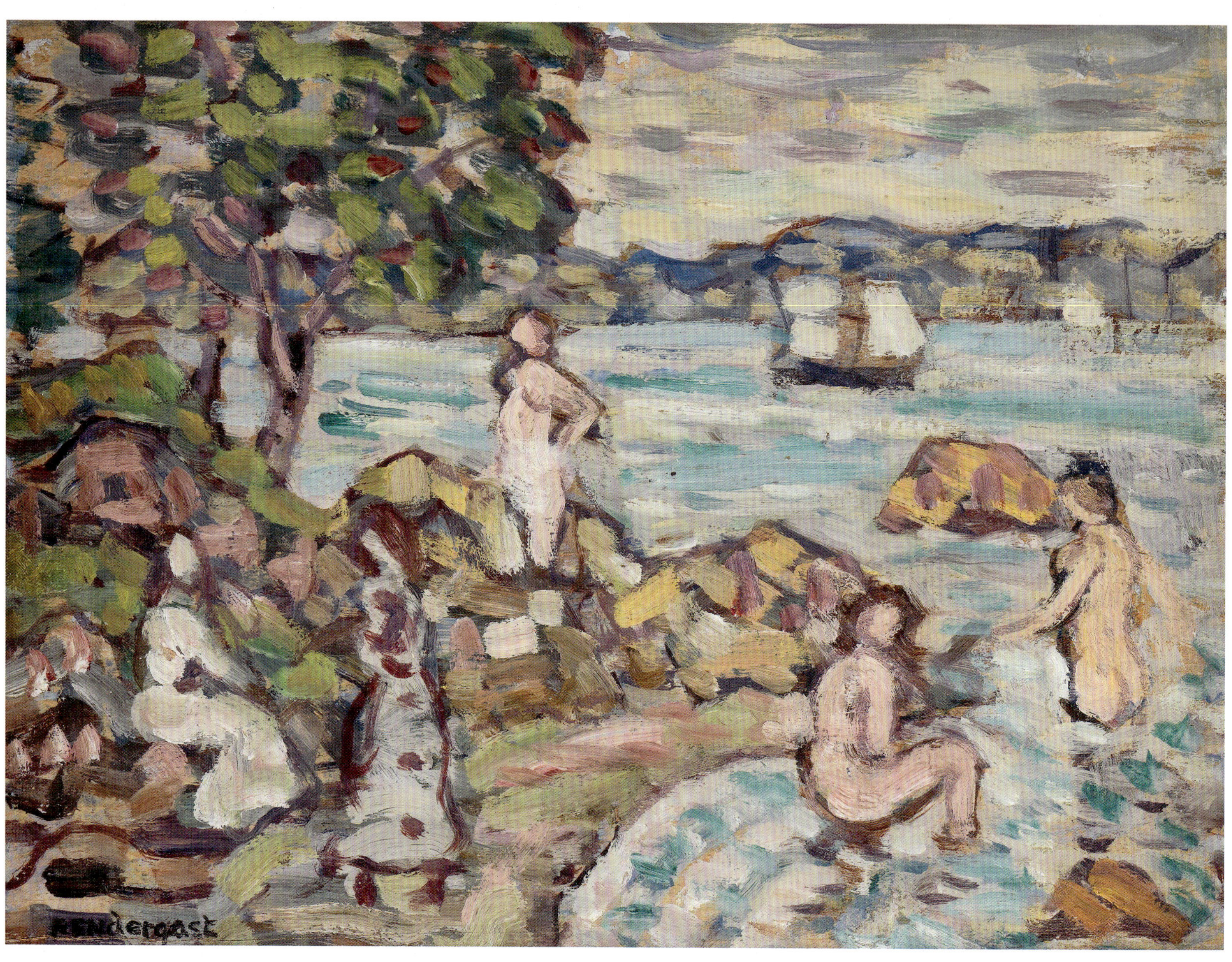

51. *Bathing*, c. 1910–13

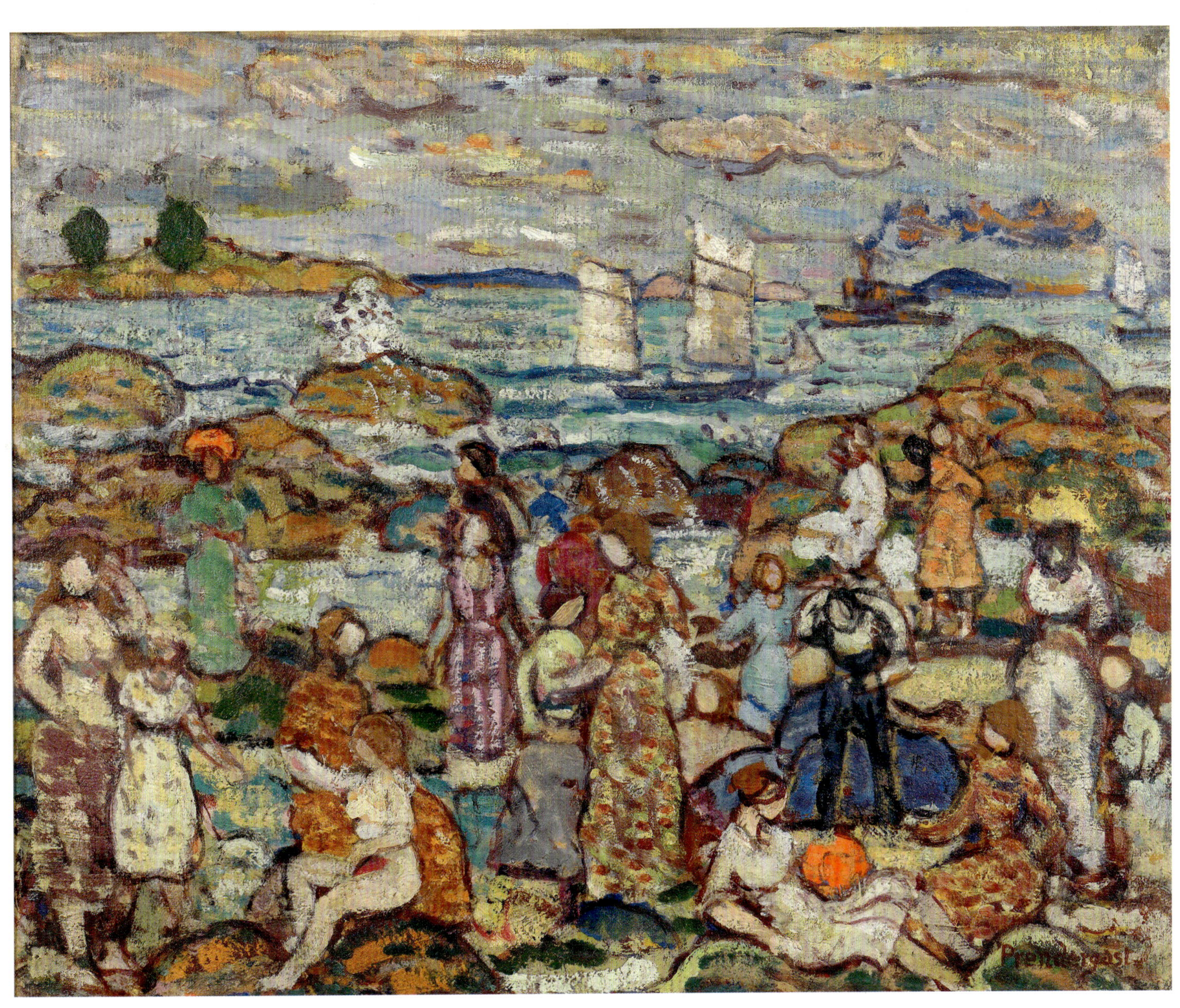

52. *Beach Scene, Maine,* c. 1910–13

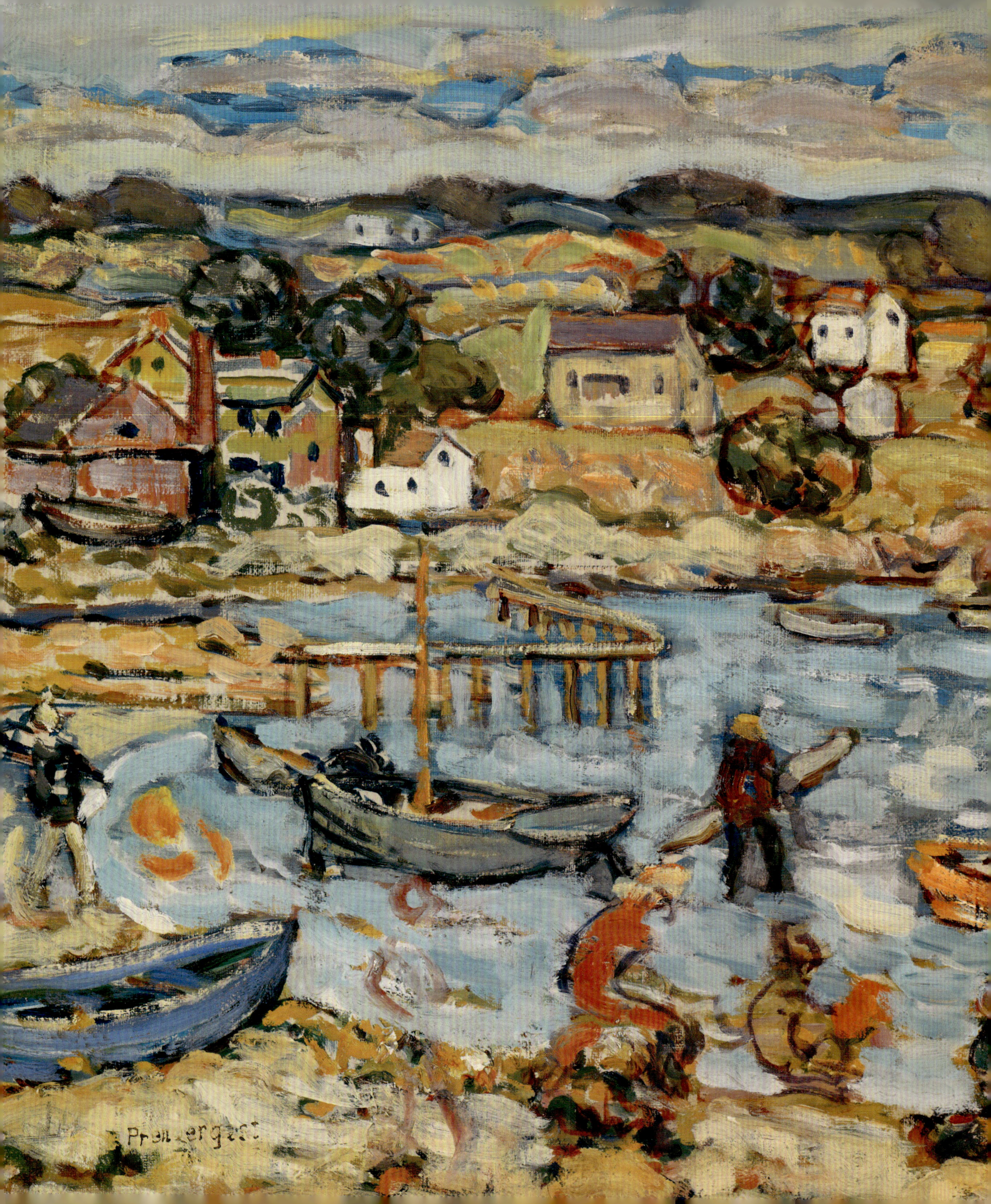

Prendergast

Maurice Prendergast:
Theme and Variations

RICHARD J. WATTENMAKER

Maurice Prendergast's progressive mastery of three disparate and challenging media—watercolor, monotype, and oils—allowed him over a career of more than three decades to shape a uniquely enchanting vision. Among his most distinctive picture motifs were the series of compositions, notably parks and beaches, drawn primarily from vantage points around the Massachusetts coastal towns of Salem, Marblehead, Cohasset, Revere Beach, Nahant, and Beachmont, where he sketched and painted all his working life. Prendergast developed a familiar repertoire of pictorial elements evoking a certain leisured innocence—adults in their holiday finery, the women often carrying parasols; children, horses, donkeys, swans, boats, surf, clouds, and sky—that epitomize his colorful sea- and park-side scenes.

At the outset of his career, in the early 1890s, Prendergast spent some three and a half years in Paris, where he intermittently took classes at various art academies and began to paint in oils. Dull grays and tans dominate in his early student works in that medium, but he soon abandoned these in favor of the brilliant luminosity that he had already explored in his French beachside watercolors and oil pochades and would later cultivate in all media after his return to Boston in the fall of 1894.[1] In sheet after sheet, his ability to imbue color and light with an airy transparency dazzles the eye, the figures glowing within the upwardly tilted perspective that was to characterize his subsequent style.

While painting abroad in Italy from 1898 to 1899, Prendergast confidently recast his New England coastal motifs. The exotic architecture of Venice—the Ponte della Paglia, the Ducal Palace, St. Mark's Square, and the Rialto Bridge—became the settings for his watercolors and monotypes, with gondolas, facades, and urban gardens replacing the sailboats, piers, and stony beaches that had preceded them. So deliberate was Prendergast in positioning his dramatis personae that, on occasion, he reused the same figure in the same attitude, incorporating it in various settings in different media. The figure of the young girl bending over in the foreground of the monotype

Detail, *Marblehead Harbor* (fig. 26)

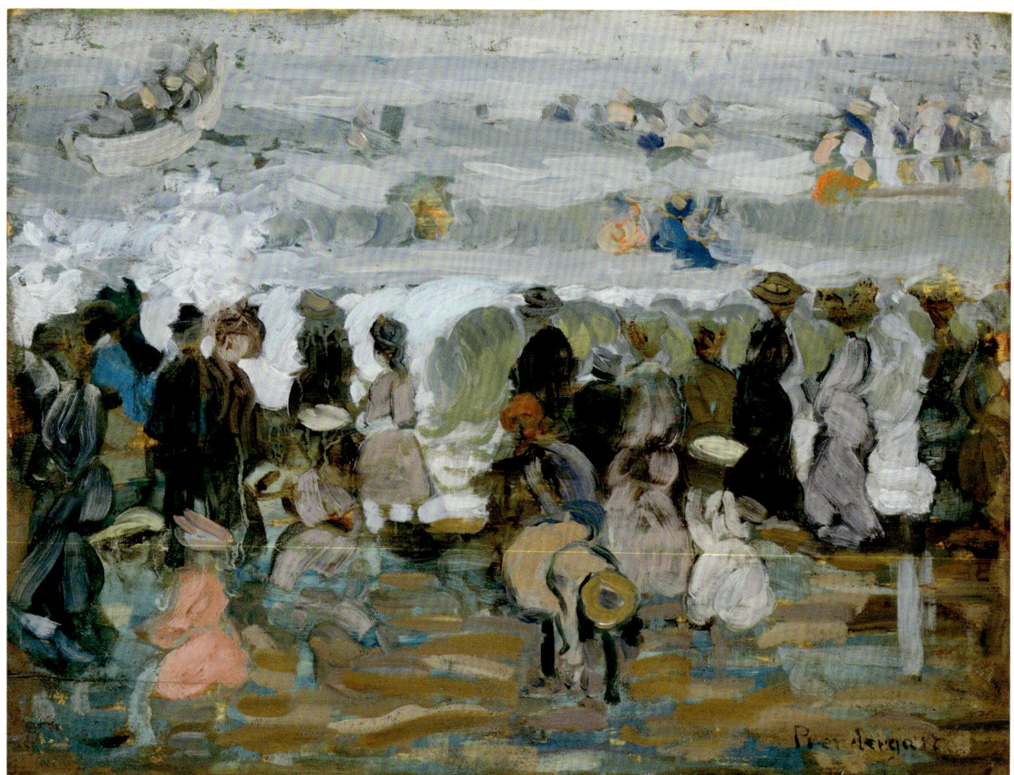

South Boston (not illustrated), for example, is repeated in an oil on panel, *After the Storm* (fig. 22), as well as *The Balloon* (plate 23).[2]

By the early twentieth century, a distinct simplification of means is evident in Prendergast's work, and after 1910 he generally gave up naming particular locales in his titles in favor of generic descriptions such as *The Beach, Beach Scene with Donkeys, In the Park, Landscape with Figures,* or *Cottages and Boats.*[3] These progressively intricate motifs were rarely landscapes per se but rather complex compositions that often relied on a horizontal placement of elements, and they were intended to be seen as picture organizations rather than mere illustrations of the New England coast. Walter Pach, one of the artist's most steadfast enthusiasts, wrote early in 1921: "Thirty years ago and more, Mr. Prendergast was treating much the same sort of theme as he depicts now. . . . Yet to-day after so many years, his painting becomes ever more vigorous . . . the tone is fuller, the design more inevitable; it is the art of a radiantly young spirit strengthened by untiring work."[4]

By this time Prendergast had already begun to exhibit his watercolors and monotypes, which he had framed by his brother, Charles, to heighten their elegance. These works, carefully selected by the artist himself, were exhibited around the country, gaining Prendergast a reputation as a serious colorist to be watched. He was eager to sell these pictures, and he priced them to be affordable. Meanwhile, back in the studio, he was working in oils, struggling to gain control of that deceptive, pasty medium.[5]

     RICHARD J. WATTENMAKER

In 1904 he was able to complete a large oil, *Salem Willows* (fig. 23), on which he
had been working for several years. The canvas essentially defines his compositional
interest in the seashore motif, which was to challenge and inspire him until his death,
in 1924.[6] Dense stands of green trees anchor the left and right sides of the canvas
with their strong silhouettes against the sea, clouds, and sky. A horizontal division
of the composition, the bottom half dark against a light top half, is reinforced by the
vertical division into thirds, with the center band of light flowing down into the white
dresses, suggesting an inverted pyramid. Here Prendergast has mastered the kind of
broad organization that he had found so inspiring in the dramatic Venetian proces-
sions of Carpaccio in the Scuolo di San Giorgio degli Schiavoni and in the large-scale
wall and ceiling decorations of Veronese and Tintoretto in the Ducal Palace and the
Scuolo di San Rocco, respectively. This Venetian influence was later recalled by the

Fig. 23. Maurice Prendergast, *Salem Willows*, 1904. Oil on canvas, 26¼ × 34¼ in. (66.7 × 87 cm). Terra Foundation for American Art, Chicago; Daniel J. Terra Collection (1999.120)

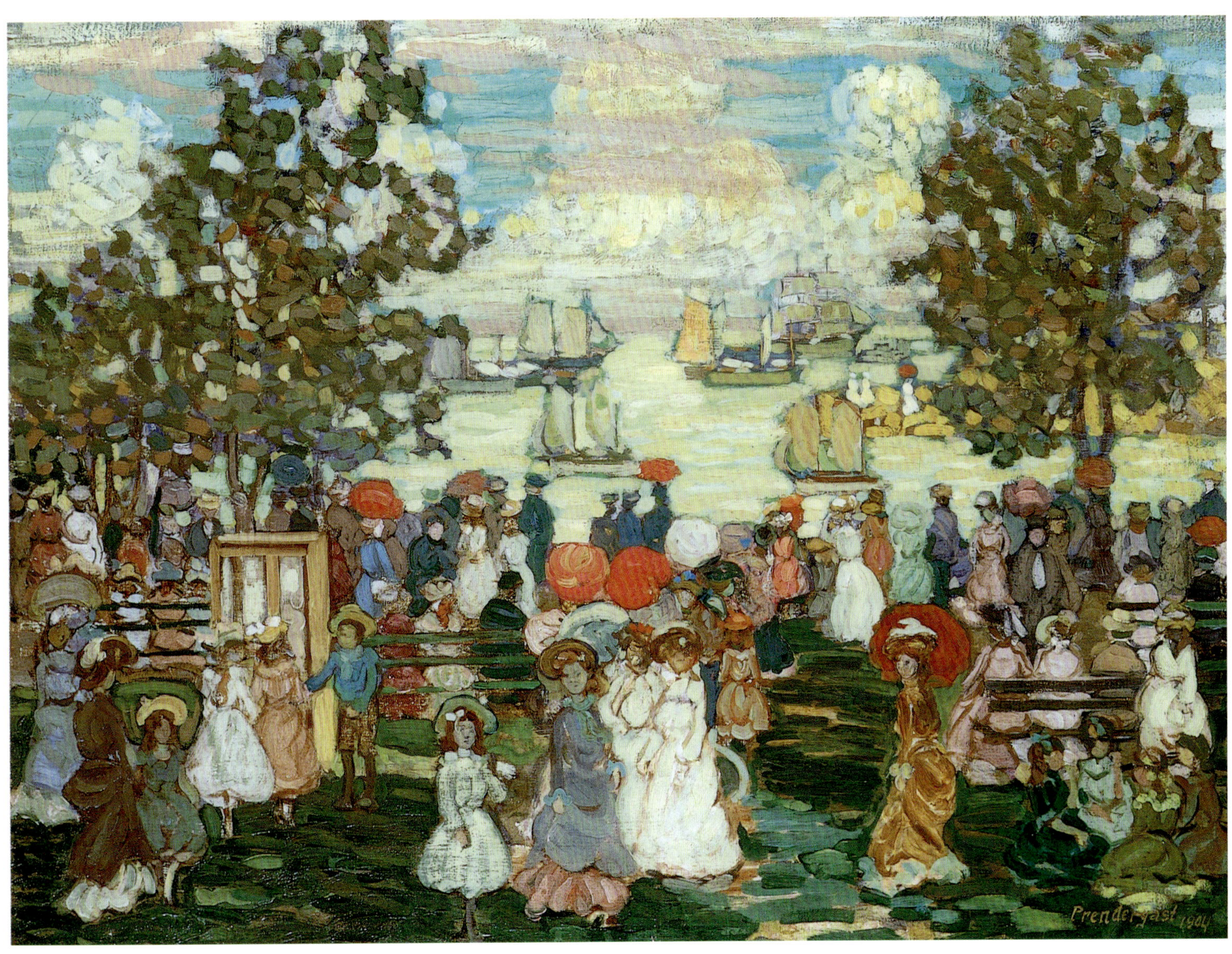

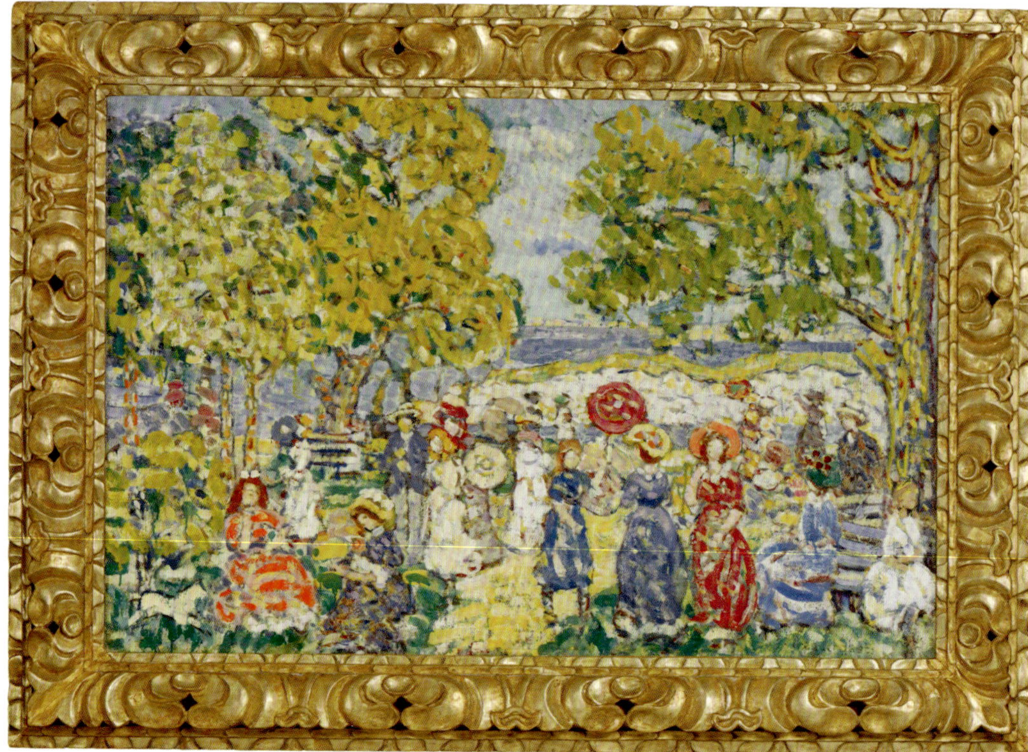

Fig. 24. Maurice Prendergast, *Landscape with Figures (The Park)*, c. 1910–13. Oil on canvas, 29⅝ × 42⅞ in. (75.3 × 108.9 cm). Frame by Charles Prendergast. Munson-Williams-Proctor Institute Museum of Art, Utica, New York; Edward W. Root Bequest (57.212)

artist's friend Charles Hovey Pepper, himself a painter, who remembered that during Prendergast's trip in 1898 he had "spent the first week studying the galleries" and "was most forcibly impressed with Tintoretto and Carpaccio."[7]

In *Salem Willows* Prendergast's brushstroke is already broken and woven into mosaic-like patterns, growing out of his study of Manet, Pissarro, and Monticelli as well as Byzantine art. He was fiercely determined to master the oil medium, to create paintings worthy of his serious intentions. This picture must have been a great effort, a touchstone, because he kept it with him for another year, until 1905, after his friend, Boston neighbor, and sometimes student, Esther Williams, expressed her desire to purchase it.[8] Prendergast was exhilarated by the sale, writing: "Getting up steam again for painting, it is a great profession . . . you are on the threshold as an artist, be firm and determined."[9]

We may gauge Prendergast's intense concentration from a notation in a sketchbook dating from the early years of the century, rebuking a would-be visitor: "I am working. My mind is virtually set to compose, to which everything else is secondary, that is, which interferes with my work."[10] Always meticulous in composing his figures and their settings, he often worked from a preliminary watercolor, as his friend Pepper noted: "He was accustomed to do water-colors [*sic*] of scenes that caught his fancy— rather complete little pictures in themselves—and then compose his larger canvases from these in the studio."[11] Transposing the lessons of the fugitive and unforgiving

   RICHARD J. WATTENMAKER

watercolor technique to the oils was a challenging task, however, and it consumed Maurice totally.

By 1907 Prendergast expressed a new vigor, and at the end of May he traveled to Paris, seeking fresh inspiration. He spent five months there, painting panels and watercolors in the Luxembourg Gardens and views along the Seine, and two months at Saint-Malo, on the Brittany coast, which offered colorful summertime beaches crowded with bathers, cabanas, and the vivid uniforms of the French soldiers. The panels Prendergast made at Saint-Malo correspond in their luminosity to the oil pochades he had painted in New England prior to 1907 (plate 29); in both, he vigorously applied patches of contrasting color, which are sometimes somber and stiff, sometimes painted with great abandon (plate 28).

In Paris, Prendergast assiduously visited all the exhibitions where modern art was on display, including a show of seventy-nine watercolors by Cézanne at Galerie Bernheim-Jeune.[12] On June 13 he wrote home to Charles, "I have seen the [Salon de] Champ de Mars. It gave me the impression I was working all right."[13] This self-confidence and sense of validation are perfectly in character. Never one to join the bandwagon, Prendergast remained clear-eyed in his own approach to contemporary painting, selectively incorporating certain plastic elements from modernism. In October he saw the Salon d'Automne retrospective exhibition of Cézanne, which comprised fifty-six works, including some watercolors.[14] In a long letter to Esther Williams, dated October 10, he related his experiences:

> I have been extremely fortunate in regard to the exhibitions, not only in the
> Spring with the Salons, but Chardins, Fragonards etc. and the delightful
> fall exhibitions which last during the month of October. They [all have] Paul
> Cézannes. . . . Cézanne gets the most wonderful color, a dusty kind of a
> grey and he had a water color [sic] exhibition late in the Spring which was
> to me perfectly marvelous. He left everything to the imagination. They were
> great for their simplicity and suggestive qualities. I have not done anything
> important, that is, anything large—mostly all sketches. But I got what I
> came over for, a new impulse. . . . I think Cézanne will influence me more
> than the others. I think so now. Cézanne died about six months ago and
> they had some photographs taken of some decorations on his studio walls
> somewhere in the country and they were done under Chinese influence.
> One can easily detect it and it came to me quite as a surprise.[15]

Prendergast's response to seeing Cézanne's watercolors was from the standpoint of a skilled master watercolorist with a formed vision, not that of a student. Cézanne's oils, however, specifically his use of color, forever marked Prendergast's work in that medium, as he described in a 1922 letter to Walter Pach: "[Cézanne's] work strengthened and fortified me to pursue my own course."[16] Accordingly, he began to focus on the built-up, sensuous multicolor and textural effects that were to dominate the majestic canvases created during the next sixteen years of his life. As he had done when he transformed his style after returning from Italy, Prendergast sought to construct a new style, working and reworking his surfaces to attain that singular, layered web of jewel-like color, light, and atmospheric space that his art at its most mature achieves.

Prendergast launched his series of post-1907 experiments with a number of large-scale canvases for which *Salem Willows* served as the compositional template. In each of them, color, paint application, and texture are considerably varied. These marked adjustments reveal his close study not only of Cézanne's multifigured compositions, still lifes, and landscapes but also of those by Watteau and other eighteenth-century French painters as well as contemporaries such as Paul Signac, Henri-Edmond Cross, and Maurice Denis (fig. 25). All of the latter had been influenced in some measure by Pierre Puvis de Chavannes, whose muted mural decorations in the Boston Public Library had been well known to Prendergast for more than a decade. These collective influences account for his frequent recourse to horizontal formats, which he had never used before in his paintings. Prendergast's works from this time also show a heightened sophistication, as he investigated tertiary color schemes and compositional motifs akin to musical harmonies and cadences.

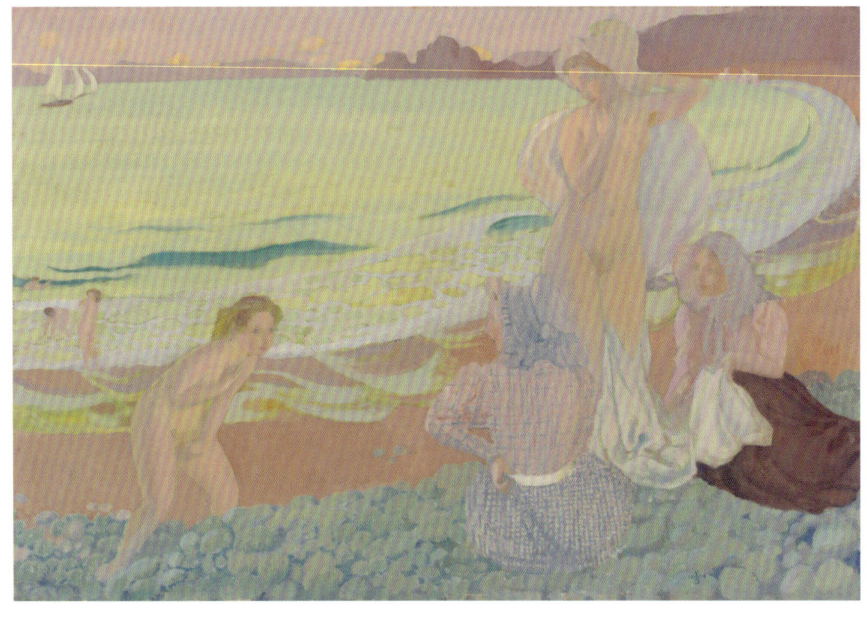

Fig. 25. Maurice Denis, *On the Beach of Trestrignel*, 1898. Oil on board, 27⅝ × 39⅜ in. (70.2 × 100 cm). The Museum of Modern Art, New York; Grace Rainey Rogers Fund (1.1964)

The most lucid and perceptive analysis of Cézanne's evident importance for Prendergast's change in style remains that of Albert C. Barnes and Violette de Mazia:

Maurice Prendergast used many elements of Cézanne's form, but modified and adapted them in a manner so individual to himself and merged them so subtly with other traditional features. . . . His drawing and modeling by small superposed dabs of color are in principle similar to Cézanne's, but show wider variation in color, shape, size, and decorative value of the individual strokes; these are much less definitely shaped, more like irregular dabs or blobs of color than Cézanne's. . . . The technique has on the whole more freedom, liveliness and decorative value than Cézanne's. The successive strokes of color that make up the pattern of overlapping patches coalesce into a series of receding planes, which build up volumes and

     RICHARD J. WATTENMAKER

define spatial intervals as they do in Cézanne. . . . Prendergast also uses
freely a broad contour-line of color. His line in general is less rigid, more
varied in color, shape and size. Because of its. . . tendency to a curvilinear
arabesque it functions more definitely as a part of the all-over scintillating
pattern of color and light than as an agent in spacing and the construction
of solid masses. . . . Prendergast's space compositions render a friezelike
or panoramic sequence of rhythms, sometimes involving the gentle movement of solid color-volumes in deep space, at other times a compact series
of glowing color-units that rival the finest of old mosaics in their texture and
patterned surface.[17]

The Holiday (plate 44), from about 1908–9, provides a marked example of
Prendergast's stylistic shift. Although the *Salem Willows* framework is still firmly in
place, albeit significantly modified, here there is a striking transition from spontaneous,
Manet-esque brushwork to a deliberate layering of color strokes of varying size, shape,
and thickness, a directionality that lends a sumptuous impasto to the paint surfaces.
The paint application creates a dense overlapping of muted pastel-colored strokes that
complement the horizontal blue patterns of the bench in the left foreground, imparting
an overall pale tonality. The narrow horizontal band of shoreline, executed in a similar
manner, knits together the two flanking trees, providing the spatial definition that
separates sea from sky. Prendergast's rich, vibrating color chords across the surface
produce a subtle, coherent, and appealing amalgam of diversified color, line, light,
and texture that exemplifies what many critics, in his lifetime and later, have called a
tapestry or embroidery effect in his oils.

That Prendergast was very conscious of this deliberate process of change is
certain. When Albert Barnes wrote to him on September 18, 1912, expressing a
desire to acquire representative examples of his work and referring to the unsold 1907
Saint-Malo panels, which the collector had seen at the Macbeth Gallery, the artist was
decisive in his response: "I have changed my style completely since you saw those
small panels in Macbeth's. When he was here 'Macbeth' . . . selected a canvass [*sic*]
to show in his galleries which I like very much[;] it would please me when you are in
N.Y. to [go] up there and see it and get [William] Glackens to go with you (for I have a
wholesome respect for him in all matters on art) . . . it is a 'coast scene.'"[18]

Prendergast, who had always been interested in how the Old Masters solved the
problems he was confronting as a painter, returned to Italy in August 1911. The primary
reason for the trip was to make another watercolor campaign on the quays and canals
of Venice, but he also went to renew his acquaintance with Carpaccio, the churches,
and the Accademia. After joining Charles in Capri, he stopped in Naples, Rome,
and Florence before settling down in Venice. Soon thereafter he fell ill, however, and

was obliged to undergo a prostate operation in early November. He convalesced for several months, during which time he did little work, instead enjoying the quiet of the off-season as well as reading, looking at pictures, and buying frames, some of which the brothers modified and adapted for Maurice's pictures. Throughout 1912 Maurice helped Charles with frame commissions, completed some of the watercolors begun in Venice, and experimented with still lifes, flower pieces, and a few portraits. In the latter part of the year he was involved in preparations for the Armory Show, and the following summer he underwent a second operation, which the Italian doctors had already counseled in 1911. The next spring, in 1914, Maurice made his last trip to France, visiting the exhibitions in Paris and making sketches of the Old Masters in the Louvre, among them Watteau and Poussin. He also saw the Camondo bequest—the group of important Impressionist and Post-Impressionist works donated to the Louvre in 1911 by Isaac de Camondo—including five paintings by Cézanne. He then traveled to Brittany, ending an extended period of repose and reflection. Reinvigorated, on November 1, 1914, the brothers moved permanently to New York, where they had a wide circle of friends who genuinely valued their work.

Along the Shore (plate 63), a painting made about this time, reveals a further diversification of Prendergast's seaside themes. The conspicuously elongated figure in white acts as a firm central focal point, a distinct amplification of the two figures in white in the center foreground of *Salem Willows*. The contrast of the subdued, principally tertiary pastel colors in the other figures subtly plays off the saturated hues of the parasols. This procession of figures is interwoven with three donkeys and riders, and the whole broad ensemble is fixed in a colorful frieze by the varied strokes that make up the sea. An element of surprise is introduced by the Cézannesque note, reminiscent of a Japanese screen, in the leafy branch at upper right, which echoes the gently undulating shapes of the distant shoreline and hills.

The final stage of Prendergast's investigation of color is represented by canvases such as *The Idlers* (plate 64), *New England Harbor* (plate 74), *Marblehead Harbor* (fig. 26), and *Acadia* (plate 73).[19] In *The Idlers*, four elongated and two kneeling figures are constructed by luscious bursting strokes and dabs of juicy pigment, the colors applied so that they fuse with the rhythmic flow of line and pattern and reverberate throughout the surface. The broad discontinuous lines of the figures, especially the kneeling girls in the foreground, are indebted to Prendergast's study of Matisse.[20] A reviewer justly noted the artist's debt to Renoir as well, whose work he was known to admire and which he had studied not only on his 1914 trip to Paris but also in the home of Dr. Barnes, where the Prendergast brothers were frequently welcomed in these years: "Mr. Prendergast's remarkably handsome and personal patchwork of greens and blues and pinks and yellows is spread over a foundation design so sturdy in its unpretentious vigor as to make us very comfortable about the strength of his composition."[21]

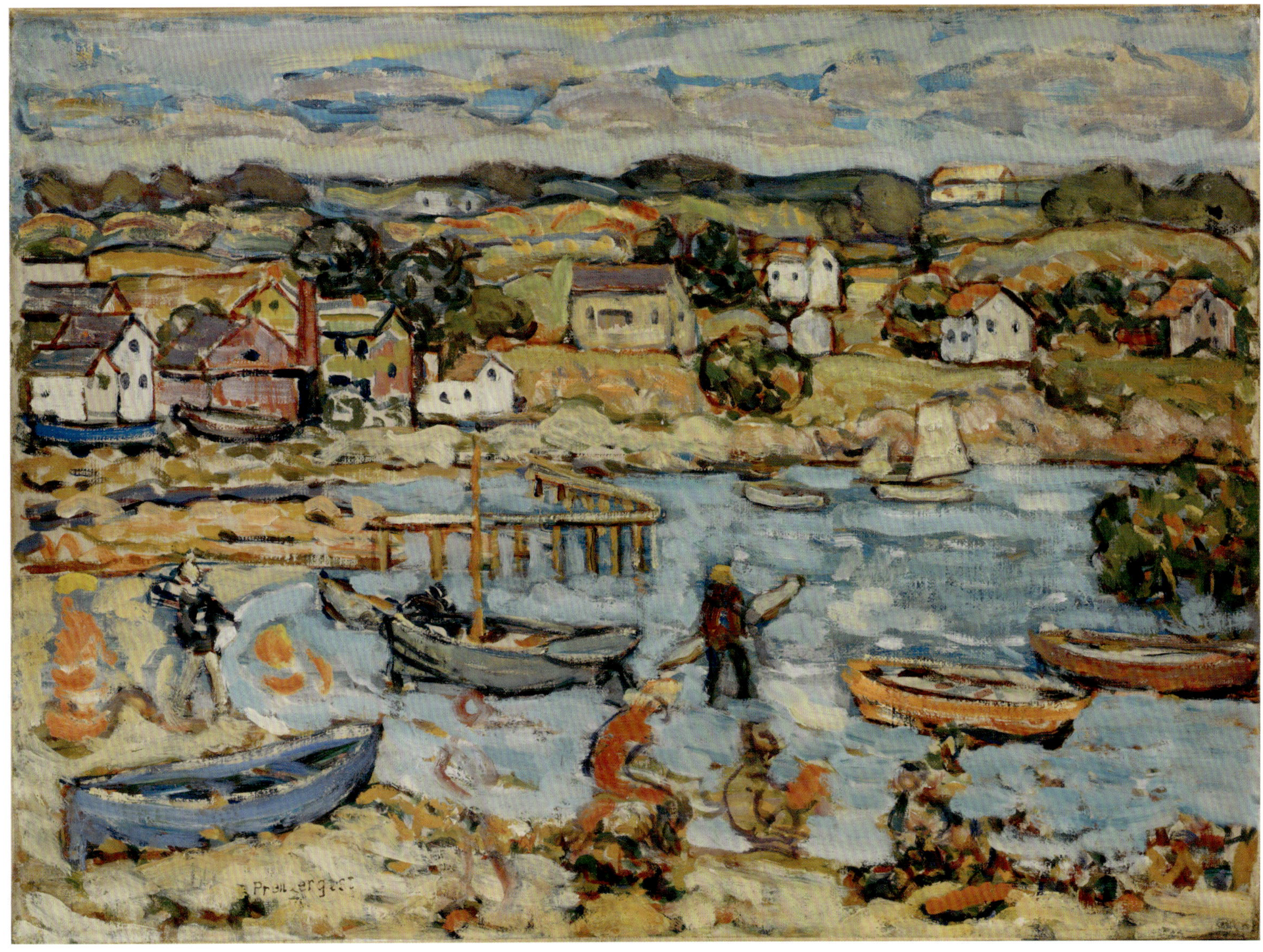

In *Acadia*, which is signed but possibly not completely finished, Prendergast bisected the composition by means of a lavender-purple tree trunk. The surrounding figures and overhanging branches are not as circumscribed as in earlier compositions; colors overflow their linear boundaries to create an opulence that is freer, richer, and more abstract than in Bonnard's canvases, which also owe a substantial debt to Renoir's post-1910 glowing color harmonies. *New England Harbor* integrates figures, landscape, and architecture in a series of stepping-stones that lead the eye into space. The composition plays the geometry of walls, roofs, chimneys, and sails against the sinuous outlines of figures, horse, and donkey in the foreground, setting these against the houses and the peninsular outcroppings in the middle ground and the sky and hills beyond. In color, this composition partly springs from the artist's contemporary pastels over watercolor and pencil (for example, plate 69). In *Marblehead Harbor*,

Fig. 26. Maurice Prendergast, *Marblehead Harbor*, c. 1918–20. Oil on canvas, 18 × 24⅛ in. (45.7 × 61.3 cm). The Barnes Foundation, Philadelphia (BF216)

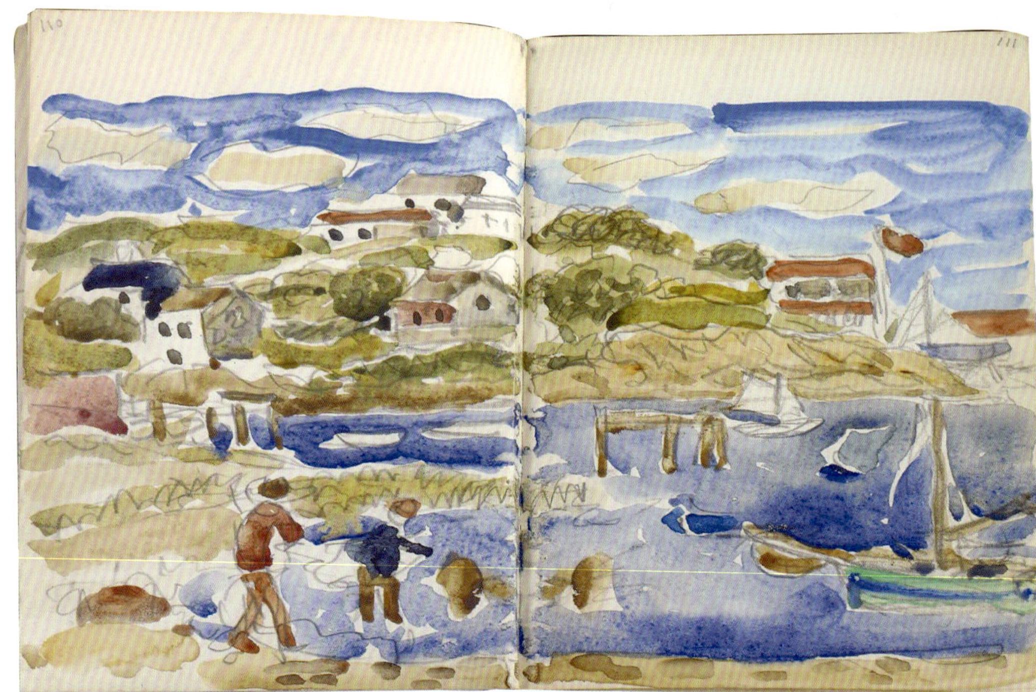

Fig. 27. Maurice Prendergast, *Sketchbook*, c. 1918–20 (cat. 79). Watercolor, pencil, and crayon on paper, 7⅞ × 5⅛ in. (20 × 13 cm). Private collection, Princeton, New Jersey; courtesy Betty Krulik Fine Arts, Ltd., New York

in contrast, such relationships—in this instance among the boats, houses, clouds, and sky—are disposed more asymmetrically. The rapid back-and-forth rhythm of small architectural units across the far shore is set into play against the angled rowboats afloat or moored on the near shore, elements that derive from the numerous, often annotated drawings and small watercolors in Prendergast's sketchbooks (fig. 27, plate 56).[22]

Ultimately, Maurice Prendergast was able to distill the dainty, exquisite color touches of his watercolors—painted on the coast of New England, along the canals of Venice and in the parks of Boston and New York—into complex symphonies of sparkling color mixtures in unorthodox juxtapositions. These large oils pull the eye across their surfaces with correspondingly intricate compositions that build upon and extend the work of the masters who were his inspiration. One of the greatest innovators of American art, he fully merits the high regard in which he was held by his contemporaries, fellow painters, critics, and collectors alike. Critic and friend Forbes Watson summed up this esteem in the artist's obituary: "The position which Maurice Prendergast occupied in American art was unique. . . . The artists . . . who gathered to pay a final tribute to Prendergast, included a distinguished group of the leaders of American art, men who knew well what the passing really meant. For Prendergast was a man who cannot be replaced."[23]

RICHARD J. WATTENMAKER

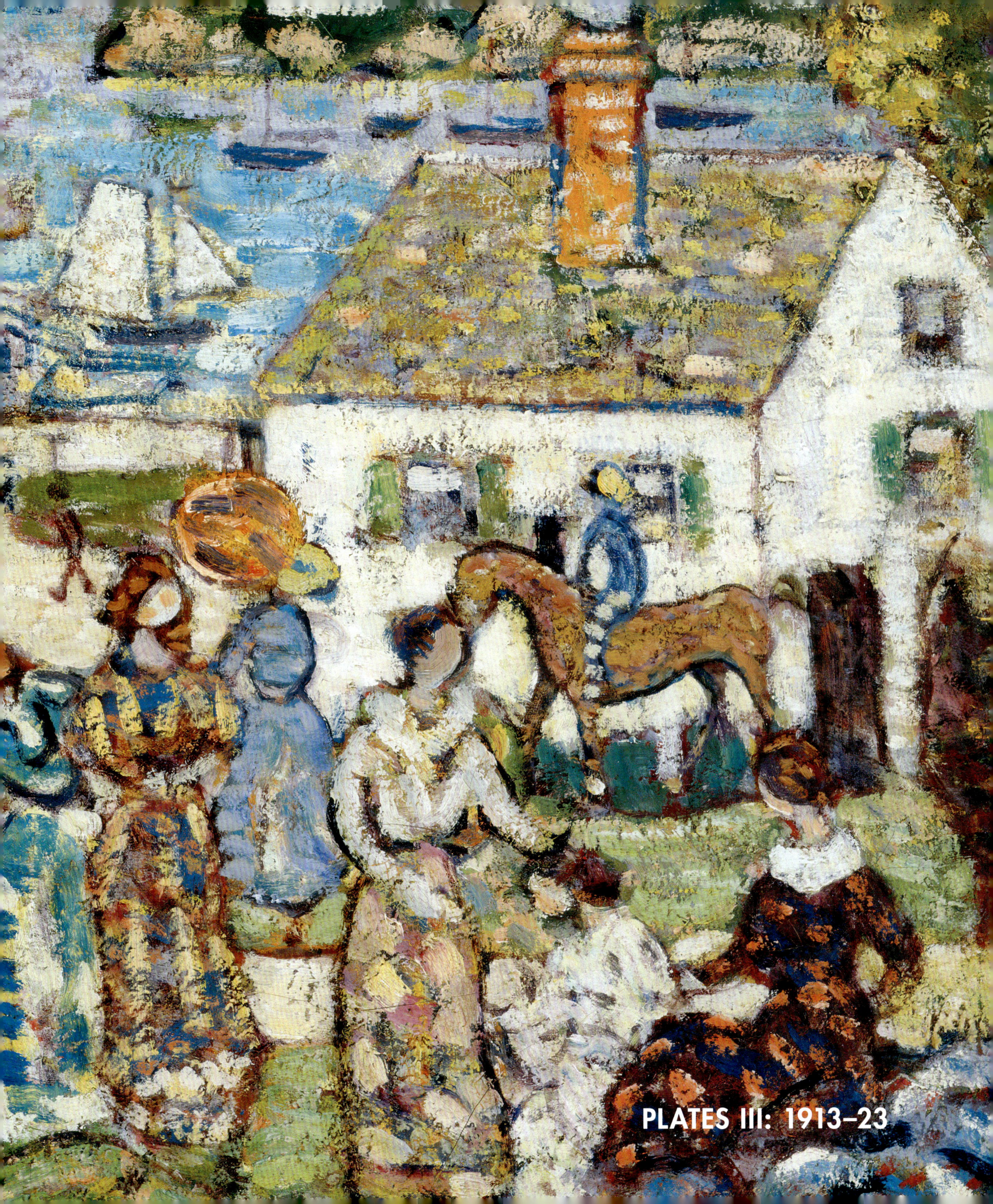
PLATES III: 1913–23

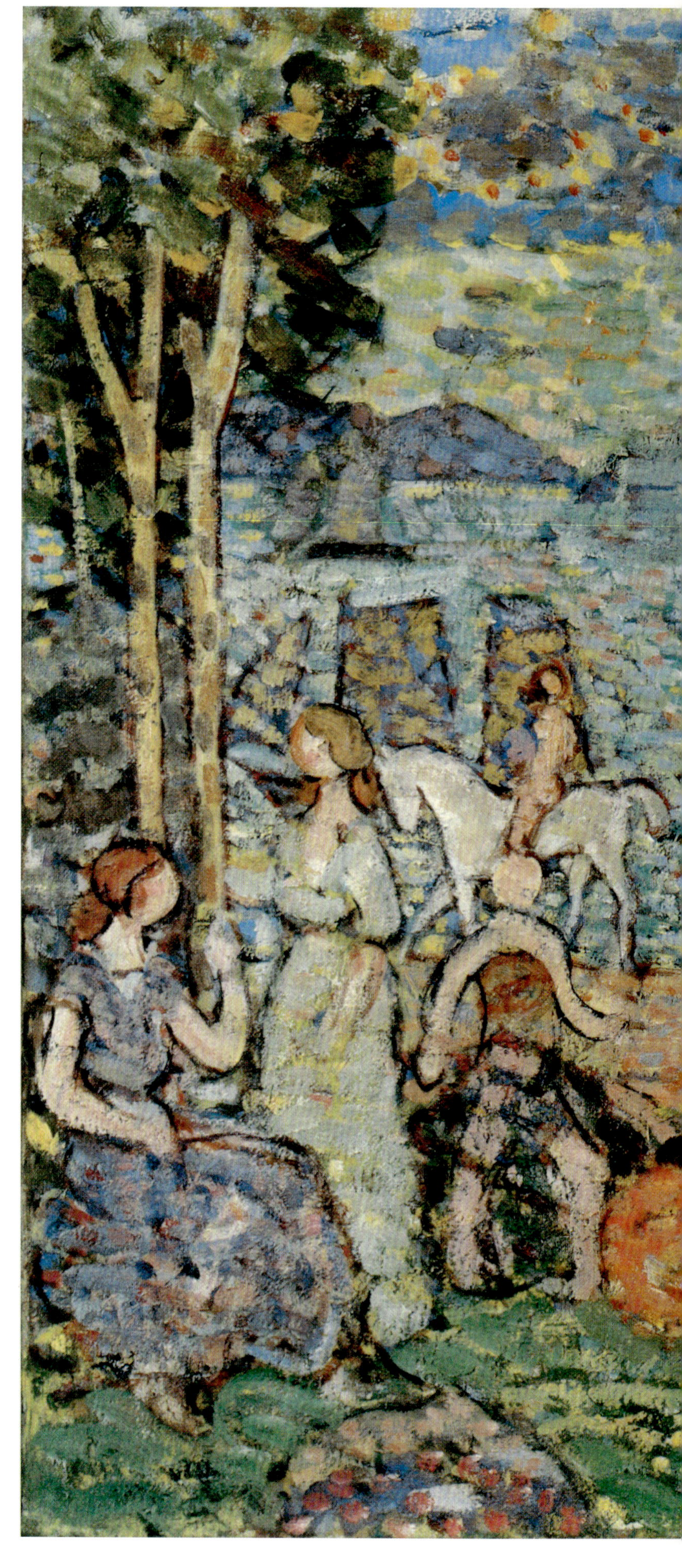

53. *The Promenade*, 1913

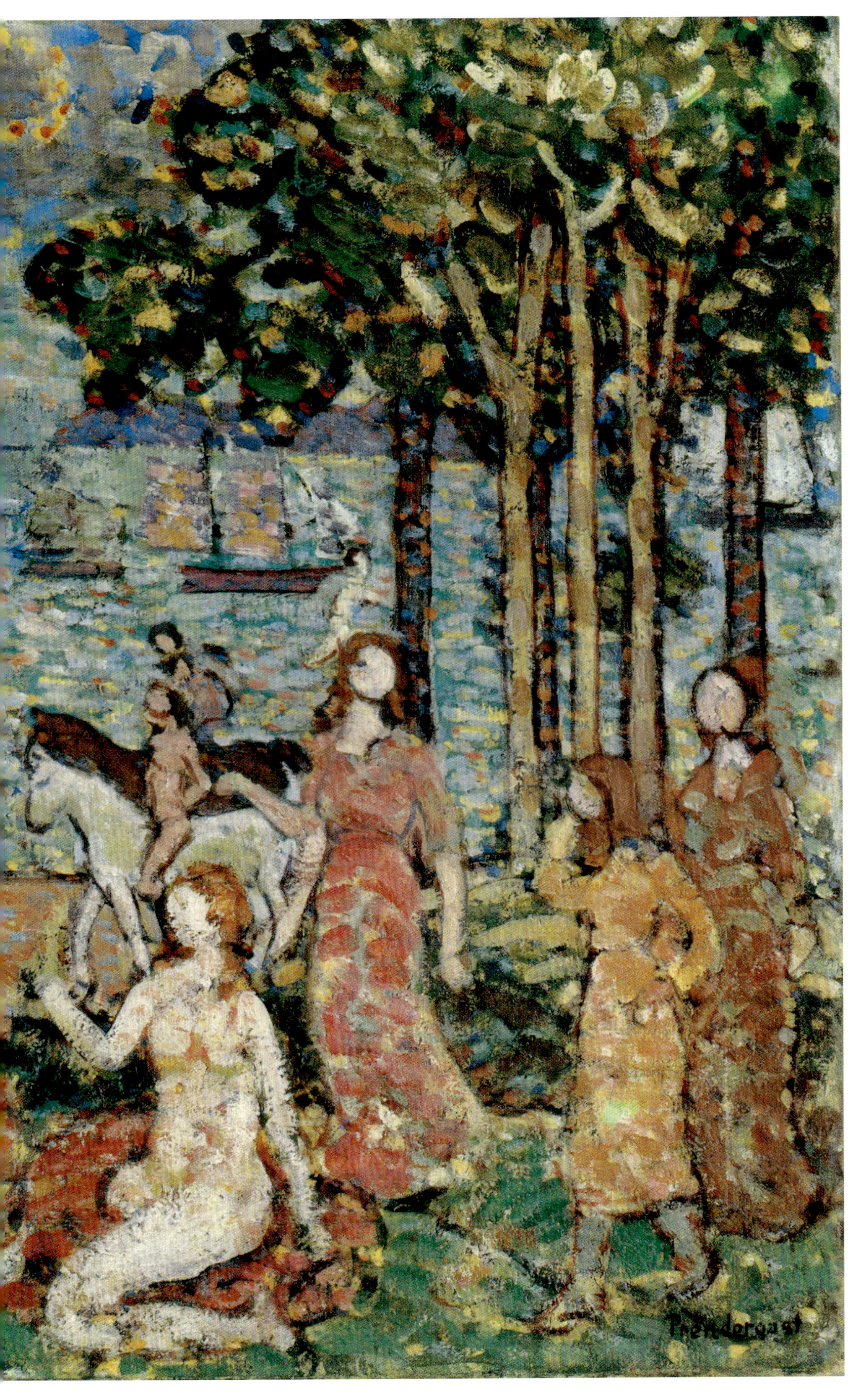

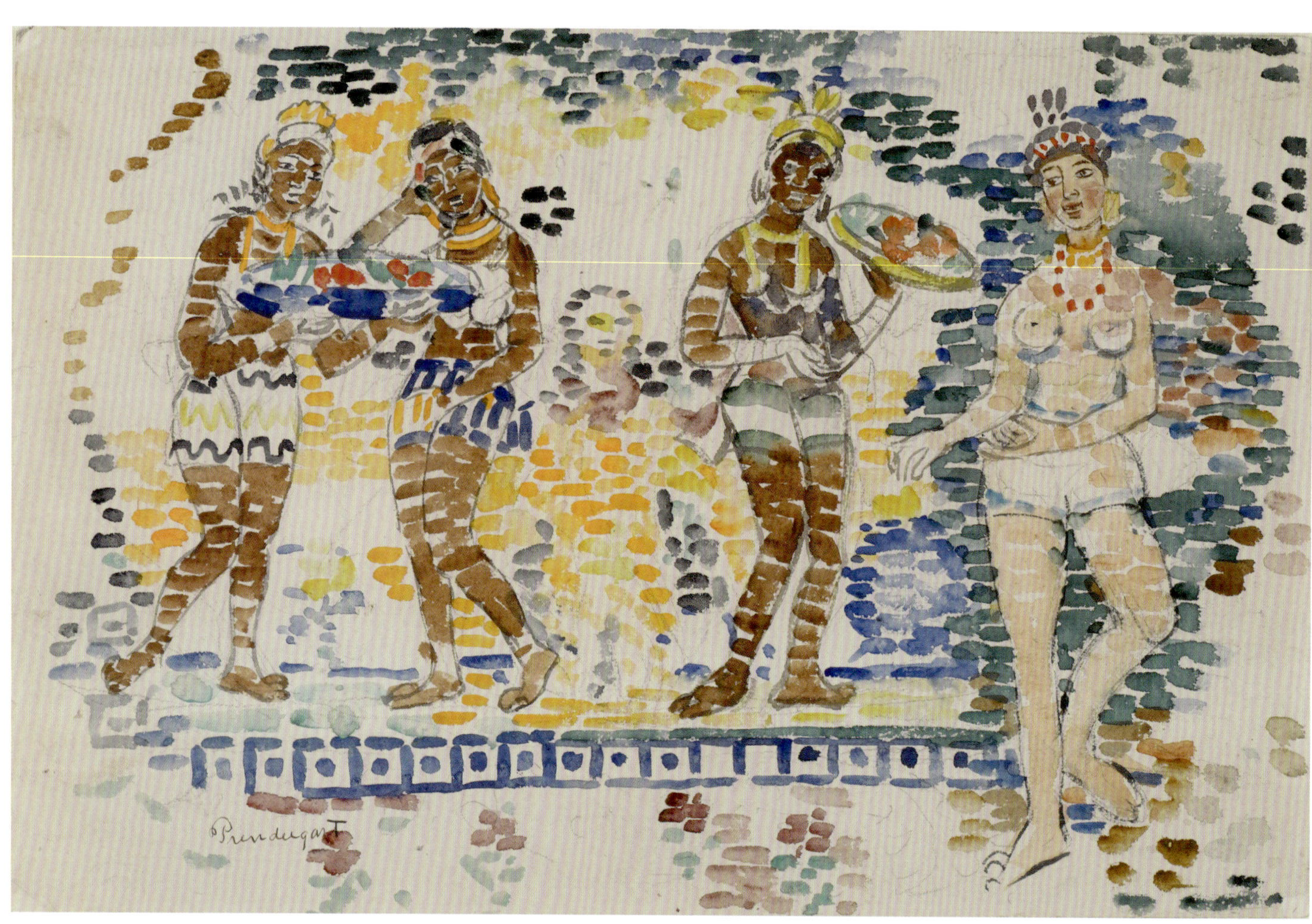

54. *Five Figures*, c. 1910–13 (verso: *Beach Scene with Boats*, c. 1896–97, plate 14)

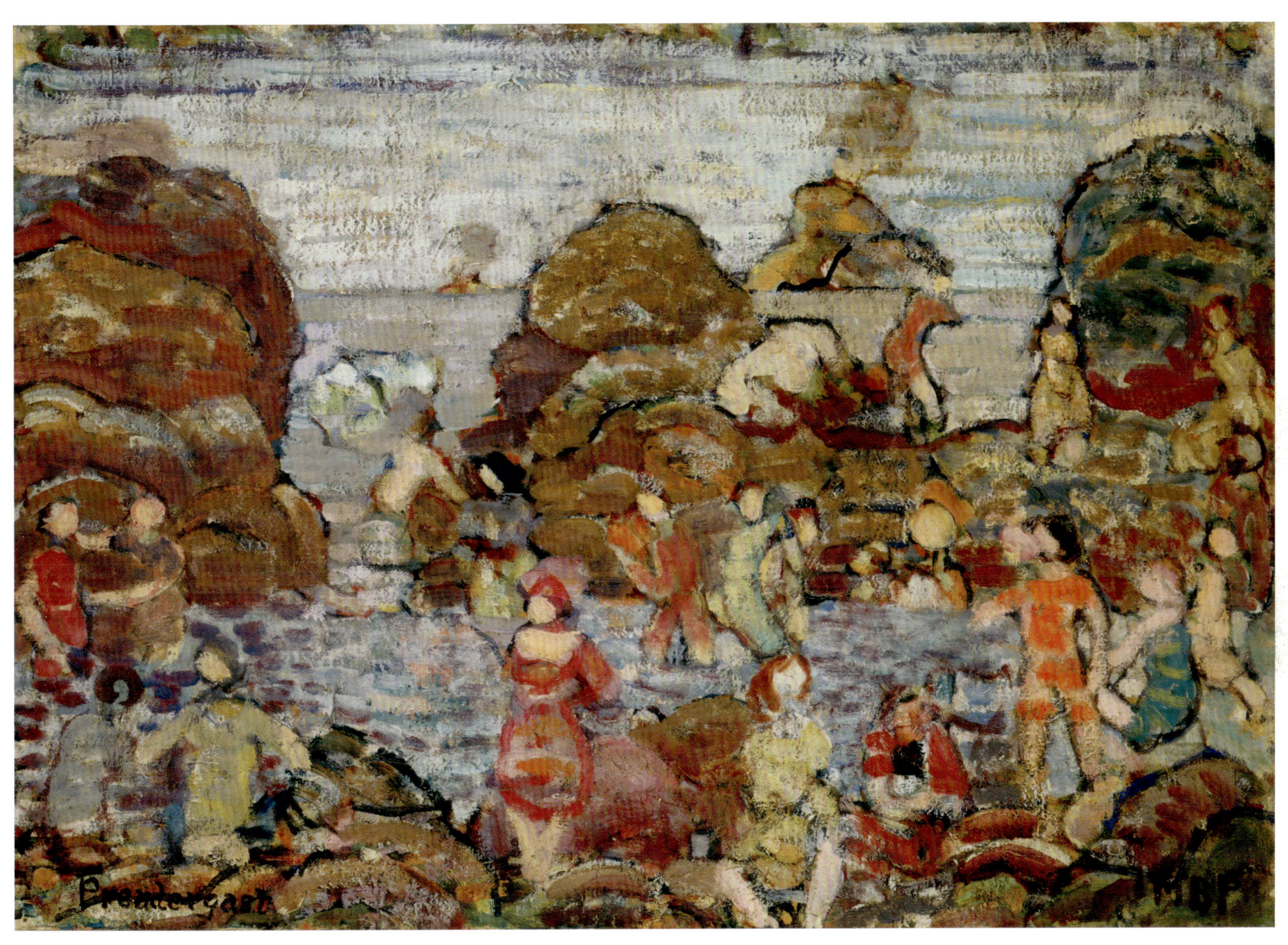

55. *Bathers in a Cove, Maine, c. 1910–13*

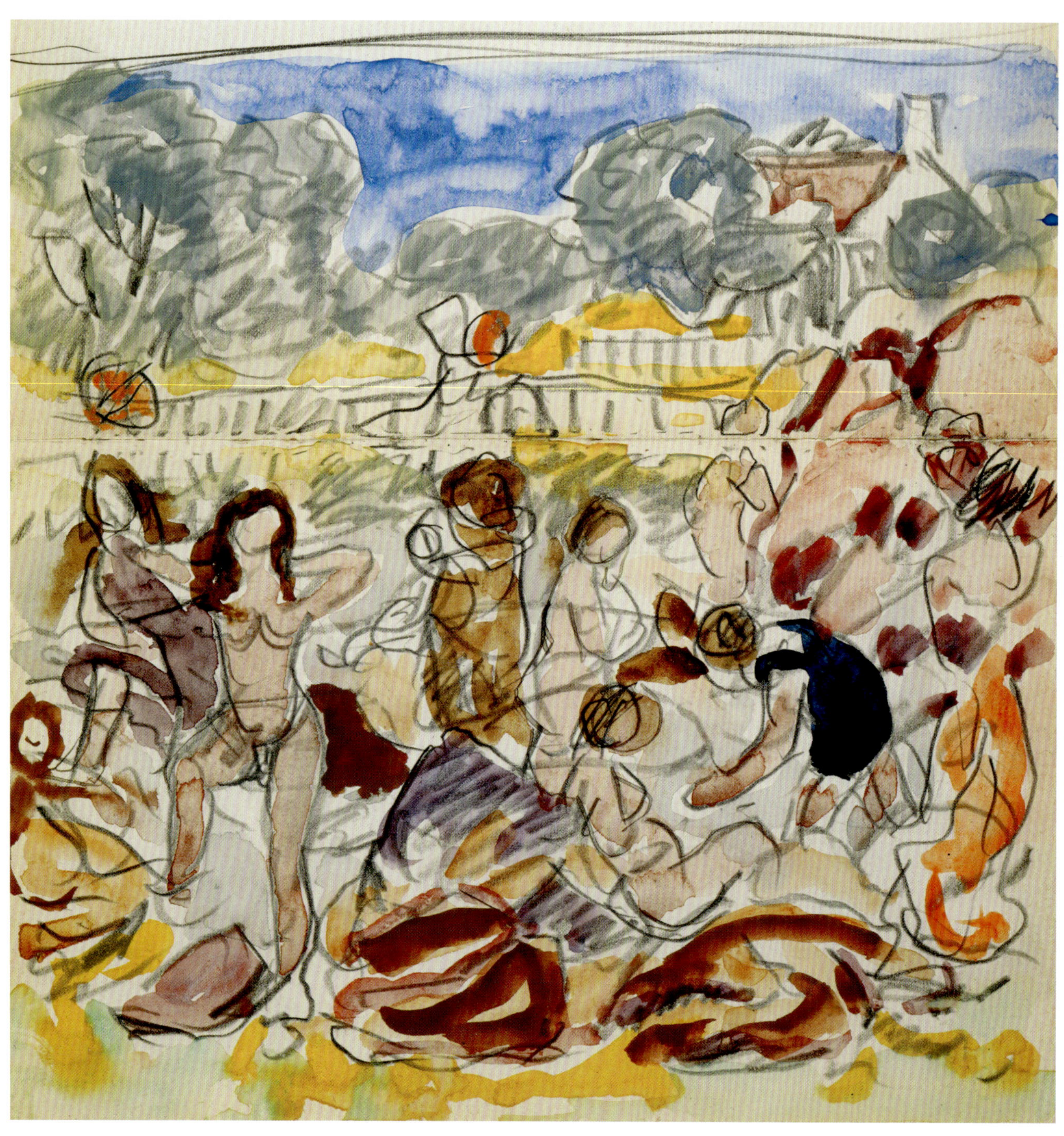

     56. *Sketchbook, c. 1916–18*

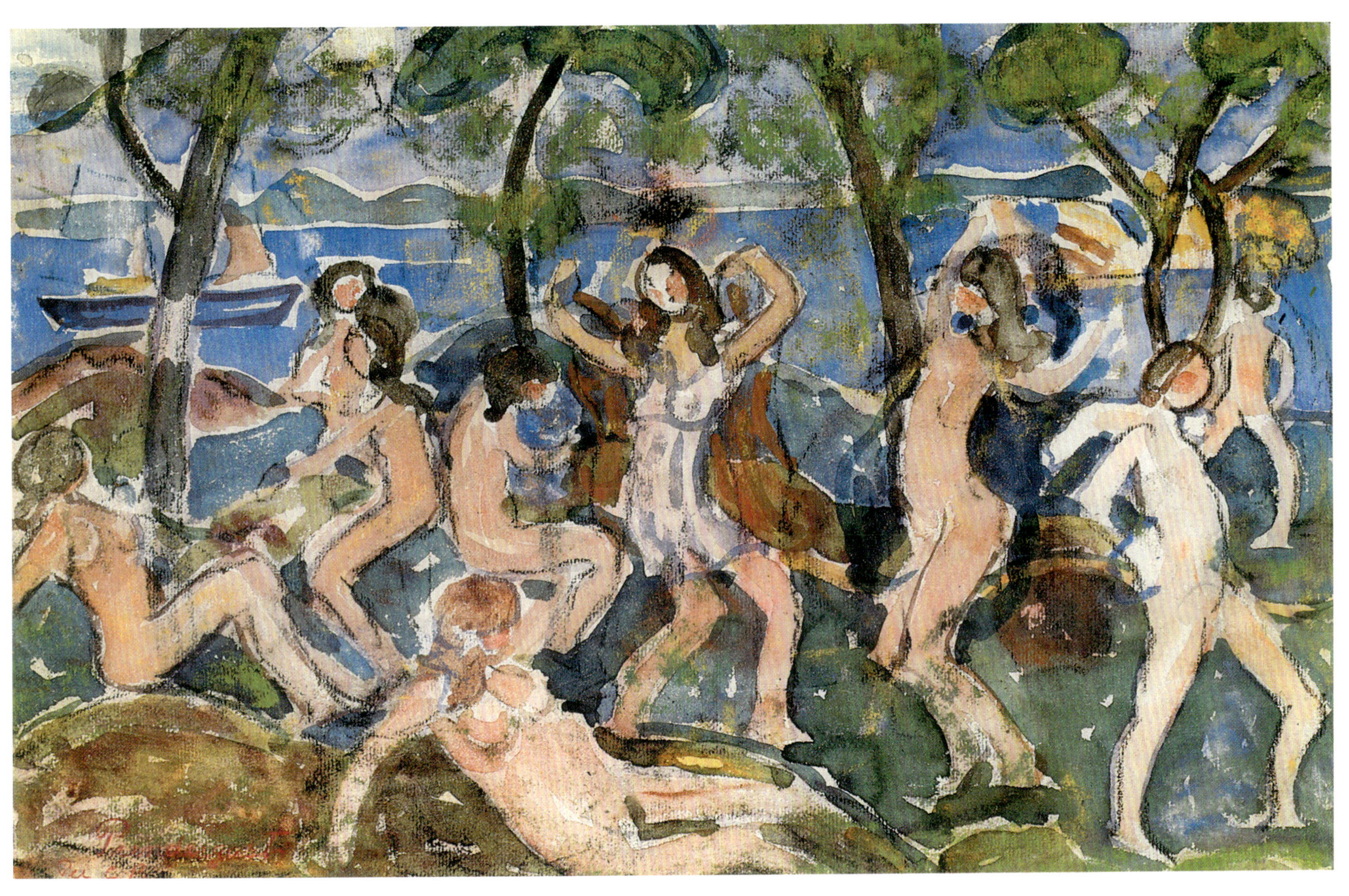

57. *Bathers*, c. 1912–15

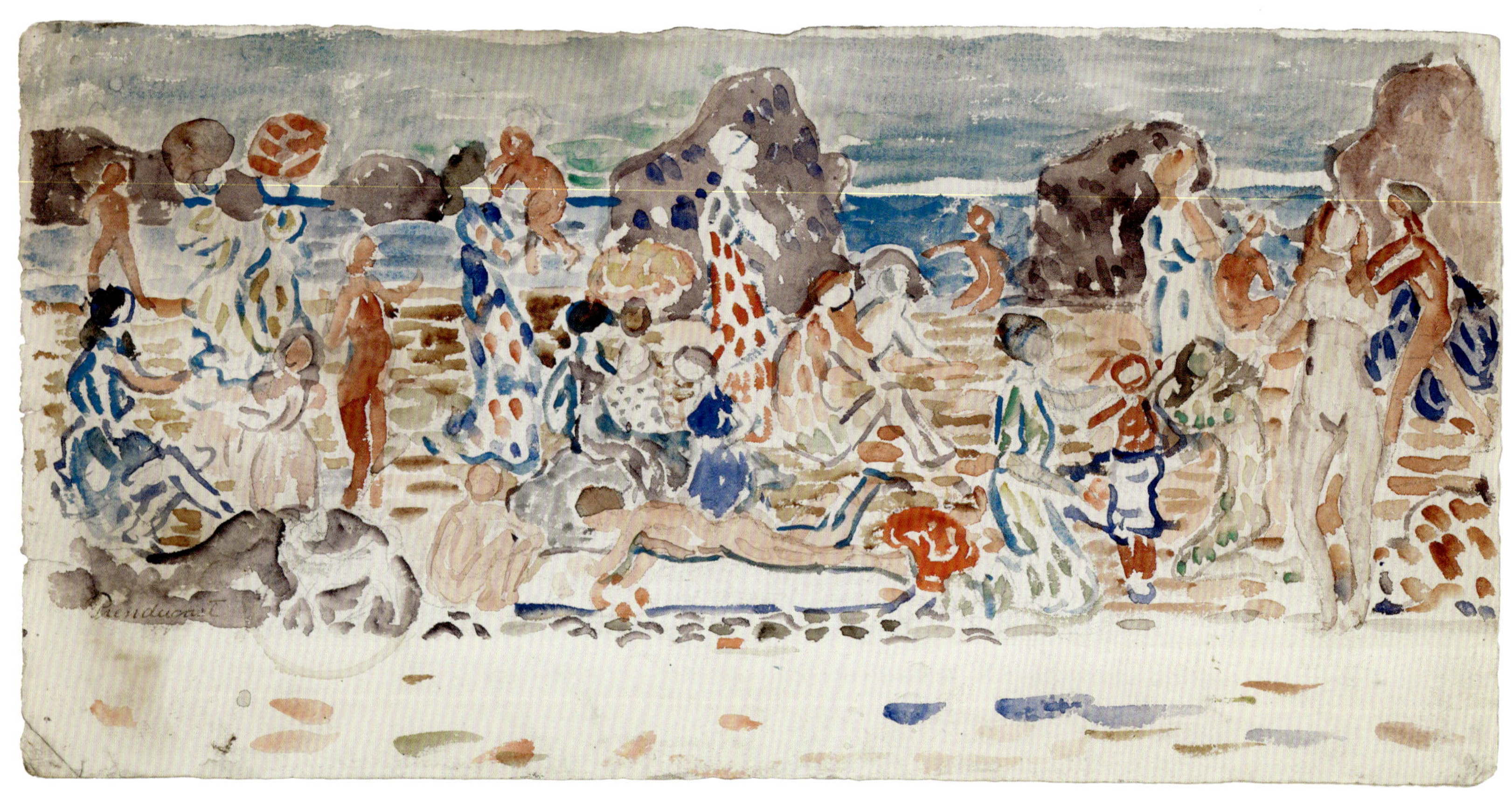

          58. *Summer Day*, c. 1913–15

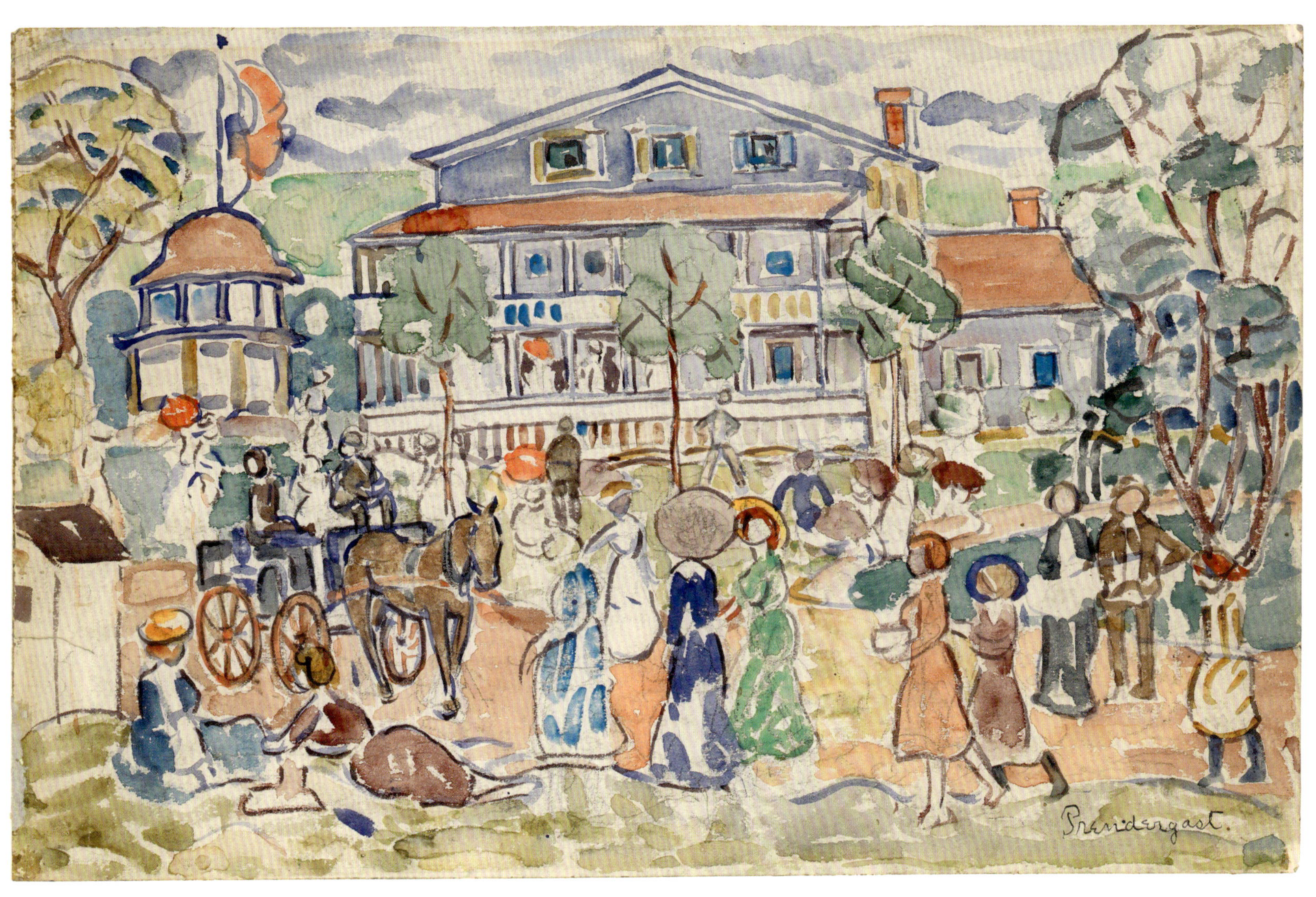

59. Summer Hotel, Maine, c. 1914–15

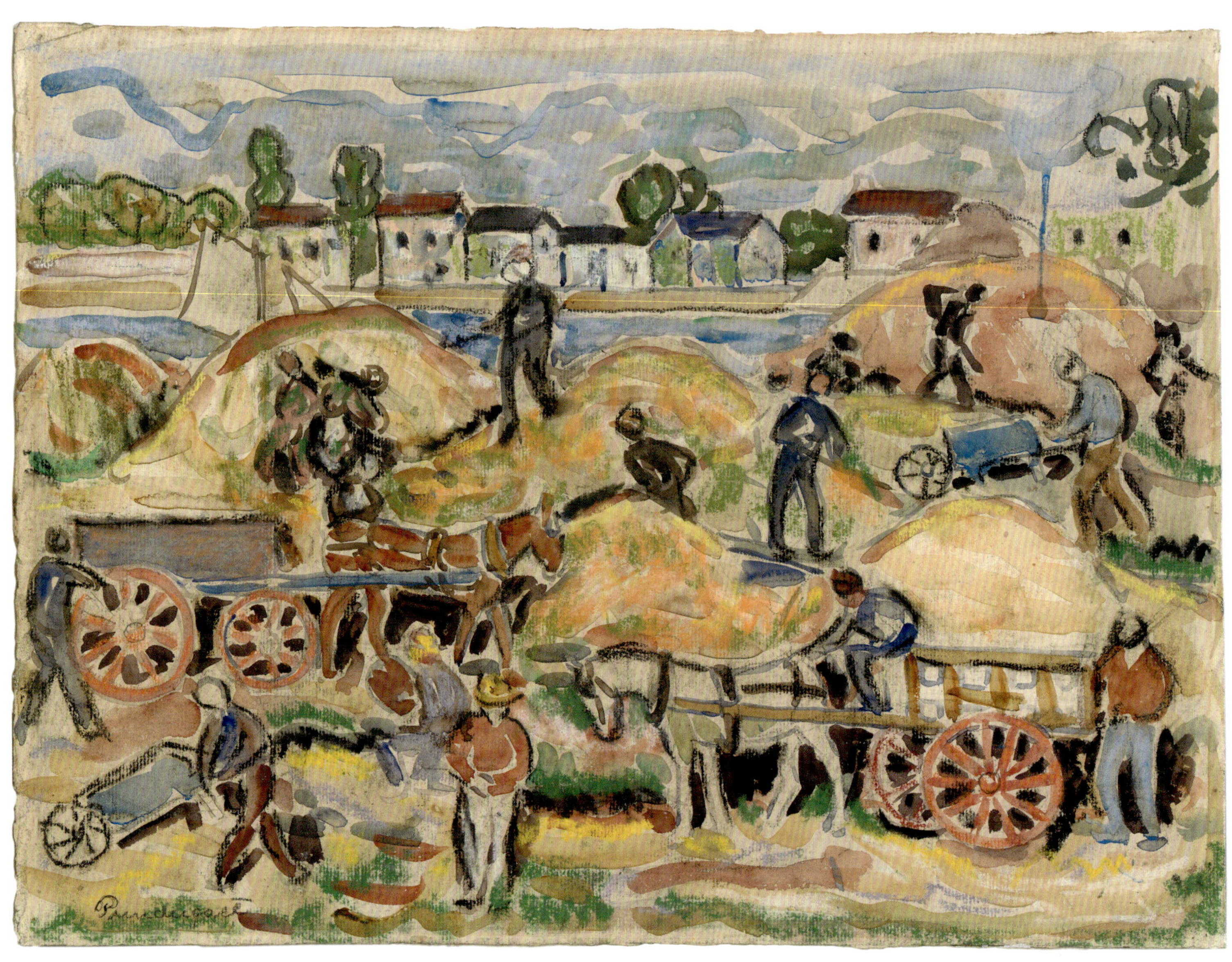

   60. *Hay Harvesting, Maine,* c. 1913–15

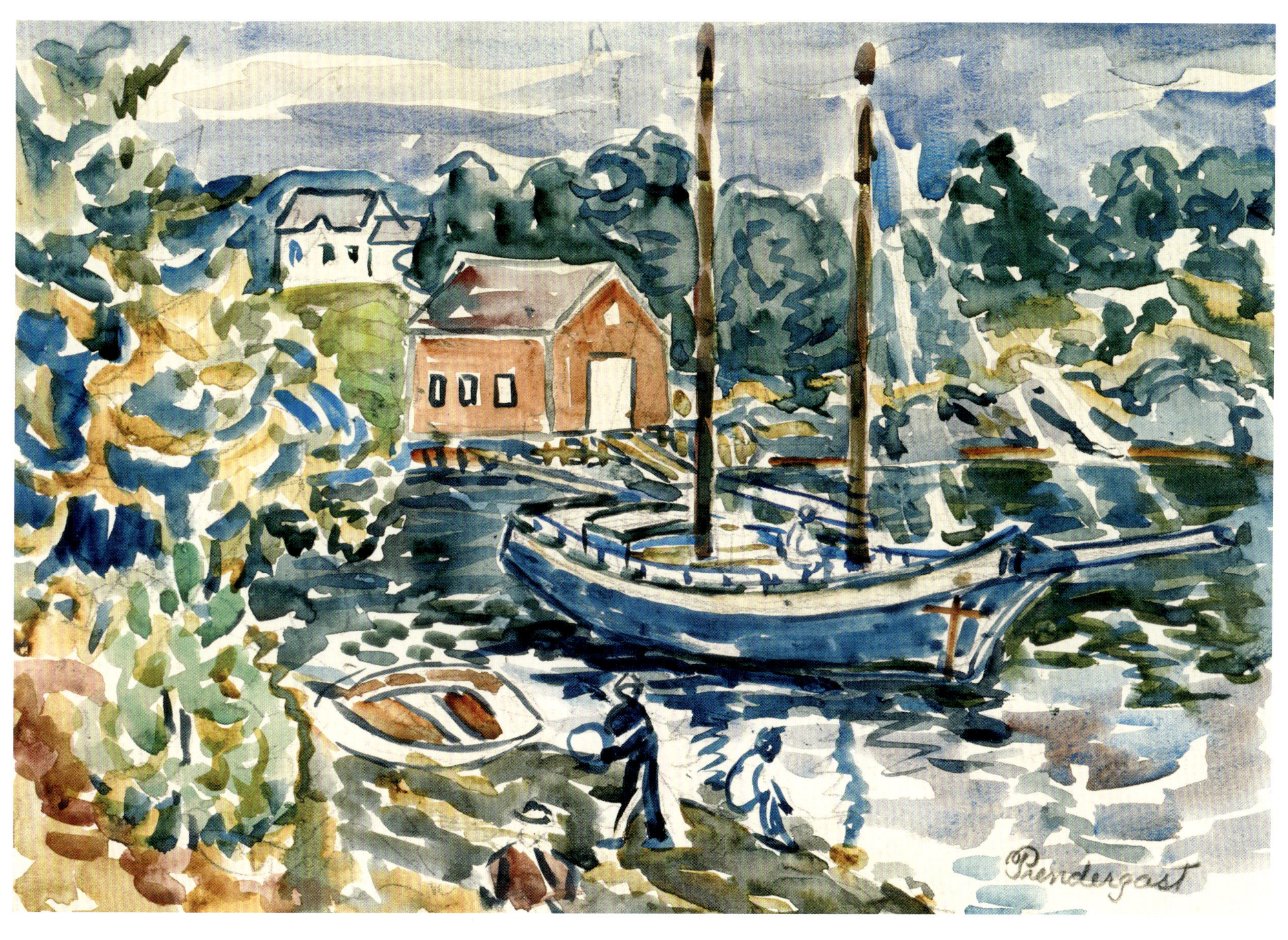

61. *The Cove*, c. 1913–15

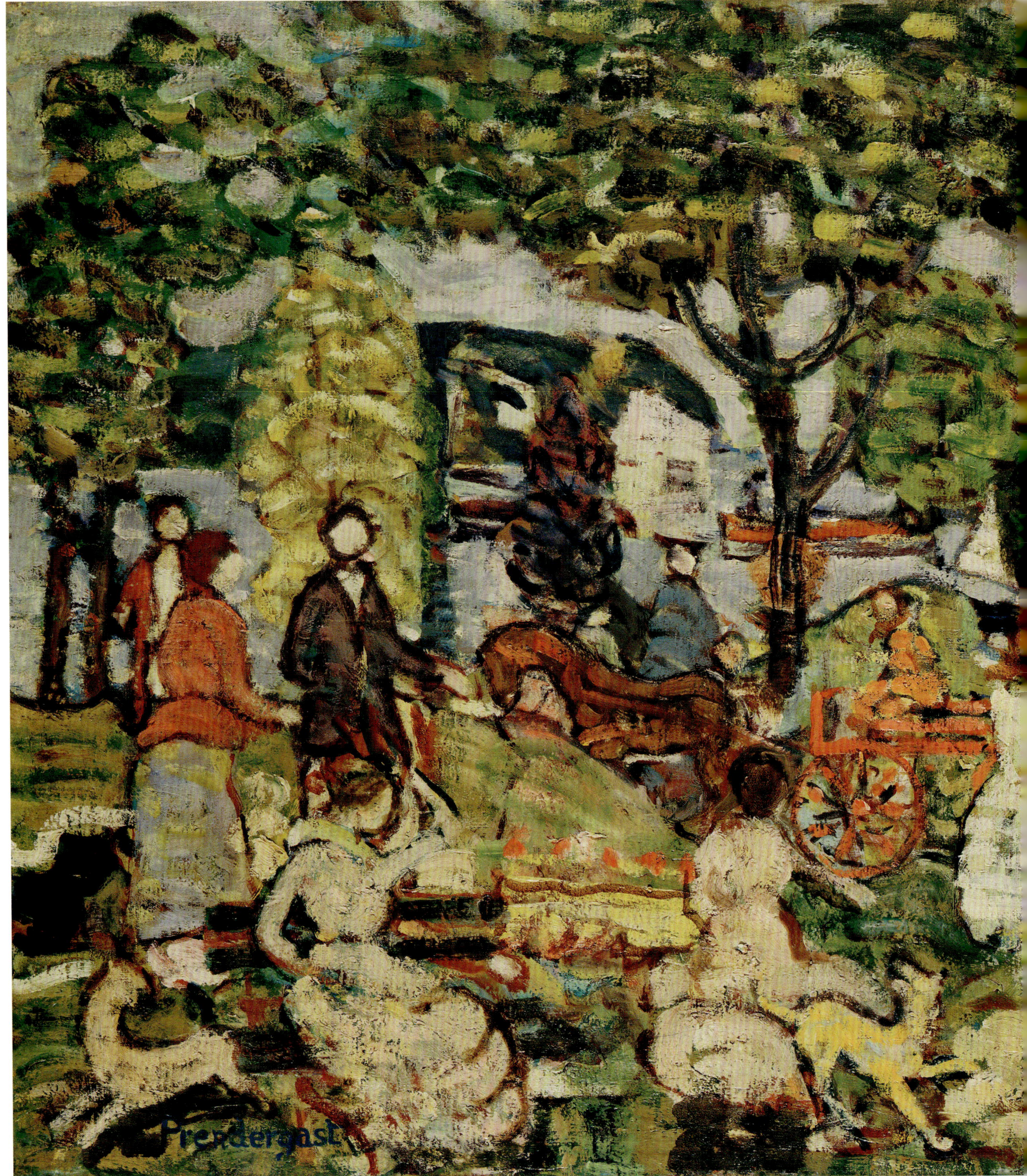

Prendergast

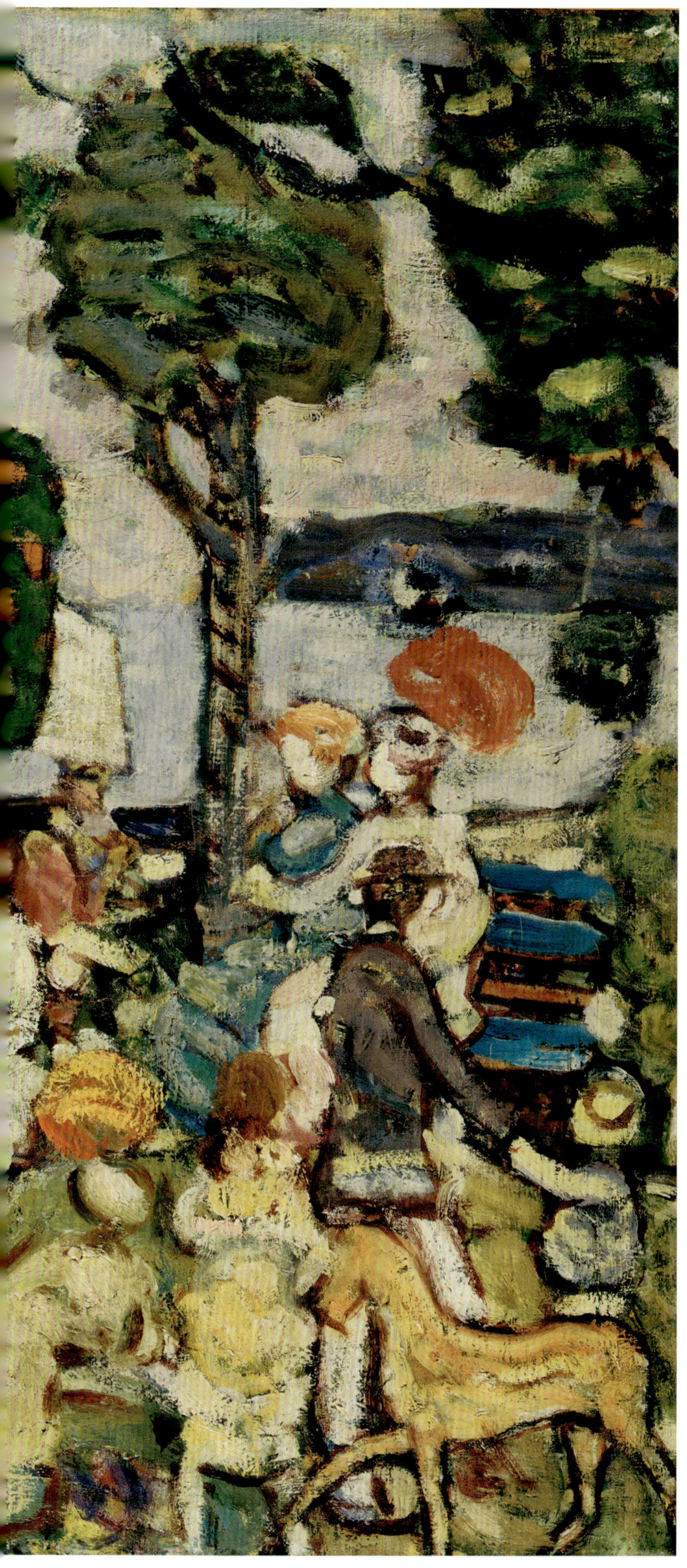

62. *Sunday Promenade*, c. 1914–15

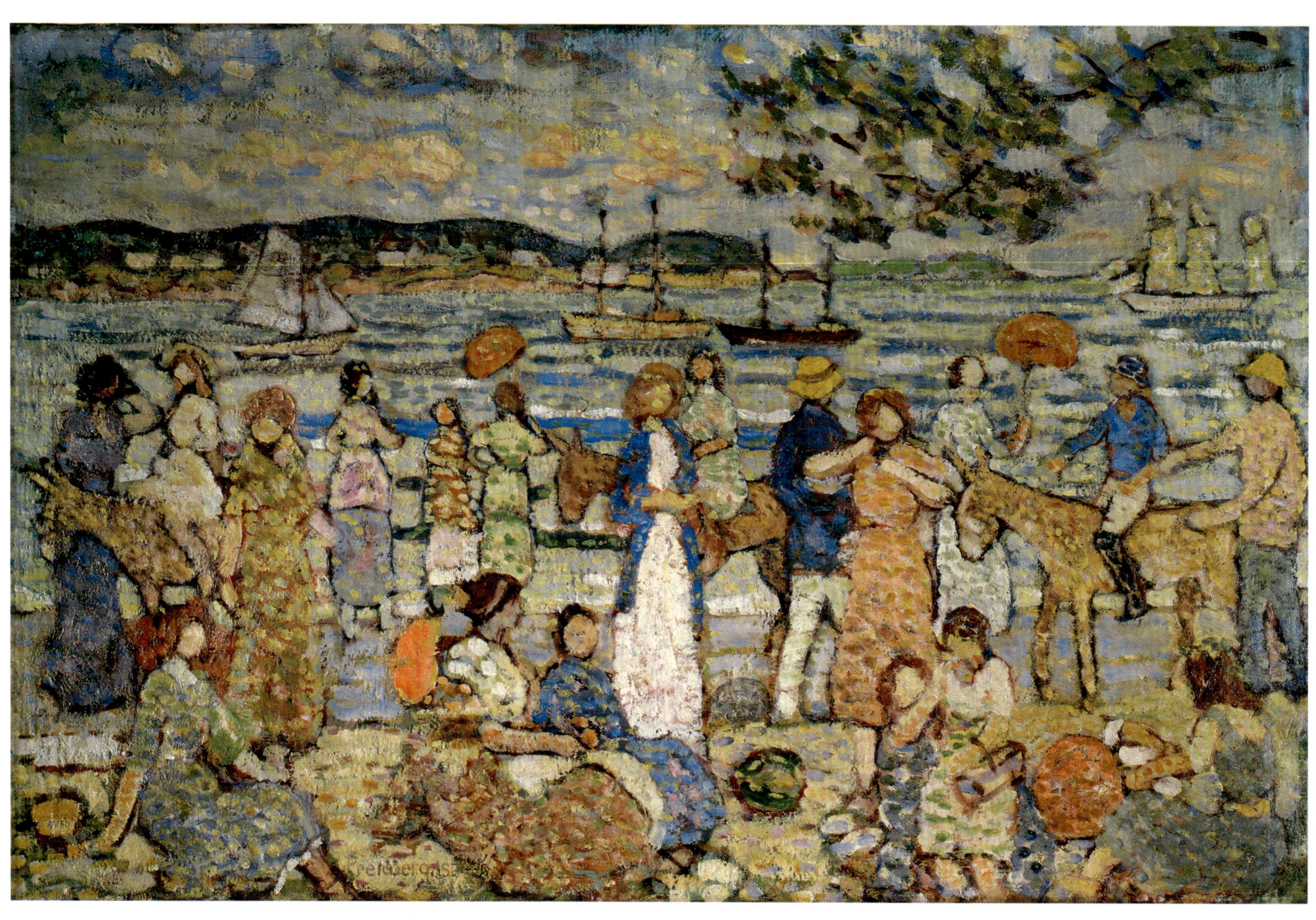

63. *Along the Shore*, c. 1914–15

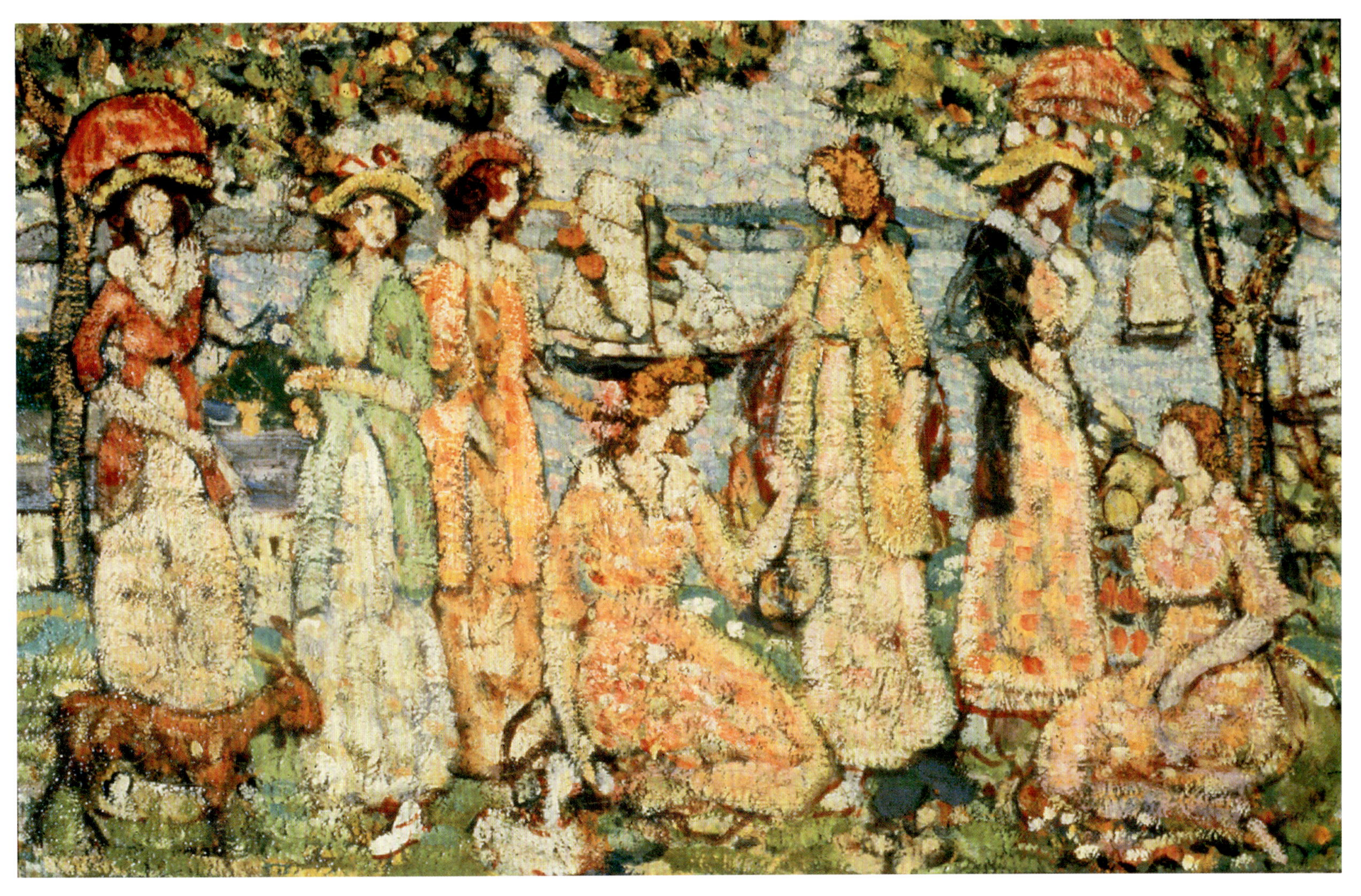

64. *The Idlers*, c. 1916–18

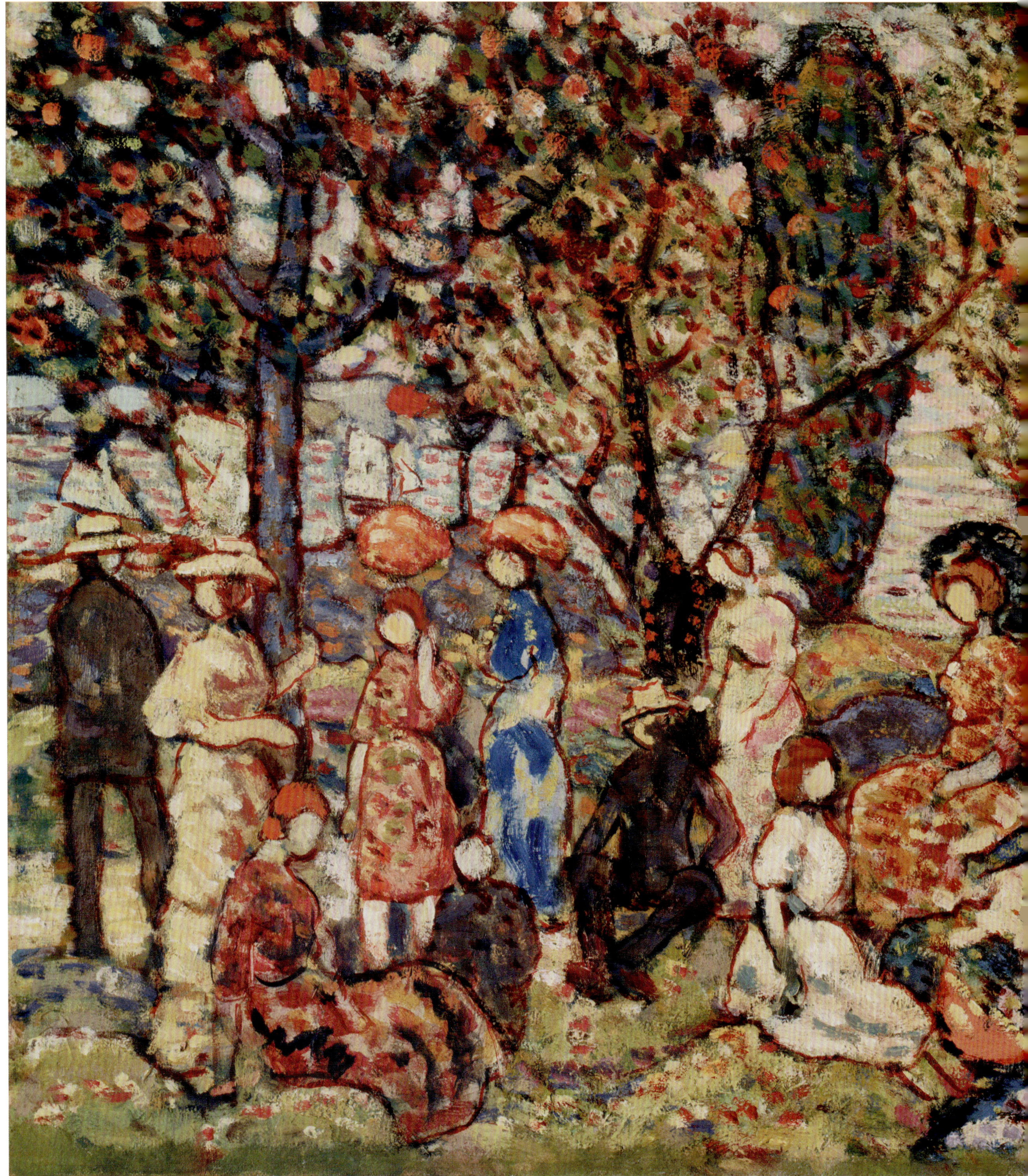

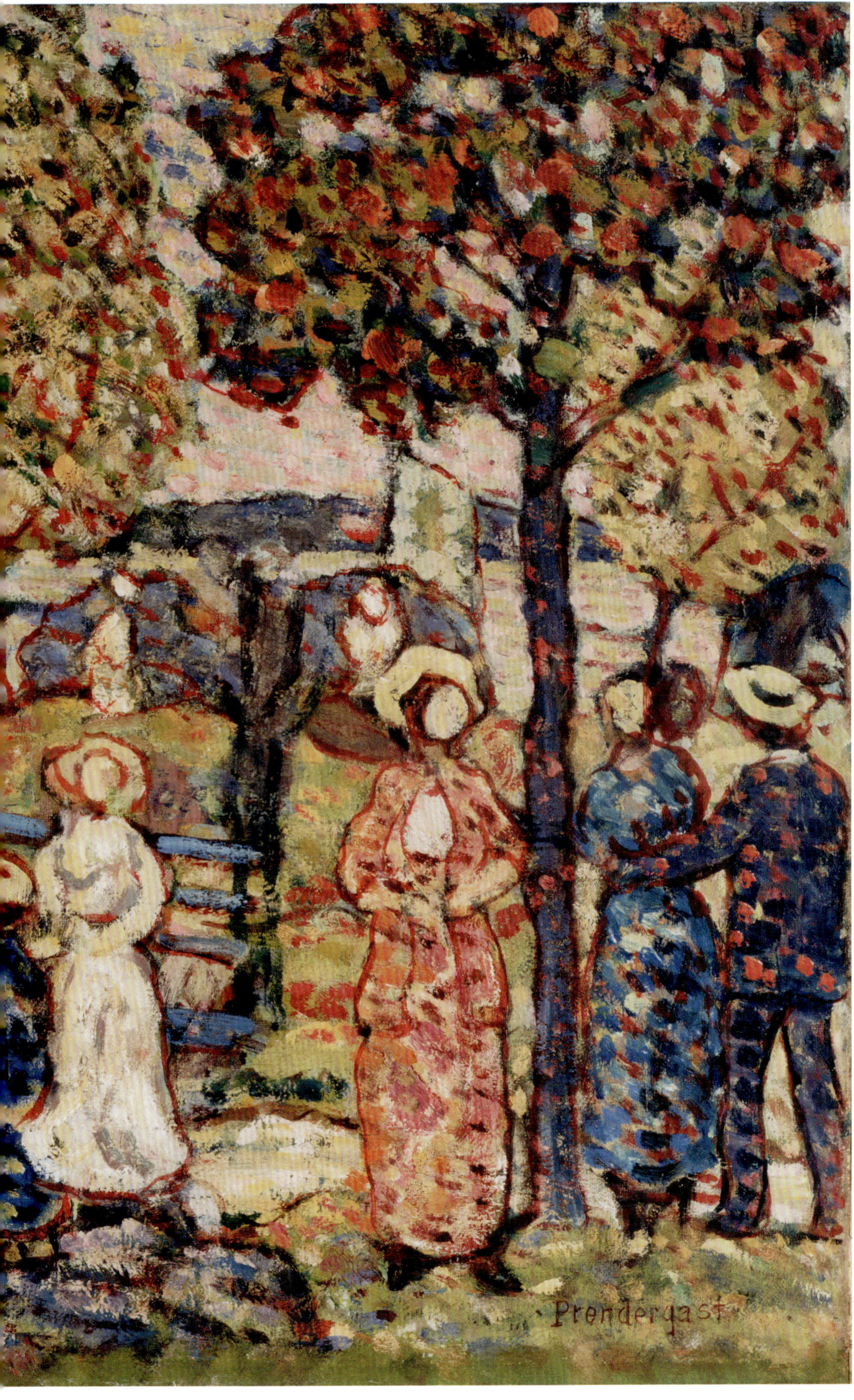

65. *Autumn,* c. 1917–18

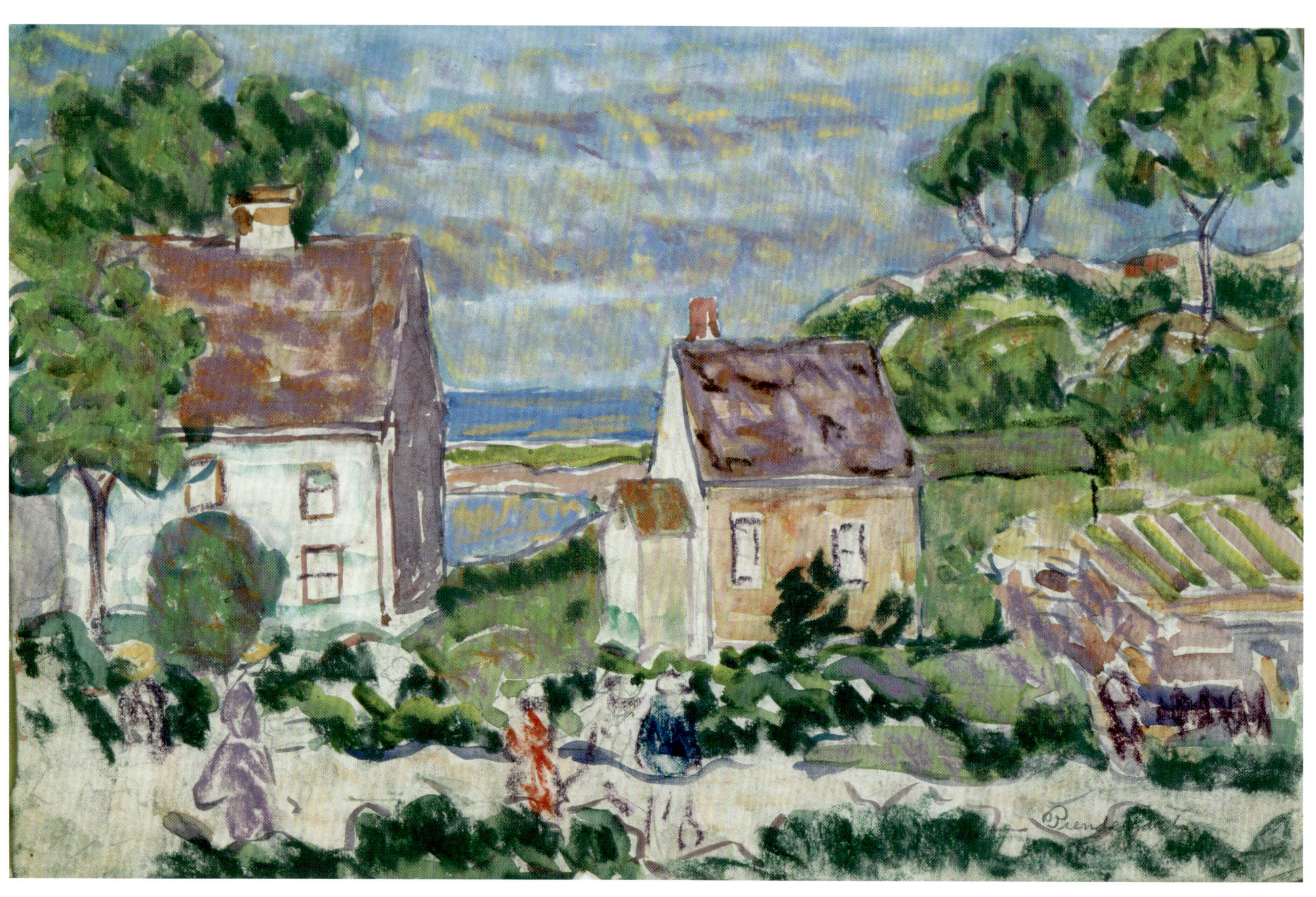

   66. *Maine Coastal Village,* c. 1916–18

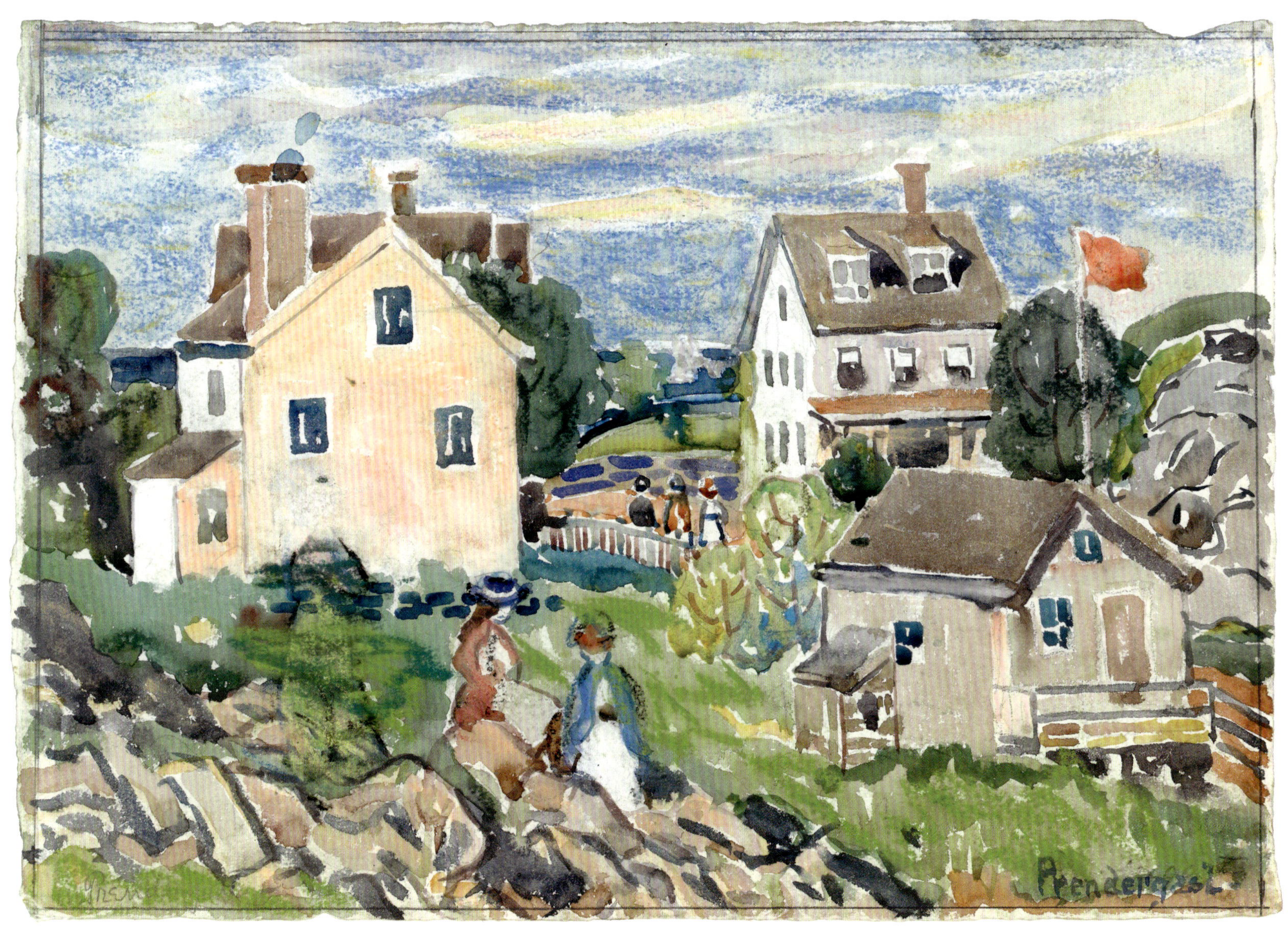

67. New Hampshire, c. 1916–19

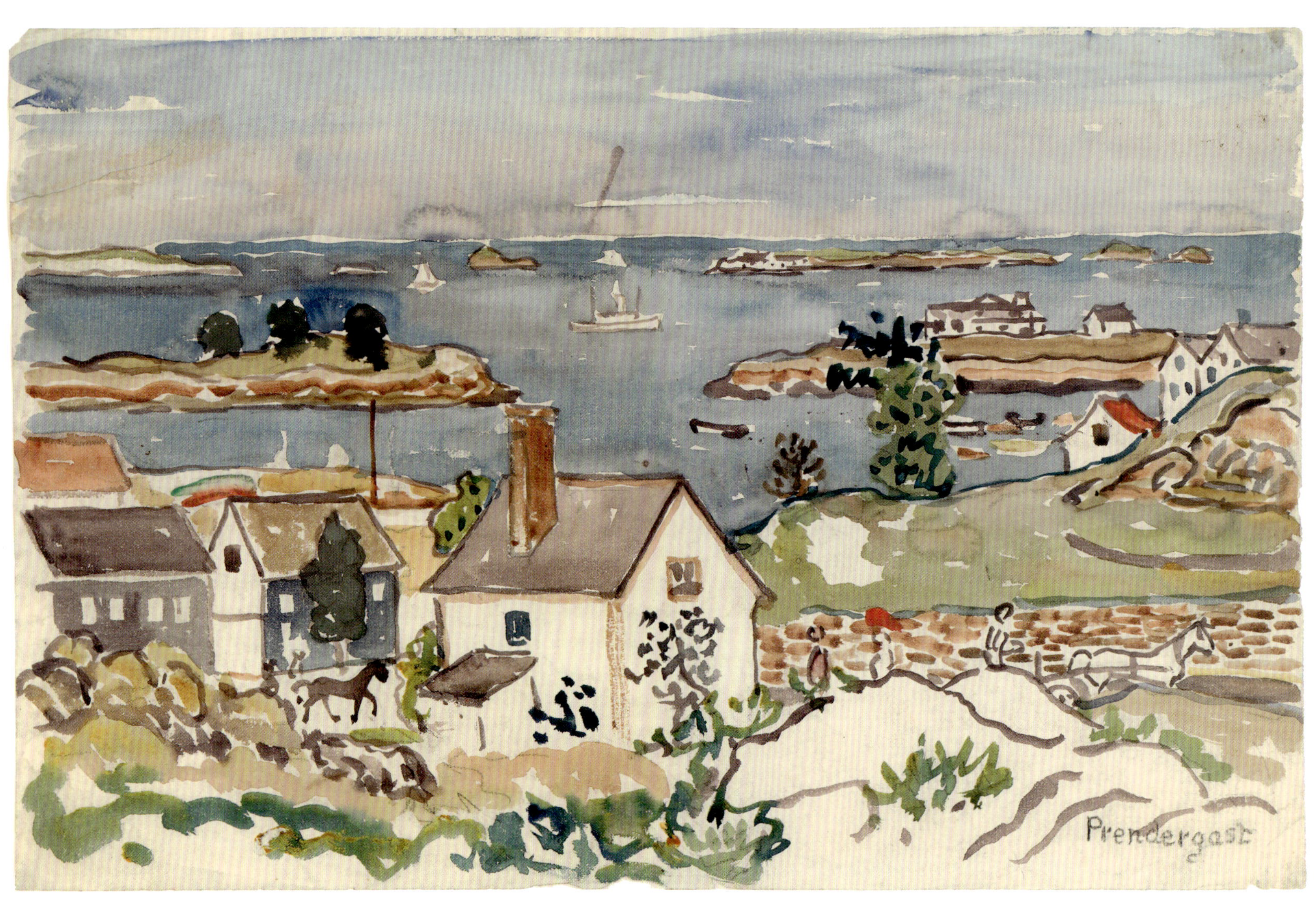

     68. *Harbor Village*, c. 1916–19

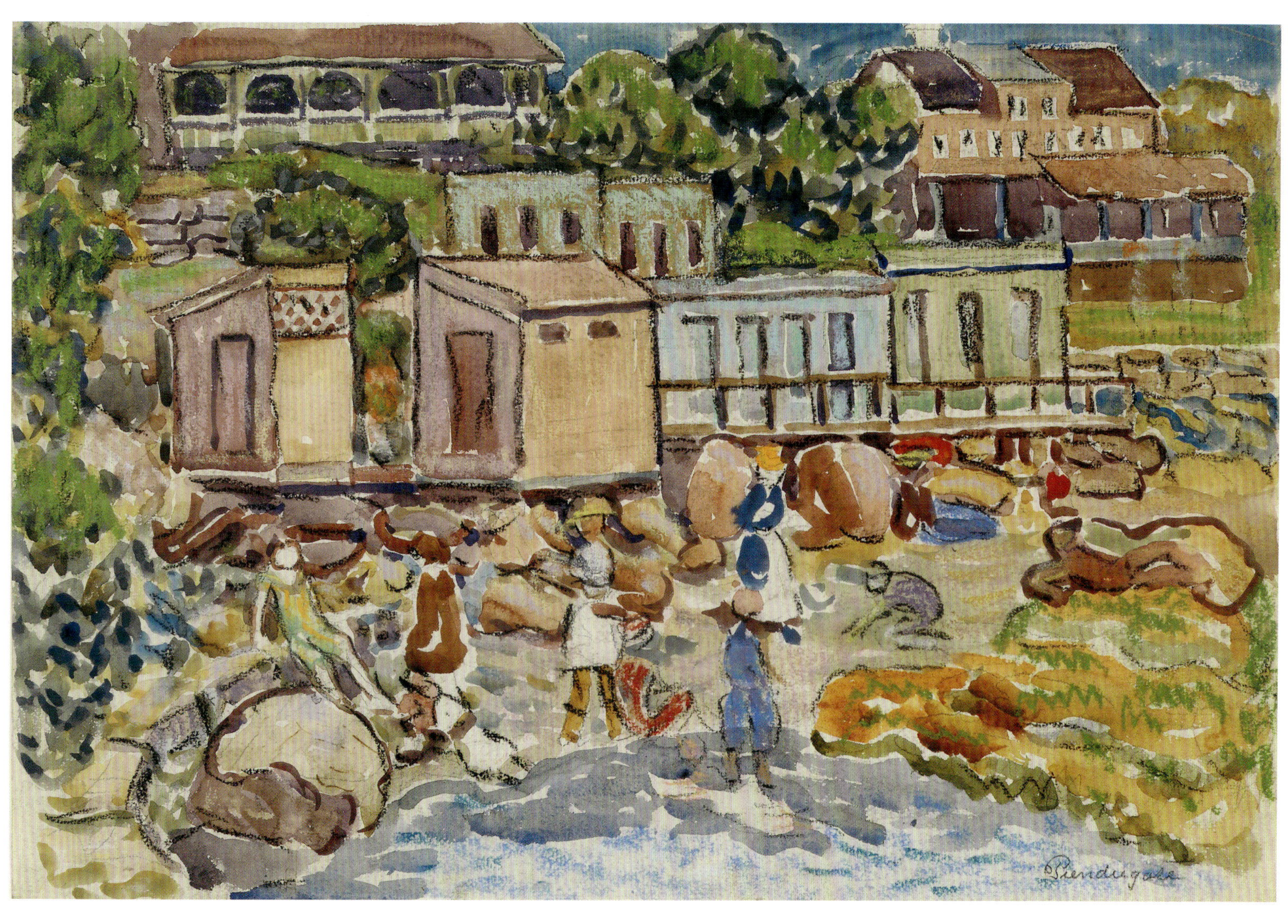

69. Beach Resort, c. 1919

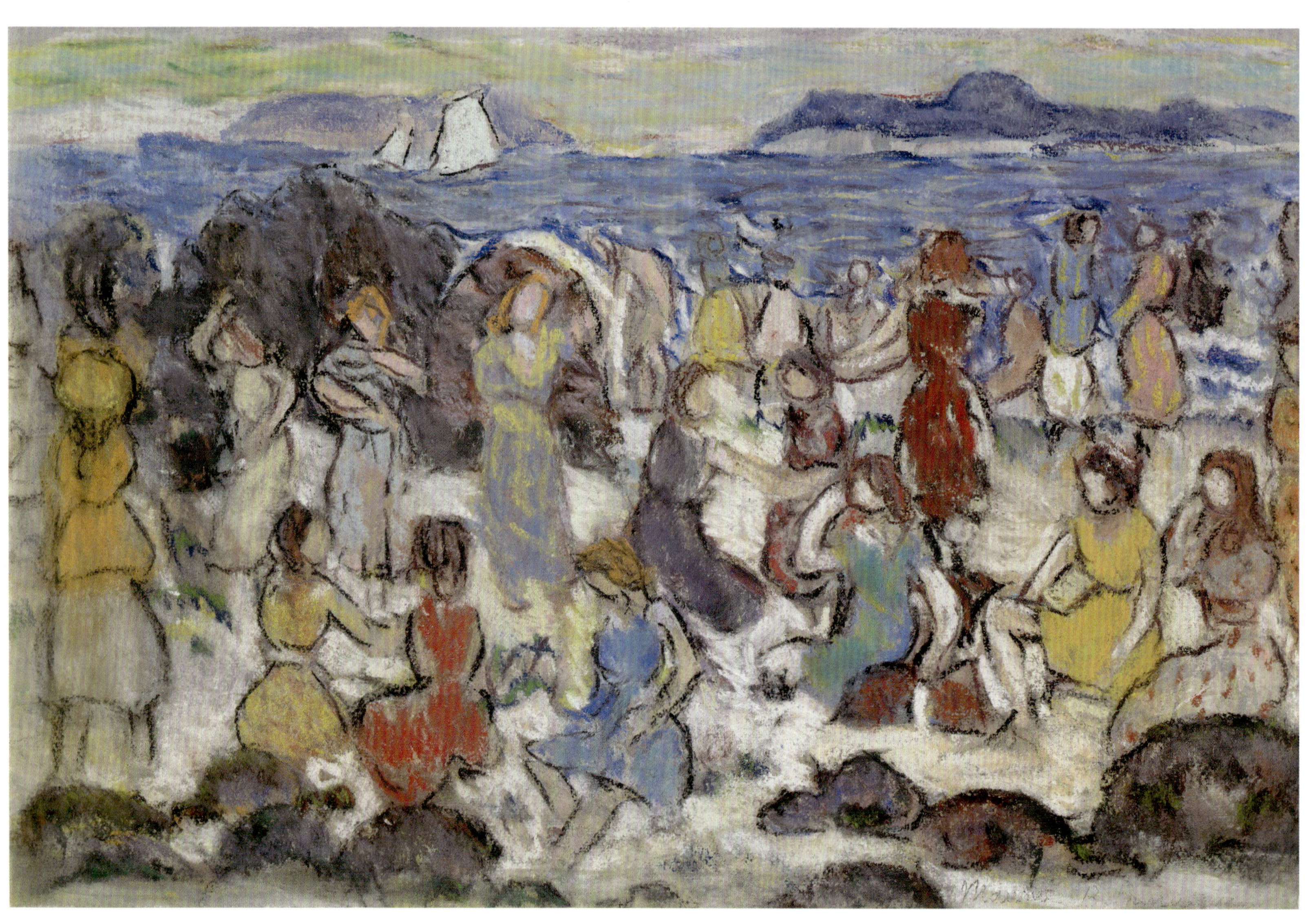

70. *Maine Beach, Late Afternoon,* 1916

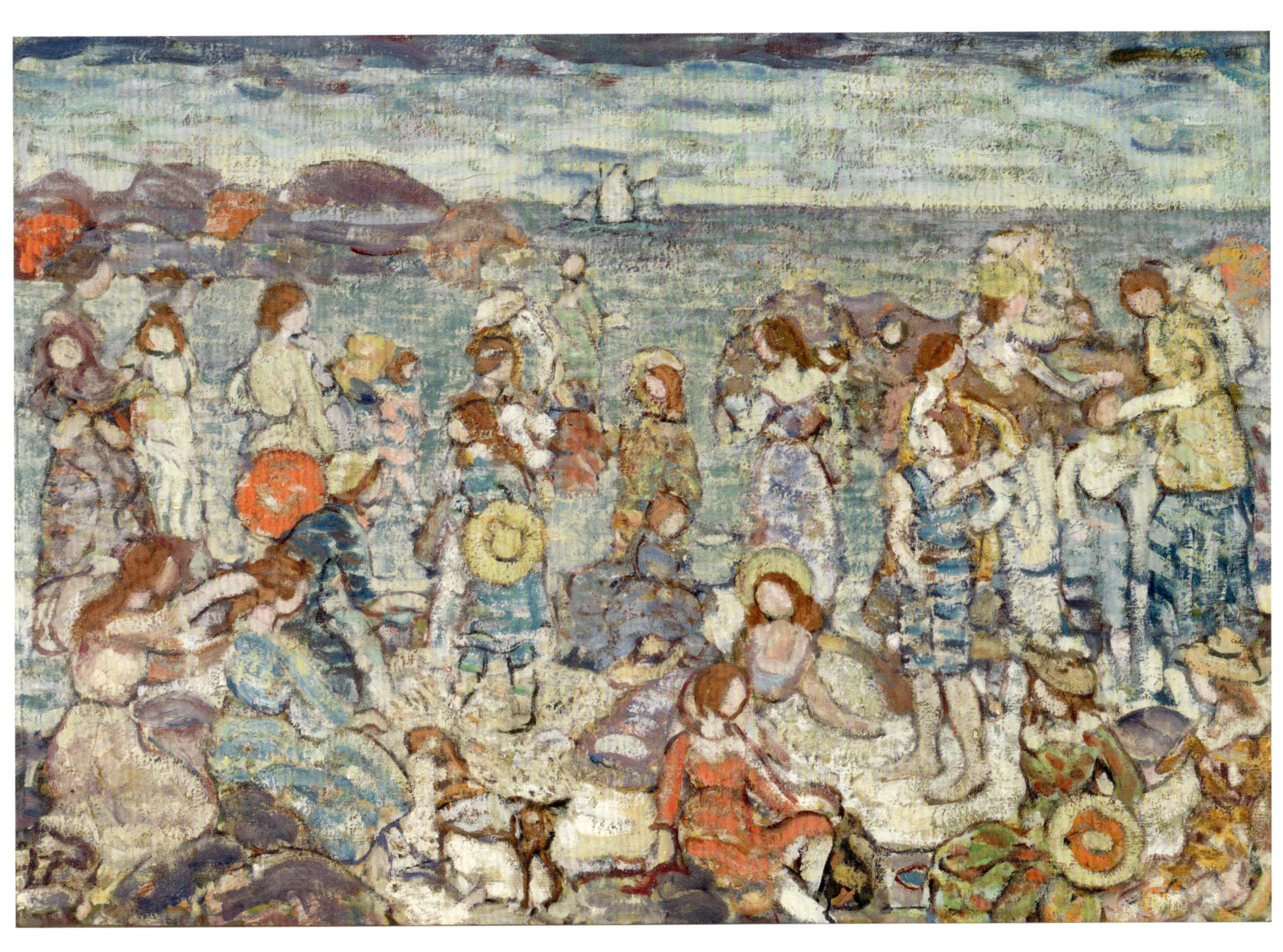

71. *The Cove*, 1916

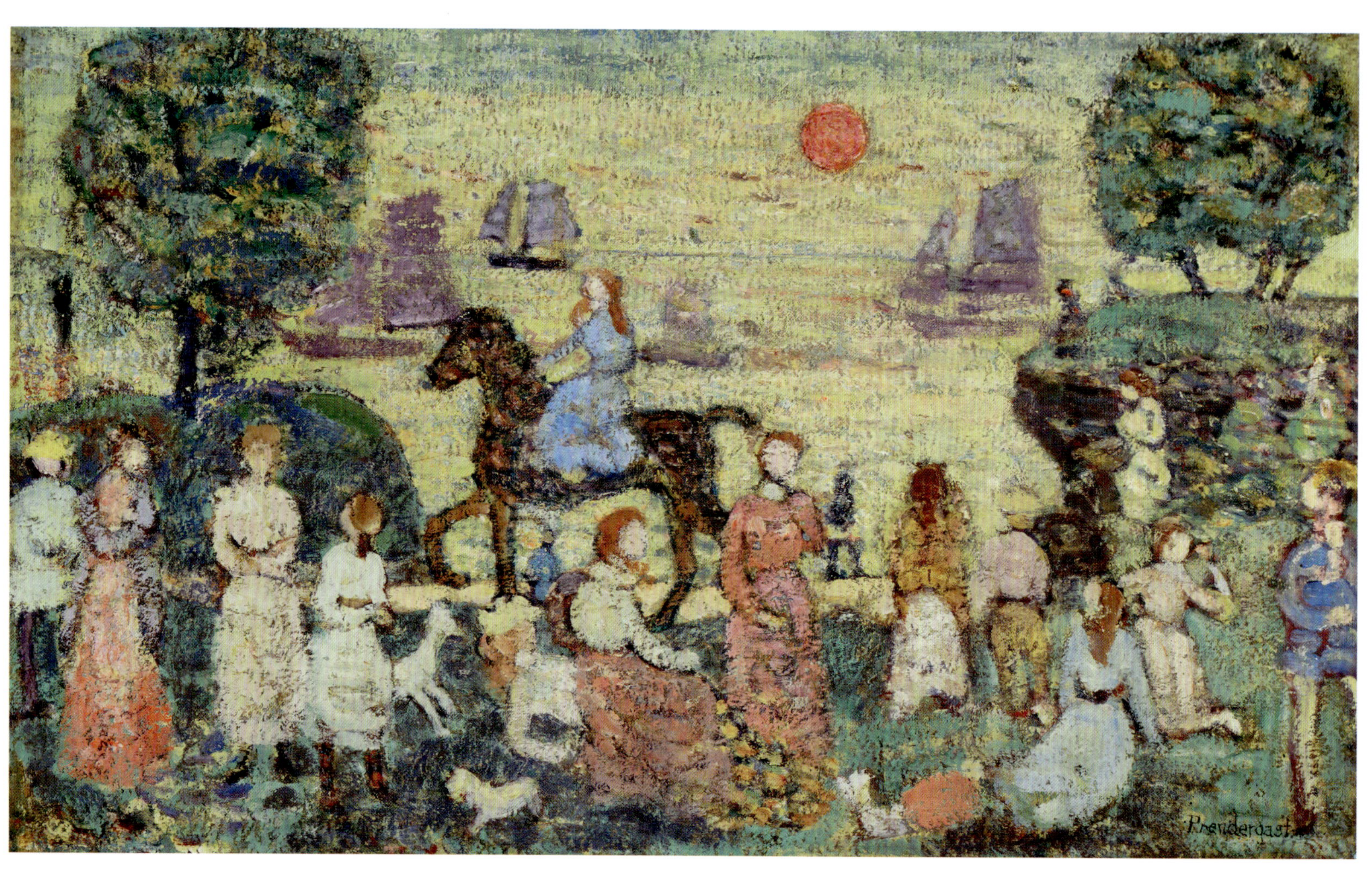

72. *Sunset and Sea Fog*, c. 1918–23

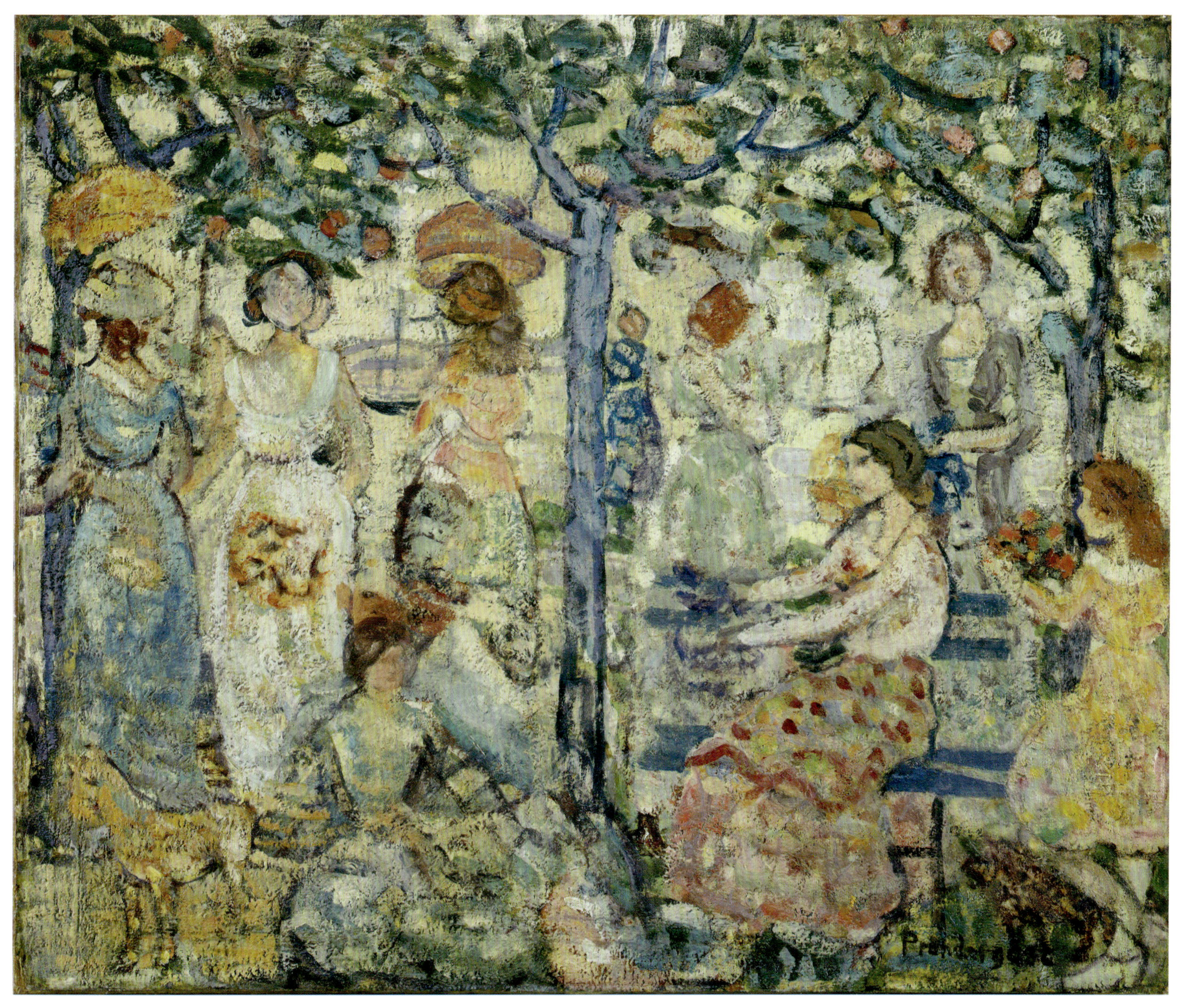

73. *Acadia, c. 1918–23*

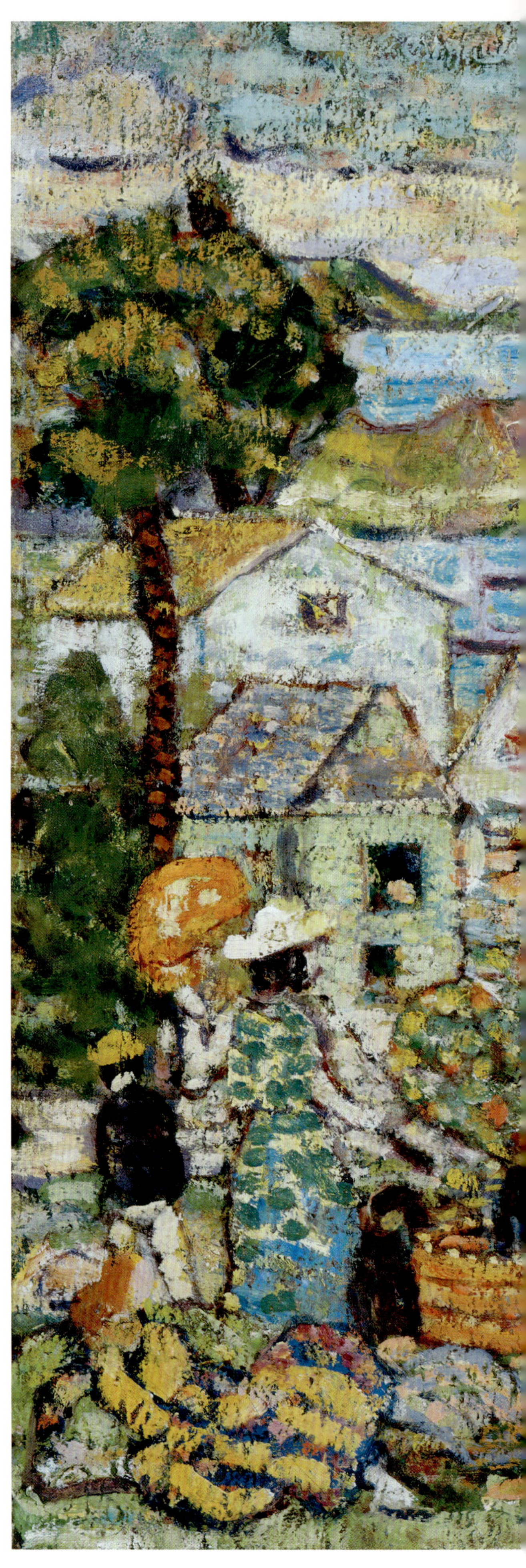

74. *New England Harbor,* c. 1919–23

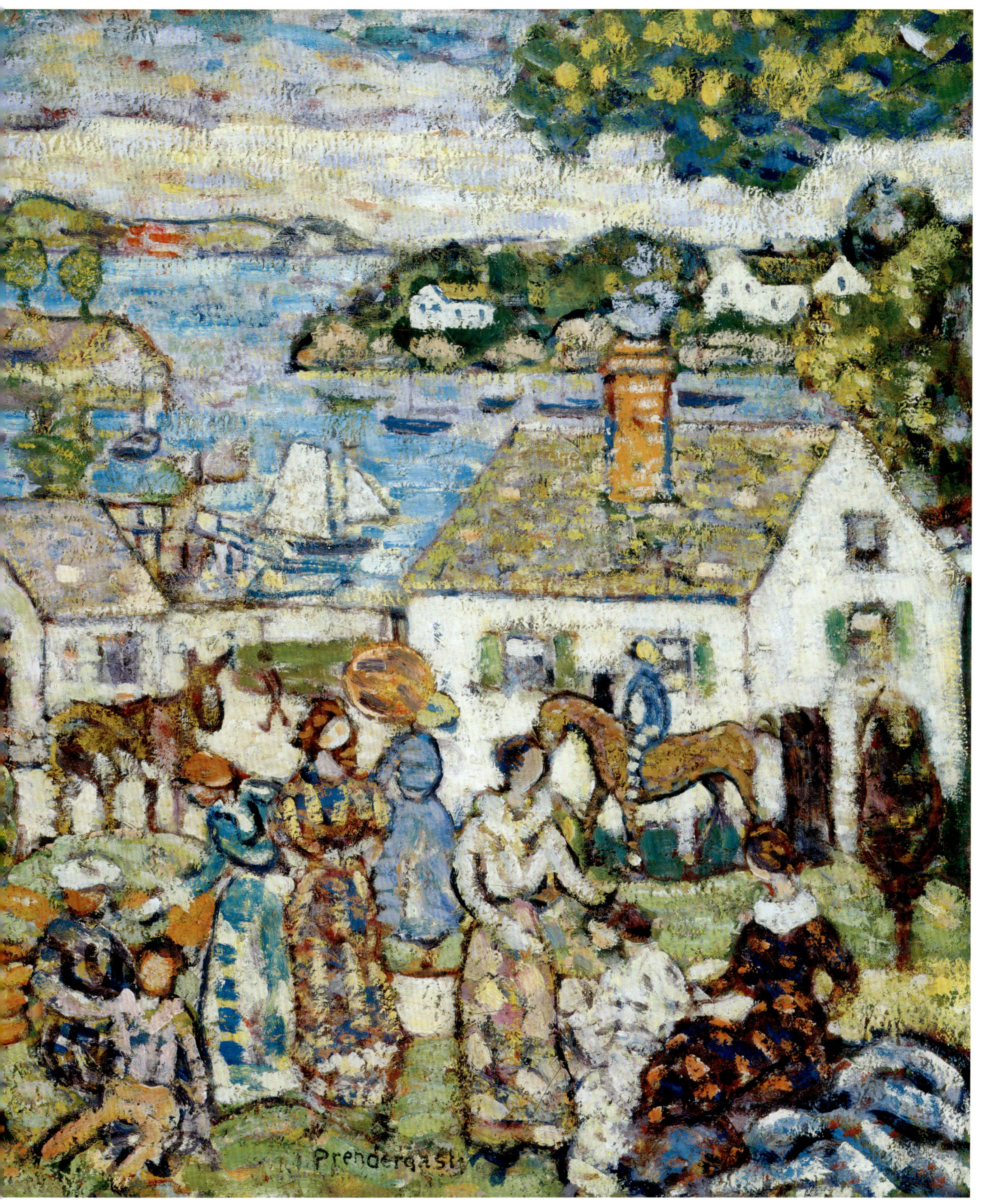
Prendergast

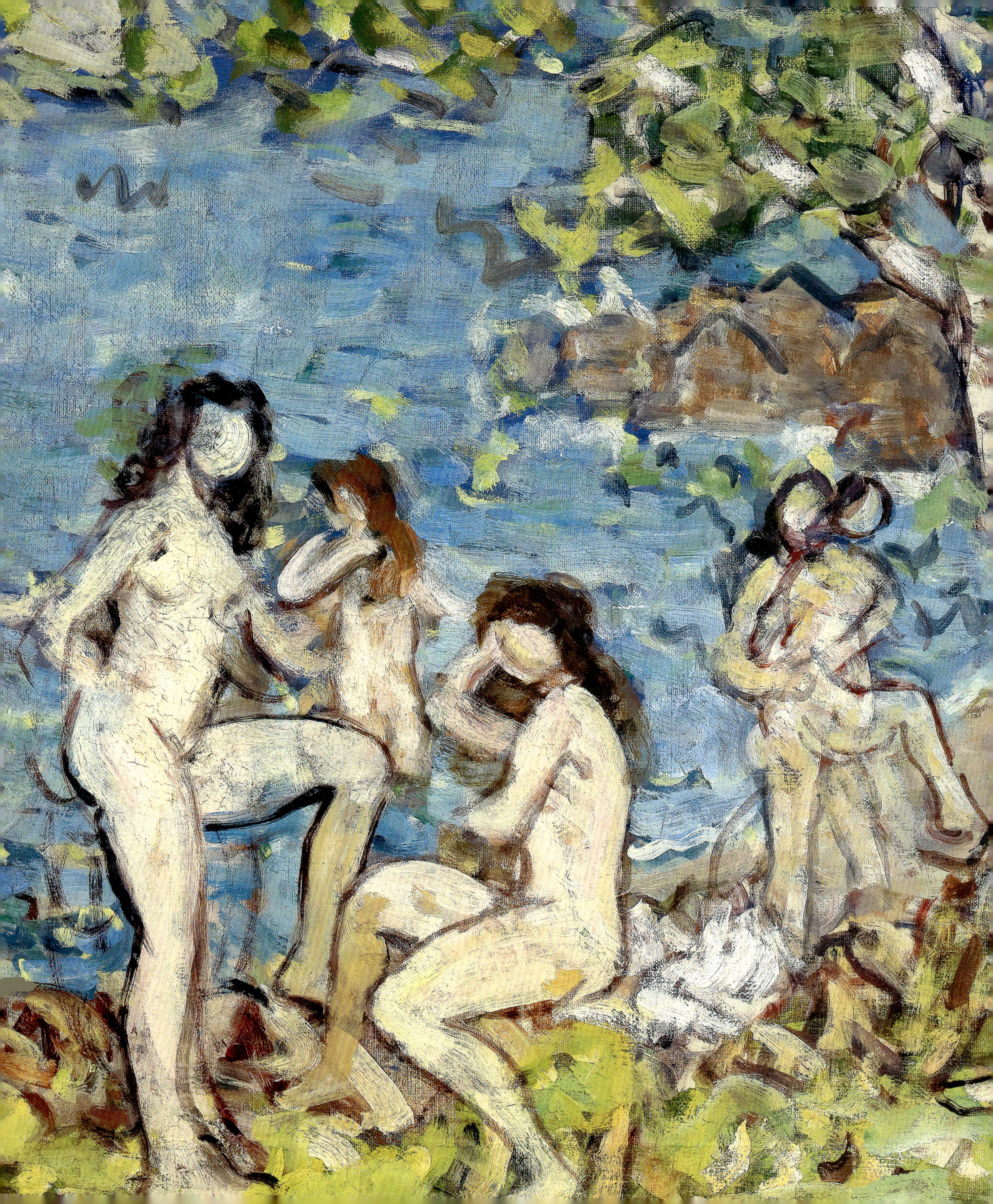

A Happy Enigma?

JOSEPH J. RISHEL

Maurice Prendergast, despite the best efforts of distinguished scholars and critics of American modernism for three generations, remains a happy enigma, and likely always will.

On the one hand, he was praised nearly from the moment of his entrance onto the public stage, in the 1890s, as one of the more progressive and innovative of that small group of artists from the United States whose involvement with new and radical artistic notions—mostly found in Paris and brought home in a myriad of adopted and adapted ways—resulted in work that forever changed the landscape of American art in the years just before and after the First World War.[1] This fact was noted early on by Prendergast's fellow American Walter Pach,[2] an exceptionally cosmopolitan figure himself, and has been charted and thoughtfully analyzed into present times by, to note just three of his most dedicated champions, Nancy Mowll Mathews, Patterson Sims, and Richard Wattenmaker.[3] The foundation for this praise is his complex (often very subtle) way of manipulating paint, sometimes in isolated dashes, drawn in part from his close looking at second-generation Impressionist techniques, and, later in his career, in blunted concoctions of diversely colored mosaics (almost caked in their density) that at times verge on abstraction (plate 62). Add to this a progressively rising horizon and flattening of visual space with a palette of great complexity that requires remarkable discipline and mobility, be it with oil paint or watercolor, and a position in the advanced guard is set.[4]

On the other hand, all of these formal and material experiments evolved, with constant pulses of invention over thirty years in a determined and applied practice of his trade, within a small repertory of subjects (one hardly needs the plural, actually), which were set in his mind early on when he established himself as a decorative artist in conservative Boston, a position essentially unchanged throughout his productive life.[5] Which places him—and here's the crux of the "enigma" of making/subjects—in small company. One can but stretch to figures (highly admired by Prendergast and his circle) such as Albert Pinkham Ryder or, even further, to Giorgio Morandi or Joseph Albers, for comparison.[6]

I speak, of course, of that wonderful, endless cascade of figures, always gathered out of doors, fashionable and affluent (with a high ratio of enchantingly dressed

Detail, *Bathers by the Sea*, c. 1910–13 (fig. 31)

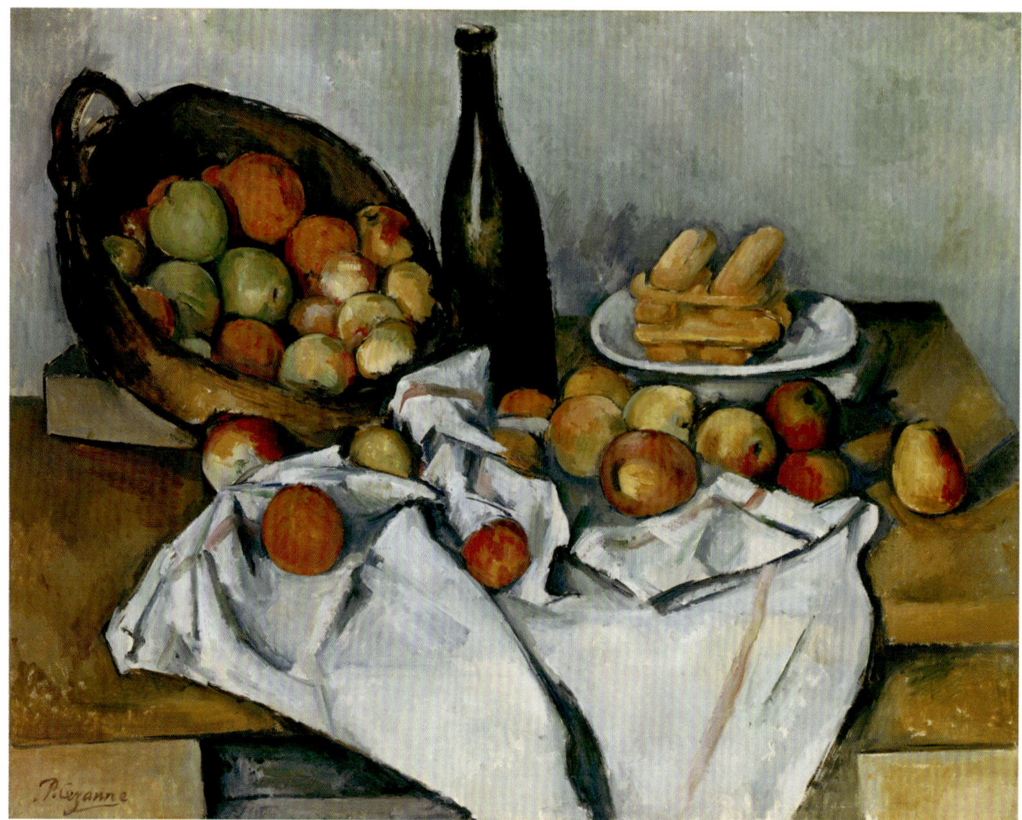

Fig. 28. Paul Cézanne, *The Basket of Apples*, c. 1893. Oil on canvas, 25⁷⁄₁₆ × 31½ in. (65 × 80 cm). The Art Institute of Chicago; Helen Birch Bartlett Memorial Collection (1926.252)

children and women) at gay and animated leisure, be it in public parks (New York or Boston), taking in the sites in Venice, or sporting on the cold beaches of New England or Normandy (our subject here). His ease with his containment was, at one low moment, held against him: "Of Mr. Prendergast there is nothing new to be said. He has become of late more and more overburdened by his own mannerisms. His work is always 'amusing,' but its range is exceedingly limited."[7]

But this soon passed with the balance we hold today of the two poles of his ambitions: the definition of his genius, finding conservative, picturesque (in other hands, conventional) subjects of which he never seems to bore and which never let him down as a vehicle for his far-ranging explorations.

Prendergast's position as a high modernist begins, of course, with Paul Cézanne, as exemplified in Pach's famous declaration in 1922 (two years before Prendergast's death but long after the fact) that the artist was "probably the first American to realize the importance of the master of the modern school" and that Cézanne's lessons were evident in "every stroke he makes."[8] This said just as Cézanne was emerging as the touchstone of modern art as it would come to be defined by Pach and the circle he gathered in New York, in company with Clive Bell and Roger Fry in London.[9]

There can be no doubt of the power of this attraction from Prendergast's first encounter with Cézanne's work in large numbers when he was in France in 1907, on

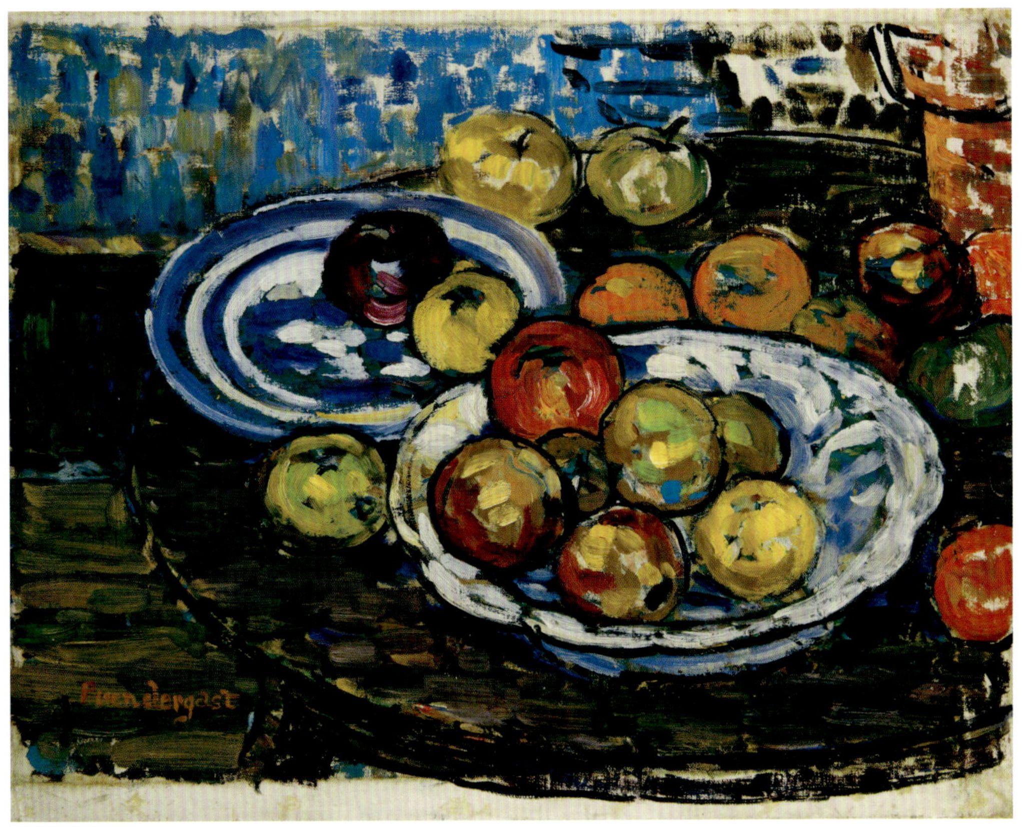

Fig. 29. Maurice Prendergast, *Still Life with Apples*, 1910–13. Oil on canvas, 14 × 17¼ in. (35.6 × 43.8 cm). Terra Foundation for American Art, Chicago; Daniel J. Terra Collection (1992.66)

an extended second trip that lasted just over five months. He was able to see the water-colors at Bernheim-Jeune during the summer—which would, in a modified series, become the first public exhibition of Cézanne in America when Alfred Stieglitz showed them in 1911—as well as the posthumous exhibition at the Salon d'Automne that October.[10] It was at this time that Prendergast wrote to his good friend, the painter Esther Baldwin Williams, praising Cézanne's "perfectly marvelous" watercolors: "He left everything to the imagination. They were great for their simplicity and suggestive qualities."[11]

The points of entry for young Americans discovering Cézanne, as so beautifully explored in the 2009–10 exhibition "Cézanne and American Modernism," were nearly infinite in possibility, some of a profound and lasting manner, others of a transient passage through a magnetic field.[12] The most literal product of Prendergast's infatuation with Cézanne are a small number of still lifes made between 1910 and 1913,[13] nearly all abounding with apples, that stand as testament to his "instinct for structure,"[14] something Pach would observe to be his greatest link to Cézanne (figs. 28, 29). The present exhibition affords us another chance to explore the Cézanne connections through its focus on the sea and "bathers," a favored subject, of course, for Cézanne, who gave it nearly a third of his working effort over his long life.[15]

Compared, for example, with an oil sketch by Cézanne (fig. 30), very simi-lar to one shown at the Armory Show in 1913,[16] the compositional arrangement of

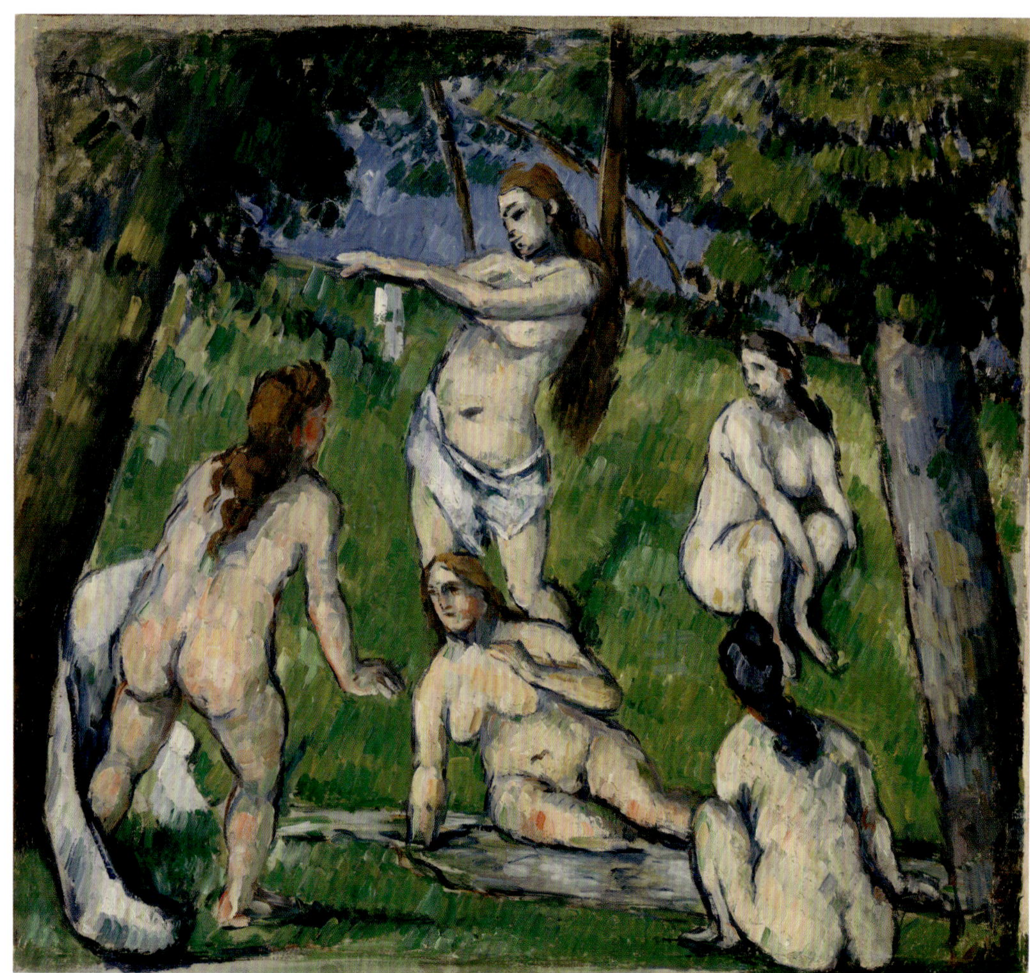

Fig. 30. Paul Cézanne, *Five Bathers*,
1877–78. Oil on canvas, 16 × 16⅞ in.
(40.6 × 42.9 cm). The Barnes Foundation,
Philadelphia (BF93)

Fig. 31. Maurice Prendergast, *Bathers
by the Sea*, c. 1910–13. Oil on canvas,
31 × 35⅛ in. (78.7 × 89.2 cm). Williams
College Museum of Art, Williamstown,
Massachusetts; Gift of Mrs. Charles
Prendergast (83.20.1)

Prendergast's *Bathers by the Sea* (fig. 31) is enough to support some general dependence on Cézanne on the part of Prendergast, but hardly the intense attention to the still lifes, which have a quality of "homage."[17] Prendergast was, I think, too sophisticated and knowing— freed by a large pool of aesthetic or narrative encounters—to hold to one dominant source for long. Wattenmaker has justly underscored the ease with which Prendergast moved through all of those advanced figures, past or present, who now form part of the modernist road map: "Trecento and Quattrocento frescoes, Carpaccio, Giorgione, Poussin, Watteau, Puvis de Chavannes, Cézanne, Renoir, Gauguin, and Maurice Denis among the classicists [fig. 25], and others such as Monticelli, Conder, Cross, K.-X. Roussel, Bonnard, and Charles Guérin."[18] And I would suggest that if one had to point to his most frequent compass, it would be to Renoir. A walk through the Barnes Foundation collection will confirm this; twenty-one Prendergast paintings hang evenhandedly between Cézanne and Renoir, but it is Renoir who more often makes the best comparison, even as Seurat, Puvis de Chavannes, and especially Matisse are brought in to dispel a too simplistic view of the puzzle of begats.

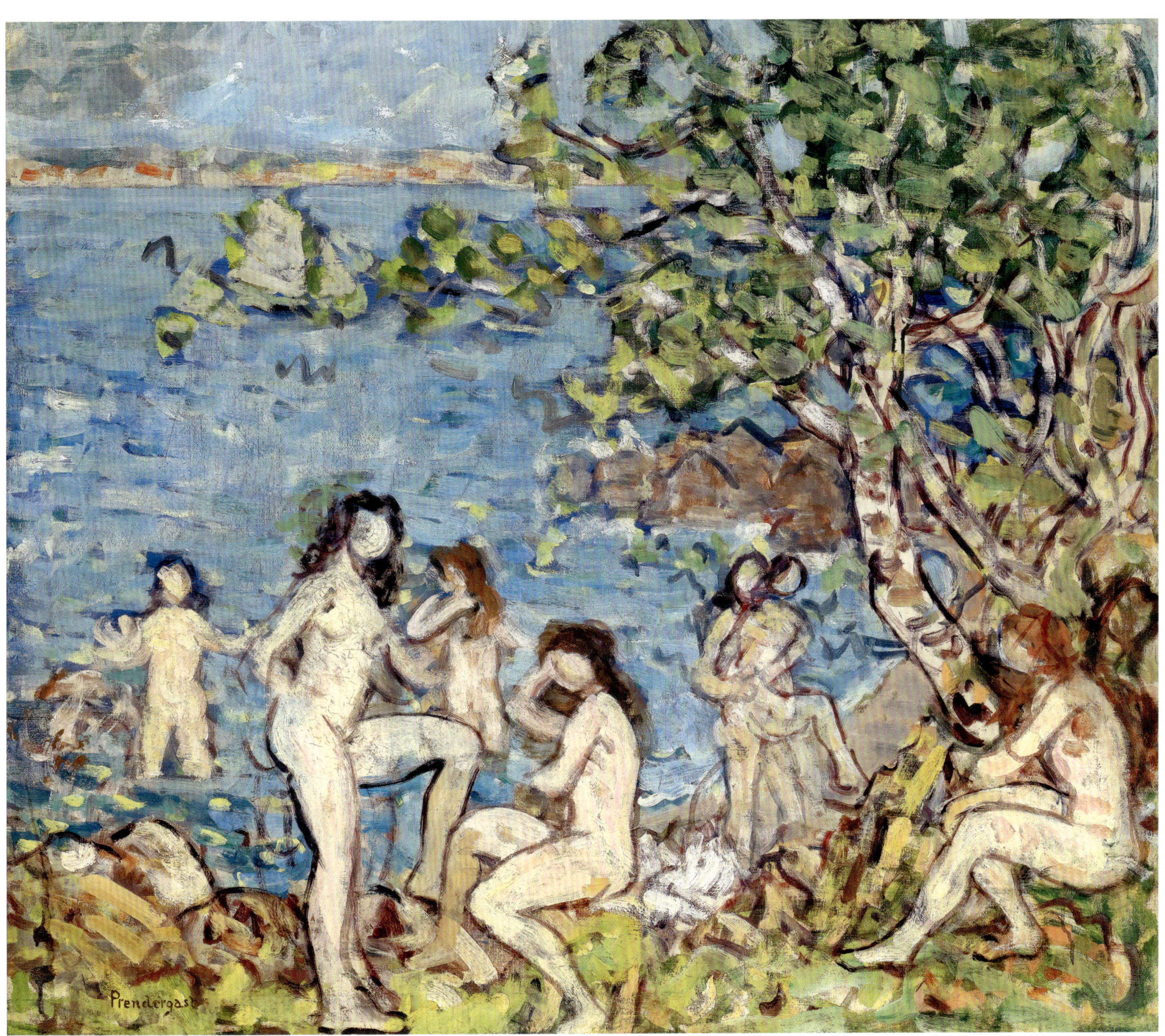

Prendergast

Some of the notions in play here were the foundation of a recent exhibition in Philadelphia, "Gauguin, Cézanne, Matisse: Visions of Arcadia,"[19] which may prove useful to bring up here since, while it did not involve American art, either historical or modern, it did attempt to reintroduce the idea of "text"—which is to say a suggested or implied narrative—into some of the most celebrated heroes of modern, formal constructions. This was not an issue ever repressed, in fact, but one set aside, to some degree, particularly since the 1940s, by the theoretical march to abstraction. The idea of an idyllic place almost but not completely out of time, as described by Virgil in his *Eclogues*, was a subject that could be (and has been) pursued in American art, two opposing and disparate examples being Frederic Edwin Church's vision of unpeopled nature as a kind of eternal paradise (*Sunset in the Berkshire Hills*, 1857, Woodmere Art Museum, Philadelphia) and, on the other end, Thomas Eakins's depiction of piping Pans in a bosky grove, cameras in the wings (*Arcadia*, c. 1883, The Metropolitan Museum of Art, New York). Neither of which gets one far with Prendergast, other than to say that there was a foundation for pastoral pursuits well instituted in nineteenth-century America to support his own explorations in that direction.

To return to the Cézanne/Renoir/Prendergast triangle, my clear bias is that, despite all the arguments to the contrary, Renoir holds the firmer ground as the preferred companion, particularly in this context, where nude bathers abound (compare, for example, fig. 32 and plate 57).[20] Cézanne is, on an emotional and

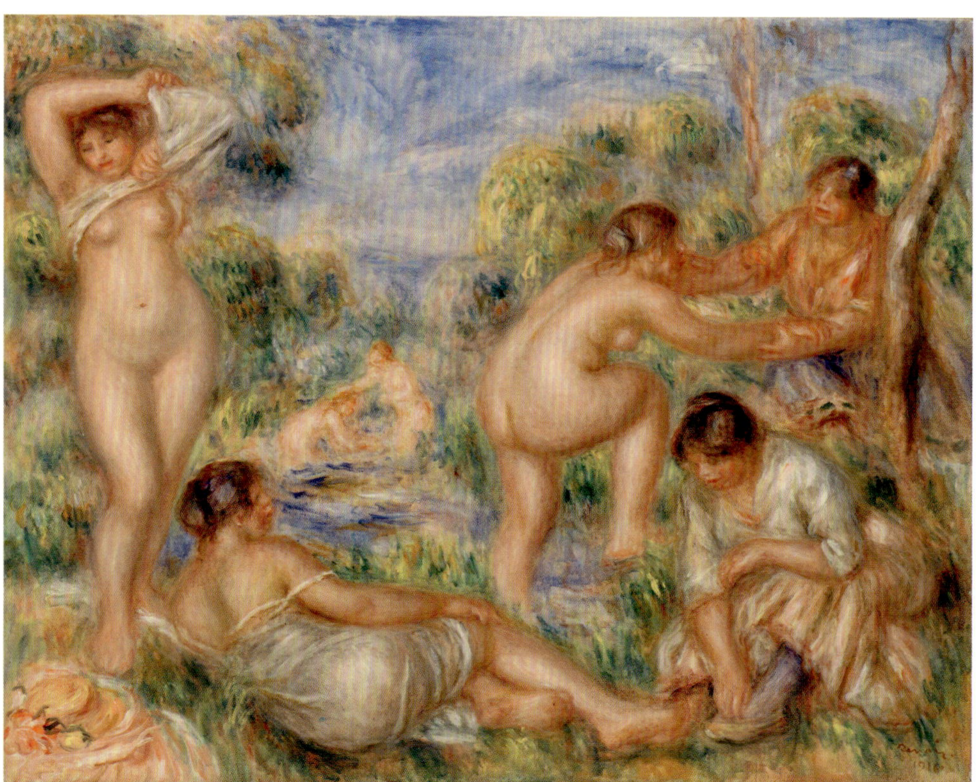

Fig. 32. Pierre-Auguste Renoir, *Bathing Group*, 1916. Oil on canvas, 28¹⁵⁄₁₆ × 36⁷⁄₁₆ in. (73.5 × 92.5 cm). The Barnes Foundation, Philadelphia (BF709)

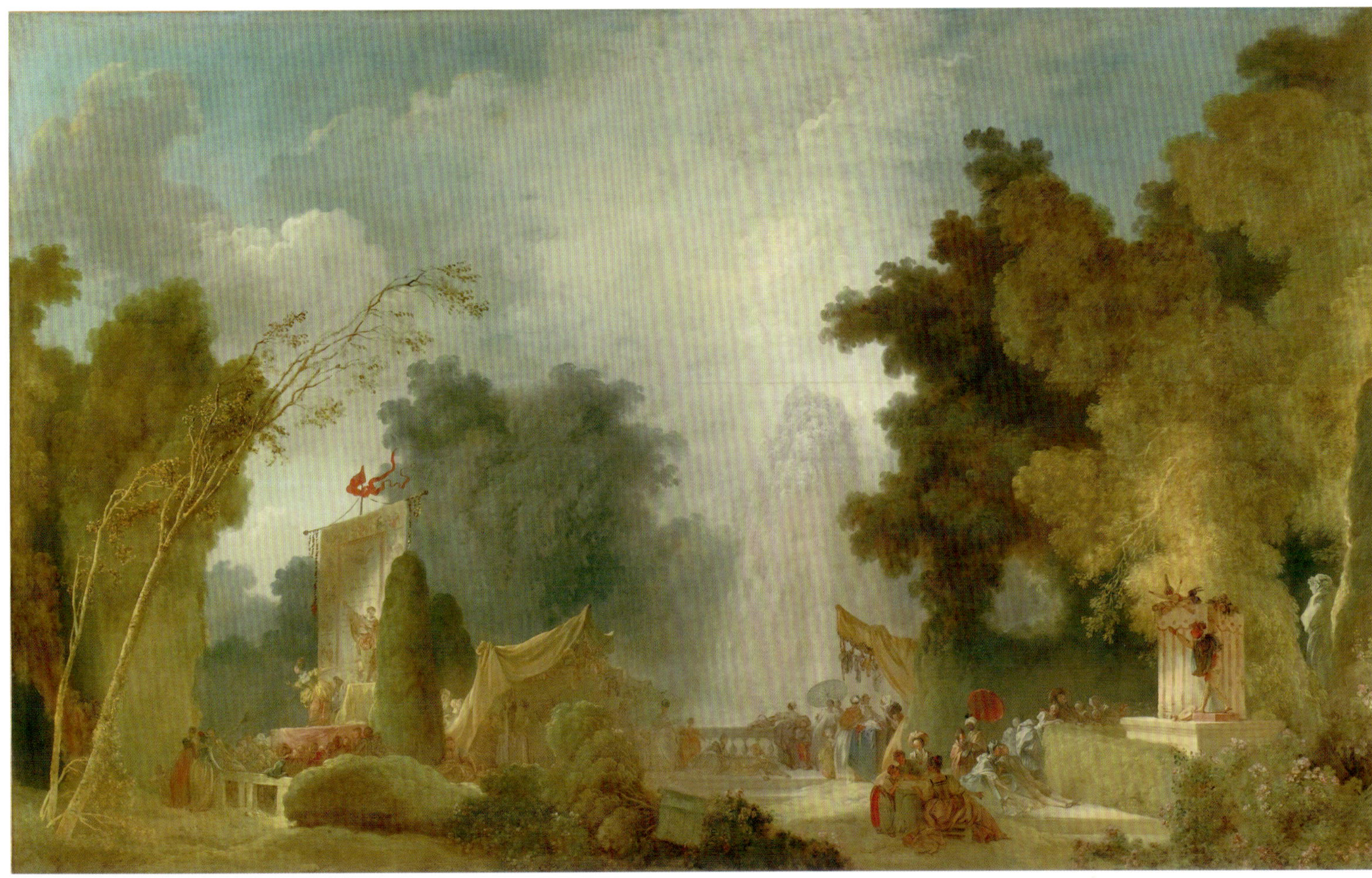

poetic level, the direct heir of Nicolas Poussin—the elevated patrician whose heroes
are stern players in the game—just as Renoir comes out of the more lyrical tradition
of the pastoral, kin to the arcadian but more playful and keen to please, with its
artistic groundings in sixteenth-century Venice, going into full bloom with Watteau
and Fragonard in the eighteenth century.[21] Is Prendergast not often inventing his
own Cytherean world of the *fête galante*?[22] This said remembering that, as keen as
Prendergast was about so much of what he saw in France during his visits, it was the
Watteaus in the Louvre that especially caught his interest, along with the Chardin-
Fragonard exhibition in 1907, where he saw Fragonard's enormous *Fête at Saint-Cloud*
(fig. 33), from the Banque de France, for the first time.[23] A template of sorts for his own
civilized and merry depictions, *Fête at Saint-Cloud* set Prendergast into a charmed
world celebrated as well by Renoir, who was an unabashed defender of the eighteenth century, vigilant against modernization, be it street lights or automobiles, and,
one often forgets, Cézanne's best and most loyal friend.[24] So our enigma—subject vs.
making—perhaps becomes a still nicer thing to muse about, particularly on the beach.

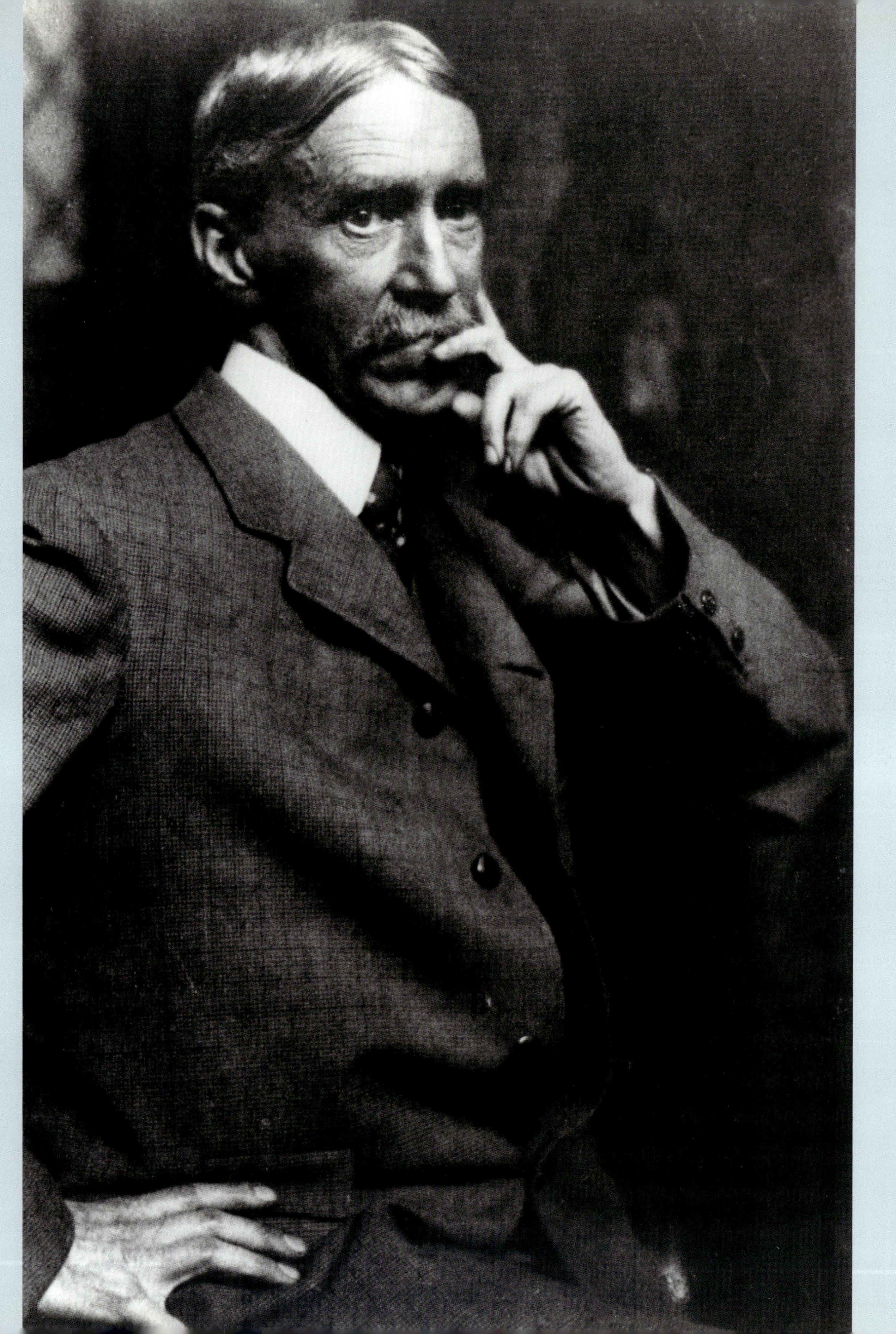

CHRONOLOGY

1858   Maurice Brazil Prendergast and his twin sister, Lucy Catherine (died c. 1877), are born and baptized on October 10 in St. John's, Newfoundland, then a colony of British North America.

1863   Charles James Prendergast is born on May 27 and baptized in St. John's on June 24.

1868   In November, the Prendergast family moves to Boston, where Maurice will live (at various residences) until 1914.

1886–87   Maurice and Charles travel to England on a cattle boat. During these travels, Maurice completes two watercolors of rural scenes in Wales, his first known works of art.

1889   During the summer Maurice paints in Westport, Maine.

1891–94   Maurice and Charles arrive in Paris by January 1891. Maurice studies at the Académies Julian and Colarossi. The brothers meet James W. Morrice, with whom Maurice spends the summers painting at Tréport, Dieppe, and Dinard, along the northwest coast of France. Maurice begins to introduce seaside motifs into his paintings. He returns to Boston on September 1, 1894.

1895   Maurice exhibits watercolors at the Boston Arts Club ("Fifty-Second Exhibition," April 6–27), the first known exhibition to include his work.

1898–99   In July 1898 Maurice travels to Italy, visiting Venice, Padua, Florence, Siena, Orvieto, Rome, Naples, and Capri before returning home in November of 1899. While he is abroad, sixteen of his watercolors are shown at the Eastman Chase Gallery, Boston, likely his first solo exhibition.

1900   Maurice's first major exhibition of watercolors and monotypes opens at the Macbeth Gallery, New York (March 9–24).

Fig. 34. Attributed to Gertrude Stanton Käsebier, *Maurice Prendergast*, c. 1907. Williams College Museum of Art, Prendergast Archive and Study Center, Williamstown, Massachusetts; Gift of Mrs. Charles Prendergast (A.1.5)

1901   Maurice wins a bronze medal at the Pan-American Exposition in Buffalo, New York.

1904   Maurice exhibits six paintings of seaside promenades at the National Arts Club, New York, and becomes associated with members of the group of influential American artists known as the "red hots" (later "The Eight"), including Robert Henri, William J. Glackens, George Luks, John Sloan, and Arthur B. Davies.

1905–6   Maurice and Charles reside at 56 Mount Vernon Street, Boston, where they will remain until moving to New York in 1914. In an effort to protect his health and cure his loss of hearing, Maurice joins the "L Street Brownies," a Boston swimming club, and begins a swimming and sunning regimen.

1907   Maurice sails to France on May 19 and arrives in Le Havre on May 28. His itinerary includes Saint-Malo, Versailles, and Paris, where he is impressed by a Cézanne watercolor exhibition as well as the Salon du Champ de Mars. He also sees fifty-six Cézannes at the Salon d'Automne. Having painted in Saint-Malo and Paris, Maurice returns home in early November.

1908   Sixteen of Maurice's paintings are included in an exhibition at the Macbeth Gallery, New York (February 3–17), known as "The Eight" show. Maurice visits the Glackens family in Yarmouth, Massachusetts, on Cape Cod.

1911   Charles sails to Italy in mid-June. Maurice joins him in Capri in August, stopping in Rome and Florence en route to Venice. Maurice becomes ill and has prostate surgery in Venice.

1912   Upon his return from Venice, on January 31, Maurice accepts an invitation to join the Association of American Painters and Sculptors. He is appointed to the foreign and American selection committees for the upcoming Armory Show.

   Maurice spends the summer with the Glackens family in Bellport, New York, on Long Island. In the fall, Dr. Albert C. Barnes purchases the first of several works by Maurice for his private collection.

1913   Maurice exhibits in the landmark Armory Show (February 17–March 15).
Maurice and Charles spend part of the summer in Brooksville, Maine.

1914   Maurice makes his last trip to France, arriving in the spring and returning
in mid-October. He spends time in Paris and visits Saint-Malo, Roscoff,
Concarneau, and locations in Brittany.

On November 1, Maurice and Charles move to New York and take up
residence at 50 Washington Square South, the same building in which
William Glackens lives.

Maurice is elected president of the Association of American Painters
and Sculptors on May 17.

1915   A retrospective exhibition at Carroll Galleries, New York (February 15–
March 6), the largest show of Maurice's works to date, includes twenty-
nine paintings and thirty-one watercolors.

Maurice and Charles are in Ogunquit, Maine, in early August. Maurice
visits Walt Kuhn, an American painter and one of the organizers of the
Armory Show, and his family in York Village, Maine.

1917   Maurice summers in Annisquam and Gloucester, Massachusetts.

1919   Maurice is appointed to the Advisory Board of the Society of Independent
Artists. He exhibits in Boston, Chicago, Detroit, Buffalo, Washington, D.C.,
Philadelphia, St. Louis, Toledo, Rochester, and the Musée du Luxembourg,
Paris.

1920   Maurice exhibits two paintings at the Venice Biennale.

1921   A joint exhibition of the work of Maurice and Charles is held at Brummer
Gallery, New York (April 4–23).

1923   Maurice is awarded the third William A. Clark Prize and a bronze medal
from the Corcoran Gallery of Art, Washington, D.C.

1924   Maurice Prendergast dies on February 1 in New York, survived by Charles
(died 1948).

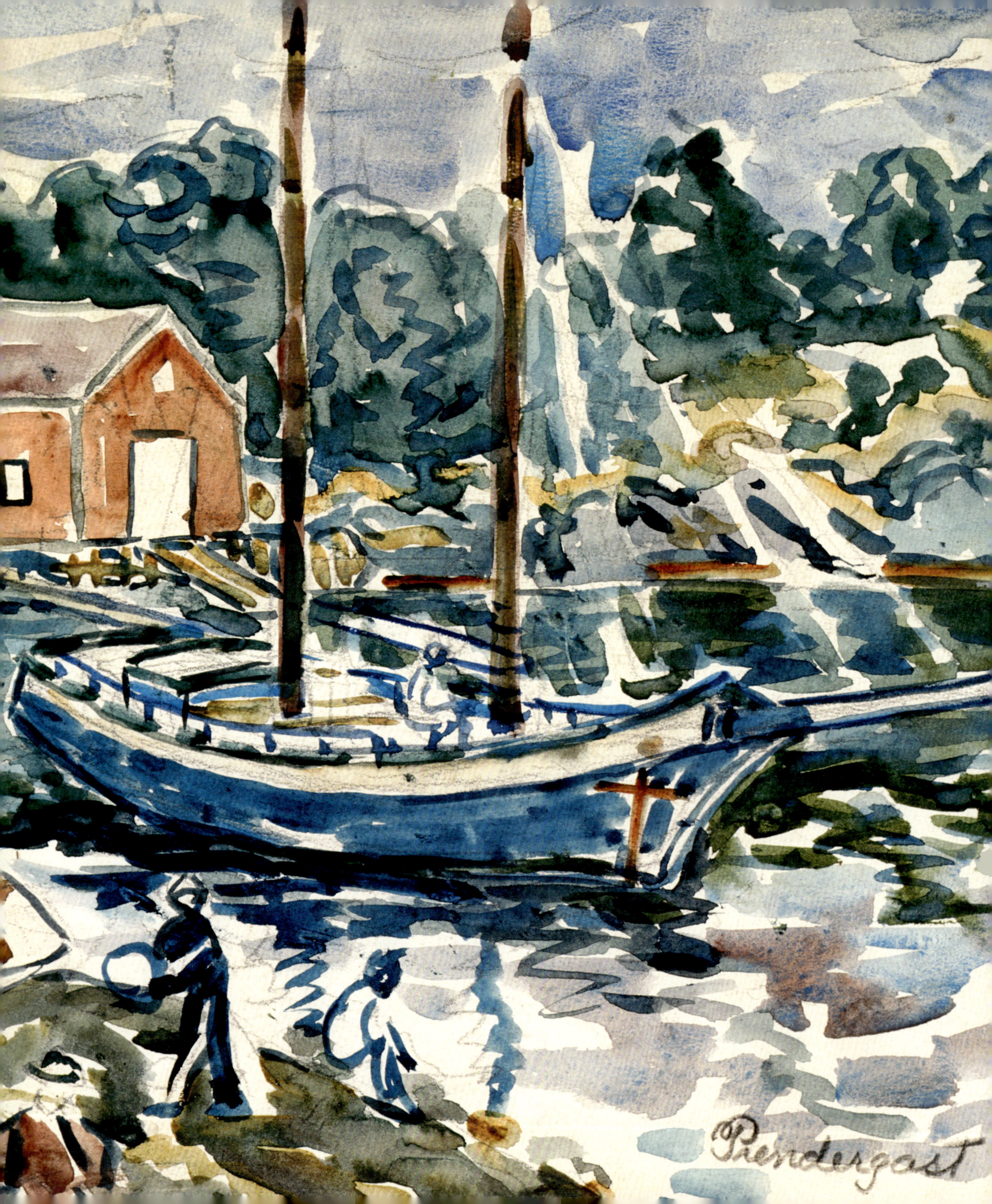
Prendergast

NOTES

Frequently cited sources are abbreviated as follows:

CR: Carol Clark, Nancy Mowll Mathews, and Gwendolyn Owens, *Maurice Brazil Prendergast, Charles Prendergast: A Catalogue Raisonné* (Williamstown, Massachusetts: Williams College Museum of Art, 1990)

Prendergast 1994: Richard J. Wattenmaker, *Maurice Prendergast* (New York: Harry N. Abrams, in association with The National Museum of American Art, Smithsonian Institution, 1994)

Wattenmaker 2010: Richard J. Wattenmaker, *American Paintings and Works on Paper in the Barnes Foundation* (Merion, Pennsylvania: The Barnes Foundation, in association with Yale University Press, 2010)

AAA: Papers held by the Archives of American Art, Smithsonian Institution, Washington, D.C.

CROWDS BY THE SEA

1. It is debatable whether an explanation is even needed. As Theodore Stebbins has observed: "Whistler, Sargent, Prendergast . . . disagreed on questions of style but were unified in finding the harbors, rivers, and even the open sea symbolic of very little, but rather most appropriate for recreational activities. . . . In most of these late [nineteenth-century] works, lakes, harbors, and ocean were included in compositions largely for the light-filled reflective surfaces they provide to the painter . . . , or simply as a backdrop, as in several of the works by Prendergast already mentioned." Theodore E. Stebbins Jr., preface to Stebbins and Derrick R. Cartwright, *Waves and Waterways: American Perspectives, 1850–1900* (Giverny: Musée d'Art Américaine de Giverny, in association with Terra Foundation for the Arts, 2000), p. 13.

2. The seaside works of artists such as Homer, Bellows, and Hopper celebrate the ocean for its unspoiled qualities, continuing a tradition of American seaside paintings that reached back more than 150 years. See Thomas Dennenberg, ed., *Weatherbeaten: Winslow Homer and Maine* (New Haven: Yale University Press, 2012); Kathleen Foster, *Shipwreck!: Winslow Homer and the Lifeline* (Philadelphia: Philadelphia Museum of Art, 2012); Sophie Lévy, ed., *Winslow Homer: Poet of the Sea* (Giverny: Musée d'Américaine, in association with University of Chicago Press, 2006); Sarah Cash, "Life at Sea, 1911–1917," in *George Bellows*, exh. cat. (Washington, D.C.: National Gallery of Art; DelMonico Books-Prestel, 2012),

pp. 159–66; Cartwright, *Waves and Waterways*; Harold B. Nelson, *Sounding the Depths: 150 Years of American Seascape* (San Francisco: Chronicle Books, in association with the American Federation of Arts, 1989).

3. Both artists exhibited in a two-person show at the Art Institute of Chicago in 1900. Murphy was also a co-owner, with Charles Prendergast, of a successful frame shop, which in 1905 moved to Boston. Trevor J. Fairbrother et al., *Bostonians: Painters of an Elegant Age, 1870–1930* (Boston: Museum of Fine Arts, 1986), pp. 219–20.

4. John Sloan, "Gist of Art: Principles and Practise Expounded in the Classroom and Studio," recorded with the assistance of Helen Farr (New York: American Artists Group, 1939), p. 218.

5. Richard J. Wattenmaker, "William Glackens's Beach Scenes at Bellport," in *Smithsonian Studies in American Art* 2 (Spring 1988), pp. 75–94.

6. "For the Americans, the French Impressionist commitment to landscape offered a corrective to the academic emphasis on the figure and encouragement to return to the traditionally American theme of nature. The French Impressionists showed Americans how to create an American art." H. Barbara Weinberg, Doreen Bolger, and David Park Curry, *American Impressionism and Realism: The Painting of Modern Life, 1885–1915*, exh. cat. (New York: The Metropolitan Museum of Art, 1994), p. 32.

7. A recent study of the political implications of paintings of the New England landscape in American art between the 1890s and the 1920s does not include Prendergast's work: Julia B. Rosenbaum, *Visions of Belonging: New England Art and the Making of American Identity* (Ithaca, New York: Cornell University Press, 2006).

8. Dominic Madormo, "The 'Butterfly Artist': Maurice Prendergast and His Critics," in *CR*, p. 62.

9. Weinberg, Bolger, and Curry, *The Painting of Modern Life*, p. 8.

10. Jean-Jacques Rousseau, "Letter to M. D'Alembert on the Theatre," quoted in James A. Leith, *Space and Revolution: Projects for Monuments, Squares, and Public Buildings in France, 1789–1799* (Montreal: McGill-Queen's University Press, 1991), p. 36. The complete letter is translated in Jean-Jacques Rousseau, *Politics and the Arts: Letter to M. D'Alembert on the Theatre*, translated with notes and an introduction by Allan Bloom (Ithaca, New York: Cornell University Press, 1968).

11. Charles Baudelaire, *The Painter of Modern Life and Other Essays*, trans. and ed. Jonathan Mayne (London: Phaidon, 1964), p. 9. For the original, see Baudelaire, *Œuvre complètes, texte établi, présenté et annoté par Claude Pichois* (Paris: Gallimard, 1976 [Bibliothèque de la Pléiade]), p. 691: "Pour le parfait flâneur, pour l'observateur passionné, c'est une immense jouissance que l'élire domicile dans le nombre, dans l'ondoyant, dans le movement, dans le fugitive et l'infini."

12. *Whitmanarchive.org/published/LG/1860/poems/122* and *Whitmanarchive.org/criticism/current/encyclopedia/entry_10.html* [1/16/2013].

13. Christian Borch, *The Politics of Crowds: An Alternative History of Sociology* (Cambridge, United Kingdom: Cambridge University Press, 2012), p. 130. Borch comments on Melville's interpretation of crowds as a predecessor to Whitman's on p. 129, n. 2.

14. Ibid., p. 137.

15. Ibid., p. 140.

16. Duncan Phillips, "Maurice Prendergast," *The Arts* (March 1924), in David W. Scott, *Maurice Prendergast*, with a reprinted essay by Duncan Phillips compiled and edited by Willem de Looper, Martha Carey, and Jan Lancaster (Mount Vernon, New York: The Artist's Limited Edition, a Medænas Monograph on the Arts, produced with The Phillips Collection, Washington, D.C., 1980), p. 12.

17. David W. Scott, "Maurice Prendergast," in Erika D. Passentino, ed., *The Eye of Duncan Phillips: A Collection in the Making* (Washington, D.C.: The Phillips Collection, in association with Yale University Press, 1999), p. 309.

18. Andrew McClellan, "A Brief History of the Art Museum Public," in Andrew McClellan, ed., *Art and Its Publics: Museum Studies at the Millenium*, 3rd ed. (Malden, Massachusetts: Blackwell, 2006), p. 19. Prendergast moved to New York in 1914 and died there in 1924.

19. In the mid-1890s, "Prendergast established a consistent pattern of placing his work before the public. He entered watercolors and monotypes in group shows in Boston, Philadelphia, and New York, subsequently assembling solo exhibitions in both private galleries and museums across the country. . . . He assiduously maintained this approach throughout his life." *Prendergast* 1994, p. 33.

20. *Museum of Fine Arts Bulletin VII* (1909), p. 19, quoted in McClellan, ed., *Art and Its Publics*, p. 58.

21. For Albert C. Barnes and Prendergast, see Richard J. Wattenmaker, "Maurice B. Prendergast (1858–1924)", in Wattenmaker 2010, pp. 143–48. For Duncan Phillips and Prendergast, see Scott, "Maurice Prendergast," p. 309.

22. "In some deep and essential sense, crowds *are* modernity. Modern times are crowded times." Jeffrey T. Schnapp and Matthew Tiews, "Introduction: A Book of Crowds," in Schnapp and Tiews, eds., *Crowds* (Stanford: Stanford University Press, 2006), p. X.

23. Herman Melville, *Moby Dick; or, The Whale*, chapter 1, p. 3.

PRENDERGAST: CHANGE AND SEA-CHANGE

1. Frederick James Gregg, "Maurice B. Prendergast," *Maurice B. Prendergast: Paintings in Oil and Watercolors* (New York: Carroll Galleries, 1915).

2. See also "Maurice Prendergast Is King at the Montross Gallery," *American Art News* 17 (January 11, 1919), p. 2.

3. Not all American writers on modern art at the time agreed with this assessment. Willard Huntington Wright (brother of Stanton MacDonald-Wright), for instance, in *Modern Art: Its Tendency and Meaning* (New York: John Lane Company, 1915) classified Prendergast as one of "the lesser moderns" (pp. 221–22). But Prendergast had powerful admirers, such as Walter Pach and John Quinn, who made him one of the most sought-after contemporary artists in the mid-1910s in New York. He and his brother, Charles, a fellow artist and frame maker with whom he lived and worked, were not only successful in exhibiting and selling but were chosen to be leaders of arts organizations and socialized with a stellar array of arts personalities. A gathering in November 1915 at the home of Walter Pach, for example, included the French artists Marcel Duchamp and Albert Gleizes, the American artist George Of, the American critic Henry McBride, and the Prendergast brothers. See Laurette McCarthy, *Walter Pach: The Armory Show and the Untold Story of Modern Art in America* (University Park: The Pennsylvania State University Press, 2011), p. 91.

4. Actually the word he uses is "represensation," which may have been a typo but is an intriguing word nevertheless.

5. From New York Prendergast wrote to John Quinn on September 7, 1915, "as a painter I like the surroundings of Boston the best, Cohasset, Marblehead, and Salem, especially appeal to me." John Quinn Papers, 1901–26, New York Public Library.

6. Maurice Denis, "Definition du Neo-Traditionisme," in *Art et critique* (August 1890), in Linda Nochlin, *Impressionism and Post-Impressionism, 1874–1904* (Englewood Cliffs, New Jersey: Prentice-Hall, 1966), p. 187.

7. For more on Prendergast and Dow, see Mathews, "Prendergast in Italy," in *Prendergast in Italy* (London and New York: Merrell Publishers, Ltd., 2009), pp. 25–26.

8. According to Bryant F. Tolles in *Summer by the Seaside: The Architecture of New England Coastal Resort Hotels, 1820–1950* (Lebanon, New Hampshire: University Press of New England, 2008), the Jocelyn House was built in 1890 and the Checkley House had undergone a major enlargement in 1895 (pp. 148–49).

9. Information on Prendergast at Brook's Cove comes from Hedley Howll Rhys, "Maurice Prendergast: The Sources and Development of His Style," Ph.D. diss. (Cambridge, Massachusetts: Harvard University, 1952), pp. 24–25.

10. For Prendergast and the leisure reform movements of the turn of the century, see Mathews, *The Art of Leisure: Maurice Prendergast in the Williams College Museum of Art* (Williamstown, Massachusetts: Williams College Museum of Art, 1999).

11. George Bellows to Joseph Taylor, April 20, 1910, in *Prendergast* 1994, p. 103 and n. 97.

12. Ibid.

13. "Exhibition of Watercolors and Monotypes in Color by Maurice B. Prendergast," Macbeth Gallery, New York, March 9–24, 1900.

14. Maurice Prendergast to J. Montgomery Sears, February 24, 1900, private collection, quoted in Erica Hirshler, "The Fine Art of Sarah Choate Sears," *The Magazine Antiques* (September 2001), pp. 320–29.

15. For instance, in 1909 he exhibited at the Rand School of Social Science ("Exhibition of Paintings, Sculptures, Etchings, and Drawings," New York, May [?]–June 1) and in 1915 at the People's Art Guild (November).

16. "Exhibition of Henri, Sloan, Glackens, Davies, Luks, Prendergast," National Arts Club, New York, January 1904, and "Exhibition of Paintings, by Arthur B. Davies, William J. Glackens, Robert Henri, Ernest Lawson, George Luks, Maurice B. Prendergast, Everett Shinn, John Sloan," Macbeth Gallery, New York, February 3–15, 1908.

17. Many of these are now in the Prendergast Archive and Study Center, Williams College Museum of Art, including Julius Maier-Graefe, *Der Moderne Impressionismus* (Berlin: Bard, J., [1904]), and Prendergast's own handwritten translation of Emile Bernard's article "Paul Cézanne," *L'Occident* (July 1904), pp. 17–30. See Mathews, "Maurice Prendergast and the Influence of European Modernism," in *CR*, pp. 35–45.

18. "Work by Henri Matisse," *American Art News* 6 (April 11, 1908), p. 6.

19. "Fourteenth Annual Exhibition of Paintings by Prominent Artists," Poland Spring Art Gallery, South Poland, Maine, opened July 27, 1908. He also exhibited there in 1906 at the "Twelfth Annual Exhibition, etc. . . . ."

20. "An Exhibition of Paintings by a Group of Boston Artists," Macbeth Gallery, New York, April 16–29, 1909.

21. Emile Bernard, "Paul Cézanne," *L'Occident* (July 1904), in Michael Doran, *Conversations with Cézanne* (Berkeley and Los Angeles: University of California Press, 2001), p. 36. Prendergast wrote out his own translation of this article (see above, note 17), but it is rough and difficult to understand.

22. "Exhibition of Independent Artists," New York, April 1–27, 1910.

23. "International Exhibition of Modern Art," Association of American Painters and Sculptors, New York, February 17–March 15, 1913.

24. James Huneker, *Promenades of an Impressionist* (New York: Charles Scribner's Sons, 1910), p. 4.

25. See Shelley Baranowski and Ellen Furlough, *Being Elsewhere* (Ann Arbor: The University of Michigan Press, 2004), or Alison Russell, *Crossing Boundaries: Postmodern Travel Literature* (New York: Palgrave, 2000).

26. Charles Hovey Pepper to William Macbeth, in *Prendergast* 1994, p. 112.

27. Few of Prendergast's works have titles that can be documented as given by the artist. Most were applied later by his brother Charles, Eugénie Prendergast (Charles's wife), or Prendergast's dealers.

28. For changes in New England tourism, see Dona Brown, *Inventing New England: Regional Tourism in the Nineteenth Century* (Washington, D. C.: Smithsonian Institution Press, 1995), esp. chap. 6, "The Problem of the Summer: Race, Class, and the Colonial Vacation in Southern Maine," pp. 169–200.

29. For instance, X-rays have shown that *The Cove* (c. 1918–23, Whitney Museum of American Art, New York) is painted over *The Beach*, a work illustrated in the exhibition catalogue for the "Thirteenth Annual Exhibition" at the Albright Gallery, Buffalo, May 24–September 8, 1919.

30. *Prendergast* 1994, p. 137 and n. 135.

31. Charles Hovey Pepper, "Is Drawing to Disappear in Artistic Individuality?" *The World To-Day* 19 (July 1910), p. 719.

"AUDACITIES": MAURICE PRENDERGAST AND THE CULTURE OF FIN-DE-SIÈCLE BOSTON

1. Walter Pach, *Queer Thing Painting: Forty Years in the World of Art* (New York: Harper and Brothers, 1938), p. 224. As early as 1909 the devoted Pach chided the Boston museum for not owning a painting by his colleague. Prendergast's art, he hinted, was more sturdy, powerful, and joyous than most of the pictures by contemporary Bostonians that the institution had already purchased. See Pach, "Boston's New Museum of Fine Arts," *Harper's Weekly* 53 (December 18, 1909), p. 16.

2. The import of this mural commission for progressive local artists is evident in a letter that Arthur Wesley Dow wrote to the Boston press after hearing a rumor that Puvis de Chavannes might create a decoration for the new public library. He welcomed this "true poet and true artist" and likened his achievements to "the art of the greatest Italians, like Giotto, Piero della Francesca, Filippo Lippi, Botticelli, Titian, and the greatest Japanese masters like Tanyu and Yeitoku, some of whose marvelous works in gold and color are now in the [Boston] Art Museum."

What the Frenchman shared with these figures, Dow argued, was a commitment to work that is "abstract, spiritual, [and] full of infinite meaning." Arthur W. Dow, "To the Editor of the Transcript," *Boston Evening Transcript*, January 23, 1892, p. 9.

3. "Reviews of Recent Publications," *The Studio* 7 (April 1896), p. 191.

4. The exhibition and the local "patrons and patronesses" are noted in "Works of Modern Painters," *Boston Sunday Herald*, March 6, 1898, p. 26. Isabella Stewart Gardner lent two landscapes by Whistler.

5. Frank T. Robinson, *Living New England Artists* (Boston: Samuel E. Cassino, 1888), pp. 101–6.

6. Progressive artists felt free to change nature's "true" or objective colors to achieve harmony between design and color. Having described the best modern posters as "veritable frescoes comforting to behold," one critic observed: "What matter if a sky be green, trees red, coursers and animals of mystic forest blue, running water a yellow sulphur tint, if the general effect of the fresco is enveloped in a pleasing atmosphere of gradations, and produces a startling unearthly impression." Octave Uzanne, "Eugène Grasset and Decorative Art in France," *The Studio* 4 (November 1894), p. 46.

7. On Prendergast's Boston contemporaries, see Trevor J. Fairbrother et al., *The Bostonians: Painters of an Elegant Age, 1870–1930* (Boston: Museum of Fine Arts, 1986), pp. 56–63.

8. "Exhibition by Messrs. Brackett, Prendergast, Noyes, and Burdick," *Boston Evening Transcript*, April 30, 1897, p. 2. Charles Peabody, "The Arts," *Time and the Hour* 9 (April 29, 1899), p. 11. "Fourteenth Annual Exhibition of the Watercolor Club," *Boston Evening Transcript*, March 2, 1901, p. 9.

9. "Exhibition of Things That Loom in the Spring Ha-Ha!" Copley Society, Boston, April 1–12, 1902 (pl. no. 80). Other spoofs on contemporary painters' names were Clawed Money, Herman Dubbed-the-Murky, F. W. Been-Seen, Mr. Tin Whistle, Mary Cusset, and J. J. Any-old-thing.

10. In early 1896 works by Mrs. J. Montgomery Sears and by Prendergast were included in the annual exhibition of the Boston Water Color Club. Sarah Sears owned at least ten of Maurice's works on paper, and supposedly she helped finance his trip to Italy in 1898–99. In the 1890s Sears was a patron of the modern painters Frits Thaulow and John Singer Sargent; she also joined the Boston Pictorialist photographer F. Holland Day in trying (unsuccessfully) to initiate an exhibition program for photography at the Museum of Fine Arts, Boston.

11. Quoted in Hedley Howell Rhys, *Maurice Prendergast* (Cambridge, Massachusetts: Harvard University Press, 1960), p. 38.

12. "Exhibition of the Eight," *Boston Evening Transcript*, February 6, 1908, p. 11. The Macbeth Gallery, New York, hosted the exhibition. At forty-nine, Prendergast was the oldest member of the Eight, and the only Bostonian. Unlike George Luks, William Glackens, Everett Shinn, and John Sloan, he did not work as an illustrator for newspapers and magazines. Indeed, his pictures diverged from the dark, Manet-inspired realist paintings that made the event so newsworthy. Prendergast may have been one of the oddballs, but, as Robert Henri, the group's most conspicuous figure, liked to declare: "We've come together because we're so unalike."

13. Letter from Prendergast to Albert C. Barnes, March 4, 1915, quoted in Wattenmaker 2010, p. 146.

MAURICE PRENDERGAST: THEME AND VARIATIONS

1. See, for example, *CR* 9–18 (watercolors) and *CR* 1584 and 1585 (monotypes); see also Carol Clark, *American Drawings and Watercolors in the Robert Lehman Collection* VIII (New York: The Metropolitan Museum of Art, 1992), no. 3, "Paris Sketchbook 1891–94" (*CR* 1476), pp. 7–59.

2. *South Boston* is dated c. 1900–1902 in *CR* (1754) but is probably earlier (c. 1897). *After the Storm* (*CR* 36, recto) is dated c. 1901–3 in *Prendergast* 1994 (pp. 75–77) and c. 1902–6 in *CR* (p. 221), but based on a review published in *The Chicago Tribune* (November 7, 1897), it would appear that both datings are too late. The review is accompanied by a satirical sketch captioned "308 'The Hilarious Shrimps' by M.B. Prendergast." The painting to which it refers was given the title *The Beach, Marine Park* (n.d.) in the "Tenth Annual Exhibition of Oil Paintings and Sculpture by American Artists," The Art Institute of Chicago, Nov. 2–Dec. 12, 1897 (no. 308). This anecdotal evidence raises the possibility that *The Beach, Marine Park* and *After the Storm* may actually be the same painting, with a date of 1897 at the very latest. The text of the article reads: "Prendergast's two oils may be deemed freakish by many visitors, and they are in a sense freakish, but they are as well original and refreshingly spontaneous. A less able man could not have painted 'The Beach' with its high, well maintained distance, the bulky boats, and the queer children with long, thin legs playing in the water."

3. Maurice Prendergast to the dealer William Macbeth, January 17, 1904, Macbeth Gallery Records, AAA. See *Prendergast* 1994, p. 75 and p. 151, n. 71. For a comprehensive discussion of Prendergast's art education prior to his first stay in Paris, see Ellen M. Glavin, "The Early Art Education of Maurice Prendergast: Art Education in Boston," *Archives of American Art Journal* 33, no. 1 (1993), pp. 2–12.

4. Walter Pach, "Art: The Independents," *The Freeman* II (March 1921), p. 617.

5. Photographs of Maurice and Charles Prendergast in their studio (c. 1900–1903), showing oil paintings hanging frame to frame on the walls behind. See *CR*, pp. 726–27.

6. Terra Foundation for American Art, Chicago, Daniel J. Terra Collection. See *Prendergast* 1994, pp. 73–74, pls. 51, 52, including the preparatory watercolor *The Yacht Race* (c. 1897/ reworked c. 1900; *CR* 673).

7. C. H. Pepper, "Is Drawing to Disappear in Artistic Individuality? A Sketch of the Work of Maurice Prendergast," *The World To-Day* XIX (July 1910), p. 719. Cited in *Prendergast* 1994, p. 150.

8. See *Prendergast* 1994, pp. 74–75 and p. 151, n. 69. See also handwritten invoice and receipt, dated 1905, from Maurice Prendergast to Esther Williams, on which is written: "one oil paint-ing/ 'The Promenade'/ Salem Harbor/ painted in 1904/ by Maurice B. Prendergast" (Esther Baldwin Williams Papers, AAA).

9. Sketchbook, c. 1905–10, *CR* 1483 ("1905 Sketchbook"), Cleveland Museum of Art, Gift of Mrs. Charles Prendergast, 1951 (51.423).

10. Sketchbook, c. 1898–1903, *CR* 1481 ("Sketchbook of Frame Studies"), Williams College Museum of Art, Williamstown, Massachusetts, Gift of Mrs. Charles Prendergast.

11. Charles Hovey Pepper, quoted in Joseph Coburn Smith, *Charles Hovey Pepper* (Portland, Maine: Southwouth-Anthoensen Press, 1945), p. 41. See *Prendergast* 1994, pp. 71, 73, and 151, n. 65.

12. "Les Aquarelles de Cézanne," Galerie Bernheim-Jeune, Paris, June 17–29, 1907.

13. Prendergast Archive and Study Center, Williams College Museum of Art, Williamstown, Massachusetts.

14. Grand Palais, Paris, October 1–22, 1907. Prendergast later had other opportunities to see some of these same works in "Water-colors by Cézanne" at Alfred Steiglitz's Photo-Secession Gallery (March 1–26, 1911) and, on his last trip to France, in "Le paysage du Midi" at Bernheim-Jeune (June 2–16, 1914), which also included works by Renoir, Cross, Bonnard, Denis, Van Gogh, Matisse, Luce, Manguin, Valtat, and Vuillard (see also *Prendergast* 1994, p. 117). In January 1916 he saw an exhibi-tion of Cézanne's paintings and watercolors at the Montross Gallery, where he had exhibited twice in 1915.

15. Maurice Prendergast to Mrs. Oliver E. Williams, October 10, 1907, Esther Baldwin Williams Papers, AAA. Cézanne had died a year before. Prendergast also indicated that he saw the Salon des Indépendants in the spring. See his letter to Walter Pach, December 6, 1909, elaborating on his reaction to Cézanne's oils (*Prendergast* 1994, pp. 99–100). In late August 1908, William Glackens and his family visited Prendergast, "staying in Boston for eight or ten day(s) before leaving for Yarmouth for the summer" (Maurice Prendergast to Mrs. Oliver E. Williams, May 3, 1908, Esther Baldwin Williams Papers, AAA). In early September of that year Prendergast visited the Glackenses on Cape Cod. Glackens, who was at a critical juncture in his development as an artist, was dramatically transforming his work by moving away from the dark palette of the pictures shown earlier that year at Macbeth's to a bright, Impressionist style. His canvas *Race Track* (1908–9) had been withdrawn from the traveling exhibition of The Eight and was in the process of being repainted in this bright new style (see discussion in Wattenmaker 2010, pp. 75–78). Prendergast must have related in detail his reactions to what he had seen in Paris the previous year, notably to Cézanne and contemporary French painting, including the Fauves. Indeed, Prendergast made a series of five pencil sketches in a sketchbook used by Glackens on Cape Cod (Glackens Sketchbook no. 92.52, "W. Glackens Cape Cod 1908," Museum of Art, Fort Lauderdale, Nova Southeastern University). Prendergast took a serious interest in Glackens's work and had an important influence over the future direc-tion of the painter's style. See his letter to Edith [Mrs. William] Glackens (August 26, 1908) stating that he would arrive on September 3 and "shall be interested to see what Glackens has done," in Ira Glackens, *William Glackens and the Ashcan Group* (New York: Crown Publishers, 1957), p. 114. In the late winter of 1908 or early 1909 Maurice wrote a letter introducing Marsden Hartley to Glackens and his colleagues in New York. When Hartley visited the Prendergasts in their studio on Mt. Vernon Street in Boston, he was especially struck by Prendergast's intense enthusiasm in speaking of Cézanne. In an entry in his draft memoirs, *Somehow a Past*, Hartley wrote, "Maurice was a person of fiery enthusiasms as regards painting. . . . He loved Cézanne devoutly—and anything that he thought good must be spoken to the world at once" (see *Prendergast* 1994, pp. 12 and 150, n. 6).

16. Maurice Prendergast to Walter Pach, February 2, 1922, Walter Pach Papers, AAA. See *Prendergast* 1994, p. 146.

17. Albert C. Barnes and Violette de Mazia, *The Art of Cézanne* (New York: Harcourt Brace, 1939), pp. 138–40.

18. Maurice Prendergast to Albert C. Barnes, undated (early 1913), The Barnes Foundation Archives. The painting, *Landscape with Figures* (The Barnes Foundation, inv. no. 480; *CR* 266), was purchased February 17, 1913. A panel, *Seascape—Saint Malo* (The Barnes Foundation, inv. no. 561; *CR* 79), was purchased from William Macbeth on November 6, 1912. See Wattenmaker 2010, pp. 144–45.

19. Other examples from this period include *Beach and Two Houses* (c. 1918, The Barnes Foundation; *CR* 462), *The Cove* (c. 1918–23, Whitney Museum of American Art, New York; *CR* 453), and *Landscape with Figures* (c. 1921, Corcoran Gallery of Art, Washington, D.C.; *CR* 492).

20. At the 1907 Salon d'Automne, Prendergast sketched Matisse's *Le luxe I*, painted at Collioure that year (Musée Nationale d'Art Moderne, Centre Pompidou, Paris), a large, freely drawn seashore composition. See *Prendergast* 1994, p. 87, fig. 65. See also ibid., pp. 114–15, figs. 90, 92, for sketches

of Matisse's *La coiffure* (c. 1907, Staatsgalerie Stuttgart) and *Nasturtiums with "The Dance" II* (1912, The Metropolitan Museum of Art, New York) made at the 1913 Armory Show (nos. 403 and 409, respectively), either at its venue in New York or when the show traveled to Boston. *Le luxe II* (c. 1907–8, Statens Museum for Kunst, Copenhagen) was also in the Armory Show (no. 407).

21. *The New York Times*, January 11, 1920, sec. 9, p. 3.

22. See *Marblehead Harbor* (c. 1918–20; *CR* 1554) and Wattenmaker 2010, pp. 166–67, which illustrates two of the twelve drawings from *Sketchbook 53* (c. 1916–19, Museum of Fine Arts, Boston; *CR* 1546). See also *Prendergast 1994*, pp. 140–41.

23. *The New York World*, February 10, 1924, p. 8. See *Prendergast 1994*, pp. 148–49.

A HAPPY ENIGMA?

1. Prendergast's critical fortunes were established with his very first exhibition, in 1895, when he showed two watercolors at the Boston Art Club. One critic commented: "Another acquisition revealed by this exhibition is that shown in the work of Maurice B. Prendergast, who has lately returned to Boston from his studies in Paris. His *Fishing Boats, Tréport, France* and his *Porte St. Denis* show a finely disciplined sense of pure and brilliant color, subordinated to a vivacious and accurate style of depiction." "The Boston Art Club's Fifty-Second Exhibition," *The Sunday Herald*, April 7, 1895, p. 33, quoted in Dominic Madormo, "The 'Butterfly Artist': Maurice Prendergast and His Critics," in *CR*, p. 60.

2. Walter Pach, "Maurice Prendergast," *Shadowland* 6 (April 1922), pp. 10–11, 74–75.

3. See especially Nancy Mowll Mathews, "Maurice Prendergast and the Influence of European Modernism," in *CR*, pp. 35–45, and *Maurice Prendergast* (Munich: Prestel-Verlag, 1990); Patterson Sims, *Maurice B. Prendergast: A Concentration of Works from the Permanent Collection*, exh. cat. (New York: Whitney Museum of American Art, 1980); Richard J. Wattenmaker, *Prendergast 1994* and "Maurice B. Prendergast (1858–1924)," in Wattenmaker 2010, pp. 143–69.

4. As it emerges with a closer look, Prendergast combined materials in ways that far expanded conventional formulas. On Prendergast's combination of pastel and watercolor, see Innis Howe Shoemaker, "Maurice B. Prendergast, Bathers, New England," in *Adventures in Modern Art: The Charles K. Williams II Collection*, exh. cat. (Philadelphia: Philadelphia Museum of Art, 2009), pp. 233–35.

5. As much as he was portrayed as reclusive, shy, frail and, over time, deaf—"outside the mainstream of American life," in Milton Brown's words—he was very knowing and observant,

demonstrated by the fact that he was the only artist to be placed on the selection committee for both U.S. and foreign submissions to the Armory Show. See Brown, "Maurice B. Prendergast," in *CR*, p. 18, and *Prendergast 1994*, p. 111.

6. Prendergast's commitment to his subject was so insistent that Eleanor Green has described his "many peopled landscapes of interchangeable titles" as almost serial in nature, remarking upon the influence that seeing Monet's Haystacks series exhibited at the Galerie Durand-Ruel in 1891 may have had on the artist. Green, *Maurice Prendergast: Art of Impulse and Color*, exh. cat. ([College Park]: University of Maryland, 1976), p. 24.

7. William Howe Downes, "Four Boston Painters," *Boston Evening Transcript*, January 13, 1914, p. 11, quoted in Madormo, "The 'Butterfly Artist,'" p. 69. Interestingly, Downes had been one of Prendergast's earliest champions in Boston.

8. Pach, "Maurice Prendergast," p. 74, quoted in Nancy Mowll Mathews, "Maurice Prendergast (1858–1924)," in Gail Stavitsky and Katherine Rothkopf, eds., *Cézanne and American Modernism*, exh. cat. (Montclair, New Jersey: Montclair Art Museum; Baltimore: Baltimore Museum of Art, 2009), p. 266.

9. On the making of Cézanne's critical reputation in the twentieth century, see Joseph J. Rishel, "A Century of Cézanne Criticism: From 1907 to the Present," in Françoise Cachin and Joseph J. Rishel, eds., *Cézanne*, exh. cat. (Philadelphia: Philadelphia Museum of Art, 1995), pp. 45–75.

10. Thirteen years after his initial trip to France, from 1891 to 1894, Prendergast arrived in Le Havre on May 28, 1907, and spent time in Paris and Saint-Malo before leaving for America on October 26. The exhibition of seventy-nine watercolors by Cézanne at Bernheim-Jeune ran from June 17 to June 29, just before Prendergast left for Brittany. Prendergast extended his stay in France through the end of October so he could study the works at the Paris Salon d'Automne, where fifty-six Cézannes were on view. On his 1907 trip to France, see Ellen Marie Glavin, "Maurice Prendergast; the Development of an American Post-Impressionist, 1900–1915," Ph.D. diss. (Boston University, 1988), pp. 93–109; *Prendergast 1994*, pp. 85–94; and Mathews, "Maurice Prendergast and the Influence of European Modernism." On the March 1911 exhibition at Stieglitz's 291 gallery in New York, often cited as a watershed moment in Cézanne's American reception, see John Rewald, "Polemics, Cézanne's First Show in New York," in *Cézanne and America: Dealers, Collectors, Artists and Critics 1891–1921* (Princeton, New Jersey: Princeton University Press, 1989), pp. 129–154.

11. Prendergast to Williams, October 10, 1907. Esther Baldwin Williams Papers, AAA. The full letter is reproduced in *Prendergast 1994*, p. 87. Before returning to America, Prendergast completed a forty-six-page translation of Émile

Bernard's article on Cézanne, published in 1904 in *L'Occident.* See *Prendergast* 1994, p. 89.

12. "Cézanne and American Modernism," Montclair Art Museum, New Jersey, September 13, 2009–January 3, 2010; Baltimore Museum of Art, February 14, 2010–May 23, 2010; and Phoenix Art Museum, June 26, 2010–September 26, 2010. For the exhibition catalogue, see Stavitsky and Rothkopf, eds., *Cézanne and American Modernism.*

13. Sometime about 1910–13 Prendergast made a series of fourteen fruit still lifes in a Cézannesque manner, his first forays in the genre. See *CR*, nos. 300–313. These may have been prompted in part by Prendergast's reacquaintance with Cézanne's work in Boston in late 1909, when he went to see a Cézanne painting (*Harvesters*, c. 1880, private collection, Paris) in the collection of Mr. John O. Sumner, a professor of art history at the Massachusetts Institute of Technology. In December, he wrote to Pach, who had arranged the introduction to Sumner, that "it was such a pleasure for me to see his work again" and also commented: "I wish Mr. Sumner [would] secure one of his [Cézanne's] 'nature mortes,' fruit pieces where he painted one thin coat over the other." Prendergast to Pach, December 6, 1909, quoted in *Prendergast* 1994, p. 99.

14. Walter Pach, *Queer Thing Painting: Forty Years in the World of Art* (New York: Harper and Brothers Publishers, 1938), p. 224, quoted in Glavin, "Maurice Prendergast," p. 106.

15. While Prendergast had long been exploring the motif of figures by the sea, his turn to nudes in a landscape began in 1910 and was also concentrated in the 1910–13 period. See *CR*, esp. nos. 281–85, 356–57, 363. On Cézanne's bathers, see Mary Louise Krumrine, *Paul Cézanne: The Bathers*, exh. cat. (New York: Harry N. Abrams, 1990).

16. Cézanne exhibited only one painting of bathers at the Armory Show: no. 216, under the title "Baigneuses," dated 1878. The picture of four bathers is now in a private collection. See John Rewald, *The Paintings of Paul Cézanne: A Catalogue Raisonné* (New York: Harry N. Abrams, 1996), no. 363.

17. Mathews, "Maurice Prendergast," in *Cézanne and American Modernism*, p. 266.

18. *Prendergast* 1994, p. 120. Prendergast had made drawings after Giorgione, Poussin, Watteau, Puvis, and Matisse during his trips to Paris in 1907 and 1914. See *Prendergast* 1994, pp. 86–87, and 118–20.

19. See Joseph J. Rishel, ed., *Gauguin, Cézanne, Matisse: Visions of Arcadia*, exh. cat. (Philadelphia: Philadelphia Museum of Art, 2012).

20. The importance of Renoir to Prendergast hardly starts with me. Both Wattenmaker and Mathews delve into it as a fertile subject. See *Prendergast* 1994, esp. pp. 117, 121, 128, and 141, and Mathews, "Maurice Prendergast and the Influence of European Modernism," p. 43.

21. On the vitality of the pastoral tradition rooted in Venetian painting, see Robert C. Cafritz, Lawrence Gowing, and David Rosand, *Places of Delight: The Pastoral Landscape*, exh. cat. (Washington, D. C.: Phillips Collection, in association with the National Gallery of Art, 1988).

22. Prendergast's affinity with Watteau and the charm of his *fêtes* has been noted by critics since the turn of the twentieth century. In 1899, one critic remarked: "Mr. Prendergast was born to paint fêtes, and he carries a whole Fourth of July in his color-box. What an irresistible spirit of happy holiday activity pervades his scintillating and Watteau-like scenes!" Two years later, William Howe Downes wrote: "He is a delightful artist of the butterfly sort, a sort of modern Watteau. The fun that he has in painting these scenes must be huge." "Twelfth Annual Exhibition of the Water Color Club," *Boston Evening Transcript*, March 4, 1899, p. 10; Downes, "Fourteenth Annual Exhibition of the Watercolor Club," *Boston Evening Transcript*, March 2, 1901, p. 9, quoted in Madormo, "The 'Butterfly Artist,'" pp. 62, 66. Ellen Glavin emphasizes the resonance between Prendergast and the tradition of the *fête galante*, especially in the work he produced immediately after his 1907 trip to France, in the third chapter of her dissertation, "A New Fête and the Influence of Watteau, 1907–1910." See Glavin, "Maurice Prendergast," pp. 92–120.

23. In 1907 Prendergast made a compositional study of Watteau's *Gathering in a Park* (1716–17, Musée du Louvre, Paris) in his sketchbook (*Sketchbook 38*, Museum of Fine Arts, Boston), inscribed below with large, scrawling print "Watteau." Of all the exhibitions he had seen in France, including the Salon d'Automne retrospectives and the Bernheim-Jeune show of Cézanne watercolors, recall that Prendergast singled out the Chardin-Fragonard show at Galerie Georges Petit, which ran from June 11 to July 12, in his October 1907 letter to Esther Williams. See Glavin, "Maurice Prendergast," pp. 98–101, 252, and also *Prendergast* 1994, p. 86.

24. "I am of the eighteenth century," Renoir once stated. "I humbly consider not only that my art descends from Watteau, Fragonard, Hubert Robert, but that I am one of them." Renoir to René Gimpel, quoted in John House, "Renoir and the Art of the Past," in Sylvie Patrie et al., *Renoir in the 20th Century*, exh. cat. (Ostfildern: Hatje Cantz, 2010), p. 36.

SELECTED BIBLIOGRAPHY

"A Significant Group of Paintings." *New York Evening Sun*, January 23, 1904, p. 4.

Brooks, Van Wyck. "Anecdotes of Maurice Prendergast." In *The Prendergasts: Retrospective Exhibition of the Work of Maurice and Charles Prendergast* (exhibition catalogue). Andover, Massachusetts: Addison Gallery of Art, Phillips Academy, 1938.

Brown, Dona. *Inventing New England: Regional Tourism in the Nineteenth Century*. Washington, D.C.: Smithsonian Institution Press, 1995.

Brown, Milton W. *The Story of the Armory Show*. New York: Abbeville Press, 1963.

Clark, Carol. *American Drawings and Watercolors*. Vol. 8, The Robert Lehman Collection. New York: The Metropolitan Museum of Art, 1992.

Clark, Carol, Nancy Mowll Mathews, and Gwendolyn Owens. *Maurice Brazil Prendergast, Charles Prendergast: A Catalogue Raisonné*. Williamstown, Massachusetts: Williams College Museum of Art, 1990.

DeKay, Charles. "Eight Painters—First Article." *New York Times*, February 9, 1908, p. 8.

———. "Six Impressionists. Startling Works by Red-Hot American Painters." *New York Times*, January 20, 1904, p. 9.

Fairbrother, Trevor J. *The Bostonians: Painters of an Elegant Age, 1870–1930* (exhibition catalogue). Essays by Theodore E. Stebbins, Jr., William L. Vance, and Erica E. Hirshler. Boston: Museum of Fine Arts, 1986.

———. *Painting Summer in New England* (exhibition catalogue). Salem, Massachusetts: Peabody Essex Museum, 2006.

Fairbrother, Trevor J., Theodore E. Stebbins, Jr., and Carol Troyen. *The New World: Masterpieces of American Painting* (exhibition catalogue). Essays by Pierre Rosenberg and H. Barbara Weinberg. Boston: Museum of Fine Arts; Washington, D.C.: Corcoran Gallery of Art; Paris: Grand Palais, 1983.

Glackens, Ira. *William Glackens and the Ashcan Group*. New York: Crown Publishers, 1957.

Glavin, Ellen M. "The Early Art Education of Maurice Prendergast: Art Education in Boston in the 1870s." *Archives of American Art Journal* 33, no. 1 (1993), pp. 2–12.

———. "Maurice Prendergast: The Boston Experience." *Art and Antiques* 5 (July–August 1982), pp. 64–71.

———. "Maurice Prendergast: The Development of An American Post-Impressionist, 1900–1915." Ph.D. dissertation. Boston: Boston University, 1988.

Glavin, Ellen M., Eleanor Green, and Jeffrey Russell Hayes. *Maurice Prendergast: Art of Impulse and Color* (exhibition catalogue). College Park, Maryland: University of Maryland Art Gallery, 1976.

Gregg, Frederic James. *Maurice B. Prendergast: Paintings in Oil and Watercolors*. New York: Carroll Galleries, 1915.

House, John, and David M. Hopkin. *Impressionists by the Sea*. London: Royal Academy of Arts, 2007.

Huneker, James. "Eight Painters." *New York Sun*, February 9, 1908, p. 8.

Ivinski, Pamela A. *Maurice Prendergast: Paintings of America* (exhibition catalogue). Introduction by Warren Adelson, essay by Nancy Mowll Mathews. New York: Adelson Galleries, 2003.

Kennedy, Elizabeth, ed. *The Eight and American Modernisms* (exhibition catalogue). Essays by Peter John Brownlee et al. Chicago: Terra Foundation for American Art; New Britain, Connecticut: New Britain Museum of American Art; Milwaukee: Milwaukee Art Museum, 2009.

Langdale, Cecily. *Monotypes by Maurice Prendergast in the Terra Museum of American Art*. Chicago: Terra Museum of American Art, 1984.

———. *The Monoypes of Maurice Prendergast*. New York: Davis and Long, 1979.

Mathews, Nancy Mowll. *The Art of Charles Prendergast from the Collections of the Williams College Museum of Art and Mrs. Charles Prendergast* (exhibition catalogue). Additional essay by Marion M. Goethals. Williamstown, Massachusetts: Williams College Museum of Art, 1993.

———. *The Art of Leisure: Maurice Prendergast in the Williams College Museum of Art*. Williamstown, Massachusetts: Williams College Museum of Art, 1999.

———. *Maurice Prendergast* (exhibition catalogue). Williamstown, Massachusetts: Williams College Museum of Art, 1990.

———. "Maurice Prendergast." In *Cézanne and American Modernism*. Montclair, New Jersey: Montclair Art Museum; Baltimore: The Baltimore Museum of Art, 2009.

Mathews, Nancy Mowll, and Elizabeth Kennedy. *Prendergast in Italy* (exhibition catalogue). Williamstown, Massachusetts: Williams College Museum of Art; Chicago: Terra Foundation for American Art, 2009.

McCarthy, Laurette. *Walter Pach: The Armory Show and the Untold Story of Modern Art in America*. University Park: The Pennsylvania State University Press, 2011.

Milliken, William M. "Maurice Prendergast, American Artist." *The Arts* 9 (April 1926), pp. 180–92.

Milroy, Elizabeth. *Painters of a New Century: The Eight and American Art* (exhibition catalogue). Additional essay by Gwendolyn Owens. Milwaukee: Milwaukee Art Museum, 1991.

"Notes on Current Art." *New York Times*, January 11, 1920, sec. 9, p. 3.

Pach, Walter. "Art: The Independents," *The Freeman* 2 (March 9, 1921), pp. 616–17.

———. "Maurice Prendergast." *Shadowland* 6 (April 1922), pp. 10–11, 74–75.

———. *Maurice Prendergast Memorial Exhibition: February Twenty-First to March Twenty-Second, Nineteen Thirty-Four*. New York: Whitney Museum of American Art, 1934.

Pène du Bois, Guy. "Eight Independent Painters to Give an Exhibition of Their Own Next Winter." *New York Sun*, May 15, 1907, p. 5.

Pepper, Charles Hovey. "Is Drawing to Disappear in Artistic Individuality? A Sketch of the Work of Maurice Prendergast." *The World To-Day* 19 (July 1910), pp. 716–19.

Perlman, Bennard B. *Painters of the Ashcan School: The Immortal Eight*. New York: Dover Publications, 1988.

"Prendergast First American Modernist." *American Art News* 19, April 9, 1921, p. 3.

Review of "Tenth Annual Exhibition of Oil Paintings and Sculpture by American Artists," The Art Institute of Chicago, November 2–December 12, 1897. *Chicago Tribune*, November 7, 1897.

Rhys, Hedley Howell, and Peter A. Wick. *Maurice Prendergast: 1859–1924* (exhibition catalogue). Boston: Museum of Fine Arts, 1960.

Rishel, Joseph J., ed. *Gauguin, Cézanne, Matisse: Visions of Arcadia* (exhibition catalogue). Essays by Stephanie D'Alessandro et al. Philadelphia: Philadelphia Museum of Art, 2012.

Rishel, Joseph J., and Colin B. Bailey. *Masterpieces of Impressionism & Post-Impressionism: The Annenberg Collection* (exhibition catalogue). Philadelphia: Philadelphia Museum of Art, 1989.

Rishel, Joseph J., and Katherine Sachs. *Cézanne and Beyond* (exhibition catalogue). Essays by Roberta Bernstein et al. Philadelphia: Philadelphia Museum of Art, 2009.

Scott, David W., Duncan Phillips, Willem De Looper, Martha Carey, and Jan Lancaster. *Maurice Prendergast*. Mount Vernon, New York: Artist's Ltd. Edition, 1980.

Sims, Patterson. *Maurice B. Prendergast: A Concentration of Works from the Permanent Collection*. New York: Whitney Museum of American Art, 1980.

Sloan, John, and Helen F. Sloan. *Gist of Art*. New York: American Artists Group, 1939.

Stebbins, Theodore E., and Derrick R. Cartwright. *Waves and Waterways: American Perspectives 1850–1900* (exhibition catalogue). Giverny: Musée d'Art Américain de Giverny, 2000.

Tottis, James W., Valerie Ann Leeds, Vincent DiGirolamo, Marianne Doezema, Suzanne Smeaton. *Life's Pleasures: The Ashcan Artists' Brush with Leisure, 1895–1925* (exhibition catalogue). With contributions from Michael E. Crane and Kirsten Olds. Detroit: Detroit Institute of Arts, 2007.

Wattenmaker, Richard J. *American Paintings and Works on Paper in the Barnes Foundation*. Merion, Pennsylvania: The Barnes Foundation, 2010.

———. *Maurice Prendergast*. The Library of American Art. Washington, D.C.: National Museum of American Art, Smithsonian Institution, 1994.

———. "Maurice Prendergast at the Whitney." *The New Criterion* 9 (November 1990), pp. 33–40.

———. *Puvis de Chavannes and the Modern Tradition* (exhibition catalogue). Ontario: Art Gallery of Ontario, 1976.

Weinberg, H. Barbara, Doreen Bolger, and David Park Curry. *American Impressionism and Realism: The Painting of Modern Life, 1885–1915*. New York: The Metropolitan Museum of Art, 1994.

WORKS IN THE EXHIBITION

Checklist numbers accord with the numbering of works in the plate sections. Works that are not illustrated in the plate sections are indicated with an asterisk (*) and cross-referenced if illustrated as comparative figures. Dimensions are in inches followed by centimeters; height precedes width precedes depth.

Maurice Brazil Prendergast (1858–1924)

1. *St. Servan Fisherman*, 1891
Oil on panel, 10 × 7½ (25.4 × 19.1)
Williams College Museum of Art, Williamstown, Massachusetts; Bequest of Mrs. Charles Prendergast (95.4.74)

2. *Low Tide*, c. 1897
Oil on panel, 13½ × 18 (34.3 × 45.7)
Williams College Museum of Art, Williamstown, Massachusetts; Gift of Mrs. Charles Prendergast (86.18.40)

3. *At the Seashore*, 1895
Monotype on cream Japanese paper, laid down on Japanese paper, 7¹¹⁄₁₆ × 5¹⁵⁄₁₆ (19.5 × 15.1)
Terra Foundation for American Art, Chicago; Daniel J. Terra Collection (1992.69)

4. *The Harbor from City Point (New England Shore and Harbor Scene)*, 1895
Watercolor over graphite indications on wove paper, 14 × 10 (35.6 × 25.4)
Hood Museum of Art, Dartmouth College, Hanover, New Hampshire; Bequest of Warren F. Upham, Class of 1916 (W.976.136)

5. *Viewing the Ships*, c. 1895–97
Watercolor and graphite on ivory wove watercolor paper, 10 × 14 (25.4 × 35.6)
Terra Foundation for American Art, Chicago; Daniel J. Terra Collection (1999.125)

6. *Marine Park*, c. 1895–97
Monotype on cream Japanese paper, 7⁷⁄₁₆ × 10⅛ (18.9 × 25.7)
Terra Foundation for American Art, Chicago; Daniel J. Terra Collection (1999.116)

7. *Telegraph Hill I*, c. 1895–97
Monotype with graphite on grayish ivory Chinapaper, 14¾ × 14⅝ (37.5 × 37.2)
Terra Foundation for American Art, Chicago; Daniel J. Terra Collection (1992.111)

8. *Evening on a Pleasure Boat*, c. 1895–97
Oil on canvas, 14⅜ × 22⅛ (36.5 × 56.2)
Terra Foundation for American Art, Chicago; Daniel J. Terra Collection (1999.110)

9. *South Boston Pier*, 1896
Brush, watercolor, and graphite on heavy white wove paper, 18¼ × 14 (46.4 × 35.6)
Smith College Museum of Art, Northampton, Massachusetts; Purchased with the Charles B. Hoyt Fund (1950.43)

10. *Float at Low Tide, Revere Beach*, c. 1896–97
Watercolor and graphite on wove paper, 13¹³⁄₁₆ × 9¾ (35.1 × 24.8)
Addison Gallery of American Art, Phillips Academy, Andover, Massachusetts; Gift of Mrs. William C. Endicott (1942.2)

11. *Rocky Shore, Nantasket*, c. 1896–97
Watercolor, pencil, and ink on paper, 17 × 12½ (43.2 × 31.8)
Williams College Museum of Art, Williamstown, Massachusetts; Bequest of Sophia W. Brumbaugh (M.2004.13.1)

12. *Handkerchief Point*, 1896–97
Watercolor and pencil on paper, 19⅞ × 13½ (50.5 × 34.3)
Museum of Fine Arts, Boston; Gift of Francis W. Fabyan in memory of Edith Westcott Fabyan (31.906)

13. *Sunny Morning, Low Tide at the Beach*, c. 1896–97
Watercolor and pencil on paper, 9 × 12½ (22.9 × 31.8)
Williams College Museum of Art, Williamstown, Massachusetts;
Bequest of Mrs. Charles Prendergast (95.4.97)

14. *Beach Scene with Boats* (verso), c. 1896–97
Watercolor and graphite on wove paper, 14¼ × 20¾ (36.2 × 52.7)
Brooklyn Museum, New York; Dick S. Ramsay Fund (40.54b)
(recto: *Five Figures*, c. 1910–13 [cat. 54])

15. *The Stony Beach, Ogunquit*, c. 1896–97
Watercolor and pencil on paper, 20⅞ × 14 (53 × 35.6)
Private collection

16. *Excursionists, Nahant*, c. 1896–97
Watercolor, gouache, and graphite on off-white wove paper,
19½ × 14³⁄₁₆ (49.5 × 36)
The Metropolitan Museum of Art, New York; The Lesley and
Emma Sheafer Collection, Bequest of Emma A. Sheafer, 1973
(1974.356.2 recto)

17. *The Lido, Venice*, c. 1898–99
Watercolor and pencil on paper, 11 × 15 (27.9 × 38.1)
Private collection; courtesy Guggenheim, Asher Associates

18. *At the Shore (Capri)*, c. 1898–99
Watercolor on paper, 10 × 14 (25.4 × 35.6)
Private collection

19. *Docks, East Boston*, c. 1900–1904
Watercolor and graphite on wove paper, 14½ × 21¼ (36.8 × 54)
National Gallery of Art, Washington, D.C.; Collection of Mr. and
Mrs. Paul Mellon, in Honor of the 50th Anniversary of the National
Gallery of Art (1992.51.12)

20. *The East River*, 1901
Watercolor and pencil on paper, 13⅞ × 20 (35.2 × 50.8)
The Museum of Modern Art, New York; Gift of Abby Aldrich
Rockefeller (132.1935a-b)

21. *The Flying Horses*, c. 1902–6
Oil on canvas, 23⅞ × 32⅛ (60.7 × 81.5)
Toledo Museum of Art, Ohio; Purchased with funds from the
Florence Scott Libbey Bequest in Memory of her Father,
Maurice A. Scott (1957.22)

22. *On the Pier, Nantasket*, c. 1900–1905
Watercolor and graphite on wove paper, 19⅜ × 21½ (49.2 × 54.6)
Addison Gallery of American Art, Phillips Academy, Andover,
Massachusetts; Gift of anonymous donor (1928.49)

23. *The Balloon*, c. 1901
Watercolor on paper, 20⅜ × 15⅛ (51.8 × 38.4)
Private collection

24. *Boston Harbor*, c. 1900–1905
Watercolor and pencil on paper, 11⅛ × 15½ (28.3 × 39.4)
Private collection

25. *On Deck, Boston (Nantasket Ferry?)*, 1902
Monotype, 10¼ × 9⅜ (26 × 23.8)
Museum of Fine Arts, Boston; Lee M. Friedman Fund (63.1531)

26. *Lighthouse*, c. 1900–1902
Monotype with watercolor and graphite on cream Japanese
paper, 9⅜ × 14 (23.8 × 35.6)
Terra Foundation for American Art, Chicago; Daniel J. Terra
Collection (1992.93)

27. *Salem*, c. 1902–4
Oil on panel, 11 × 11 (27.9 × 27.9)
Williams College Museum of Art, Williamstown, Massachusetts;
Bequest of Mrs. Charles Prendergast (95.4.77)

28. *Approaching Storm*, c. 1902–4
Oil on panel, 10½ × 13⅞ (26.7 × 35.2)
Williams College Museum of Art, Williamstown, Massachusetts;
Bequest of Mrs. Charles Prendergast (95.4.76)

29. *Yacht Race*, c. 1902–4
Oil on panel, 10½ × 13¾ (26.7 × 34.9)
Maier Museum of Art, Randolph College, Lynchburg, Virginia;
Gift of Mrs. Charles Prendergast, 1991 (M.1991.3.2)

30. *Figures Under the Flag*, c. 1900–1905
Watercolor and pencil on paper, 20½ × 10¼ (52.1 × 26)
Williams College Museum of Art, Williamstown, Massachusetts;
Gift of Mrs. Charles Prendergast (86.18.70)

31. *Surf, Cohasset*, c. 1900–1905
Watercolor and pencil on paper, 11 × 15¼ (27.9 × 38.7)
Williams College Museum of Art, Williamstown, Massachusetts;
Gift of Mrs. Charles Prendergast (91.18.9)

32. *April Snow, Salem*, c. 1906–7
Watercolor and pencil on paper, 15¼ × 22⅛ (38.7 × 56.2)
The Museum of Modern Art, New York; Gift of Abby Aldrich
Rockefeller (129.35)

PLATES II: 1907–13
33. *Study St. Malo, No. 32*, c. 1907
Oil on panel, 10½ × 13¾ (26.7 × 34.9)
Williams College Museum of Art, Williamstown, Massachusetts;
Gift of Mrs. Charles Prendergast (91.18.26)

34. *Lighthouse at St. Malo*, c. 1907
Oil on canvas, 20⅛ × 24⅝ (51.1 × 62.6)
William Benton Museum of Art, University of Connecticut, Storrs;
Gift of Mrs. Eugénie Prendergast (72.31)

35. *St. Malo*, c. 1907
Oil on panel, 10½ × 13¾ (26.7 × 34.9)
Bowdoin College Museum of Art, Brunswick, Maine; Anonymous
Gift (1991.9)

36. *Study St. Malo, No. 12*, c. 1907
Oil on panel, 10½ × 13¾ (26.7 × 34.9)
Williams College Museum of Art, Williamstown, Massachusetts;
Gift of Mrs. Charles Prendergast (91.18.8)

37. *St. Malo*, c. 1907
Watercolor, pencil, and gouache on paper, 15¼ × 11 (38.7 × 27.9)
Williams College Museum of Art, Williamstown, Massachusetts;
Gift of Mrs. Charles Prendergast (86.18.74)

38. *At the Shore, St. Malo No. 1*, c. 1907
Watercolor and graphite on wove paper, 13⁹⁄₁₆ × 19⅞ (34.5 × 50.5)
Addison Gallery of American Art, Phillips Academy, Andover,
Massachusetts; Bequest of Lizzie P. Bliss (1931.92)

39. *St. Malo, No. 2*, c. 1907–10
Watercolor, graphite, and crayon on paper,
12⅞ × 19⅜ (32.7 × 49.2)
Columbus Museum of Art, Ohio; Gift of Ferdinand Howald
(1931.247)

40. *On the Beach, St. Malo*, c. 1907
Watercolor and graphite on wove paper, 13½ × 19⅞ (34.3 × 50.5)
Addison Gallery of American Art, Phillips Academy, Andover,
Massachusetts; Bequest of Lizzie P. Bliss (1931.94)

41. *St. Malo, No. 1*, c. 1907–10
Watercolor on paper, 13⅛ × 19½ (33.3 × 49.5)
Columbus Museum of Art, Ohio; Gift of Ferdinand Howald
(1931.246)

42. *St. Malo*, c. 1907
Watercolor and pencil on paper, 11¼ × 15¼ (28.6 × 38.7)
Williams College Museum of Art, Williamstown, Massachusetts;
Gift of Mrs. Charles Prendergast (86.18.75)

43. *Winter Day*, c. 1908
Oil on wood board, 10⅜ × 13⅝ (26.4 × 34.6)
Picker Art Gallery, Colgate University, Hamilton, New York;
Gift of Mrs. Charles Prendergast (1991.38)

44. *The Holiday*, 1908–9
Oil on canvas, 27 × 34⅜ (68.6 × 87.3)
The Fine Arts Museums of San Francisco, de Young Museum;
Museum purchase, gift of the Charles E. Merrill Trust with matching
funds from the M. H. de Young Museum Society (68.14)

45. *Landscape Near Nahant*, c. 1908–12
Oil on canvas, 20¼ × 27⅞ (51.4 × 70.8)
The Phillips Collection, Washington, D.C. (1606)

46. *Seaside, Maine*, c. 1911
Oil on wood panel, 10⁵⁄₁₆ × 13¾ (26.2 × 34.9)
Picker Art Gallery, Colgate University, Hamilton, New York;
Gift of Mrs. Charles Prendergast (1991.37)

47. *Lake in Maine*, c. 1910–13
Oil on canvas, 18¾ × 22½ (47.6 × 57.2)
Williams College Museum of Art, Williamstown, Massachusetts;
Bequest of Mrs. Charles Prendergast (95.4.14)

48. *Rocky Coast Scene*, 1912–13
Oil on canvas mounted on panel, 13¾ × 19½ (34.9 × 49.5)
The Fine Arts Museums of San Francisco, de Young Museum;
Gift of Mrs. Charles Prendergast (1965.10)

49. *Maine Barn*, c. 1910–13
Oil on coated paperboard panel, 11 × 14 (27.9 × 35.6)
Williams College Museum of Art, Williamstown, Massachusetts;
Gift of Mrs. Charles Prendergast (84.16.2)

50. *Maine*, c. 1910–13
Oil on wood panel, 10⅜ × 13⅞ (26.4 × 35.2)
Williams College Museum of Art, Williamstown, Massachusetts;
Gift of Mrs. Charles Prendergast (84.16.1)

51. *Bathing*, c. 1910–13
Oil on panel, 10 × 13¾ (25.4 × 34.9)
Williams College Museum of Art, Williamstown, Massachusetts;
Bequest of Mrs. Charles Prendergast (95.4.113)

52. *Beach Scene, Maine*, c. 1910–13
Oil on canvas, 30½ × 34½ (77.5 × 87.6)
Williams College Museum of Art, Williamstown, Massachusetts;
Gift of Mrs. Charles Prendergast (86.18.51)

PLATES III: 1913–23
53. *The Promenade*, 1913
Oil on canvas, with wood frame, 32⅜ × 34¼ (82.2 × 87)
Whitney Museum of American Art, New York; Alexander M. Bing
Bequest (60.10a-b)

54. *Five Figures* (recto), c. 1910–13
Watercolor on paper, 14¾ × 20¾ (37.5 × 52.7)
Brooklyn Museum, New York; Dick S. Ramsay Fund (40.54a)
(verso: *Beach Scene with Boats*, c. 1896–97 [cat. 14])

55. *Bathers in a Cove, Maine*, c. 1910–13
Oil on canvas, 20 × 27¾ (50.8 × 70.5)
Palmer Museum of Art, The Pennsylvania State University,
University Park; Gift of Eugénie Prendergast (77.24)

56. *Sketchbook*, c. 1916–18
Watercolor and pencil on paper, 7⅝ × 5 (19.4 × 12.7)
Delaware Art Museum, Wilmington; Gift of Helen Farr Sloan
(1974-33)

57. *Bathers*, c. 1912–15
Watercolor and pencil on paper, 11⅜ × 17½ (28.9 × 44.5)
William Benton Museum of Art, University of Connecticut, Storrs;
Gift of the Eugénie Prendergast Foundation (74.8.2)

58. *Summer Day*, c. 1913–15
Watercolor on paper, 9⅞ × 19⅛ (25.1 × 48.6)
Williams College Museum of Art, Williamstown, Massachusetts;
Gift of Mrs. Charles Prendergast (86.18.42)

59. *Summer Hotel, Maine*, c. 1914–15
Watercolor and pencil on paper, 11½ × 17¾ (29.2 × 45.1)
Williams College Museum of Art, Williamstown, Massachusetts;
Bequest of Mrs. Charles Prendergast (95.4.70)

60. *Hay Harvesting, Maine*, c. 1913–15
Watercolor and pastel on paper, 12¼ × 16¾ (31.1 × 42.6)
Williams College Museum of Art, Williamstown, Massachusetts;
Gift of Mrs. Charles Prendergast (91.18.16)

61. *The Cove*, c. 1913–15
Watercolor and pencil on paper, 10⅜ × 14 (26.4 × 35.6)
Colby College Museum of Art, Waterville, Maine; Gift of
Mrs. Charles Prendergast (1964.032)

62. *Sunday Promenade*, c. 1914–15
Oil on canvas, 24 × 32 (61 × 81.3)
Philadelphia Museum of Art; Gift of Meyer P. Potamkin and
Vivian O. Potamkin, 2001 (1964-116-1)

63. *Along the Shore*, c. 1914–15
Oil on canvas, 23¼ × 34 (59.1 × 86.4)
Columbus Museum of Art, Ohio; Gift of Ferdinand Howald
(1931.252)

64. *The Idlers*, c. 1916–18
Oil on canvas, 21 × 32 (53.3 × 81.3)
Maier Museum of Art, Randolph College, Lynchburg, Virginia;
Seventh purchase made possible by the Louise Jordan Smith Fund,
1949 (M.1949.5)

65. *Autumn*, c. 1917–18
Oil on canvas adhered to panel, 22½ × 32⅛ (57.2 × 81.6)
The Phillips Collection, Washington, D.C. (1603)

66. *Maine Coastal Village*, c. 1916–18
Gouache and pastel over graphite on off-white wove paper,
12 × 17¾ (30.5 × 45.1)
Bowdoin College Museum of Art, Brunswick, Maine;
Gift of Mrs. Charles Prendergast (1982.25.a)

67. *New Hampshire*, c. 1916–19
Watercolor, pastel, and pencil, 11¼ × 15⅛ (28.6 × 38.4)
Williams College Museum of Art, Williamstown, Massachusetts;
Gift of Bernard Heineman, Jr., Class of 1945 (73.43)

68. *Harbor Village*, c. 1916–19
Watercolor and pencil on paper, 11¹⁵⁄₁₆ × 17⅞ (30.4 × 45.4)
Williams College Museum of Art, Williamstown, Massachusetts;
Gift of Mrs. Charles Prendergast (91.28.13)

69. *Beach Resort*, c. 1919
Watercolor, pastel, and pencil on paper,
13⅞ × 19⅞ (35.2 × 50.5)
Williams College Museum of Art, Williamstown, Massachusetts;
Gift of Mrs. Charles Prendergast (86.18.58)

70. *Maine Beach, Late Afternoon*, 1916
Pastel on paper, 15½ × 22½ (39.4 × 57.2)
Museum of Fine Arts, Boston; Abraham Shuman Fund (59.404)

71. *The Cove*, 1916
Oil on canvas, 28⅛ × 39¾ (71.4 × 101)
Whitney Museum of American Art, New York; Gift of Gertrude
Vanderbilt Whitney (31.322)

72. *Sunset and Sea Fog*, c. 1918–23
Oil on canvas, 18 × 29 (45.7 × 73.7)
The Butler Institute of American Art, Youngstown, Ohio (955-O-128)

73. *Acadia*, c. 1918–23
Oil on canvas, 31¾ × 37½ (80.6 × 95.3)
The Museum of Modern Art, New York; Abby Aldrich Rockefeller
Fund (167.1945)

74. *New England Harbor*, c. 1919–23
Oil on canvas, 24 × 28 (61 × 71.1)
Cincinnati Art Museum; The Edwin and Virginia Irwin Memorial
(1959.51)

75. *Maine Beach*, c. 1910–13*
Oil on wood, 9⅛ × 16¼ (23.2 × 41.3)
Private collection

76. *Sketchbook 24*, 1910–13*
Graphite pencil on blank paper in notebook,
7⅞ × 5³⁄₁₆ × ⅝ (20 × 13.2 × 1.6)
Museum of Fine Arts, Boston; Gift of Mrs. Charles Prendergast in
honor of Perry T. Rathbone (1972.1114)

77. *Sketchbook 26*, 1913–15*
Graphite pencil on blank paper in notebook,
7¾ × 5³⁄₁₆ × ¹¹⁄₁₆ (19.7 × 13.2 × 1.8)
Museum of Fine Arts, Boston; Gift of Mrs. Charles Prendergast in
honor of Perry T. Rathbone (1972.1116)

78. *Sketchbook 29*, 1915–16*
Graphite pencil on blank paper in notebook,
7¾ × 5³⁄₁₆ × ⁹⁄₁₆ (19.7 × 13.2 × 1.4)
Museum of Fine Arts, Boston; Gift of Mrs. Charles Prendergast in
honor of Perry T. Rathbone (1972.1119)

79. *Sketchbook*, c. 1918–20*
Watercolor, pencil, and crayon on paper, 7⅞ × 5⅛ (20 × 13)
Private collection, Princeton, New Jersey; courtesy Betty Krulik Fine
Arts, Ltd., New York
See fig. 27 (p. 116) for illustration.

80. *Sketchbook*, c. 1920–23*
Pencil and watercolor on paper, 7¾ × 5 × ⅝ (19.7 × 12.7 × 1.6)
Williams College Museum of Art, Williamstown, Massachusetts;
Gift of Mrs. Charles Prendergast in honor of President John W.
Chandler (85.11.1)

81. *Sketchbook*, c. 1920–23*
Watercolor, pencil, and crayon on paper, 7¾ × 3¾ × ⁹⁄₁₆
(19.7 × 9.5 × 1.4)
Williams College Museum of Art, Williamstown, Massachusetts;
Gift of Mrs. Charles Prendergast in honor of President John W.
Chandler (85.11.2)

Eugène Louis Boudin (1824–1898)
82. *Port of Le Havre*, 1887*
Oil on canvas, 25¾ × 35⅝ (65.4 × 90.5)
Bowdoin College Museum of Art, Brunswick, Maine; Bequest of
Mildred Curtis Hughson, in memory of her father, William John
Curtis, Class of 1875 (1991.71)

Maurice Denis (1870–1943)
83. *On the Beach of Trestrignel*, 1898*
Oil on board, 27⅝ × 39⅜ (70.2 × 100)
The Museum of Modern Art, New York; Grace Rainey Rogers Fund
(1.1964)
See fig. 25 (p. 112) for illustration.

William J. Glackens (1870–1938)
84. *W. Glackens Cape Cod* (sketchbook), 1908*
Graphite on paper, 5⅛ × 8¼ (13 × 21)
Museum of Art | Fort Lauderdale, Nova Southeastern University;
Gift of the Sansom Foundation (94.132)

85. *Captain's Pier*, 1912–14*
Oil on canvas, 25⅛ × 30⅛ (63.8 × 76.5)
Bowdoin College Museum of Art, Brunswick, Maine;
Gift of Stephen M. Etnier, Honorary Degree, 1969 (1957.127)
See fig. 3 (p. 12) for illustration.

Hermann Dudley Murphy (1867–1945)
86. *The Beach*, 1905*
Oil on canvas, 20 × 27⅛ (50.8 × 68.9)
Bowdoin College Museum of Art, Brunswick, Maine;
Bequest of Mrs. Ella Pratt (1969.46)
See fig. 1 (p. 10) for illustration.

Charles Prendergast (1863–1948)
87. *Hill Town*, c. 1928*
Tempera, graphite, and gold leaf on incised, gessoed panel,
38⁹⁄₁₆ × 48¼ (98 × 122.6)
Addison Gallery of American Art, Phillips Academy, Andover,
Massachusetts; Bequest of Lizzie P. Bliss (1931.91)

John Sloan (1871–1951)
88. *South Beach Bathers*, 1907–8*
Oil on canvas, 31¹³⁄₁₆ × 36 (80.8 × 91.4)
Walker Art Center, Minneapolis; Gift of the T.B. Walker
Foundation, Gilbert M. Walker Fund, 1948 (1948.27)
See fig. 2 (p. 11) for illustration.

LENDERS TO THE EXHIBITION

Addison Gallery of American Art, Phillips Academy, Andover, Massachusetts
Brooklyn Museum, New York
The Butler Institute of American Art, Youngstown, Ohio
Cincinnati Art Museum, Ohio
Colby College Museum of Art, Waterville, Maine
Columbus Museum of Art, Ohio
Delaware Art Museum, Wilmington
The Fine Arts Museums of San Francisco, de Young Museum
Hood Museum of Art, Dartmouth College, Hanover, New Hampshire
Maier Museum of Art, Randolph College, Lynchburg, Virginia
The Metropolitan Museum of Art, New York
Museum of Art | Fort Lauderdale, Nova Southeastern University
Museum of Fine Arts, Boston
The Museum of Modern Art, New York
National Gallery of Art, Washington, D.C.
Palmer Museum of Art, The Pennsylvania State University, University Park
Philadelphia Museum of Art
The Phillips Collection, Washington, D.C.
Picker Art Gallery, Colgate University, Hamilton, New York
Private collection, courtesy Guggenheim, Asher Associates
Private collection, Princeton, New Jersey, courtesy Betty Krulik Fine Arts, Ltd., New York
Smith College Museum of Art, Northampton, Massachusetts
Terra Foundation for American Art, Chicago
Toledo Museum of Art, Ohio
Walker Art Center, Minneapolis
Whitney Museum of American Art, New York
William Benton Museum of Art, University of Connecticut, Storrs
Williams College Museum of Art, Williamstown, Massachusetts
And anonymous lenders

ACKNOWLEDGMENTS

This catalogue and exhibition are the achievement of many. Nancy Mowll Mathews, co-curator of the exhibition and former Eugénie Prendergast Senior Curator of 19th and 20th Century Art at the Williams College Museum of Art, contributed her encyclopedic knowledge to all phases of this project with unbounded generosity, cheerfully welcoming the exhibition organizers and catalogue contributors into Prendergast's colorful world. The Prendergast Archive and Study Center at the Williams College Museum of Art is a major lender to the exhibition and graciously provided crucial organizational help. We thank Christina Olsen, Class of 1956 Director, and her staff, especially Diane Hart, Kathryn Price, Edith Schwartz, and Miriam A. Stanton. We also gratefully acknowledge collegial support from Warren Adelson, Adelson Galleries, New York; Eric Widing and Lydia Kimball, Christie's; Elaine Banks Stainton, Doyle, New York; and Katherine Degn, Kraushaar Galleries, New York.

We are deeply grateful to all of the public and private lenders to the exhibition for sharing fragile and light-sensitive works that together constitute a panorama of Prendergast's seaside art. We are especially indebted to the following for their invaluable assistance: Brian T. Allen, Juliann D. McDonough, and James M. Sousa, Addison Gallery of American Art, Phillips Academy, Andover, Massachusetts; Arnold L. Lehman and Elizabeth Largi, Brooklyn Museum, New York; Louis A. Zona and Rebecca Davis, The Butler Institute of American Art, Youngstown, Ohio; Aaron Betsky, Anita J. Ellis, Julie Aronson, and Carola Bell, Cincinnati Art Museum, Ohio; Sharon Corwin, Patricia King, Elizabeth Finch, and Lorraine DeLaney, Colby College Museum of Art, Waterville, Maine; Nannette V. Maciejunes and Melinda L. Knapp, Columbus Museum of Art, Ohio; Danielle Rice and Jennifer Holl, Delaware Art Museum, Wilmington; Michael Taylor and Cynthia Gilliland, Hood Museum of Art, Dartmouth College, Hanover, New Hampshire; Martha Kjeseth Johnson and Deborah Spanich, Maier Museum of Art, Randolph College, Lynchburg, Virginia; Thomas P. Campbell, Emily Foss, and Nesta Mayo, The Metropolitan Museum of Art, New York; Malcolm Rogers, Clifford S. Ackley, Stephanie Stepanek, Erica Hirshler, and Kim Pashko, Museum of Fine Arts, Boston; Glenn D. Lowry, Whitney Snyder, and Kathleen Hill, The Museum of Modern Art, New York; Earl A. Powell III, Andrea Romeo Jain, and Shannon Schuler, National Gallery of Art, Washington, D.C.; Jan Muhlert and Beverly Sutley, Palmer Museum of Art, The Pennsylvania State University, University

Park; Timothy Rub and Nancy Leeman, Philadelphia Museum of Art; Dorothy Kosinski, Klaus Ottmann, Eliza Rathbone, Susan Nichols, Joseph Holbach, and Trish Waters, The Phillips Collection, Washington, D.C.; Anja Chávez and Sarisha Guarneiri, Picker Art Gallery, Colgate University, Hamilton, New York; Jessica Nicoll and Louise Laplante, Smith College Museum of Art, Northampton, Massachusetts; Elizabeth Glassman and Catherine Ricciardelli, Terra Foundation for American Art, Chicago; Brian Kennedy, Carolyn Putney, Lawrence Nichols, Andrea M. Mall, and Lori Mott, Toledo Museum of Art, Ohio; Olga Viso and Loren Smith, Walker Art Center, Minneapolis; Adam D. Weinberg, Barbara Haskell, Arielle Schraeter, and Jessica Pepe, Whitney Museum of American Art, New York; Thomas P. Bruhn, Carla Galfano, and Ally Walton, William Benton Museum of Art, University of Connecticut, Storrs; Julian Cox and Timothy Anglin Burgard, Fine Arts Museums of San Francisco, de Young Museum; and Jorge Santis and Rachel Diana, Museum of Art | Fort Lauderdale, Nova Southeastern University. We are also grateful for the collegial support of Mary Murray and Michael D. Somple, Munson-Williams-Proctor Arts Institute, Utica, New York.

Catalogue authors Trevor J. Fairbrother, Nancy Mowll Mathews, Joseph J. Rishel, and Richard J. Wattenmaker provide new and engaging perspectives on Prendergast's art. Mary DelMonico of DelMonico-Prestel has been a delightful and enthusiastic collaborator and her team was nothing short of spectacular. We are immensely grateful to production manager Karen Farquhar, editor Dale Tucker, and designer Laura Lindgren for crafting this publication. Avis Berman, Ellen M. Glavin, Natasha Goldman, Bob London, Lillian Morris, Richard and Adria Pepp, Jennifer Vanim, Eva Wattenmaker, and Gwendolyn M. Wells all contributed to the success of this project.

The Bowdoin College Museum of Art staff embraced *Maurice Prendergast: By the Sea* from the outset and brought both the exhibition and its accompanying publication to fruition with great excitement and efficiency. We thank Kevin Salatino, former Director, and Frank Goodyear III and Anne Collins Goodyear, Co-directors; Martina Duncan, Associate Director for Museum Operations; Andrea Rosen, Curatorial Assistant; Sarah Montross, Andrew W. Mellon Post-Doctoral Curatorial Fellow; Laura Latman, Registrar; Michelle Henning, Assistant to the Registrar; Suzanne Bergeron, Assistant Director for Communications; Victoria Baldwin-Wilson, Assistant to the Director; José Ribas and Joseph Hluska, Preparators; Liza Nelson, Shop Manager; and the security officers under Supervisor Tim Hanson.

At Bowdoin College, we greatly appreciate the unwavering commitment to the exhibition expressed by students, faculty, and administrators. We are sincerely grateful to Barry Mills, President; Cristle Collins Judd, Dean for Academic Affairs; S. Catherine Longley, Senior Vice President for Finance and Administration and Treasurer; Ann Ostwald, Director of Academic Budget and Operations; Margaret Broaddus, Senior Leadership Gifts Officer; Hieu Nguyen, Associate Vice President, Development

Administration; Grace Garland, Director, Corporate/Foundations Relations; the late Susan Danforth, Associate Director of Communications; Scott Hood, Vice President for Communications and Public Affairs; Doug Cook, Director of News and Media Relations; and Kevin Travers, Lead Designer, Interactive Media Group.

Without our donors, this ambitious and groundbreaking exhibition would not be possible. We are deeply appreciative to our major sponsors: the Devonwood Foundation, The Mr. and Mrs. Raymond J. Horowitz Foundation for the Arts, Eric '85 and Svetlana Silverman, and the Elizabeth B. G. Hamlin Fund at Bowdoin College. Generous additional support has been provided by The Robert Lehman Foundation, Carolyn Logan P'12, the Morton-Kelly Charitable Trust, Thomas A. McKinley '06, and an anonymous donor; we are also grateful to Furthermore: a program of the J. M. Kaplan Fund for support of our exhibition catalogue.

Joachim Homann

Published on the occasion of the exhibition *Maurice Prendergast: By the Sea*, on view at the Bowdoin College Museum of Art, Brunswick, Maine, June 29–October 13, 2013, organized by Joachim Homann and Nancy Mowll Mathews.

Major support is provided by the Devonwood Foundation, The Mr. and Mrs. Raymond J. Horowitz Foundation for the Arts, Eric '85 and Svetlana Silverman, and the Elizabeth B. G. Hamlin Fund at Bowdoin College. Additional support has been provided by The Robert Lehman Foundation, Carolyn Logan P'12, the Morton-Kelly Charitable Trust, Thomas A. McKinley '06, and an anonymous donor; Furthermore: a program of the J. M. Kaplan Fund supported the exhibition catalogue.

Published by the Bowdoin College Museum of Art and DelMonico Books, an imprint of Prestel Publishing

Bowdoin

Bowdoin College Museum of Art
9400 College Station
Brunswick, Maine 04011
Tel.: 207 725 3275
www.bowdoin.edu/art-museum

Prestel, a member of Verlagsgruppe Random House GmbH

Prestel Verlag
Neumarkter Strasse 28
81673 Munich, Germany
Tel.: +49 (0)89 41 36 0
Fax: +49 (0)89 41 36 23 35

Prestel Publishing Limited
14–17 Wells Street
London W1T 3PD, United Kingdom
Tel.: +44 (0)20 7323 5004
Fax: +44 (0)20 7323 0271

Prestel Publishing
900 Broadway, Suite 603
New York, NY 10003
Tel.: 212 995 2720
Fax: 212 995 2733
E-mail: sales@prestel-usa.com

www.prestel.com

Copyright © 2013 Bowdoin College and Prestel Verlag Munich · London · New York.

Editor: Dale Tucker
Designer: Laura Lindgren
Production Manager: Karen Farquhar
Printed and bound in China

Library of Congress Cataloging-in-Publication Data
Maurice Prendergast : by the sea / Joachim Homann ; with essays by Trevor Fairbrother, Nancy Mowll Mathews, Joseph J. Rishel, and Richard J. Wattenmaker.
     pages   cm
   Issued in connection with an exhibition held June 29, 2013–October 13, 2013, Bowdoin College Museum of Art, Brunswick, Maine.
   Includes bibliographical references.
   ISBN 978-3-7913-5290-9
   1. Prendergast, Maurice, 1858–1924—Exhibitions. 2. Seashore in art—Exhibitions. I. Homann, Joachim. Crowds by the sea. II. Bowdoin College. Museum of Art.
   N6537.P68A4 2013
   740.92—dc23   2013007207

Jacket illustrations: front, detail of *St. Malo, No. 2* (plate 39); back, *Low Tide* (plate 2). Endpapers: detail of *Harbor Village* (plate 68). Additional illustrations: p. 1, *St. Servan Fisherman* (plate 1); pp. 2–3: detail of *Study of St. Malo, No. 32* (plate 33); p. 4, *Along the Shore* (plate 63); p. 31, *The Stony Beach, Ogunquit* (plate 15); p. 81 *Landscape Near Nahant* (plate 45); p. 117, *New England Harbor* (plate 74); p. 156, *The Cove* (plate 61).

PHOTOGRAPHY CREDITS
Unless otherwise stated below, photographs were provided by the owners of the works of art and are published with their permission; their generosity is gratefully acknowledged. Additional credits are as follows:

The Art Institute of Chicago / Photography © The Art Institute of Chicago: fig. 28. Banque de France, Paris, France © RMN-Grand Palais / Art Resource, NY (photo: Gérard Blot): fig. 33. The Barnes Foundation, Philadelphia / image © 2013 The Barnes Foundation: figs. 26, 30, 32. Cincinnati Art Museum, Ohio / The Edwin and Virginia Irwin Memorial / The Bridgeman Art Library: plate 74. Los Angeles County Museum of Art, digital image © 2013 Museum Associates / LACMA. Licensed by Art Resource, NY: fig. 12. The Metropolitan Museum of Art, New York, image copyright © The Metropolitan Museum of Art. Image source: Art Resource, NY: plate 16. The Museum of Modern Art, New York, image © The Museum of Modern Art/Licensed by SCALA / Art Resource, NY: plates 20, 32, 73; fig. 25. Munson-Williams-Proctor Institute Museum of Art, Utica, New York, digital image © Munson-Williams-Proctor Arts Institute / Art Resource, NY: fig. 24. Museum of Fine Arts, Boston, photography © 2013 Museum of Fine Arts, Boston: plates 12, 25, 70; figs. 15, 17, 19. Picker Art Gallery, Colgate University, Hamilton, New York (digital photography by Peter Siegel): plates 43, 46. Private collection, photo © Christie's Images / The Bridgeman Art Library: plate 15. Private collection, Princeton, New Jersey, courtesy Betty Krulik Fine Arts, Ltd., New York, photo courtesy Spanierman Gallery, LLC, New York: fig. 27. Smithsonian American Art Museum, Washington, D.C., image © Smithsonian American Art Museum, Washington, D.C. / Art Resource, NY: fig. 7. Sterling and Francine Clark Art Institute, Williamstown, Massachusetts / The Bridgeman Art Library: fig. 9. Terra Foundation for American Art, Chicago, image © Terra Foundation for American Art, Chicago / Art Resource, NY: plates 3, 5, 6, 7, 8, 26; figs. 8, 23, 29. Wadsworth Atheneum Museum of Art, Hartford, image © Wadsworth Atheneum Museum of Art / Art Resource, NY: fig. 21. Whitney Museum of American Art, New York, digital image © Whitney Museum of American Art: plates 53 (photography by Sheldan C. Collins), 71.

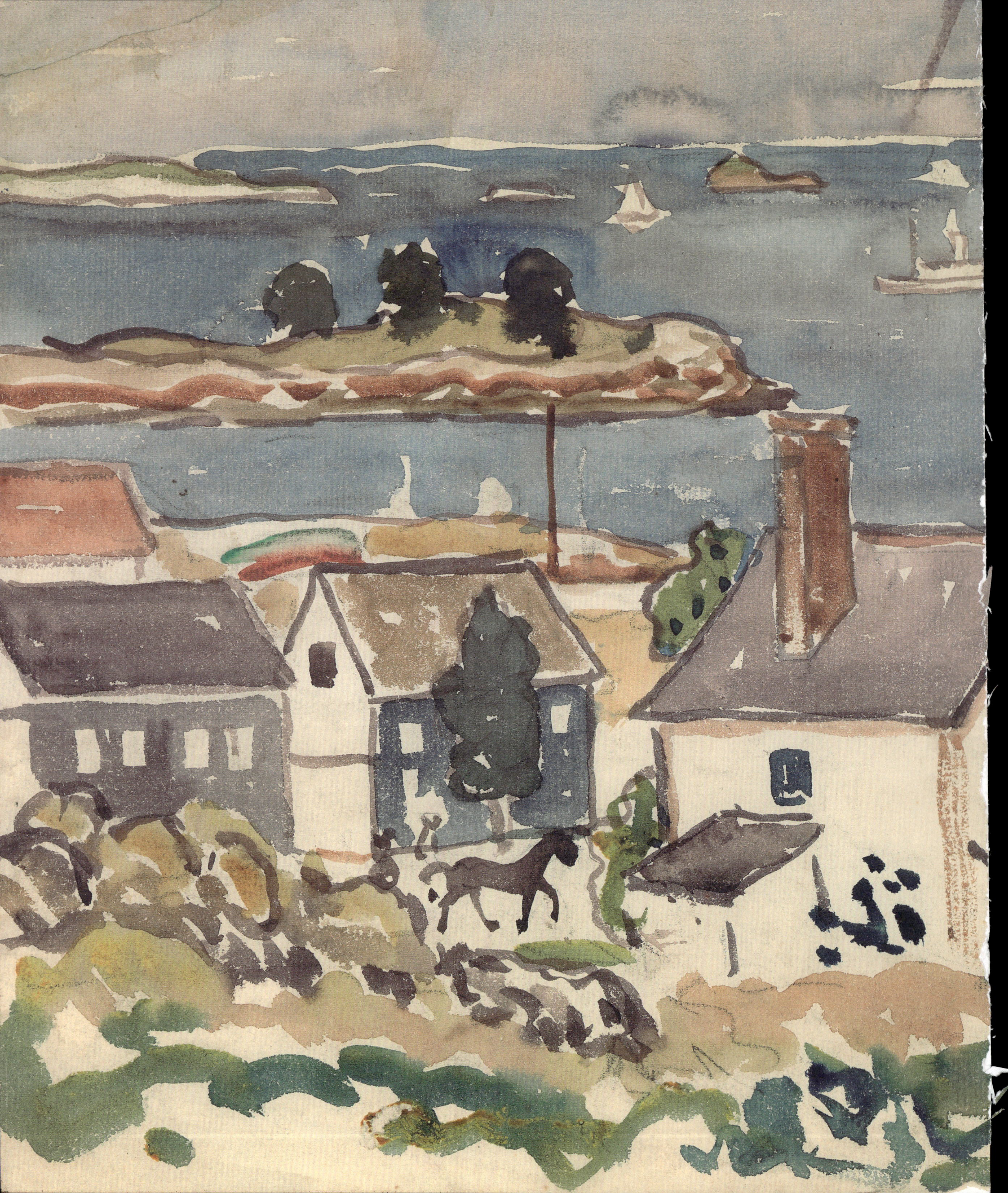